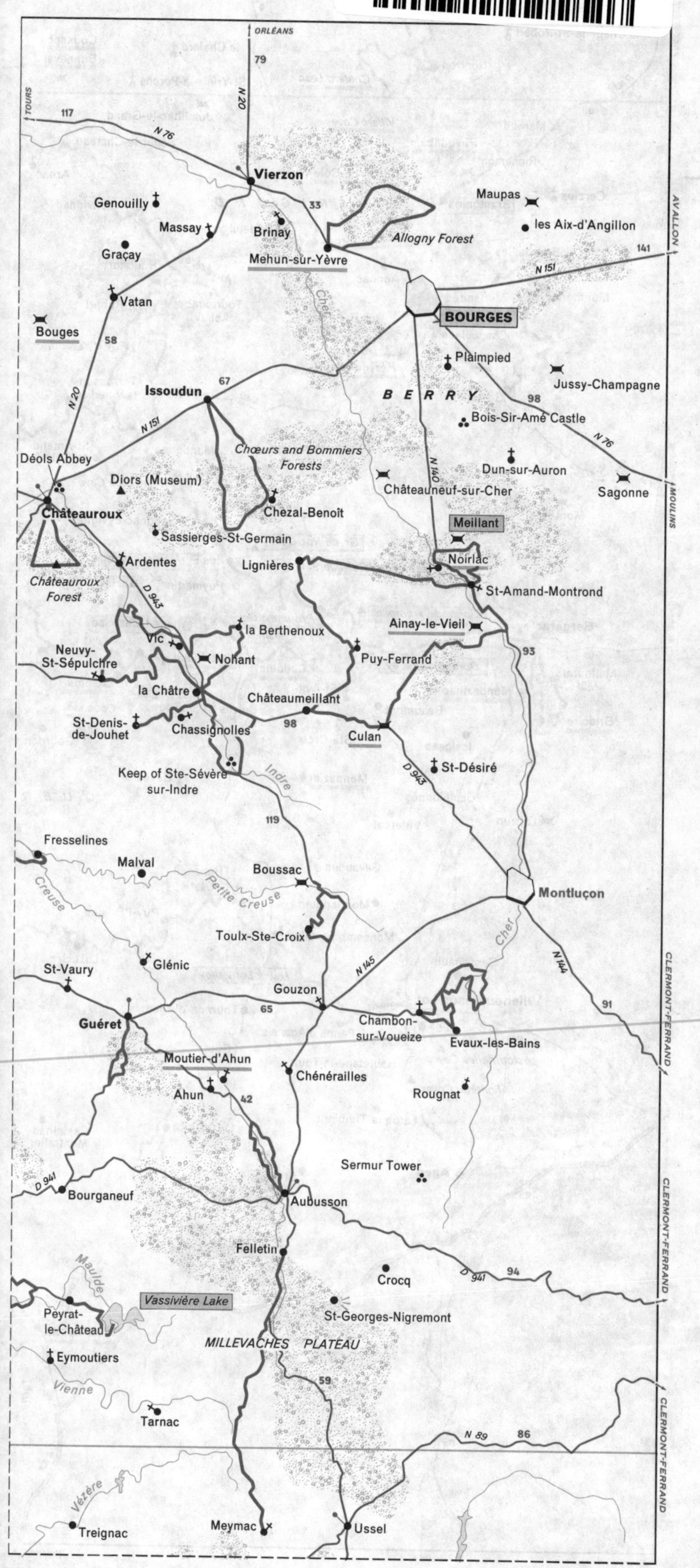
ORLÉANS
TOURS
117
N 76
79
N 20
Vierzon
33
Genouilly
Massay
Brinay
Maupas
les Aix-d'Angillon
AVALLON
Allogny Forest
141
Graçay
Mehun-sur-Yèvre
N 151
Vatan
Cher
BOURGES
Bouges
58
Plaimpied
Jussy-Champagne
67
Issoudun
B E R R Y
98
N 20
N 151
Bois-Sir-Amé Castle
Chœurs and Bommiers
Forests
N 76
Déols Abbey
N 140
Dun-sur-Auron
Diors (Museum)
Châteauneuf-sur-Cher
Sagonne
MOULINS
Châteauroux
Chezal-Benoît
Meillant
Sassierges-St-Germain
Ardentes
Lignières
Noirlac
Châteauroux
Forest
St-Amand-Montrond
D 943
Ainay-le-Vieil
la Berthenoux
Neuvy-
St-Sépulchre
Vic
Nohant
Puy-Ferrand
93
la Châtre
Châteaumeillant
St-Denis-
de-Jouhet
Chassignolles
98
Culan
St-Désiré
Keep of Ste-Sévère
sur-Indre
Indre
D 943
119
Fresselines
Malval
Boussac
Montluçon
Creuse
Petite Creuse
Toulx-Ste-Croix
Cher
N 144
Glénic
CLERMONT-FERRAND
St-Vaury
N 145
Gouzon
91
Guéret
65
Chambon-
sur-Voueize
Evaux-les-Bains
Moutier-d'Ahun
Chénérailles
Ahun
42
Rougnat
Sermur Tower
D 941
Bourganeuf
Aubusson
CLERMONT-FERRAND
Felletin
Maulde
D 941
94
Crocq
Vassivière Lake
Peyrat-
le-Château
St-Georges-Nigremont
MILLEVACHES PLATEAU
Eymoutiers
Vienne
59
CLERMONT-FERRAND
Tarnac
N 89
86
Vézère
Treignac
Meymac
Ussel

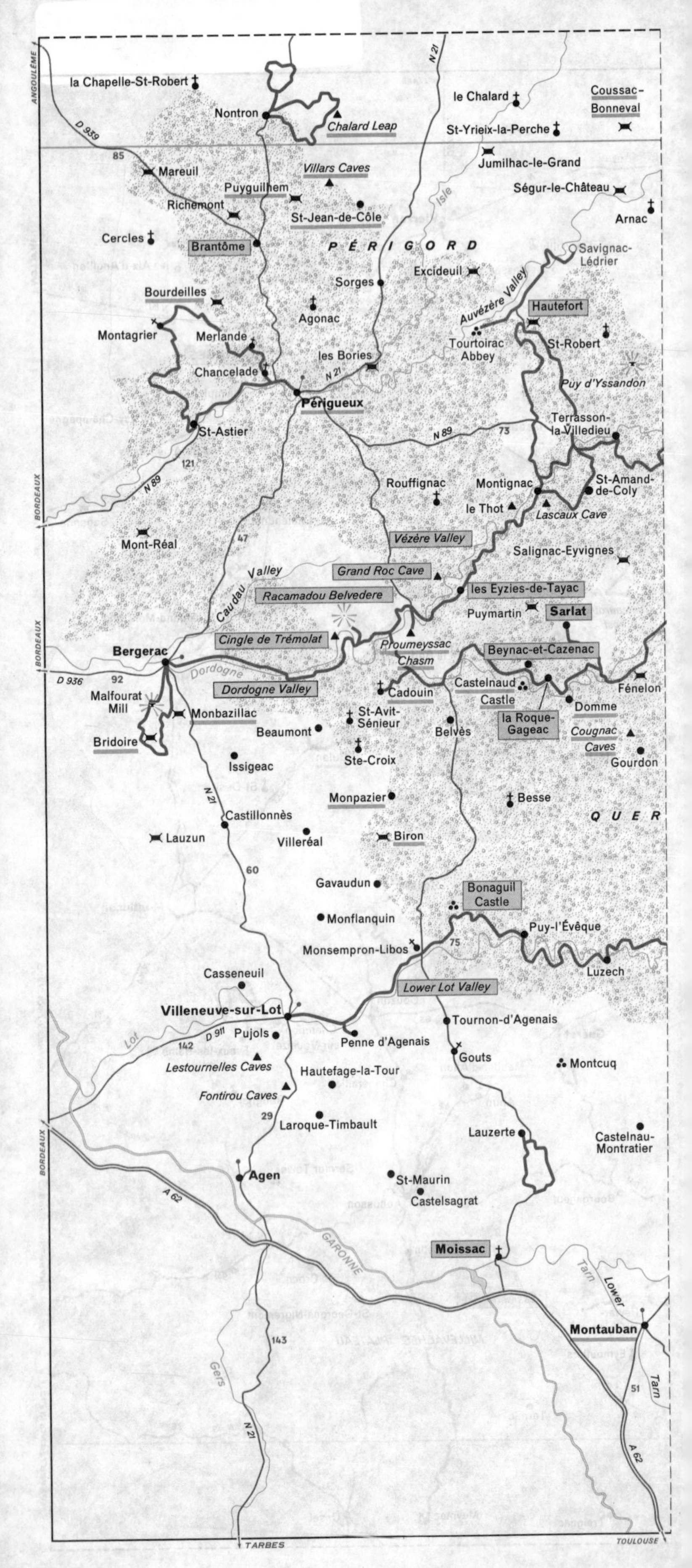
ANGOULÊME
la Chapelle-St-Robert
Nontron
Chalard Leap
D 939
85
Mareuil
Villars Caves
Puyguilhem
Richemont
St-Jean-de-Côle
Cercles
Brantôme
PÉRIGORD
Bourdeilles
Agonac
Sorges
Montagrier
Merlande
Chancelade
les Bories
N 21
Périgueux
St-Astier
121
N 89
BORDEAUX
Mont-Réal
47
Caudau Valley
Bergerac
Dordogne
D 936
92
Malfourat Mill
Monbazillac
Bridoire
Issigeac
N 21
Castillonnès
Lauzun
60
Casseneuil
Villeneuve-sur-Lot
Lot
142
D 911
Pujols
Lestournelles Caves
Fontirou Caves
29
Agen
A 62
GARONNE
143
Gers
N 21
TARBES
N 21
le Chalard
St-Yrieix-la-Perche
Coussac-Bonneval
Jumilhac-le-Grand
Ségur-le-Château
Arnac
Isle
Savignac-Lédrier
Excideuil
Auvézère Valley
Hautefort
Tourtoirac Abbey
St-Robert
Puy d'Yssandon
Terrasson-la-Villedieu
N 89
73
Rouffignac
Montignac
St-Amand-de-Coly
le Thot
Lascaux Cave
Vézère Valley
Salignac-Eyvignes
Grand Roc Cave
Racamadou Belvedere
les Eyzies-de-Tayac
Puymartin
Sarlat
Cingle de Trémolat
Proumeyssac Chasm
Beynac-et-Cazenac
Dordogne Valley
Castelnaud Castle
Fénelon
Cadouin
St-Avit-Sénieur
la Roque-Gageac
Domme
Beaumont
Belvès
Cougnac Caves
Gourdon
Ste-Croix
Monpazier
Besse
QUER
Villeréal
Biron
Gavaudun
Bonaguil Castle
Monflanquin
Puy-l'Évêque
Monsempron-Libos
75
Luzech
Lower Lot Valley
Tournon-d'Agenais
Penne d'Agenais
Gouts
Montcuq
Hautefage-la-Tour
Laroque-Timbault
Lauzerte
Castelnau-Montratier
St-Maurin
Castelsagrat
Moissac
Tarn
Lower
Montauban
51
Tarn
A 62
TOULOUSE

St-Germain-les-Belles
Mount Gargan
Masseret
Treignac
Meymac
Ussel
N 20
Vézère
Suc-au-May
N 89
St-Angel
CLERMONT-FERRAND
Uzerche
Monédières Massif
Egletons
St-Nazaire Site
Pompadour
Ventadour Castle
Marèges
Bort-les-Orgues
90
Ajustants Tourist Road
Naves
Ruffaud Pool
le Saillant
Tulle
Gimel-les-Cascades
Allassac
l'Aigle
la Valette
N 120
Valley
Dordogne
Brive-la-Gaillarde
Corrèze
Puy de Pauliac
le Chastang
D 922
Aubazines
Murel Waterfall
Servières-le-Château
Vic Rock
Argentat
Enchanet
Maronne
la Fage Chasm
Collonges-la-Rouge
Merle Towers
Turenne Castle
Dordogne Valley
Curemonte
Puy d'Issolud
Beaulieu-sur-Dordogne
Cère
Gorges
Laroquebrou
St-Etienne-Cantalès
Martel
Carennac
N 120
Copeyre Belvedere
Castelnau
Aurillac
Souillac
Loubressac
Padirac Chasm
St-Céré
Notre-Dame de Verdale
Montal
Lacave Cave
Presque Cave
N 122
91
Rocamadour
Gramat
N 140
Rudelle
Lacapelle-Marival
101
GRAMAT CAUSSE
Assier
C Y
Labastide-Murat
Célé
N 20
Espagnac-Ste-Eulalie
Figeac
Capdenac
Valley
Bellevue Cave
Lot
Marcilhac-sur-Célé
65
Pech-Merle Cave
Célé
Foissac
Cabrerets
La Mounine's Leap
St-Cirq-Lapopie
Lower Lot Valley
Cahors
Calvignac
Villeneuve
D 911
N 140
122
Aveyron
RODEZ
Loc Dieu
D 926
D 911
Saux
61
Lacapelle-Livron
Puylaroque
Montpezat-de-Quercy
Caylus
Beaulieu-en-Rouergue
St-Antonin-Noble-Val
Varen
Gorges
N 20
Aveyron
Montricoux
Penne
Bruniquel
Puycelci
72
Valley
D 999
Albi

PRACTICAL INFORMATION

The French Government Tourist Offices at 178 Piccadilly, London WIV OAL, Tel (01) 49 76 22 and 610 and 628 Fifth Avenue, New York, Tel (212) 757 – 1125 will provide information and literature.

How to get there. – You can go directly by scheduled national airlines, by commercial and package tour flights, possibly with a rail or coach link-up or you can go by crosschannel ferry or hovercraft and on by car or train. Enquire at any good travel agent and remember if you are going in the holiday season or at Christmas, Easter or Whitsun, to book well in advance.

When to go there. – This inland region extending from the river Cher in the north to the Garonne in the south is open to maritime influences from the Atlantic. The climate on the whole is mild. In winter frosts are infrequent, spring is early and warm and summer is hot. The rainfall is evenly distributed throughout the year.

Autumn is a good time to visit the region. In Berry and Limousin the heather in flower covers hills and plateaux, while the limestone plateaux of Quercy and the plains of Périgord blend the grey or ochre of their rocks with the yellow and browns of the changing leaves. Clear skies enhance the beauty of the countryside.

The high tourist season in France is during July and August, so book in advance if you plan to visit then.

Before Leaving

Papers and other documents. – A valid national passport, identity card or British Visitor's Passport is all that is required in the way of personal documents. The minimum driving age is 18 years old.

For the car a valid driving licence, international driving permit (not required for France but is necessary for Spain) car registration book and a nationality plate of the approved size. Insurance cover is compulsory and although the Green Card (an International Insurance Certificate) is no longer a legal requirement for France it is the most effective form of proof of insurance cover and is internationally recognized by police and other authorities.

Caravan owners must in addition produce the caravan log-book and an inventory for customs clearance. Endorse the Green Card for caravan and trailer. A carnet is required to import temporarily certain vehicles: pleasure craft over 5.5 m long and motor boats.

Certain motoring organisations run accident insurance and breakdown service schemes for their members. Enquire before leaving. A red warning triangle is obligatory in case of a breakdown.

In France it is compulsory for the front passengers to wear seat belts if the car is equipped with them. Children under ten should be on the back seat.

The speed limits although liable to modification are: motorways 130 kph - 80 mph (110 kph when raining); national trunk roads 110 kph - 68 mph; other roads 90 kph - 56 mph (80 kph – 50 mph when raining); in town 60 kph - 37 mph.

Regulations on speeding and drinking and driving are strictly interpreted – usually by an on the spot fine and/or confiscation of the vehicle. Remember to cede priority to vehicles joining from the right. There are tolls on the motorways.

Medical Treatment. – For EEC countries it is necessary to have Form E III which testifies to your entitlement to medical benefits from the Department of Health and Social Security. With this you can obtain medical treatment in an emergency and after the necessary steps, a refund of part of the costs of treatment from the local Social Security offices (Caisse Primaire d'Assurance Maladie). It is however advisable to take out comprehensive insurance cover.

Customs

Currency. – Regulations are liable to alteration: find out the latest allowances permitted when obtaining travellers' cheques and the permitted amount of foreign currency at one of the international travel agencies or banks before leaving.

Take your passport when getting currency and cheques and you will always need it as identification when cashing cheques in banks. (Commission charges vary: hotels, where they will change cheques, charge more highly than banks and very highly indeed when "obliging" non residents on holidays or at weekends!).

Going into France from the UK: your personal luggage may include, 1 bottle of spirits, 300 cigarettes or 75 cigars or 400 grammes of tobacco for those over 17; 2 cameras, 10 rolls of film per camera, a portable radio, record player (and 10 records) and a musical instrument. Returning to the UK: you may bring back duty free purchases to the value of £ 10, 300 cigarettes or 175 small cigars or 75 cigars or 400 grammes of tobacco, 1 bottle of spirits, 2 litres of wine. See also note above on currency.

Duly Arrived

Consulates: British – Bordeaux 33081, 15 Cours de Verdun (tel 52 28 35)
American – Bordeaux 33080, 22 Cours du Maréchal Foch (Tel 52 65 95)

Local Tourist Information Offices or *Syndicat d'Initiative* are to be found in most large towns and many tourist resorts. They can supply large scale town plans, time-tables and local information on entertainment facilities, sports and sightseeing.

Where to stay. – In the Michelin Red Guide France you will find a selection of hotels at various prices in all areas. It will also list local restaurants again with prices. If camping or caravanning consult the Michelin Guide Camping Caravaning France.

Electric Current. – Mostly 220/230 volts, in some places however it is still 110 volts. European circular two pin plugs are the rule – remember an electrical adaptor.

Poste restante. – Name, Poste restante, Poste centrale, Department's postal number followed by the town's name, France.

Public Holidays in France. – National museums and art galleries are closed on Tuesdays. The following are days when museums and other monuments may be closed or may vary their hours of admission:

New Year's Day	Ascension Day	The Assumption, **15 August**
Easter Sunday and Monday	Whit Sunday and Monday	All Saints' Day, **1 November**
May Day **(1 May)**	France's National Day, **14 July**	Armistice Day, **11 November**
Fête de la Libération **(8 May)**		Christmas Day

Prices and tipping (late 1983). – In shops and on menus, items are clearly marked; small extras cost approximately the following:

English newspapers (dailies)	6.00 to 7.00F
American newspapers (dailies)	5.00F
Petrol (per litre)	4.57 to 4.69F
Petrol-Super (per litre)	4.86 to 5.03F
English cigarettes	7.40 to 9.50F
American cigarettes	7.40 to 8.30F
French cigarettes	4.30 to 7.70F
Postage: to UK	letter 2.30F; card 1.60F
to USA - Airmail	Aerogramme 3.30F; card 2.20F
Coffee - *un café* (black espresso)	4.05F
Coffee and milk - *un café au lait*	5.70F
Fresh lemon or orange juice - *citron pressé, orange pressée*	9.30F
A beer (bottled) - *une bière bouteille*	9 to 15.50F
A beer (draught) - *une bière pression*	6.60 to 9.80F

Service is often included on the bill; if in doubt ask; if it is not, add on 15 %.

Opening times and admission prices. – The **visiting times** indicate the hours of opening and closing and it is important to remember that many châteaux, museums, etc, refuse admittance from up to an hour before the actual closing time.

When **guided tours** are indicated, the departure time for the last tour of the morning or afternoon will once again be prior to the given closing time. Most tours are conducted by French speaking guides but in some cases the term guided tour may cover group visiting with recorded commentaries. Some of the larger and more frequented châteaux offer guided tours in other languages. Enquire at the ticket or book stalls. Other aids for the foreign tourist are notes, pamphlets or audio guides.

The **admission prices** indicated are for adults, however reductions for children, students and parties are common. In some cases admission is free on certain days, eg Wednesdays, Sundays or public holidays.

THE REGION

A brief description. – Regions which are totally different in character lie side by side in the area between Berry and the plains of Agenais, the Massif Central and the Aquitaine Basin. Périgord, Limousin and Quercy are the chief provinces which together with parts of neighbouring Marche, Combraille, Rouergue and Agenais make up a tourist area of many attractions and great interest.

This region of contrasting countrysides is one of great natural beauty: the wide horizons of Berry succeeded by the green mountain country of Limousin; the limestone plateaux of Quercy stretching out in stark loneliness; the wooded plateaux of Périgord divided by the picturesque valleys and the rich orchard country of Agenais.

The works of man from the earliest prehistoric shelter to the most modern dam merit also the attention of a visiting tourist. Rich in prehistoric sites the area has many visible traces of the earliest inhabitants.

The religious buildings ranging from charming churches to the solid sanctuaries of Limousin and the hundreds of fortresses, castles, manors and mansions in a variety of architectural styles are witness to the rich historical past of the region. Added to this are thoughts of good food – an art here – accompanied by local wines, an added enticement to a tour.

BOOKS TO READ

In addition to the books listed below, there is much information to be gained on the region from the works of authors such as George Sand (p 146).

Original editions of works mentioned below can be obtained through public libraries.

Dordogne – Joy Law (Macdonald – 1981)

Three Rivers of France by Freda White (*Faber & Faber* – 1962); revised edition by Henri Myhill 1972.

Dordogne – Patrick Turnbull (Batsford – 1979)

Ways of Aquitaine by Freda White (*Faber & Faber* – 1968)

The Lascaux Cave Paintings by F. Windels *(Faber & Faber)*

Lascaux by A. Laming *(Penguin)*

The Hungry Archaeologist in France by Glyn Daniel (*Faber & Faber* – 1963)

The Cave Artists by A. Sieverking (*Thames & Hudson* – 1979).

Customs and Cookery in the Perigord and Quercy by Anne Penton (*David & Charles*)

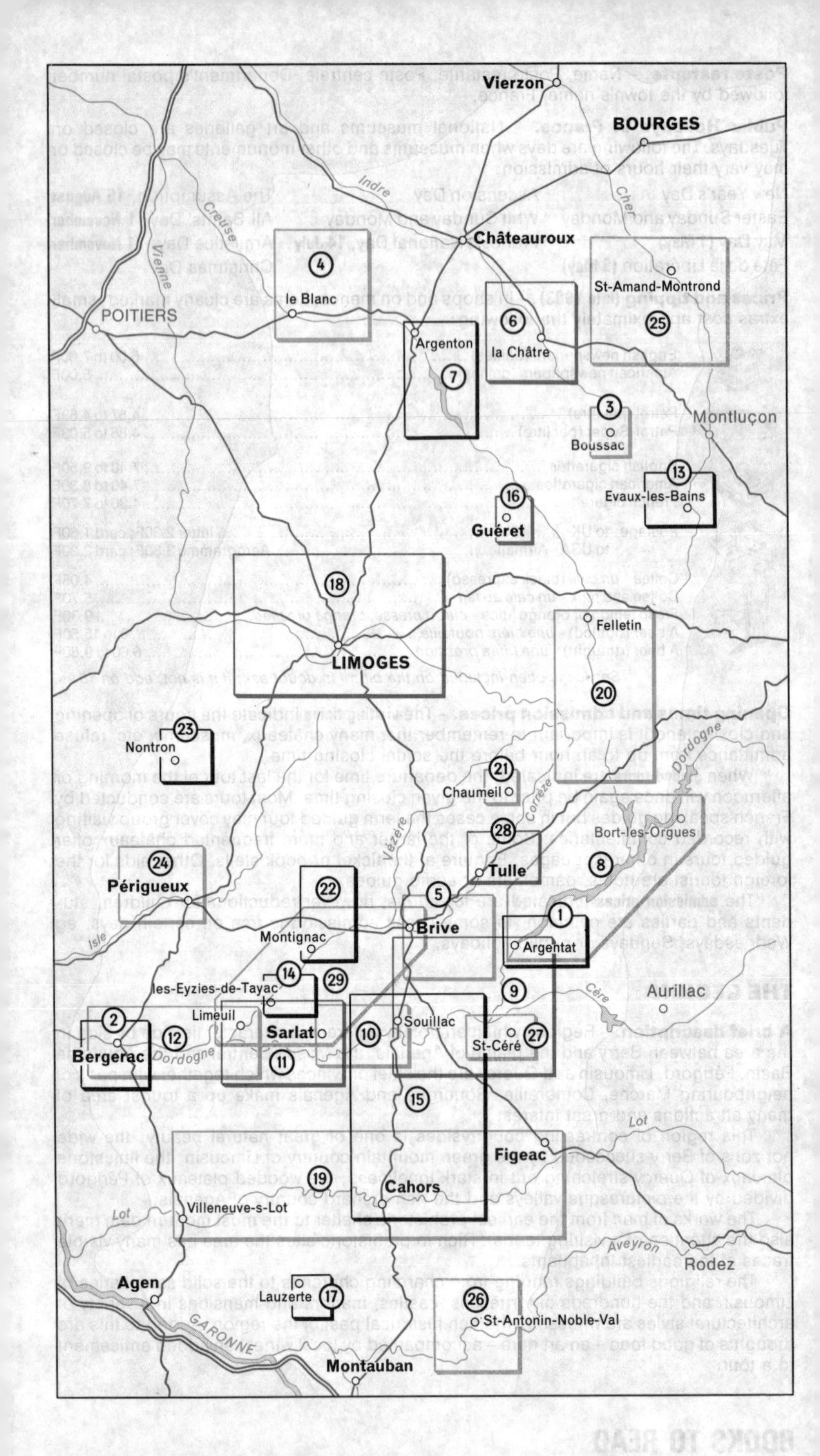

Local maps to be found in this guide

① ARGENTAT
② MONBAZILLAC Vineyard
③ BOUSSAC
④ La BRENNE
⑤ BRIVE-LA-GAILLARDE
⑥ La CHARTRE
⑦ CREUSE Valley

DORDOGNE Valley
⑧ Bort-les-Orgues-Argentat
⑨ Argentat-Souillac
⑩ Souillac-Sarlat
⑪ Sarlat-Limeuil
⑫ Limeuil-Bergerac

⑬ EVAUX-LES-BAINS
⑭ LES EYZIES-DE-TAYAC
⑮ GRAMAT Causse
⑯ GUÉRET
⑰ LAUZERTE
⑱ LIMOGES
⑲ LOT, Lower Valley
⑳ MILLEVACHES Plateau
㉑ MONÉDIÈRES Massif
㉒ MONTIGNAC
㉓ NONTRON
㉔ PÉRIGUEUX
㉕ ST-AMAND-MONTROND
㉖ ST-ANTONIN-NOBLE-VAL
㉗ ST-CÉRÉ
㉘ TULLE
㉙ VÉZERE Valley

INTRODUCTION TO THE TOUR

Appearance of the country. – They are many types of countryside between Bourges and Montauban: the dry and monotonous plains of Berry-Champagne, the granite plateaux of the Limousin Marche which one reaches almost without noticing, the high plateaux of the Limousin Montagne with their look of wooded farmland, the causses or limestone plateaux of Périgord and Quercy cut by deep valleys, and the rich alluvial plain of the Garonne which is Agenais.

Relief. – The highest peaks described in this guide are to be found in eastern Limousin, in the part of the country known as the **Limousin Montagne.** Limousin, western bastion of the Massif Central, differs from the neighbouring countrysides in its soil which derives from the ancient crystalline rocks. The region consists of highlands so worn by erosion that none of the peaks is more than 1 000 m - 3 300 ft in altitude (Mount Bessou and Puy Pendu are 977 m - 3 205 ft, the Audouze Beacon 953 m - 3 126 ft). The impression of being in a mountainous area comes more from the harshness of the climate – snow sometimes lies for four months – than from such worn and indistinguishable heights as one may see when crossing the Millevaches Plateau. The latter is the watershed between the drainage basins of the Loire and the Dordogne.

Plateaux make up the most important part of the region and they are extremely varied.

West of the Limousin Montagne, there are a series of low lying plateaux at an altitude of 400 to 500 m - 1 300 to 1 650 ft. These almost regular slopes, the Blond and the Ambazac Hills belong to the crystalline formation of the Massif Central. Heavy rainfall enables trees and bushes to flourish. South of the Montagne and the Monédières Massif, between the Vézère and the Dordogne, are the plateaux of Bas-Limousin. These lie one below the other, facing southwest and enjoy a comparatively mild climate: the Brive Basin, a sandstone depression, has a particularly warm sheltered climate.

The Périgord and Quercy plateaux are different. Porous limestone covers the ancient base: the Périgord plateaux are primarily of Cretaceous limestone, whereas the Quercy plateaux of the older Jurassic limestone. In Quercy may be seen the causses or limestone plateaux with their caves, chasms, and underground rivers as in the Martel, Gramat and Limogne Causses.

Berry, between Bourges and Châteauroux, unfolds the monotonous horizons characteristic of Berry-Champagne, another limestone platform. A top soil of alluvium, sands and clay on the calcareous foundation enables cereal crops to be grown and some reafforestation to have been undertaken.

The **valleys** of the Dordogne, the Lot and the Vézère cut deeply into the plateaux and attract the greater part of the economic life of the region. The fertile alluvial soil in the sheltered valleys, produces rich crops; the majority of the people have been drawn to live in the valleys. Between Moissac and Agen, the alluvial valley of the Garonne spreads out widely, its soil fertilised by the river floods.

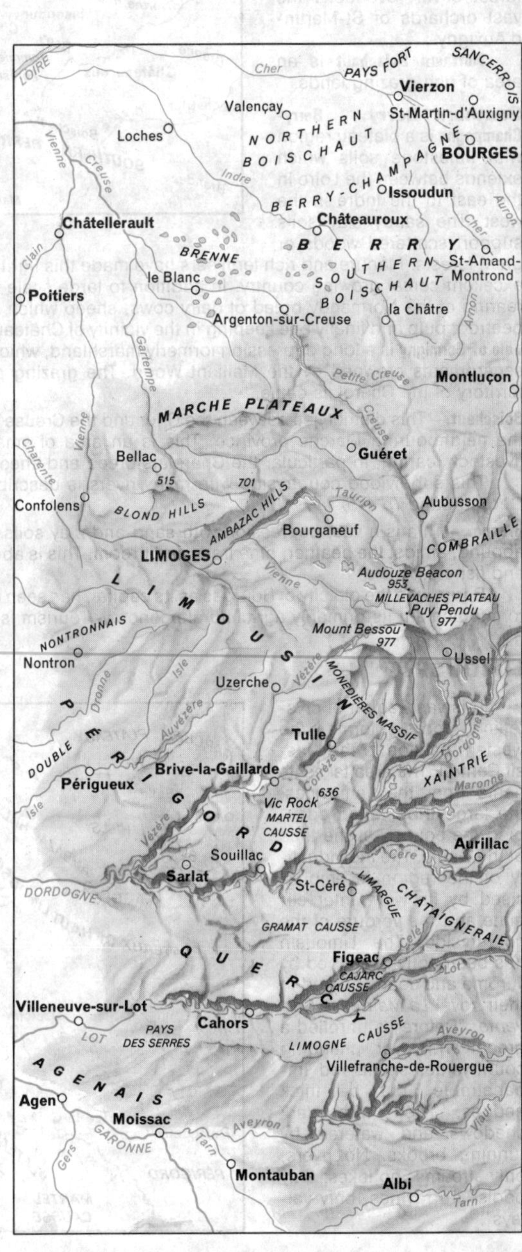

THE REGIONS

BERRY

This province extending across the Departments of Cher and Indre is one of the oldest agricultural regions of France. It owes its unity more to its common historical background rather than its existence as a geographical region. Geologically Berry forms the contact zone between the Paris Basin and the Massif Central. Berry consists of a vast low lying plateau, rising in the northeast to the Sancerre Hills (the Humbligny Beacon 434 m - 1 424 ft) and tilting westwards in a series of steps towards the Brenne depression. In the south the countryside is more undulating with many isolated hills and escarpments. The Cher and Indre belong to the Loire drainage system while the Creuse is a tributary of the Vienne.

Northern Berry. – The **Pays Fort** and **Sancerrois** are transitional areas bordering the Loire country. The former with its marl and clay soils slopes towards the Sologne while the latter's chalk slopes often vine clad rise above the river banks. This once forested landscape has been reduced to *bocage* (wooded farmland). The Allogny Forest *(p 131)*, the last important outpost of the primitive forest cover, overlooks the vast orchards of St-Martin-d'Auxigny.

Northern Boischaut is an area of rich grazing lands.

Southern Berry. – **Berry-Champagne** is a plateau region with limestone soils which extends between the Loire in the east to the Indre in the west. The sandy clay soils support scattered woods or great forests. Manure and rich fertilisers have made this light and easily worked soil into excellent cereal growing country. In addition to large scale arable farming there is the rearing of the Normandy breed of dairy cows, sheep which are kept inside and fed on beetroot pulp and finally bee keeping in the vicinity of Châteauroux. Away to the east, the **Vale of Germigny** is a long depression formerly marshland, which runs along the foot of the escarpments crowned by the Meillant Wood. The grazing pastures have become the territory of the Charolais cattle.

Boischaut. – This district lies between the Cher and the Creuse and its clay soils overlap to the neighbouring Marche province. This is an area of small farms concentrating on livestock rearing, in particular the Charolais breed and sheep.

This subdivided countryside with many rivers is described by the woman novelist George Sand *(p 145)*.

Brenne. – This is a vast depression with sand and clay soils where pools and marshes abound, amidst the heather, pine trees and broom. This is above all a haven for shooters and fishers.

Berry, with the old city of Bourges as its capital, has seen the arrival of new industries to supplement its primarily agricultural economy. Tourism is also being developed.

LIMOUSIN

This vast region of crystalline rocks, forms the western bastion to the Massif Central. The area takes its name from the Lemovices, the large tribe which occupied the country at the time of the Gauls. The individuality of the region is emphasised by its wet winter climate and the verdure of the countryside. The Limousin has been aptly described by Jérôme and Jean Tharaud in their novel *La Maîtresse Servante:* "Before us unrolled a green and ever changing countryside, silent and impenetrable, cut by thick hedges, filled with dark shadows and watered by running brooks. No rivers, only streams; no lakes, only pools; no ravines, only valleys".

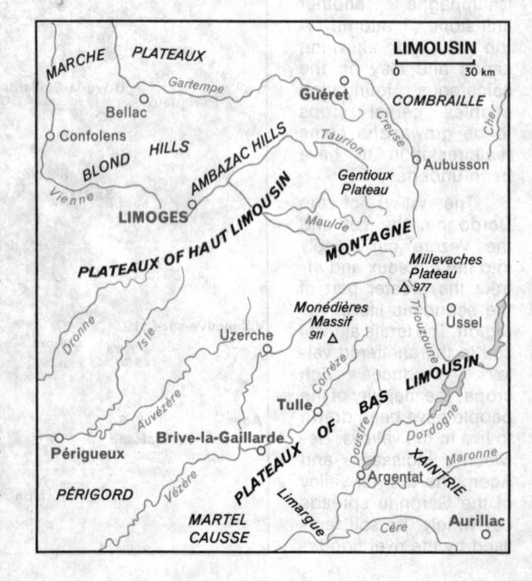

Montagne. – This vast series of plateaux, rising to 1 000 m - 3 300 ft has been levelled by erosion. The Montagne or mountain area is also a watershed where the sources of many rivers rise. Pools of water cover an area of more than 4 000 ha - 9 900 acres; their creation was favoured by the clay soil and in the Middle Ages was often undertaken by religious communities. The weather on these highlands, is rugged, the rains heavy, the winds strong and snow has been known to lie on the ground for four months at a time. Farms are few and far between and stony wastes and sheep grazing moors are more common than ploughed land, particularly on the Millevaches Plateau *(p 133)* and in the Monedières Massif *(p 136)*. With the introduction of liming, wheat has replaced rye or buckwheat and plantations of pines have been added to the existing beech woods. The Montagne is surrounded on three sides by regions with differing physical aspects.

The Plateaux of Haut-Limousin. – Those to the northwest form an undulating area – **Ambazac** and **Blond Hills** – with alternating escarpments and deeply incised valleys. This is a highly compartmented *bocage* (wooded farmland) area. Trees thrive with the wet climate – oak and beech on the uplands and chestnut trees lower down. Quickset hedges surround fields and meadows. The pastures enriched by manure and artificial fertilisers make good cattle grazing country *(p 18)*. Further north the drier less wooded **Marche** area is a marchland between the Massif Central and the Loire country. The Haute-Marche, drained by the Creuse, is an area of stock rearing while arable farming prevails in the Basse-Marche, around Bellac.

(After a photo by Arthaud, Grenoble)

The wooded Limousin landscape

To the west the **Confolentais** district with its lush meadows is an area specializing in the fattening of livestock: beef and dairy cattle, sheep from the Montagne and white pigs.

The Plateaux of Bas-Limousin. – This area, where the influence of Périgord and Quercy may already be seen, is characterised by a greater luminosity, milder climate and fertile basins. The depression of the **Brive Basin** is a dividing zone between the crystalline escarpments of the Uzerche plateau and the limestone ridges of the Causses. In the green valleys with screens of poplars, fruit growing flourishes. To the south of Brive, on the **Corrèze Causse** (causse = limestone plateau), crossed by the N 20 there is sheep rearing, renewed exploitation of the truffle oak plantations and the keeping of geese for the production of *foies gras*. In the valleys walnut production is increasing as is the growing of maize as a fodder crop. The **Xaintrie** *(p 48)* is an area alternating with pine and silver birch woods. This granite plateau is deeply incised by the Dordogne, the Maronne and numerous other rivers.

Industrially the Limousin has been enriched by the development of the hydro-electric potential of the area and the exploitation of the uranium deposits *(p 19)* in the Ambazac Hills.

PÉRIGORD

Périgord, lying between Limousin and the valleys of Aquitaine, covers an area which since the Revolution of 1789 is approximately the same as the Dordogne Department. The region is named after the Petrocorii who lived here at the time of the Gauls. Primary rocks constitute the southwestern edge of the Massif Central. Secondary limestone makes up the greater part of the plateaux cut by the valleys of the Dronne, the Isle, the Auvézère, the Vézère and the Dordogne. There are Tertiary sands in the nearby Aquitaine Basin. The diversity of the landscape is as striking as the already cited geological variety. The numerous forests occupy 40 % of the area.

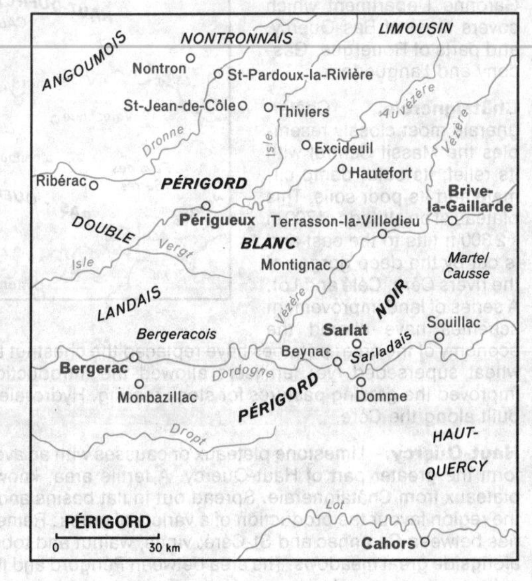

Nontronnais. – Situated in the northwest, this area has a high rainfall and it closely resembles Limousin with its pastures, chestnut woods, heather and gorse moors and its isolated farms. A narrow band of limestone following the line Nontron, Thiviers, Excideuil and Montignac, links Angoumois and Quercy. On this outcrop of minor scarps and flat topped hills are coppices of small truffle oaks and juniper shrubs. Only the valleys are cultivated. Lush green basins appear in the areas of less resistant rocks such as at St-Pardoux-la-Rivière, St-Jean-de-Côle, Corgnac-sur-l'Isle and Cherveix. Near the Brive Basin the red sandstone hills are covered in places with vines, cherry trees, market gardens, tobacco plantations and walnut trees.

Double and Landais. – Lying in the west between the rivers Dronne and Isle the **Double** is an area of forests where tall oak and chestnut trees predominate. The clay nature of the soils favours the formation of numerous pools. The **Landais** lying to the south of the Isle is a less rugged region where fruit trees flourish. The chestnut gives way to the maritime pine and meadows become more abundant. The rich hillsides of Bergeracois, overlooking the fertile Dordogne valley, enjoy warmer temperatures which enable crops usually produced farther south to be grown. The vineyard of Monbazillac *(p 57)* heralds the arrival of the Bordelais region.

Périgord Blanc. – White Périgord is named thus because of the frequent outcrops of chalky limestone which in this open and less forested countryside imparts a whiteness to the landscape. Coppices of black oaks with light coloured downy leaves divide up the artificial pastures for the rearing of dairy cattle especially around Ribérac which have replaced orchards and wheat fields. Numerous agricultural markets are held in the local towns.

Périgord Noir. – Dissected by the Vézère and Dordogne valleys this area owes its name to the greater density of trees to be found growing on the sandy soils covering the limestone areas and also to the presence of the holm oak with its dark, dense foliage, which is particularly numerous in the Sarladais. The alluvial soil of the valleys whose river courses are lined with screens of poplars or willows, supports a variety of crops: wheat, maize, tobacco and walnuts. The lively and prosperous markets sell excellent nuts, mushrooms, truffles and *foies gras*. In the limestone areas resurgent springs *(p 16)*, grottoes with concretions, caves and shelters with sculpted or painted walls *(p 24)* all attract the tourist. Along the river Dordogne landscapes are gentle and harmonious, as seen from the viewpoints of the Domme Barre and Beynac and Castelnaud Castles. The former capital of Black Périgord, Sarlat has been brought to life by tourism.

QUERCY

Quercy corresponds to the region which stretches from the Massif Central to the plains of Aquitaine and was occupied by the Cadurques who made Cahors their capital. The region has a strong historical unity. In the Middle Ages Quercy belonged to the province of Guyenne. Under the *Ancien Régime* two regions were recognized, the Haut-Quercy centred on Cahors and seat of the main administrative departments and Bas-Quercy, depending on Montauban. During the Revolution they were reunited under the Lot Department. However in 1808 Napoleon separated them again, creating the Tarn-et-Garonne Department which covers most of Bas-Quercy, and parts of Rouergue, Gascony and Languedoc.

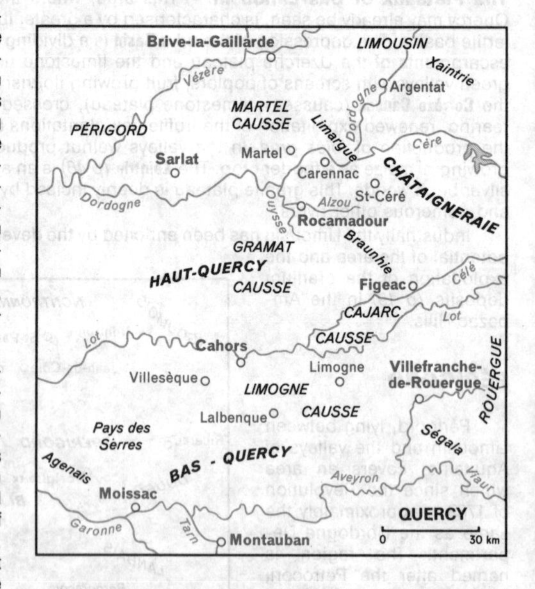

Châtaigneraie. – Châtaigneraie most closely resembles the Massif Central with its relief, its cold, damp climate and its poor soils. This plateau at an altitude of 700 m - 2 300 ft tilts to the east and is cut by the deep gorges of the rivers Cère, Célé and Lot. A series of land improvement schemes have altered the economy of the area: potatoes have replaced the chestnut tree; later with the use of lime, wheat superseded rye; fertilisers allowed the introduction of market gardening and improved the grazing pastures for stock rearing. Hydro-electric undertakings have been built along the Cère.

Haut-Quercy. – Limestone plateaux or causses with an average height of 300 m - 1 000 ft form the greater part of Haut-Quercy. A fertile area, known as **Limargue**, separates the plateaux from Châtaigneraie. Spread out in flat basins and over vast plains, the soils of the region favour the production of a variety of crops: Reine Claude plums and strawberries between Carennac and St-Céré, vines, walnut and tobacco plantations which stand alongside great meadows. The area between Périgord and the N 20, with its sand and clay soils supports moorlands, coppices of chestnut trees and woodlands. The tapping of maritime pines for the resin, the timber industry and the sale of livestock, chestnut and walnuts form the basis of the region's economy.

The **causses** present a completely different picture. Flocks of sheep graze on the sparse grass of the pastures which are sub-divided by dry stone dykes. Stunted oaks and maple are the only trees. In the valleys there are temporary pastures, vineyards and other crops. The local landscapes and the unusual attractive rural houses make this a picturesque area to which must be added the interest of the subterranean features.

The characteristic Quercy house, roofed with flat stones or tiles has on the ground floor a large vaulted room or cellar which is often used as a shelter for the sheep, and on the first floor the living quarters. In the south the second floor or attic is used as a tobacco drying room.

The decorative features of the Quercy house are the outside stone staircase that enables the inhabitants to reach the living rooms without going through the cellar or sheep pen, the large stone step at the top sometimes sheltered by a porch – the *bolet* – and the dovecote. The architecture of these dovecotes, which often stand apart from the main building, is often very varied. Built between 1750 and 1850, they were intended less for the keeping of pigeons but for their droppings, an excellent manure for the small holdings. So important was this manure that when the property was divided on the death of the owner, the pigeon droppings were divided among the heirs in the same way as the land and the poultry.

(After a photo by Yvon)

Lavergne (Lot)
Quercy dovecote.

The **Martel Causse** is a vast arid plain covered in stones, which is crossed by a relatively fertile zone. The many dry stone dykes were built by shepherds as they cleared stones from the ground to allow sheep to graze and mark the field boundaries.

The **Gramat Causse**, a great limestone plateau, at an average height of 350 m - 1 150 ft offers many natural phenomena and unusual landscapes. Magnificent canyons break the monotonous but grand horizons: in the north lie the Ouysse and Alzou Canyons to whose cliff-face clings Rocamadour *(p 156)*; in the south the much longer Célé Canyon *(p 81)*. Between the narrow gashes of the Alzou and the Célé lies the waterless **Braunhie** (pronounced Brogne – rhyming with Dordogne). This arid region is riddled with caves and ravines *(p 16)*.

The **Cajarc Causse**, a low lying plateau, is hemmed in by the banks of the Célé and Lot rivers, whose meanders are richly cultivated.

The **Limogne Causse** with its drier climate has a very different appearance. Bordered by the valley of the Lot *(p 124)*, the plateau is dotted with dolmens and megaliths which appear amidst the clumps of white truffle oaks, the juniper shrubs and the fields of lavender. Here and there are to be found the curious shepherds' shelters built of flat stones with strange conical roofs, known as *garriottes* or *cazelles*. There are few big towns, although Limogne-en-Quercy and Lalbenque remain the busiest centres of the truffle market.

Bas-Quercy. – This area is linked to the Garonne by the valleys of the Tarn and Aveyron. In the region of Villesèque and Lalbenque a series of chalky plateaux are traversed by escarpments of a harder rock forming spurs or isolated outcrops. This is the country of long narrow ridges *(serres)* which continues into the Agenais. The crests of these ridges are planed down to a height of 200 m - 660 ft and provide sheep grazing land as well as supporting oak woods and crops in the areas of clay soil.

The low lying river areas form fertile strips. The meadows bordered by poplars produce several crops: fruit, vines, cereals and tobacco. Despite the difficult environment the population has remained stable mainly due to the arrival of farmers from Spain and North Africa.

Quercy made up of very diverse regions, formerly had a closed economy, but now is increasing its commercial links with Toulouse and Paris.

AGENAIS

This region covers the Lot-et-Garonne Department and is a transition zone between southern Périgord, Bas-Quercy and the Landes to the west. It owes its unity to the Garonne valley.

In the north with its wet climate, the clay soils around Lauzun are covered with lush pastures grazed by dairy cattle. Further to the east, towards Gavaudun, chestnut, oak and pine woods appear. In the Fumel area the exploitation of the sands rich in iron ore, has encouraged the implantation of iron and small metallurgical works.

Pays des Serres. – This area of narrow ridges separated by wide valleys, extends to the south of the River Lot. Mixed arable farming has been abandoned in favour of specialization. Wheat predominates on the alluvial plateaux around Tournon-d'Agenais and La Roque-Timbaut. Vines are becoming increasingly common on the slopes *(Chasselas de Preyssas)*.

The Lot Valley. – This is an immense orchard interspersed with gardens and tobacco plantations. The peas, green beans and melons of Villeneuve-sur-Lot are reputed.

The Garonne Valley. – A variety of crops, even some of the more demanding ones flourish on the terraces, being favoured by the alluvial soil and the mild climate. Almost every town has its own speciality: prunes and onions from Agen; peaches and cherries from Ste-Marie; tomatoes and pumpkins from Marmande on the borders of Bordelais. The planting of poplars since the 18C has lessened the risk of flooding, while the wood itself is exploited for timber and paper.

Agenais distributes its products to such major towns as Paris, Limoges, Bordeaux, Toulouse and to the Mediterranean region.

CAVES AND CHASMS

In contrast to the deeply dissected green valleys with their many settlements, the Quercy limestone plateaux roll away to the far horizon, stony, grey and deserted. The dryness of the soil is due to the calcareous nature of the rock which absorbs rain like a sponge. Though the surface is arid, below ground there is intense activity.

Water infiltration. – Rainwater, charged with carbonic acid, dissolves the carbonate of lime to be found in the limestone. Depressions, which are usually circular in shape and small in size and are known as **cloups**, are then formed. The dissolution of the limestone rocks containing especially salt or gypsum, produces *terra rossa* a rich soil particularly suitable for growing crops; when the *cloups* increase in size they form large, closed depressions known as **sotchs**.

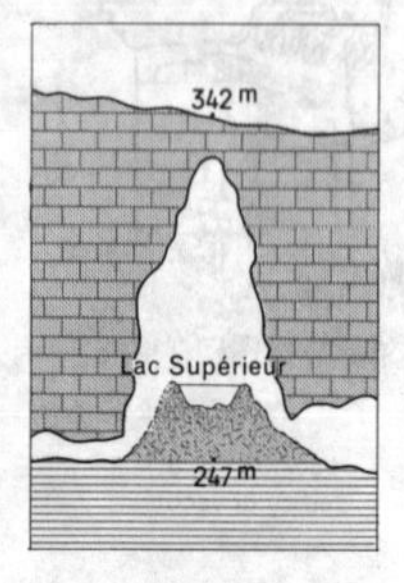

Formation of the Padirac Grand Dôme.

Where rainwater infiltrates deeply through the countless fissures in the plateau, the hollowing out and dissolution of the calcareous layer produces wells or natural chasms which are called **igues.**

Underground Rivers. – The infiltrating waters finally produce underground galleries and collect to form a more or less swift flowing river. The river widens its course and often changes level, to fall in cascades. Where the rivers run slowly they form lakes, as at Padirac, above natural dams known as **gours** which are raised layer by layer by deposits of carbonate of lime. The dissolution of the limestone also continues above the water-level in these subterranean galleries: blocks of stone fall from the roof and domes form. Such is the case with the Grand Dôme of Padirac which lies only a few metres beneath the surface of the plateau *(see diagram)*. When the roof of the dome caves in, a chasm will have been formed.

Cave Formation. – As it circulates below ground the water deposits the lime with which it has become charged thus building up concretions of fantastic shapes which defy the laws of gravity and equilibrium. In some caverns, the seeping waters produce calcite (carbonate of lime) deposits which form pendants, pyramids and draperies.

Stalactites form from the cave roof. Every droplet of water seeping through to the ceiling deposits upon it, before falling, some of the calcite with which it is charged. Gradually layer by layer the concretion builds up.

Stalagmites are formed in the same way but rise from the floor towards the roof. Drops of water, falling always in the same place deposit their calcite particles which build up to a candle-like shape. This rises towards a stalactite with which it ultimately joins to form a pillar linking the cave floor with the ceiling.

Concretions form very slowly indeed; the rate of growth in a temperate climate is about 1 cm in every 100 years.

The **sports** or **eccentrics** are very fine protuberances which seldom exceed 20 cm - 8 ins in length. They emerge at any angle either as slender spikes or in the shape of small, translucent fans. They are formed by crystallisation and seem to disregard the laws of Gravity. The Grotte du Grand-Roc near Les Eyzies-de-Tayac, contains remarkable specimens.

Cave with concretions
1 Stalactites - 2 Stalagmites
3 Pillar in formation - 4 Completed pillar.

Resurgent Springs. – Underground rivers form either by the disappearance of a water course into a rift *(igue)* in a plateau, or by an accumulation of infiltrated water reaching non-porous strata (marl or clay). The water then finds a way through by following the line of the stratum. When the impermeable layer breaks through on the side of a hill the water emerges once more above ground and is known as a resurgent spring *(see diagram)*.

The river at Padirac, for example, flows underground for some miles, disappearing roughly in the spot where the tour of the Salle des Grands Gours ends *(p 147)* and reappearing some 11 km - 7 miles away in the Montvalent Amphitheatre in the valley of the Dordogne.

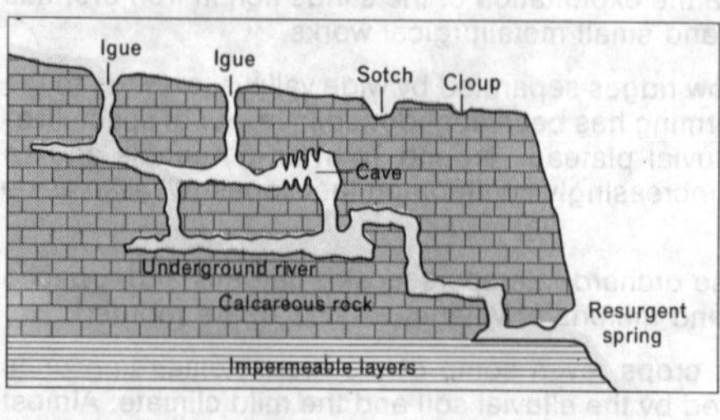

Development of a resurgent spring.

From Prehistory to Modern Exploration. – The caves and grottoes were first inhabited by animals and then by man who drove the animals away and only left these natural shelters after the Magdalenian Era had ended about 10 000 years ago.

At the end of last century the methodical and scientific exploration of the underground world, with which the name of E.A. Martel is associated, led to the discovery of a certain number of caves and their organisation as a tourist attraction. Knowledge of the underground system is at present very incomplete and a great many chasms remain unknown to speleologists.

THE ECONOMY

Man's chief activity remains the husbanding of the soil in such a region as the edge of the Massif Central, where a scarcity of mineral wealth and raw materials has not allowed the establishment of industrial centres as in northern and eastern France.

AGRICULTURE

Between Berry-Champagne and the Garonne plain husbandry takes the most diverse forms. The nature of the soil, the differences in relief, the predominant weather characteristics, the possibilities of commercial outlets, the ability of the local people to adapt themselves to modern methods, are all factors that give each province its own individual economic character.

The Intensive Agriculture of Berry-Champagne. – This is the region of large holdings – 100 to 200 ha - 250 to 500 acres are not uncommon – where wide expanses lend themselves to large scale cultivation. The use of fertilisers and modern machinery, which is helped by the absence of quickset hedges and fences, has improved the yield per hectare. The traditional cereals of wheat and barley remain the staple crops although there is a tendency to grow more maize. Oil yielding plants such as colza and sunflower are becoming increasingly important. The production of cereals has reached about 1.8 million tons a year for the Departments of Cher and Indre which form part of Berry-Champagne.

The Multiple Crop Growing of Périgord and Quercy. – Rural development in Périgord and Quercy presents a completely different picture. The Dordogne Department is the prime example of an area where the most diverse crops are grown simultaneously; the strawberry crop has made the Dordogne the leading producer in France: 18 600 tons in 1981. The mildness of the climate allows the same crops to be grown as in southwest France. The Lot Department has a similar advantage. The country has been so divided that it is now a region of small holdings, and properties rarely exceed 15 to 20 ha - 37 to 50 acres. Cereals and fodder crops take up most of the land that can be cultivated but three crops, above all, symbolise this particular region: truffles, walnuts and tobacco.

Truffles *(p 20)*, are a kind of underground mushroom which grow round certain types of oak known as truffle oaks.

There are some thirty types of truffle, but the best is the variety known as the Périgord truffle. The main centres of production and sale in Dordogne are Brantôme, Thiviers, Excideuil, Périgueux, Thenon, Terrasson, Sarlat, Domme and Sorges; and Cahors, Limogne, Sauzet and especially Lalbenque in the Lot Department. Production, which reached 1 500 tons a century ago, has dropped slightly these last few years. New plantations of truffle oaks have recently been completed, and production is likely to increase.

(After a photo by Dr. J. Merly, Périgueux)

Truffle digging near Périgueux.

Walnuts are grown on a large scale (10 000 tons a year). The Brantôme walnut, which ripens early, is often sold fresh as is the Marbot nut, a variety common in the Lot Department; from the Sarlat and Gourdon areas comes the Grandjean nut which is the variety most commonly used green or half ripe in Périgord and Quercy. The Corne walnut grows best on the better soils of the causses while the Franquette nut is planted in the new plantations.

The Dordogne Department is the leading producer of walnuts in France. Walnuts are cultivated in the south of Corrèze and throughout the Lot Department: the Dordogne valley, in the Limargue from Figeac to St-Céré, the Martel Causse and around Gourdon. New plantations are being created in the Lot and Dordogne valleys.

Conditions in Périgord and Quercy and in all parts of southwest France, are highly favourable to **tobacco** growing. It is a vigorous plant which was imported from America in the 16C and was first used for medicinal purposes before becoming the joy of all those who smoke.

Tobacco growing, was until recently strictly controlled by the Régie Nationale des Tabacs, which holds the state monopoly. The plant requires assiduous care and a large labour force, but it is a useful addition to the cash income of the small farmer. It is grown particularly on the alluvial soils of the valleys of the Dordogne and the Lot and on the mud terraces of the Périgord and Quercy hills; sowing takes place from the end of March; throughout the summer work goes on pricking and planting out seedlings, land dressing, earthing-up plants and disbudding. Harvesting is done stem by stem, each stem being covered with leaves 60 to 80 cm - 24 to 32 ins long. Drying takes place in airy sheds and lasts about six weeks. The dried leaves are then sent to the Régie Nationale's warehouse where processing takes place.

The greatest proportion of tobacco grown for snuff is cultivated on the Causse.

There are 20 000 planters in the Dordogne, Lot and Lot-et-Garonne Departments; it is essentially a family business although mechanisation is increasing.

The Lot-et-Garonne Department is the greatest producer with an area of 4 200 ha - 10 400 acres out of a national total of 20 500 ha - 50 700 acres and a production of 8 000 tons (France 43 500 tons).

Bergerac has an interesting tobacco museum *(p 57)*.

The Cornucopia of Fruit and Early vegetables: the Brive Basin and Agenais. – The **Brive Basin**, which lies between Limousin and the Quercy Plateau, is a depression made up of sandstones and schists where the headwaters of the Corrèze and the Vézère collect.

A group of gently sloping hills facing the sun and a light and fertile soil make it a good area for cereals and fruit trees. The Brive Basin specialises in the growing of vegetables, fruit and tobacco. Strawberry growing has greatly increased.

The fruit trees in the area include: plums, walnuts, peaches, cherries, pears and apples.

(After a photo by S.P.I.E.A. Ed. Larousse)
Plum drying in Agenais.

Agenais has alluvial soils in the Garonne and Lot valleys which are often remarkably fertile and also a mildness of climate that enables early crops to be grown. Vegetables are sown in open fields and in greenhouses on the plain and on hillside terraces facing the sun: peas, tomatoes, asparagus, artichokes, cauliflowers and melons are produced for the great vegetable markets of Toulouse, Bordeaux and Paris. The vast number of fruit trees give the valley the appearance of a huge orchard; there are peaches, apples, pears, cherries and above all the Agen plum to add to the area's riches.

Plum trees are particularly numerous in the Lot-et-Garonne, which has 75% of the national total. The orchards are thickest in the valleys of the Lot and Garonne and to the north of these two rivers.

The Agen prune is produced from a ripe plum which is graded on picking and then dried in an oven or drying-room *(see above)*. The plum comes from a tree that has been grafted and is known as a *prunier d'ente* (*enter* meant to graft in former times). There are several varieties of grafted plum trees, though the Robe-Sergent is now planted in nearly all orchards.

The history of grafting plum trees goes back to the time of the Crusades. In the 16C the monks of Clairac near Tonneins were cultivating plums systematically; they were the first to see the full use to which the fruit could be put. Two centuries later plum sales had expanded so greatly that they had to be controlled.

Today some 8 000 ha - 19 760 acres produce 27 000 tons of prunes. The Agen prune in spite of competition from the Californian variety, enjoys considerable success not only in France but in other common market countries.

STOCK RAISING

Each province directs its stock raising according to the natural fertility of its soil - rich pastureland provides cattle fodder, the more arid plateau areas are suitable for sheep rearing.

The Sheep of Berry and Quercy. – Sheep rearing was the only way of earning a living long ago when a lack of money and materials were major obstacles to the improvement of the Berry plains. The traditional sheep rearing has lost considerable ground since last century (there are now 315 000 sheep in the Indre and Cher).

The Berry breed is declining in numbers and is being replaced by the English Southdowns or the Charmois breed. Sought after for their meat they are now reared inside in sheepfolds and no longer roam the open pasturelands. Goat keeping is also increasing with the production of cheese as the main by-product.

The limestone plateaux of Quercy are an important sheep area with some 240 000 head. The plateau sheep is known as the «spectacled» breed for it has white fleece and black rings round its eyes. It bears good quality wool, but it is for its meat especially that this hardy, prolific breed is known.

Stock raising in Limousin. – Natural features make Limousin first and foremost into a cattle rearing area. To the indigenous meadowland must be added the specially sown pastures which have greatly increased grass production. Sheep rearing is also an important activity and the Haute-Vienne is the leading sheepmeat producer.

Limousin beef-cattle with their short withers and pure red hides were already widely known in the 17 and 18C. Improved by severe culling and better feeding, the breed now produces some of the finest meat in the world.

To supply market requirements, Limousin farmers have turned to the production of young calves for the white veal that is so much sought after in Paris and the south; bull calves of eight to fifteen months are sent to the markets at Lyons, Grenoble and St-Étienne and heifers of two to three years to the Bordeaux slaughter-houses. Some eight month old calves are sent to Italy for fattening.

The export of prize specimens has shown that the Limousin breed can acclimatise itself to other Mediterranean countries, South America, Canada, Russia... There are about 800 000 head of cattle (about 25 per cent of French production) in Haute-Vienne and the adjacent departments, making the area an important breeding centre.

Stock raising in Dordogne. – Dordogne, above all a region where a wide variety of crops are grown, is at present adding another branch to its economy: stock raising is becoming ever more important. In 1981 there were in Dordogne 200 000 head of sheep and 100 000 pigs; 300 000 cattle produced just over 53 million gallons of milk and about 28 340 tons of meat.

Poultry production is rising especially that of geese (about 130 000) and ducks. Taking livestock as a whole the total production of meat including poultry is 57 000 tons.

INDUSTRY

Apart from Limousin, where several industries have been established for some 200 years, all the many industries to be found today in the region between Berry and Agenais have only existed since the start of the 20C and, in most cases, derive from the natural richness of the soil.

The Food Production Industries. – Large canning factories which have been set up in Périgueux and Sarlat preserve truffles, poultry, *foies gras,* mushrooms and fruit. This industry which is more interested in quality than quantity has contributed to Périgord's gastronomic fame.

A parallel industry has grown up in Quercy: at Souillac and Martel are to be found a certain number of factories that prepare truffles, make *pâtés* from poultry, *foies gras* and their by-products and also produce jams and fruit and vegetable preserves.

The Brive Basin and Agenais have developed the food production industries in the same way, with fruit and vegetable preserving in Agenais and, in addition in the Brive Basin the making of jam, fruit compotes, *crème de marron* (a chestnut dessert), salting factories, pork butchery and *foies gras* factories, flour-mills, distilleries and biscuit-making factories.

(After a photo by M. Brigaud, E.D.F. photographic library)

Le Chastang Dam

The Enamel, Porcelain and Leather Industries. – The presence underground in Limousin of the metallic oxides needed for the production of enamelware favoured the establishment of an enamelling industry in Limoges.

After three centuries of decline, the craft in the last fifty years has regained its reputation which is now as high as it was in the days of such master-enamellers as the Nardon Pénicauds, the Limosins and the Nouailhers.

The discovery at the end of the 18C, of important deposits of kaolin near St-Yrieix, is the basis of the china industry *(p 118).* The first factories were scattered in the southern area of Haute-Vienne, the wood needed for the kilns otherwise being liable to city tolls on entry into Limoges.

Nevertheless, by the beginning of the 19C a group of industrialists were working in the city of Limoges itself, benefiting from its situation on the banks of the Vienne, on which timber could be floated down.

Later, when coal replaced wood as fuel in the kilns, the town had a still greater advantage to offer for coal was brought direct by rail to Limoges from the Carmaux and Commentry coalfields.

By the end of the 19C, due to improvements in the production processes, porcelain had become a major industry in the city.

The leather industry and its many offshoots were able to develop, thanks to abundant water supplies, the tanning resins got from the forests and the hides obtained from large-scale stock raising. Since the beginning of the 19C, there have been some fifty tanneries established in the towns of Limoges, Bellac, St-Junien, Tulle, Uzerche and Issoudun. Today shoes are made at Limoges and St-Amand-Montrond and St-Junien is famous for its gloves *(p 167)* and other items.

Electricity. – The hydro electric undertakings constructed along the upper Dordogne *(p 93)* and its tributaries and the similar projects undertaken on the rivers, Maulde and Taurion make a noticeable increase in the energy potential of France.

Uranium. – Prospection of the old Limousin granite massifs led to the discovery of the first uranium deposit near Crouzille in 1948. Several mines are being worked and annual production totals 700 000 tons of ore which are processed to 1 000 tons of metal by the largest western European processing plant at Bessines. Uranium reserves exceed 20 000 tons which are equal to 200 million tons of oil.

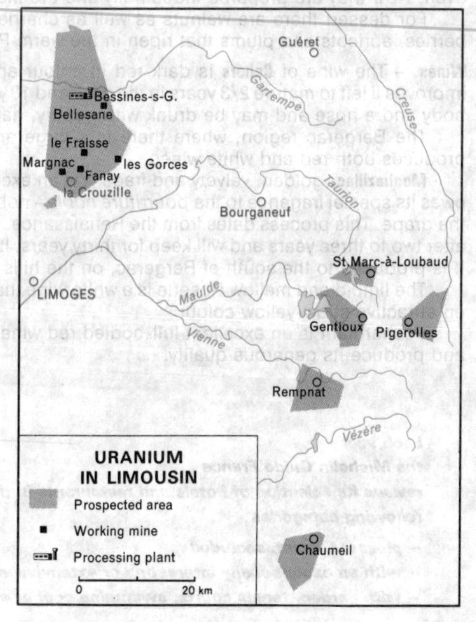

FOOD AND WINE

Gastronomy is highly honoured from the banks of the Cher to the banks of the Garonne. The food and wine reflect the character of each province and help to keep alive its individual reputation. Cookery has remained very regional like all other traditions in this part of the country.

Berry Cookery. – This makes use of farm products and is plain and simple. While vegetable, pickled pork or bread soup blended with a little cream is the principal regional dish, the true Berry speciality is *poulet en barbouille* - "chicken on the chin". This is chicken set alight with brandy, cut in pieces and cooked in a sauce of blood blended with cream, an egg yolk and the chopped liver.

Other Berry dishes are: eggs in wine, ox-tongue *au gratin* and sheep and calves' kidneys. Pumpkin *pâté, truffiat* or *bourre-chrétien* – potatoes covered in pastry – and for dessert, plum flan, *sanciaux* (honey fritters) and *millats* (stewed black cherries), complete the usual local fare.

Wines. – Berry wines are good quality wines. The Sancerre wines and those from the hillsides of the Val de Loire, Quincy and Reuilly are produced from the Sauvignon grape and have a «gun-flint» taste. The slopes of the Arnon, the Cher and Châteaumeillant are planted with *pinot, gamay* and *muscadet* vines which produce light red, white, *rosé* or "smoky" wines. All these fairly light wines go especially well with *hors-d'œuvre* and goats-milk cheese.

Limousin Cookery. – The typical soup is the *bréjaude,* a bacon (*bréjou*-bacon rind) and cabbage soup garnished with rye bread.

Pâtés with truffles or in pastry, which are sometimes garnished with a mixed veal and pork stuffing, and especially the *pâtes de foies gras,* the speciality from Brive-la-Gaillarde, are deservedly famous.

Lièvre en chabessal is hare stuffed with veal, fresh pork, ham and seasoned with salt, pepper, spices and condiments.

Cabbage plays an important part in several dishes: these are *bréjaude,* partridge and cabbage and red cabbage braised with chestnuts. Chestnuts, which for a long time remained the staple of the people, garnish turkey and goose, black pudding, veal or pork stew and, as a *purée,* venison.

Clafoutis, a kind of flan obtained by mixing short pastry with black cherries, is the Limousin dessert.

Périgord and Quercy Cookery. – Truffles, *foie gras* and potted game are among the culinary glories of Périgord. Périgord *pâté* was originally made from partridges stuffed with chicken livers and truffles. Later the *pâté* was made with truffled goose liver.

Quercy and Périgord have a common gastronomic tradition.

The Épicure's Black Diamond. – The truffle is a kind of underground mushroom which grows particularly round certain types of oak known as truffle oaks. It has no stem or root and when fully grown, weighs about 100 gm-3 1/2 ozs.

Truffles are gathered in winter when they are really ripe and fragrant. They are detected by the faint smell they give off. To unearth the treasure, the digger uses a helpmate with a keener smell than himself – a pig or a dog.

The truffle can be tasted in all *foies gras, pâtés,* poultry, sweetbreads, omelettes, *ballottines* and galantines. Both stuffings and sauces are flavoured with truffles.

Potted Meats. – Potted meats *(confit)* are the traditional basis of Périgord cookery. Pork, duck, goose and turkey are cooked in their own fat and preserved in earthenware pots. Pure goose fat is always used instead of butter.

Foies gras. – Forced feeding of geese and ducks enables livers of considerable weight to be obtained. Formerly *foies gras* were prepared as *pâtés* and cooked in terrines in the oven. Now they are prepared industrially and are included in *ballottine.*

For dessert there are walnuts as well as cherries, grapes, peaches, pears, strawberries, apricots and plums that ripen in the warm Périgord and Quercy valleys.

Wines. – The wine of **Cahors** is dark red in colour and full-bodied in flavour. The wine improves if left to mature 2/3 years in the cask and 10 years in the bottle; then it acquires a body and a nose and may be drunk with poultry, game, roasts and cheese.

The Bergerac region, where there is a large area planted with Sauvignon stock, produces both red and white wines.

Monbazillac, golden, velvety and fragant is an excellent dessert wine. This great wine owes its special fragance to the *pourriture noble* – noble rot – which reduces the acidity of the grape. This process dates from the Renaissance. Monbazillac acquires its full flavour after two to three years and will keep for thirty years. It is on a par with the greatest wines. It is produced to the south of Bergerac, on the hills south of the Dordogne.

The limpid and mellow Rosette is a white wine that is fragrant and fruity and takes on an attractive straw-yellow colour.

Pécharmant is an excellent full-bodied red wine which takes a long time to mature and produce its generous quality.

The earth's crust was formed, according to the most authoritative estimates, about three thousand million years ago after the gradual cooling of the planet. The Pre-Cambrian Age, when the oldest rock formations of the earth took place, was followed by the Primary (Palaeozoic), Secondary (Mesozoic), Tertiary (Cainozoic) and Quaternary Ages.

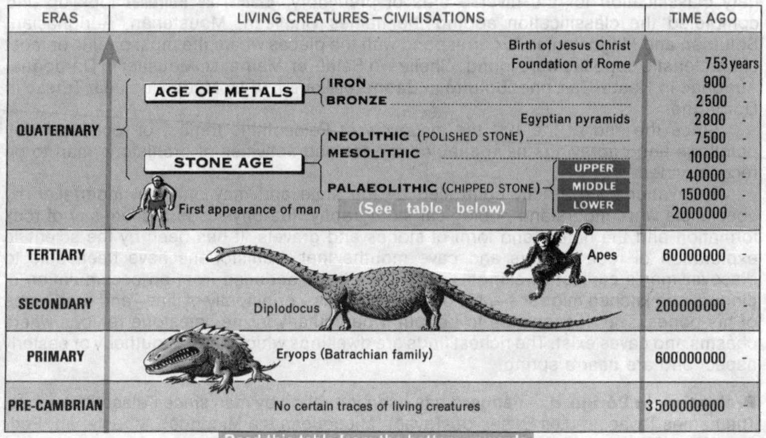

The First Ages of Man. – The Quaternary Age is relatively new since it began only about two million years ago. Nevertheless it is in this period that the evolution of man has taken place *(see table below)*.

There is no definitive evidence of life having existed on the earth in the Pre-Cambrian Age; reptiles, fish, and tail-less amphibians appeared in the course of the Primary Era, mammals and birds during the Secondary Era.

The primates, the most ancient ancestors of man, appeared at the end of the Tertiary Era and were followed in the course of the Quaternary by types ever more advanced: Pithecanthropus, Neanderthal man and finally *homo sapiens*. This last is characterised by his vertical stance, the great size of his cranium and articulate speech.

The slowness of man's evolution during the Palaeolithic Age confounds the imagination: nearly two million years had to pass before he had learnt how to polish stone; in contrast, the few thousand years that followed saw in the Near and Middle East and later in Egypt the development of brilliant civilisations which reached their climax in the construction of the Great Pyramids. A few centuries later a new step was taken with the discovery of bronze and later still, in approximately 900 BC, of iron.

PALAEOLITHIC PERIOD THE CHIPPED STONE AGE

	CULTURE	CLIMATE	FAUNA	HUMAN TYPE	TOOLS AND WEAPONS
UPPER	MAGDALENIAN SOLUTRIAN AURIGNACIAN PERIGORDIAN	Würm Glacial Age	Age of the reindeer, the mammoth, the bear, cave hyena, the hairy rhinoceros.	Chancelade Man Cro-Magnon Man Grimaldi Man Homo sapiens	Eyed needle, gravers, harpoons, blade with rounded bevelled back, assegais, various bone implements. 40,000 years ago
MIDDLE	MOUSTERIAN LEVALLOISIAN TAYACIAN	Warm period	The hippopotamus Age of the mammoth the elephant	Mousterian Man La Ferrassie Man La Chapelle-aux-Saints Man Neanderthal Man	Oval flakes, blades, discs, points, scrapers, flint biface industry. 150,000 years ago
LOWER	ACHEULEAN	Riss Glacial Age	First appearance of the mammoth	Fontechevade Man (Charente)	Chipped flint or quartz coups de poing, points, scrapers, barbed saws.
		Warm period	The bull the lion the bison the rhinoceros the tiger	Swanscombe Man (England)	
		Mindel Glacial Age			
	CLACTONIAN ABBEVILLIAN	Warm period	the hippopotamus the rhinoceros the great bear	Java Man Pithecanthropus (Indonesia)	Coups de poing Flints chipped away on two sides or bifaces.
		Günz Glacial Age			2,000,000 years ago

Read this table from the bottom upwards

The Researchers. – The study of prehistory was a science essentially French in origin and began in the very early years of the 19C. In spite of the scepticism of most learned men, the early researchers continued their investigations in Périgord, Lozère and in the valley of the Somme. To **Boucher de Perthes** (1788-1868) falls the honour of having prehistory, the science of man before the invention of writing, recognised. His discoveries at St-Acheul and Abbeville were the starting-point for an important series of studies. **Édouard Lartet** undertook many excavations in the valley of the Vézère and established a preliminary classification for the diverse eras of prehistory. **Grabiel de Mortillet** took up and completed the classification adding the names Chellean, Mousterian, Aurignacian, Solutrian and Magdalenian to correspond with the places where the most prolific or most characteristic deposits were found: Chelles in Seine-et-Marne, Le Moustier in Dordogne, Aurignac in Haute-Garonne, Solutré in Saône-et-Loire and La Madeleine near Tursac in Dordogne.

Since the end of the 19C the discovery of Palaeolithic tombs, of tools and wall paintings and engravings have enabled the life and activities of prehistoric man to be reconstructed.

Excavations are strictly controlled by the state and may only be undertaken by specialists who understand geological stratigraphy, the physics and chemistry of rock formation and the nature and form of stones and gravels. It has been by the scientific exploration of rock shelters and cave mouths that prehistorians have been able to discover man's earliest dwellings – facts have been deduced from an accumulation of cinders and kitchen middens –, his diversity of tools – principally of flint – and even some of his bones. The deposits are to be found particularly in the limestone regions where chasms and caves exist. The richest finds are dwellings which have a southerly or easterly aspect and are near a spring.

Prehistory in Périgord. – Périgord has been inhabited by man since Palaeolithic times. The names Tayacian (Les Eyzies-de-Tayac), Micoquean (La Micoque), Mousterian, Perigordian and Magdalenian are evidence of the importance of these prehistoric sites. Nearly 200 deposits have been discovered of which more than half are in the valley of the Vézère near Les Eyzies-de-Tayac *(description p 102)*.

The Evolution of Man in the Palaeolithic Age. – The discovery of prehistoric human skeletons in different parts of the world has enabled archaeologists to define a certain number of separate races from the apparent differences.

The Pre-Hominidae. – Man's most distant ancestors, collectors of food and makers of the Abbevillian biface were Australopithecus in East and South Africa, who used only split flints, Pithecanthropus or the Java man (from the Greek – *pithecos* = ape, *anthropos* = man) discovered by a Dutchman, Dr. Dubois, with a cranium half-way in size between the most highly developed ape and the least developed man, Sinanthropus or Pekin man discovered by Dr. Pei, and Atlanthropus, studied in North Africa by Professor Arambourg.

Three parts of a skull found in 1935, 1936 and 1955 in gravels at Swanscombe in England have been identified as predating Neanderthal man.

Neanderthal Man. – Neanderthal man lived on earth about 150 000 years ago. In 1856, near Düsseldorf in the Düssel valley (also known as the Neander valley), the remains of a man were found with the following characteristics: Cranium capacity approximately 1 500 cu cms, elongated cranium (dolichocephalus), extremely receding forehead, prominently developed jawbones and a stature of 5 ft 3 in only.

Skeletons of marked similarity to this were found in France at La Chapelle-aux-Saints (Corrèze) in 1908, at Le Moustier (Dordogne) in 1909 and at La Ferrassie (Dordogne) in 1909 and 1911.

Neanderthal man after existing for a long period in Africa – a characteristic cranium was discovered in Rhodesia buried among bones of contemporary wild animals – completely disappeared from the surface of the globe during the Upper Palaeolithic Age.

Homo Sapiens. – *Homo sapiens* habitation of France goes back approximately 40 000 years. His essential characteristics – a perfect vertical stance, a cranium capacity of from 1 500 to 1 700 cu cms, a high forehead and only slightly projecting eyebrows – show him to be highly developed and comparable with man today (*sapiens* = intelligent).

Several races have been traced as belonging to this same family from discoveries made in scientifically undertaken excavations.

The **Grimaldi Race** (skeletons discovered in the Grimaldi Grotto near Monaco), recalls, from its characteristics, certain races such as the Hottentots and Bushmen now living in South Africa. The Grimaldi man stood about 5 ft 3 in tall, had a dolichocephalic skull, a wide nasal opening, prominent lower jaw and a fore-arm and leg long by comparison with the upper arm and the thigh.

The **Cro-Magnon Race** (skeletons found in the rock shelters of Cro-Magnon in Dordogne and Solutré in Saône-et-Loire) were tall – about 5 ft 11 in – with long, robust limbs denoting considerable muscular strength; the skull was dolichocephalic in shape. This race lived from the Upper Palaeolithic to the Neolithic Age; traces of its existence are to be found today among the Berber populations and even among the people of southwest France.

The **Chancelade Race** (skeletal type discovered in 1888 at Chancelade near Périgueux) appeared in the Magdalenian Period. These men came either from eastern Europe or Asia and possessed characteristics extraordinarily similar to the Eskimos now living in Greenland and North America: a large cranium of a pronounced dolichocephalic form, a long, wide face, pronounced cheek bones and a height no more than 5 ft 1 in. Some of these reindeer hunters may perhaps have followed their game when it migrated north when the climate became less cold at the end of the Magdalenian Period; the remainder adapted themselves to the new conditions of life.

LIFE AND ART IN THE PALAEOLITHIC ERA (1)

The habitation of Périgord by man goes back to the beginning of the Quaternary Era, but the oldest Neanderthal skeletons to be discovered only go back to the Mousterian Age, the period when the first tombs were built.

Later, tribes came, it is believed, from eastern Europe and installed themselves in the caves and shelters which afforded many natural advantages: protection from the cold, the existence, nearby, of springs and rivers rich in fish, the possibility of attracting game to the narrow ravines where its capture was easier.

The Palaeolithic Age (*paleos* = ancient, *lithos* = stones) covers the period in which men knew only how to chip flints. An intermediate age, the Mesolithic (*mesos* = middle), separates it from the Neolithic Age (*neos* = new or late) when man learnt to polish stone. Skill in flint knapping evolved very slowly and therefore enables the Palaeolithic Age to be subdivided into three: the Lower, Middle and Upper Palaeolithic periods.

Lower Palaeolithic Age (beginning about two million years ago). – Men living in this period in Périgord knew how to use fire and hunted big game. The earth suffered three successive ice ages known as the Günz, the Mindel and the Riss Ice Ages after the tributary valleys of the Danube where they have been studied. Between each ice age, France and Britain had a tropical climate.

Flint knapping began with a cut made by striking two stones violently one against the other, or by striking one against a rock which served as an anvil.

These two methods gave rise to the two types of industry shown below.

Abbeville biface.
Cleared of its flakes on two sides, the flint kernel is fined down and takes the form of an unevenly peeled fat almond. In the Acheulean Period better finished arrow-heads were obtained.

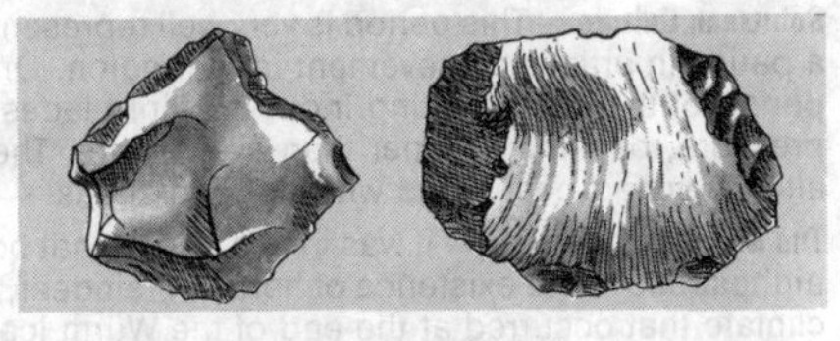

Clacton Flints (flakes)
By using the flakes a relatively smooth or worked face could be obtained.
This Clacton industry (it has been pin-pointed to Clacton-on-Sea) existed in the Tayacian Period and produced smaller pieces.

Middle Palaeolithic Age (beginning about 150 000 years ago). – With Neanderthal man there appeared better finished and more specialised tools. Mousterian industry used both bifaces and flakes. New methods – the fashioning of flints by a bone or wooden striker – enabled triangular points to be produced, also scrapers, used probably for working skins, and flints adapted to take a wooden handle and serve as hunting clubs.

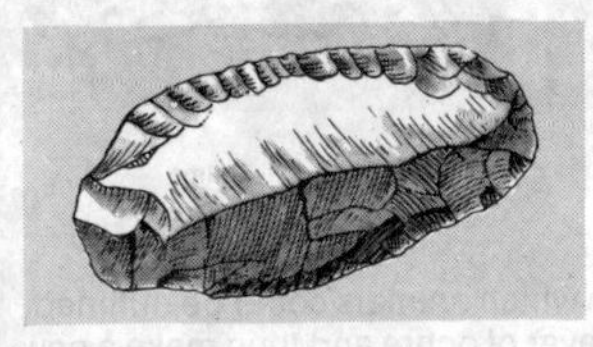

Scraper-point.

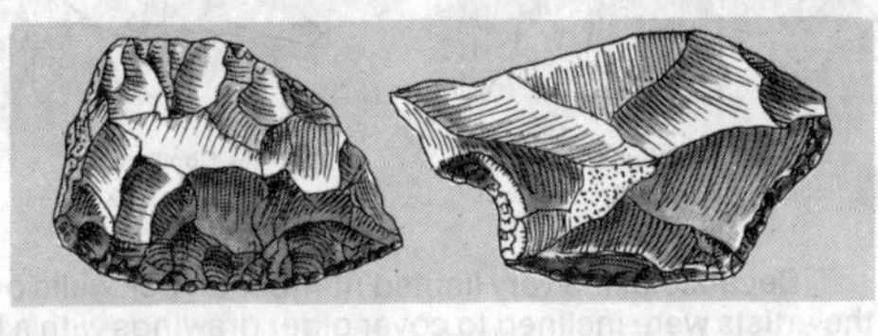

Points.

It seems likely that in the Mousterian period some cave mouths were used as dwelling places. Man by this time possessed more sophisticated weapons with which to hunt big game and protected himself from the cold with the help of animal skins.

Upper Palaeolithic Age (beginning in Périgord about 40 000 years ago). – *Homo sapiens* replaced Neanderthal man. From this time onwards there was constant improvement in the production of tools, life also became easier with the perfection of new hunting methods, so that men felt free to devote themselves to artistic expression.

The Périgordian and Aurignacian Cultures. – These two names designate contemporary industries in the same region. So far as tools were concerned, flint blades were, by this time, knapped so finely that they cut like a knife; bone points were split at the base and given a shaft to serve as javelins.

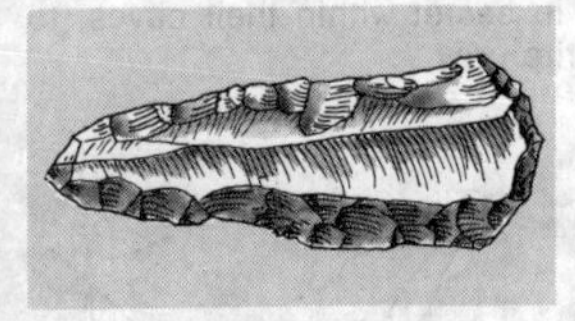

Scraper on the end of a blade.

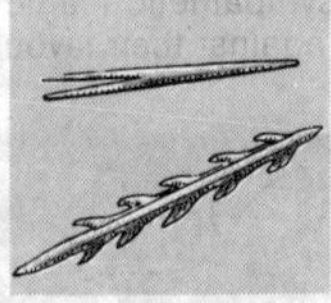

Harpoon-point.

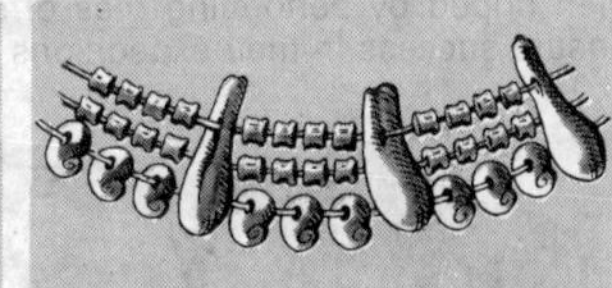

Necklace.

The tombs reveal skeletons coloured with red ochre and, more often than not, bedecked with bone pendants. Many ornaments – shells, ivory wands, knapped flints – show the desire for decoration and an already advanced artistic sense: the bracelets and ivory necklaces are made with round beads strung alternately with teeth or shells.

(1) For more information read « World Prehistory » by G. Clark (Cambridge 1969)

In the artistic field the oldest discoveries are line drawings such as those contained in the Bara-Bahau Cave. The oldest sculptures discovered were generally executed in the round and go back to the Aurignacian and Perigordian periods. Nearly all are of human figures mostly feminine, and have as their theme the cult of fertility (luxuriant figures and an exaggeration of the sexual organs); such is the "Laussel Venus" known as the "Venus with the horn of plenty".

The Laussel Venus.

Le Pech-Merle
outlined hands and black spots.

Bara-Bahau
rock engraving of a horse.

The first examples of wall decoration appear as hands placed flat against the rock and outlined in black or red: these are to be found at Font-de-Gaume and at Le-Pech-Merle. The animals are only rudimentarily sketched. By the end of this period, man had become a true artist as may be seen by the sculptures at the Abri du Poisson and the drawings and paintings of Font-de-Gaume and Lascaux.

Solutrean Culture. – This period is very well represented in the Dordogne and seems to mark a pause in artistic achievement in the region. On the other hand, it is the most brilliant period of the stone-cutting industry: flint blades, following a method of splitting under pressure, became slimmer than ever before. The flawed points were used as weapons after they had been fitted with wooden shafts.

The Magdalenian Period. – It was in this period that bone and ivory craftsmanship reached its highest peak. The existence of herds of reindeer, which is accounted for by the very cold climate that occurred at the end of the Würm Ice Age, influenced man towards working bone and horn. The many harpoons used for hunting and fishing and the perforated batons made from reindeer horn and adorned with drawings whose use has not been definitely established, are evidence of this skill.

It is also the period when cave art reached its climax. It was above all the depiction of animals. Living in the shelters and caves, the men of the Magdalenian Era used the cave walls to express their artistic emotions in painting and drawing.

Rouffignac
rock engraving of a mammoth.

Les Combarelles
rock engraving of a reindeer.

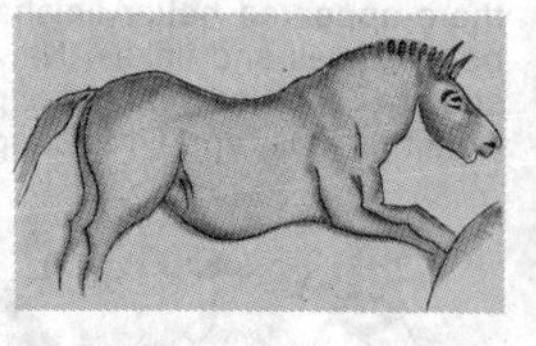
Font de Gaume
black relief of a horse.

Because of the very limited number of rock walls on which animals could be outlined, the artists were inclined to cover older drawings with a layer of ochre and then make a new drawing on top. The disappearance of the coloured backgrounds makes examination of the drawings today more difficult: drawings are juxtaposed or superimposed.

In drawing and in painting the style became more definite and technique evolved towards a greater precision of outline. It is hard to imagine the peculiarly difficult conditions under which these artists worked: by the wavering light of torches or stone lamps using animal fat as fuel, the artist managed to draw from memory the many animals he knew. This technique reached its height in the multicoloured frescoes in which flat colours were used and sometimes combined with drawing. The fact that these paintings have been discovered in very isolated caves where it is certain that man never lived makes them seem almost magical. The first designs in the series begin as far as 71 yds from the cave entrance at Font-de-Gaume, 104 yds at La Mouthe and 131 yds at Les Combarelles.

The magical quality is evident in the depiction of animals pierced by assegais or arrows: disembowelled bison lose their entrails at Lascaux, horses or stags are marked with black or red lines or have hand prints superimposed and other signs which have been taken as representing sympathetic magic. It would appear that Palaeolithic huntsmen hoped by performing rites of sympathetic magic in secret within their caves, to ensure success in their expeditions against their favourite prey.

Font de Gaume
multicoloured bison.

Lascaux
horse pierced by arrows.

Lascaux
charging bison.

After the Magdalenian Era art was in almost total eclipse. As the climate grew milder some of the reindeer hunting tribes moved northwards. Later, in their place, came tribes from Italy and southern Spain. Art was not to reappear before the Neolithic Age.

HISTORICAL FACTS OF INTEREST

Eleanor's Dowry. – In 1137, Prince Louis, son of the King of France, married Eleanor, only daughter of Duke William of Aquitaine. She brought as her dowry, the Duchy of Guyenne, Périgord, Limousin, Poitou, Angoumois, Saintonge, Gascony and suzerainty of Auvergne and the County of Toulouse. But it was an ill-assorted marriage; Louis, who had become king as Louis VII, might be said to be a monk crowned while his wife was lighthearted in character. After fifteen years of conjugal misunderstanding, the king on his return from a crusade, had the Council of Beaugency (1152) pronounce his divorce. Eleanor recovered not only her liberty but also her dowry. Her marriage, two months later, with **Henry Plantagenet,** Count of Anjou and Lord of Maine, Touraine and Normandy, was a political disaster for the royal house of France, the Capetians. Eleanor's and Henry's joint domains were already as great as were those of the King of France. Two years later Henry Plantagenet inherited the throne of England which he ruled as Henry II. The balance of power was destroyed and a war broke out between England and France that was to last three centuries.

By the building of *bastides (p 32)* in the 13C the Kings of France and England hoped to consolidate their positions and justify their territorial claims. The Capetians and Plantagenets each tried to get a foothold in the other's territories but the Dordogne acted as a dividing line between them. The Treaty of Paris in 1259, between St. Louis and Henry III of England, was in reality, only a truce. Guyenne remained English until the end of the Hundred Years War in 1453.

The Albigensian Crusade. – In the 12C the faith of the Catharists which had its origins in a religious movement of 3C Persia, made fantastic progress throughout the Languedoc. The Catharists or Albigenses (named after the town of Albi to the northeast of Toulouse) rejected church sacraments and the ecclesiastical hierarchy. It was Pope Innocent III who in 1208 preached that a crusade should be undertaken against the Albigensian heresy.

Simon de Montfort, an ambitious fanatic led the crusade (1209-1229). After two years of struggle the southern armies were vanquished at Muret (1213). Simon de Montfort was killed in 1218 laying siege to Toulouse for the second time. Peace came with the signing of the Treaty of Paris in 1229. The last of the Albigenses took refuge in Montsegur Castle but were massacred in 1244. Simon de Montfort's son moved to England in 1229 and as Earl of Leicester was to lead the baronial revolt against King Henry III and was later to become one of the leading statesmen.

The Hundred Years War (1337-1453). – In 1328 Edward III, was an unsuccessful claimant to his uncle, the French King's throne. Differences continued and Edward renewed his claim to the French throne. Philip VI then declared Guyenne confiscate in 1337 and hostilities began. Edward embarked for the continent in 1338. The victories at Crécy (1346) and the Siege of Calais (1346-1347) were decisive battles in the early years of the war, which were followed by a period of truces and the Black Death (1348).

The Dordogne became the battlefield of the war with the taking of Tulle (1346) and Domme (1347). In 1355 **Edward the Black Prince** landed at Bordeaux and at the battle of Poitiers (1356) he took the French King, John II, prisoner. The Old Duchy of Aquitaine was ceded to the English as part of the ransom for John II's liberty. The intervening period saw continental campaigns by the Black Prince and **John of Gaunt** in opposition to the great Constable of France, Du Guesclin. Both royal houses were troubled by dynastic problems. In France the assassination of the Duke of Orléans resulted in the civil war between the Burgundians and Armagnacs. Both factions sought English aid. Fighting reopened when **Henry V** revived his claims to the French throne. The battle of Agincourt 1415 was an English and Burgundian victory. In 1420 the Treaty of Troyes recognized Henry V as heir to the mad King of France and arranged the marriage between Henry and Catherine of Valois. It was however Charles, Duke of Berry who became King as Charles VII of France in 1429. The situation was critical: half the kingdom was in the hands of the English who had, as an ally, the Duke of Burgundy. Until 1429 when Joan of Arc intervened, **Charles VII,** who had been proclaimed King at Mehun-sur-Yèvre Castle, was derided by his enemies as "King of the town of Bourges". Berry was then the Capetian monarchy's surest stronghold. It was here that Charles found the support he needed to wage war against the English – Jacques Cœur put his vast fortune at the King's disposal. The English rule in Aquitaine ended with the defeat of John Talbot, Earl of Shrewsbury, at the Battle of Castillon near Libourne in 1453.

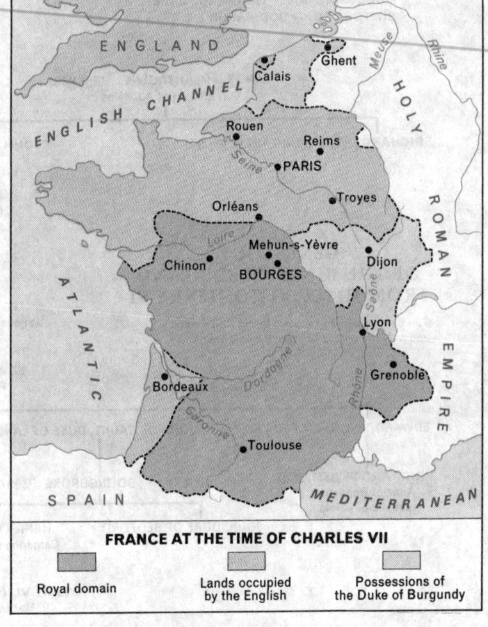

FRANCE AT THE TIME OF CHARLES VII

A few facts of regional historical note, up to the Wars of Religion, are given below in their chronological relation to the best known events of general history.

BC	In DORDOGNE
	Local tribes inhabit the area: Bituriges (Bourges): Caduici (Cahors); Petrocorii (Périgueux)
	Druids resist the Romans *(p 136)*
4C	During the Roman occupation Bourges is capital of the province, Aquitaine
	The Puy d'Issolud is the last site of Gaulish resistance to Caesar *(p 130)*
AD	
250	St. Martial evangelizing in the region
300	Périgueux destroyed by the Alemans
407	Barbarians followed by Visigoths, who make Toulouse their capital (419)
6C	Period of the Limousin saints: Junien, Leonard and Eligius
732	Charles Martel crushes the Saracens at Poitiers *(p 180)*
1183	Henri Court Mantel dies at Martel
1199	Richard Lionheart dies at Châlus
1209-1229	Albigensian Crusade *(p 25)*
1259	Treaty of Paris. Périgord and Bourdeilles ceded to the English by St. Louis
1279	Treaty of Amiens. Agenais ceded to the English
1286	Treaty of Paris. Saintonge passes to the English
1337	Philip VI declares Guyenne confiscate and Edward III renews his claim to the French throne
1337-1453	Hundred Years War *(p 25)*
1574	Monpazier delivered by treason to Geoffroi de Vivans *(p 91)*
1594	Croquants revolt, a peasant uprising
1598	Montauban, St-Antonin, Bruniquel and Bergerac – bastions of Protestantism
1621	Montauban resists a Catholic siege by Louis XIII
1685	Many Huguenots flee France. Aubusson and Bergerac suffer a sharp drop in population

BC	GENERAL HISTORY
	Celts invade Gaul
59-51	Conquest of Gaul by Caesar
52	Caesar forces the Gauls to capitulate at Alesia
AD	
313	Edict of Milan: Christians are granted freedom of worship
476	The Roman Empire crumbles under the attacks by Barbarians
711	Iberian peninsula invaded by Saracens
1066	William the Conqueror lands in England
1215	The Magna Carta
13C	Period of *bastide* building
1562	Start of the Wars of Religion
1576	Founding of the Catholic or Holy League to combat the Calvinists
1598	Edict of Nantes granted freedom of worship to Huguenots
1685	Revocation of the Edict of Nantes

GENEALOGY OF THE KINGS OF ENGLAND FROM HENRY II TO HENRY VI

The dates given correspond to the king's reign and only the names of French wives are shown.

HENRY II PLANTAGENET (1154-1189)
Eleanor of Aquitaine

RICHARD I, THE LIONHEART (1189-1199)

JOHN LACKLAND (1199-1216)

HENRY III (1216-1272)
Eleanor of Provence

EDWARD I (1272-1307)

EDWARD II (1307-1327)
Isabella, daughter of Philip the Fair

EDWARD III (1327-1377)
Philippa of Hainaut

EDWARD, THE BLACK PRINCE

JOHN OF GAUNT, DUKE OF LANCASTER

EDMUND OF YORK

RICHARD II (1377-1399)
Anne of Bohemia
Isabella of Valois

HENRY IV, BOLINGBROKE (1399-1413)

JOHN, DUKE OF BEDFORD

HENRY V (1413-1422)
Catherine of Valois, daughter of Charles VI

HENRY VI (1422-1461/1470-1471)
Margaret of Anjou

ART AND ARCHITECTURE

The first known manifestations of art in France occur in the valley of the Vézère and the prehistoric sites of the Les Eyzies region. But in periods closer to our time, Périgord, Quercy and Limousin have been the setting of intense artistic activity.

In the Middle Ages, the growing inspiration of religion was given expression in countless pilgrimages which called for huge churches and the foundation of monasteries which became centres of learning. In the 14 and 16C churches, castles and châteaux multiplied, reflecting in their style the individual character of each province.

GALLO-ROMAN ART

Of the buildings constructed by the Gauls and the Romans only a few have withstood the test of time. Souvenirs of the period of the Gauls do survive however: at the Puy d'Issolud near Vayrac, it is believed that the site can be located of the Uxellodunum encampment – this was the last bastion of the Gauls in their resistance to the all-conquering Caesar. At Luzech, also, there are traces of the Impernal encampment which commanded a bend in the river Lot and, near the Vers valley, the ruins of the Murcens encampment.

In Berry, excavations undertaken at **Drevant,** near St-Amand-Montrond, have established that on the site of a small Gaulish market town developed a large Gallo-Roman centre. The theatre, baths and a vast walled area which may have been a forum or a temple of Gallo-Roman times, have all been uncovered. The amphitheatre at **Chassenon** near Rochechouart which once stood outside the walls of the city was still being used by its citizens in the Middle Ages.

At Limoges an amphitheatre was built on the northwest outskirts of the old town; it was razed to the ground in the 16C and its ruins are now hidden beneath the Orsay Gardens. Évaux-les-Bains was known to the Romans as can be seen from the floor of a bathing establishment tiled in marble and porphyry.

Traces have been discovered at Périgueux of the ancient Vesunna, capital of the Petrocorii. The finds include the Vesunna Tower, the arena and the perimeter wall.

ROMANESQUE ART

After the troubled times of the early Middle Ages, marked by the Norman invasions, the decadence of the Carolingian dynasty and the struggles between the great feudal barons, the year 1 000 marks the beginning of a new era in the art of building.

Simultaneously with the affirmation of the royal power came a vast surge of faith throughout France: Carolingian buildings which were too cramped and no longer suited to the needs of the times, were replaced by churches of much greater size built by bolder methods. This religious art, known as the Romanesque style, appeared in regional guises so different that several separate schools of architecture developed out of their individual characteristics.

Religious Architecture

We describe below the architectural terms used in religious buildings.

Plan. – This is in the form of a Latin cross; the chevet is nearly always in the east, that is pointed in the approximate direction of Jerusalem. The two arms of the cross form the transept. The nave, where the faithful stand, is sometimes preceded by a kind of antechamber known as the narthex. The larger churches contain an apse built beyond the chancel and reserved for the clergy: this apse is normally semicircular. In pilgrimage churches the aisles continued right round the chancel forming an ambulatory which enabled the faithful to circulate easily in the interior of the building. Chapels were sometimes built on to either side of the apse (apsidal chapels) and on to the arms of the transept.

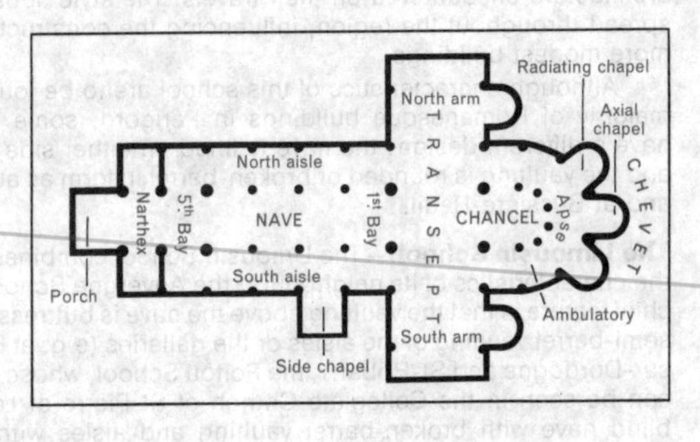

Vaulting. – The Carolingian churches with their timber roofs were very vulnerable to fire. From the 11C onwards roofing in stone became widespread. **Barrel vaulting** was the first to be practised; this is a semicircular vault placed along the axis of the structure to be covered *(see diagram).* **Groined vaulting** was adopted a little later and is formed by the intersection of two semicircular barrel vaults. This type of vaulting was often used in the building of crypts and aisles. **Domes,** common in Périgord, sometimes replaced barrel and groined vaulting.

Semicircular barrel vaulting

1 Vault - 2 Arch supporting the vault.

Carved decoration. – The carved decoration of buildings developed, in the Romanesque period, as an adornment of faces and of capitals. Larger compositions were carved on doorway tympana. But though Romanesque art kept its incontestable unity, each province was able to express its individual style.

The Romanesque Schools

The Périgord School. – The Romanesque period in Périgord produced churches with characteristics in common. The use of a fine golden limestone with warm overtones mellowed the severe appearance of the buildings. The exteriors were startling for the extreme simplicity of their decoration: the façades were often adorned only with two blind arches placed one on either side of the main doorway as at Bussière-Badil and La Chapelle St-Robert and sometimes with blind arcades placed high up; long arcades supported on pilasters that served as buttresses broke the monotony of the walls of the nave outside.

The interiors were plain: most of the buildings contained but a single nave, the vaulting rested on powerful supports linked by massive arches. The side walls were often adorned with arcades which supported galleries and two or three tall windows (clerestory) lit each bay. The small country churches were without transepts, but larger churches all possessed them and they frequently extended far out from the nave. Apsidal chapels opened off the chancel.

Le Dorat Collegiate Church
Dome on pendentives
1 Circular dome - 2 Pendentive
3 Arches of the transept crossing.

While domes were used in most Romanesque churches to cover the transept crossing, domes on pendentives *(see diagram)* became so popular an architectural feature in Périgord that their use was further extended to serve as a covering for all parts of a church.

A **dome** is a vault in the shape of a skull cap, a hemisphere intended to replace barrel vaulting. The transition from a square to a circular base is made by the construction of "pendentives", concave inverted triangles built at the four corners of the square to be covered; the upper parts of the triangles meet, forming the circular base on which the dome is constructed.

The nave is divided into several square sections, each topped by a dome on pendentives; in contrast the arms of the transept are usually roofed in barrel vaulting.

In addition to the Périgueux Cathedral of St-Front, which was rebuilt last century with additions which overpower the original character of the building, and the Church of St-Étienne-de-la-Cité, also in Périgueux, Périgord has a considerable number of domed churches: Agonac, Le Dorat, St-Jean-de-Côle, St-Astier, Grand-Brassac, Trémolat, Paunat, Souillac, Vieux-Mareuil and Ajat. Some of these, however, have been restored with the result that the domes have been replaced by ogive vaulting.

Domed buildings are to be found outside Périgord in Quercy as in Cahors in the Cathedral of St-Étienne, in Limousin in the abbey church at Solignac and even as far away as Agenais, Anjou, Poitou and Auvergne.

St-Front in Périgueux and St-Étienne in Cahors may be taken as prototypes of the Périgord school. St-Front with its plan in the shape of a Greek cross and its thrusting domes looks as though it were a copy of the Church of the Apostles in Constantinople. It is generally agreed that Périgord and Quercy pilgrims, returning from the Levant, may well have had the idea of copying the style of architecture encountered on their travels. The style subsequently spread throughout the region, influencing the construction of far more modest buildings.

Although characteristics of this school are to be found in the majority of Romanesque buildings in Périgord, some churches have a different design: the nave is lined on either side by aisles and the vaulting is rounded or broken-barrel in form as at Cadouin and at Bussière-Badil.

The Limousin School. – The Limousin School combines many of the characteristics of its neighbours: the Auvergne School, whose chief feature is that the vaulting above the nave is buttressed by the semi-barrel vaulting of the aisles or the galleries (e.g. at Beaulieu-sur-Dordogne and St-Robert); the Poitou School, whose influence can be seen in the Collegiate Church of St-Pierre at Le Dorat – blind nave with broken-barrel vaulting and aisles with groined vaulting; and the Périgord School – the domes on the church at Solignac.

(After a photo by Éd. La Cigogne)

St-Léonard
The belfry.

Nevertheless, certain elements can be considered as purely Limousin. Firstly in the use, as a building material, of granite which is found throughout the region and whose colour, while usually grey, sometimes verges on a golden tone.

Secondly in the peculiar design of some belfries: the octagonal spire which crowns them is joined to the square tiers that form the base of the tower by one or two octagonal storeys; the gables that stand on the topmost of the square tiers are not only ornamental but play a part in the overall construction since they divide and balance the weight of the upper octagonal tiers; the best examples of this style are the belfries at St-Léonard, Collonges, Uzerche and Brantôme (in Périgord). The belfry at St-Junien was probably planned to follow this pattern as the beginning of a steeply sloping gable can be seen above the second square tier.

Finally the façades present a more or less uniform style: massive belfry-porches adorned with blind arcades of various sizes and forms, as at Le Dorat, Bénévent and St-Junien; doorways with recessed elongated arcades on either side (La Souterraine and St-Junien); a first storey flanked by bell turrets which are pierced at Le Dorat and La Souterraine and encircled by a corbelled gallery at St-Junien and lastly doorways with twin doors framed by recessed covings which in some cases are scalloped showing the influence of Mohammedan art (Le Dorat, La Souterraine).

In Berry. – Though characteristics of the Poitou School may frequently be seen, most Romanesque churches in Berry have a precise plan with certain features peculiar to the area: the chancel generally consists of two bays flanked by aisles which communicate with the choir through arches resting on columns adorned with historiated capitals; the apse is semicircular; the transept has a dome on squinches above the crossing and barrel vaulting above the arms; the nave is wider than the transept crossing and communicates with the arms of the transept by narrow passages known as **Berrichon passages.**

The abbey churches are based on the Benedictine design, for the Order of St-Benedict spread throughout Berry and built abbeys at Fontgombault, Chezal-Benoît and at Châteaumeillant where the Church of St-Genès has an unusual arrangement of the chevet with six parallel apsidal chapels. Noirlac was created by the Cistercians, Plaimpied and Puy-Ferrand by the Augustinian Canons Regular. One church alone in the Bourges diocese is designed quite differently: it is the basilica of Neuvy-St-Sépulcre which is built in the form of a rotunda and was inspired by the Church of the Holy Sepulchre in Jerusalem.

Sculpture

Sculpture began to find great favour early in the 11C and spread widely throughout the 12C, taking up the decorative motifs of the Roman period and the Oriental and Byzantine themes brought back by pilgrims from their journeys to the holy places. These influences were noticeable in Aquitaine and Languedoc.

Galloons, a type of ribbonwork used by the Greeks as decoration, appear in the most overworked manner on doorways at Moissac and Beaulieu. The galloons, when crossed form a series of festoons or Greek keys: among numerous examples in Poitou and Limousin are the churches at Vigeois (side door) and Le Dorat. Roses adorn the lintel over the main doorway at Moissac.

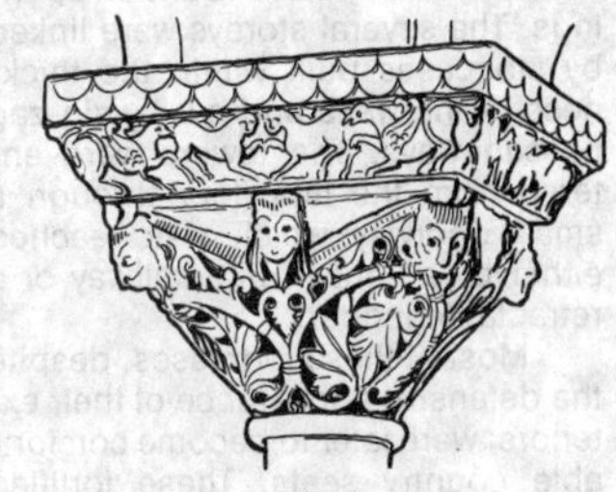

(After a photo by Éd. Privat)

Moissac – Cloister capital.

The Languedoc School. – The school, whose centre was at Toulouse, was one of the most famous, both for the quantity and the quality of work produced.

From its workshops issued wonderful capitals: capitals adorned with scrollwork and palm fronds as can be seen in the cloisters at Moissac; historiated capitals on which the personages depicted illustrate scenes from the Old and New Testaments, the Life of Christ or the Passion.

The Moissac Cloister possesses several bas-reliefs executed by artists of the Toulouse school in the early part of the 12C.

This school also produced carved doorways which were among the most beautiful in France at that time. The tympanum of the abbey doorway at Moissac appears to have inspired that of Beaulieu-sur-Dordogne: the principal theme of both is the Last Judgment; the carving at Moissac, however, has greater style, although the same decorative motifs are used in each.

The remains of the Souillac doorway, the tympana of Cahors Cathedral, and the churches at Martel and Carennac, appear from their sculpture to belong to the same school.

The Poitou School. – From Poitiers, where the school reigned in full force, its influence was deeply felt not only in Poitou but also in Limousin. Poitou designers excelled in the abundance and variety of their sculptured decoration, which was always executed with surprising skill.

At St-Junien you see, in the figures carved on the tomb of St. Junien, the same poses, often marked by a certain stiffness, that you see on the statues crowding the doorways of the larger churches of Poitou and Angoumois.

In Limousin although there were no workshops as famous as those at Toulouse, interesting work was nevertheless produced: the use of granite for the capitals of St-Léonard gives them a particular character. A strange fauna of fronting goats, lions and birds standing back to back, may be seen carved upon them. The tympanum of the church at Collonges is devoted to Christ's Ascension.

In Berry, the churches of La Celle and Châteaumeillant and the former abbey at Plaimpied possess remarkable capitals.

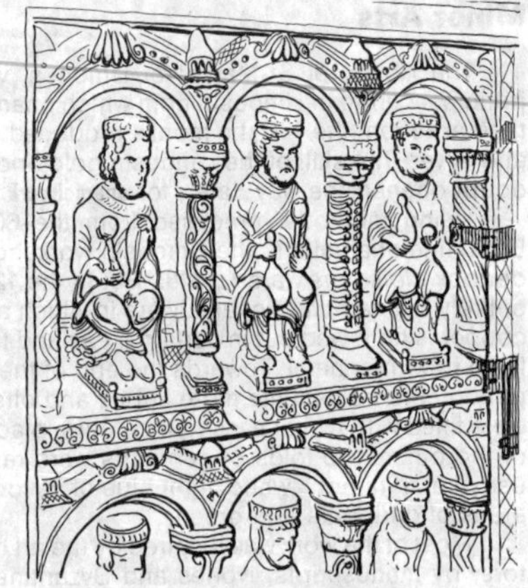

(After a photo by Éd. J. Delmas)

St-Junien – Detail from St. Junien's tomb.

Painting

Fresco work (from the Italian word *fresco* = fresh) is mural painting done with water colours on fresh plaster, with which the colours combine. The number of colours was limited, since only earth or iron oxides were used, thus producing only shades between yellow and red and two or three other colours such as green, purple and cobalt blue.

Although not in the same class as the extraordinary wall paintings to be found at St-Savin-sur-Gartempe *(see the Michelin Green Guide Côte de l'Atlantique, French edition only)*, the frescoes of Berry are worthy of attention. There is no evidence of a local school and it would seem that each artist wandered at will executing his works in his own particular style. The matt paintings were of pastel colours on light backgrounds. At Vic the figures are boldly outlined in red-ochre or brown. The frescoes at Brinay with their subdued colours show a greater use of light and shade. Like a tapestry the scenes unfold on horizontal bands against green, yellow, light brown or white backgrounds. The figures are vividly expressive.

The frescoes at Rocamadour in Quercy have more vivid colours on a dark blue background.

Civil and Military Architecture

There are few traces left of civil architecture of the Romanesque period. The former town hall of St-Antonin-Noble-Val in Quercy, although it has been considerably restored, is an interesting example of municipal Romanesque architecture of the 12C, with its sculptured gallery, arcaded portico and tall square belfry.

Montbrun Castle

The feudal fortresses erected in the 10 and 11C were greatly altered in later centuries and can scarcely be said to have resisted the warfare and destruction of the times.

The keeps, last refuge of the defence systems, were usually square in Limousin in the 12C. In the 13C they were pierced by small rounded openings. The several storeys were linked by staircases built within the thickness of the walls and cut by zig-zag passageways. The towers were entered from the first floor through a small doorway which was reached either by a lightly built stairway or a retractable ladder.

Most of these fortresses, despite the defensive appearance of their exteriors, were later to become comfortable country seats. These fortified castles show clearly the evolution of military architecture in the Middle Ages.

Castelnau Castle in Quercy with its strongly fortified keep is a good example of a feudal construction built on a hilltop site.

In Périgord parts of the castles of Biron and Beynac built on cliff-top sites and Bourdeilles, Mareuil and Commarque date back to the Romanesque period.

The Fortresses of Turenne, Merle and Ventadour, Châlus, Montbrun and Chalusset all existed in Limousin in the 13C. The ruins of Crozant overlooking the valley of the Creuse evokes what was once the powerful stronghold of the counts of Marche.

Numerous castles were built in Berry during the Middle Ages: on Henry II's accession to the throne of England in 1154 the English controlled Aquitaine and threatened neighbouring Berry. The local lords therefore fortified their castles better to resist the enemy. Culan castle taken by Philip Augustus in 1188 was rebuilt in the 13C but retained its severity of appearance emphasised by its three round towers topped by wooden hoardings. Ainay-le-Vieil is protected by its perimeter wall with nine towers. Meillant château still possesses its seven haughty-looking feudal towers.

Minor Arts

The Abbey of St-Martial of Limoges, with its many dependent priories, was the principal centre in Limousin from which enamellers and gold and silversmiths developed their art. From the 10C the monks produced shrines, episcopal rings and statues in gold and silver. The skill of the Limousin gold and silversmiths and their proven technique no doubt opened the way, later, for **enamelwork.**

Using methods, practised from the 6C onwards by Byzantine enamellers, the Limousin workshops at first undertook *cloisonné* ware *(p 118)*. But in the 12C they turned entirely to *champlevé* enamelware in which a thick sheet of copper is hollowed out in certain areas and the cavities are filled in with enamel. Towards the end of the Romanesque period colours became more subtle and often the cavities were filled with two or even four colours, placed one on top of the other. The folds of garments were rendered by the use of a highlight – white, light blue or yellow – around the areas of dark blue and green.

(After a photo by Arch. photo. Paris)

Limousin School: detail from a Eucharistic coffer.

Most of the work was inspired by the art of the illuminators, by manuscripts, ivories and Byzantine and Oriental silks. From the beginning of the 12C small enamelled figures were represented on a background of smooth gilded copper. From 1170 onwards this background was chiselled with decorative foliage motifs. A strange fauna mingled with religious symbols. The compositions although often naive, had a very strong artistic sense. Of the many objects *(see illustration)* produced in this way the most remarkable are the reliquary shrines of Ambazac *(illustration p 47)*, Gimel and Bellac. The municipal museums of Limoges and Guéret contain rich collections of enamelwork.

GOTHIC ART

Gothic architecture was born in the first half of the 12C, apparently in the Ile-de-France, and very gradually superseded the Romanesque style.

Religious Architecture

The essential elements of Gothic art are vaulting based on diagonal ribs and the systematic use of the pointed arch. Diagonal ribs revolutionised construction. The architect became master of the thrust and balance of a building; he was able to direct the weight inside through the ogival arches, the arches and the stringers on to four pillars and outside to suspend it against flying buttresses.

Columns alone could support a church: walls were no longer needed structurally and could be replaced by windows whose development was thus encouraged. The main part of the church was to become lofty and could be as light as the architect pleased.

Vaulting on diagonal ribs
1 Ogive arch - 2 Arch
3 Stringer - 4 Flying buttress
5 Keystone

In **Berry** the most important Gothic building is the Cathedral at Bourges. It bears no resemblance to any of the other great cathedrals of France; its high nave covered with sexpartite vaulting, its double side aisles which extend round the chancel and the absence of a transept make it unique.

The **Languedoc School** emerged only slowly and is characterised by the construction of naves almost as wide as they are high, many-sided belfries and by the use of brick in architecture. These features are to be seen at Moissac in St-Pierre, at Montauban in St-Jacques, at Montpezat-de-Quercy in St-Martin, and at Gourdon, Martel and St-Cirq-Lapopie.

Limousin felt simultaneously the influences of the Languedoc School and the schools of northern France. The passion for building in the 13 and 14C is illustrated in the Cathedral of St-Étienne and the Churches of St-Pierre-du-Queyroix and St-Michel-des-Lions at Limoges, in the nave of the Church of St-Martin at Brive, the collegiate Church at St-Yrieix, and the belfry-porch of Tulle Cathedral.

In **Périgord** the characteristics of the Poitou and Périgord Schools are combined.

Churches with three aisles in the Poitou style are found near churches built with a single nave in the Périgord manner. Both types of building were frequently roofed with Angevin vaulting, a method devised in Anjou in the middle of the 12C and based on a compromise between diagonal ribs and the Périgord Romanesque dome. Its special feature is that the keystone to the ribs is higher than those of the stringers or the arches whereas in other types of Gothic vaulting the keystones are all level.

Monasteries and Fortified Churches. – Monastic architecture produced some remarkable groups of buildings which have not always been able to withstand the ravages of time: of the former Cistercian Abbey of Beaulieu in Quercy only the abbey church remains. On the other hand there remain at Cadouin and Cahors, cloisters built in the Flamboyant style and at Périgueux the cloisters which took from the 12 to the 16C to build.

(After a photo by Arthaud, Grenoble)

Rudelle – The fortified church.

The insecurity that reigned throughout southwest France in the 13 and 14C was the reason why churches were fortified. These churches, which were used as sanctuaries, constituted the surest refuge against the violence of marauding armed bands. The churches were veritable fortresses with crenellated towers, watch-paths and, sometimes, palissades and moats. The most famous are Rudelle and St-Pierre-Toirac in Quercy, Compreignac and St-Angel in Limousin and St-Amand-de-Coly and Tayac in Périgord.

Sculpture

Berry, in about the middle of the 14C became, under the guidance of Duke Jean de Berry, a great intellectual and artistic centre.

The duke collected together excellent artists but most of the masterpieces executed in the studios and workshops in Bourges have unfortunately disappeared: of Duke Jean's tomb originally placed in the Sainte-Chapelle in Bourges which has since been demolished, only a few fragments remain and can be seen in Bourges Cathedral and in Jacques Cœur's Palace. The greater part of the cathedral statuary, however, dates from this period and has survived. At Issoudun, in the chapel of the former Hôtel-Dieu, there is a fine carved Tree of Jesse.

In Limousin, the art of statuary is best seen at Aubazines in the tomb of St. Stephen, a magnificent shrine carved in limestone in the second half of the 13C.

At Limoges, the Cathedral of St-Étienne contains in the ambulatory around the chancel two tombs executed in the purest 14C style. The village of Reygade in Corrèze possesses an Entombment dating from the 15C resembling the one at Carennac.

In Quercy, statuary flowered at Espagnac (the Cardaillac tomb) and in the collegiate church at Montpezat-de-Quercy (the figures of Pierre Des Près and his nephew).

Civil and Military Architecture

Among the most representative castles of the Gothic period are Bourdeilles (keep and the 13C part of the building), Château-l'Évêque, Beynac-et-Cazenac and Castelnaud in Périgord; Castelnau and Cabrerets in Quercy and Rochechouart and Coussac-Bonneval in Limousin. Bonaguil is in a class of its own for although it was built at the end of the 15C and early part of the 16C, it has all the features of a mediaeval fortress.

The ramparts of several cities in Quercy constitute a feature of military architecture: Martel, Puy-l'Évêque and Cahors with its remarkable Valentré Bridge.

The best example of civil architecture is late Gothic: Jacques Cœur's Palace at Bourges. The Hôtel des Moneyroux at Guéret, the Hôtel de la Monnaie at Figeac and several houses or mansions in Sarlat, Gourdon, Martel and Cahors are also typical.

The "Bastides". – These new more or less fortified towns (from the Provençal word: *bastidas*), were built in the 13C in Guyenne and Gascony; and in the 14C their fortified aspect was developed.

The Founders. – Alphonse of Poitiers (1249-71) – Count of Toulouse and brother to Saint Louis – founded most of the *bastides* in the Agenais between 1253-1270. However, as of 1272 the lords acting upon the orders of Philip the Bold, Philip the Fair and King Edward I, also Duke of Aquitaine, also began building the *bastides*.

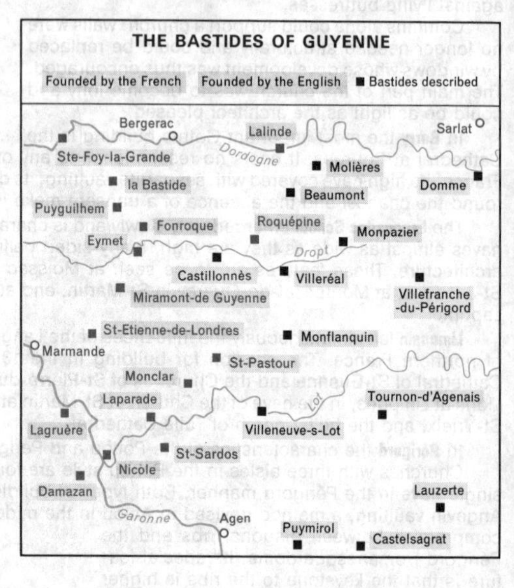

Development. – Their construction satisfied economic, military and political needs. Alphonse of Poitiers took advantage of the growth of the population, which since the 11C had occurred in the southwest, and encouraged people to settle on his land which had been previously divided up in equal parcels. They in return for the land (land to live on and land to cultivate) were granted a charter, guaranteed protection; had no military service and had the right to inherit.

The bailie represented the king, dispensed justice and collected taxes, however, the consuls, elected by the people, administered the town. After the Albigensian Crusade *(p 25)*, the Count of Toulouse, Raymond VII built about 40 *bastides;* with the outbreak of hostilities between the French and English over the Perigord, Quercy and Agenais borders, the political and military advantages of the *bastide* were confirmed. The French built Eymet, Castillonnès and Villeréal along the Dropt River as well as Villeneuve-sur-Lot, Monflanquin, Villefranche-du-Périgord and Ste-Foy-la-Grande. The king of England constructed Beaumont (1272), Molières, Lalinde and Monpazier (1285), while in 1281 Philip the Bold founded Domme. The English expansion along the Garonne pushed the French into building Damazan, Laparade, St-Sardos.

Urbanism. – All the *bastides,* whether French or English, were built to an identical plan: a chequered square or rectangular plan. In addition, the *bastide* was at times built around a pre-existing building – a fortified church as in Beaumont or a castle. The plan of Montauban, designed in 1144 by a Count of Toulouse inspired the plan of the *bastides* of that period, however, Ste-Foy-la-Grande built in 1255 and Monpazier built in 1285 were of an almost perfect design.

Monpazier *(p 137)* is on a quadrilateral plan with straight streets (**3**) which crossed alleys known as **carreyrous** (**4**) at right angles; while narrow spaces or **andrones** divided the house and served as fire breaks, drains or even latrines; in the centre of town the "square" (**1**) was surrounded with covered arcades, incorrectly known as **cornières** – which are in reality angles which form narrow passageways – and contained a wooden covered market. The church (**2**) and cemetery stood either near the main square or its periphery; the outer walls were punctuated with towers and gateways and surrounded the *bastide.*

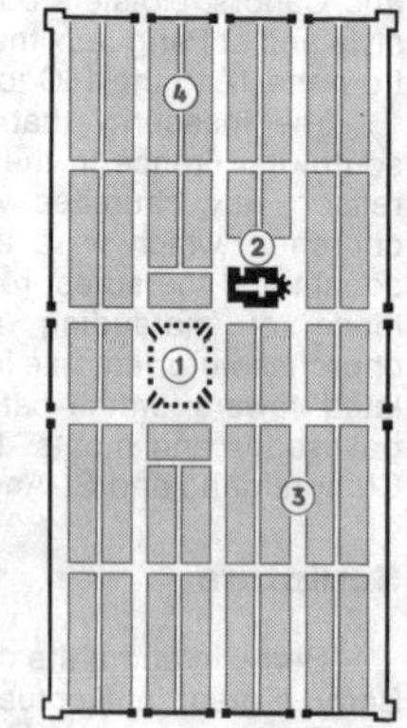

Plan of a bastide

Painting and the Minor Arts

During the Gothic period and as late as the 15C, the decoration of ecclesiastical buildings was accomplished by means of vast mural compositions.

In Quercy, the west dome of Cahors cathedral is entirely covered with 14C frescoes and interesting groups of mural paintings adorn the small Chapel of St-André at Les Arques and the churches of Martignac and Soulomès.

Art in stained glass reached its climax in Bourges with the completion in the 13C of a remarkable series of windows. In Limousin, the church at Eymoutiers is ornamented with interesting stained glass dating from the 15C.

Limousin enamelwork which flourished in the Romanesque period was transformed in the 15C with the appearance of painted enamels produced under the direction of such famous master-craftsmen as Monvaerni and Nardon Pénicaud.

THE RENAISSANCE

At the beginning of the 16C the artistic movement in France was revitalised by the influence of Italy. The military campaigns that in the last years of the 15C had taken Charles VIII as far south as Naples explain this new orientation.

Artistic treasures in Italy awoke in the king and noblemen, the desire to copy the architecture and sculpture and introduce it to their native land. This they did by employing Italian artists.

Architecture. – It took a long time for the Italian influence to be felt in Berry where Gothic art was so strongly implanted. The Renaissance style appeared in Bourges in certain parts of the Hôtels Lallemant and Cujas and in several of the châteaux bordering the Cher and the Indre, including Culan, Ainay-le-Vieil, Meillant and Lys-St-Georges.

In Périgord and Quercy the new style flowered at Assier where the château and the church were built at the beginning of the 16C on the orders of Galiot de Genouillac. Montal and Puyguilhem Châteaux have an architectural grace which links them with the châteaux of the Loire, but the castles at Bourdeilles and Les Bories and Rouffignac Church were only partly transformed by the Renaissance.

The graceful Italian style may be seen in civil architecture in such buildings as Roaldès Mansion at Cahors, the Consul's Mansion at Périgueux, the Hôtel de Maleville at Sarlat, the Hôtel de Labenche at Brive and the Maison de Loyac at Tulle.

Sculpture and the Minor Arts. – Sculpture may be seen at Limoges in the magnificent rood screen erected between 1533 and 1535 and the tomb of Jean de Langeac.

In Quercy, Assier Church is decorated outside with a frieze adorned with warlike symbols; inside is the tomb of Galiot de Genouillac. The inner court of Montal Château is an outstanding example of the Italian style with a frieze which runs between the ground and first floors, busts placed in medallions and luxuriously decorated dormer windows; inside, the remarkable staircase rivals those of the châteaux of the Loire.

(After a photo by M. Foucault, Éd. Tel)

Montal Château – The Renaissance courtyard.

Limousin enamelwork, after the exceptional developments of the 12 to 14C found new favour in the 16C with the families of the Pénicauds, the Nouailhers and the Limosins whose founder Léonard Limosin through sureness of technique, reached heights never previously attained.

In the Marche tapestry making progressed rapidly: throughout the 16C the Aubusson, Bourganeuf and Felletin workshops profited from the part played in contemporary furnishings by tapestries and hangings which came to be considered indispensable.

Aubusson and Felletin continued to take pride in making tapestries and even as late as the Revolution produced *verdures* or "greeneries" in which plants and fantastic animals appeared against a background of foliage.

CLASSICAL ART

Art, copying the styles of Paris and Versailles, lost all its regional character in the 17C.

In Berry, François le Vau, brother of the architect who designed the Louvre, Vaux and Versailles, planned Lignières Château in the style of the *Grand Siècle*: the frontons are supported by pilasters, the main buildings are reflected in sheets of water beyond which extend the French-style gardens.

Hautefort Château, on the borders of Limousin and Périgord – ravaged by fire in 1968 and since completely restored – is a very good example of Classical architecture in its planning and unity of design. Rastignac Château was only built at the end of the 18C: the purity of its lines and harmony of its proportions place it among the most interesting buildings of the period.

The only example of religious architecture at this time is the Cathedral at Montauban, a vast Classical building constructed between 1692 and 1739.

Civil architecture is represented at Limoges by the former Episcopal Palace which now houses the Municipal Museum.

The wood sculpture that remains is interesting: at Moutier d'Ahun there is a group of late 17C carvings in the chancel and at Naves the church contains a monumental retable in the Baroque style.

MODERN ART

Since last century only painting and sculpture have emerged as art forms. Ingres and Bourdelle, both from Montauban, are the most eminent representatives of Quercy of this period. Auguste Renoir and Suzanne Valadon, who were born in Limousin, left their native region when young. Corot, on the other hand, although born in Paris, often came to stay in Limousin and had a particular affection for the charming valley of the Glane near St-Junien. His student Berthe Morisot, from Bourges, was influenced by Renoir and Manet.

In recent years, tapestry making has taken on a new impetus, thanks to the inspiration and modern techniques of Dufy, Marc Saint-Saëns, Lurçat (Tapestry Museum at Aubusson) and Gromaire.

TOURING PROGRAMMES

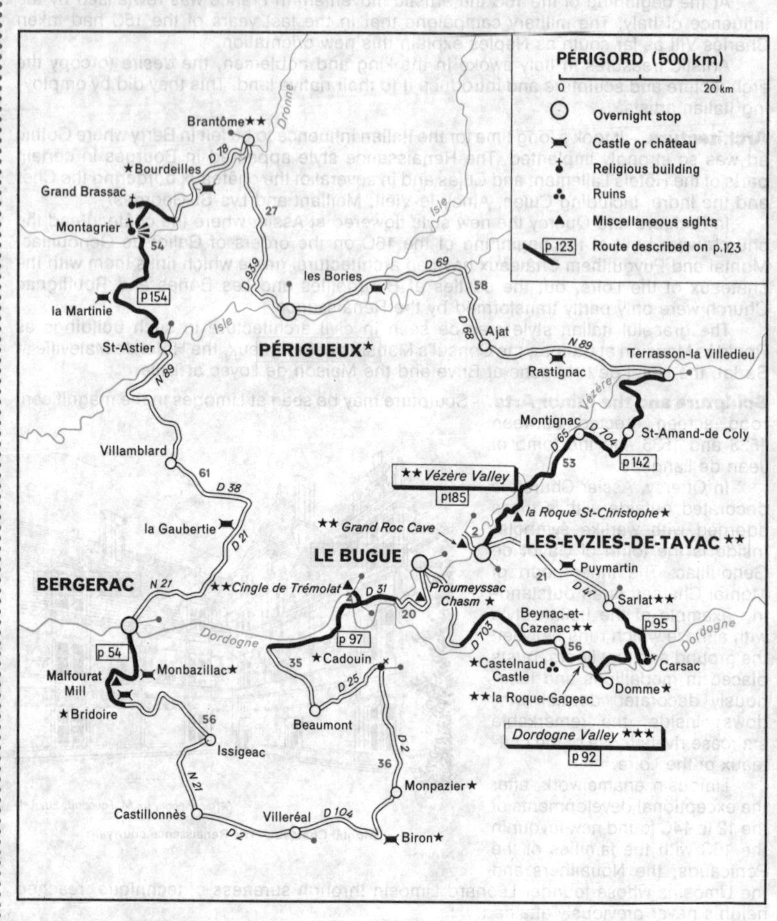

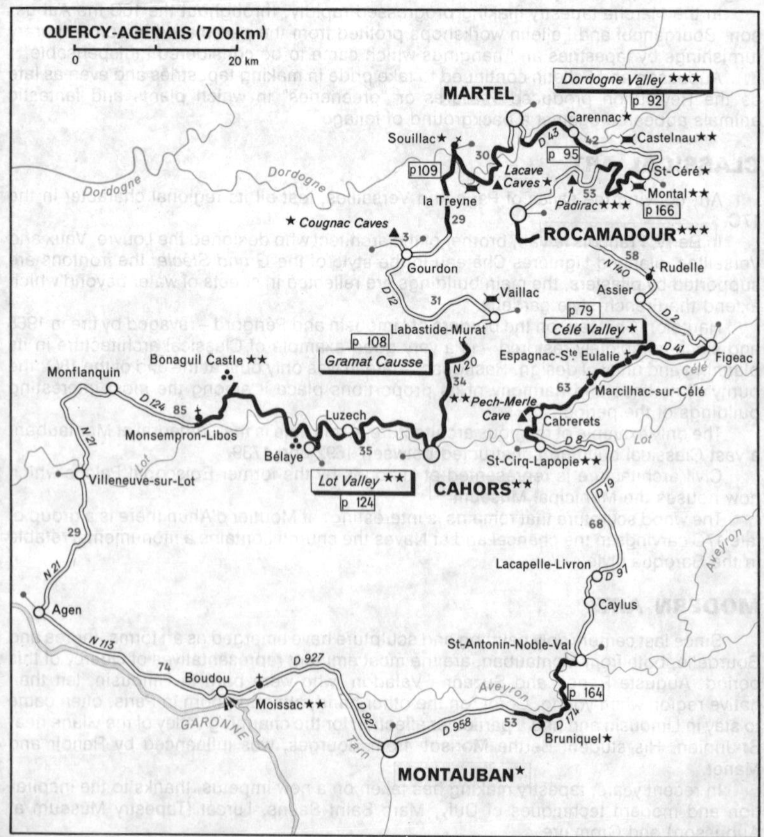

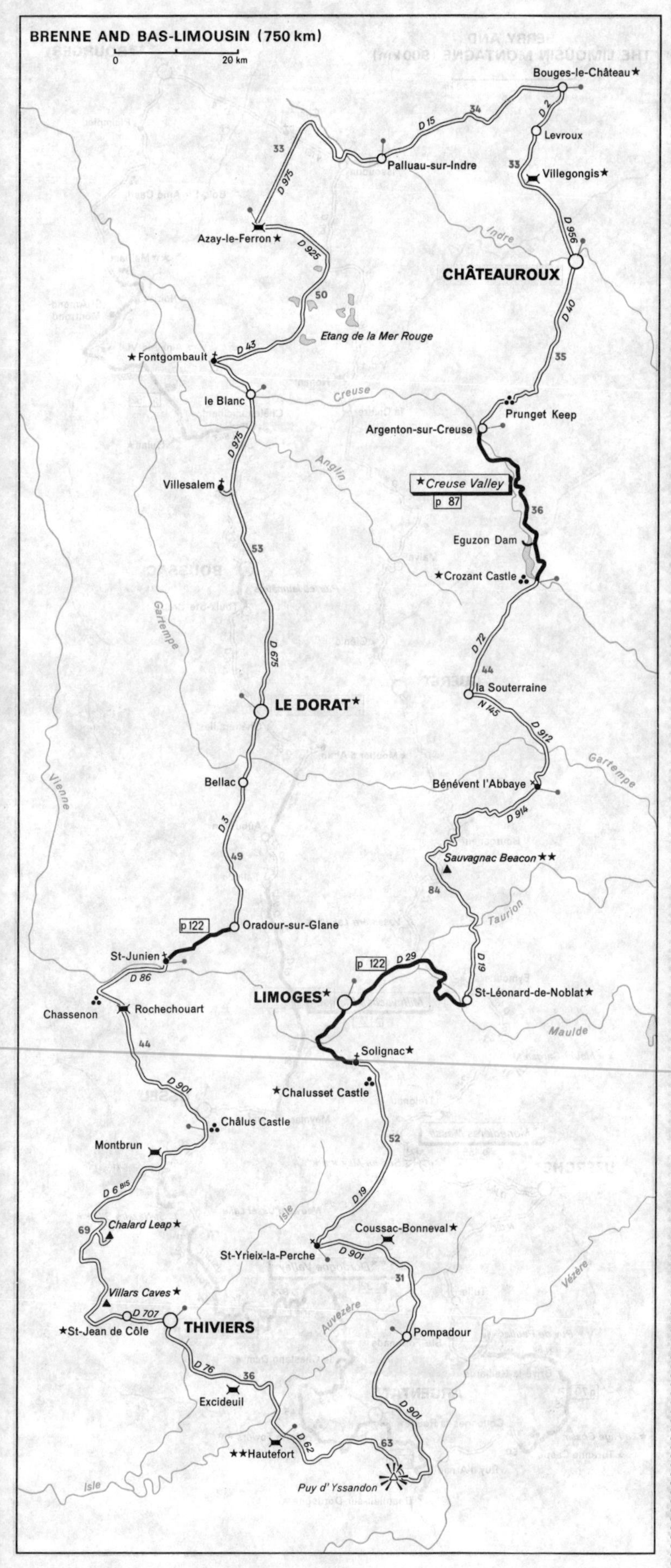
BRENNE AND BAS-LIMOUSIN (750 km)
0
20 km
Bouges-le-Château ★
Levroux
Villegongis ★
Palluau-sur-Indre
D 15
34
D 2
33
33
D 975
Azay-le-Ferron ★
D 925
D 956
Indre
CHÂTEAUROUX
50
Etang de la Mer Rouge
D 40
★ Fontgombault
D 43
35
le Blanc
Creuse
Prunget Keep
Argenton-sur-Creuse
D 975
Anglin
Villesalem
★ Creuse Valley
p 87
36
Eguzon Dam
★ Crozant Castle
53
Gartempe
D 675
D 72
44
la Souterraine
LE DORAT ★
N 145
D 912
Gartempe
Bellac
Bénévent l'Abbaye
D 914
D 3
Vienne
Sauvagnac Beacon ★★
49
84
Taurion
p 122
Oradour-sur-Glane
St-Junien
p 122
D 29
D 19
D 86
LIMOGES ★
St-Léonard-de-Noblat ★
Chassenon
Rochechouart
Maulde
44
Solignac ★
D 901
★ Chalusset Castle
Châlus Castle
Montbrun
52
D 6 BIS
D 19
Isle
Chalard Leap ★
69
Coussac-Bonneval ★
St-Yrieix-la-Perche
D 901
31
Vézère
Villars Caves ★
Auvezère
★ St-Jean de Côle
D 707
THIVIERS
Pompadour
D 76
36
Excideuil
D 901
D 62
★★ Hautefort
63
Isle
Puy d' Yssandon

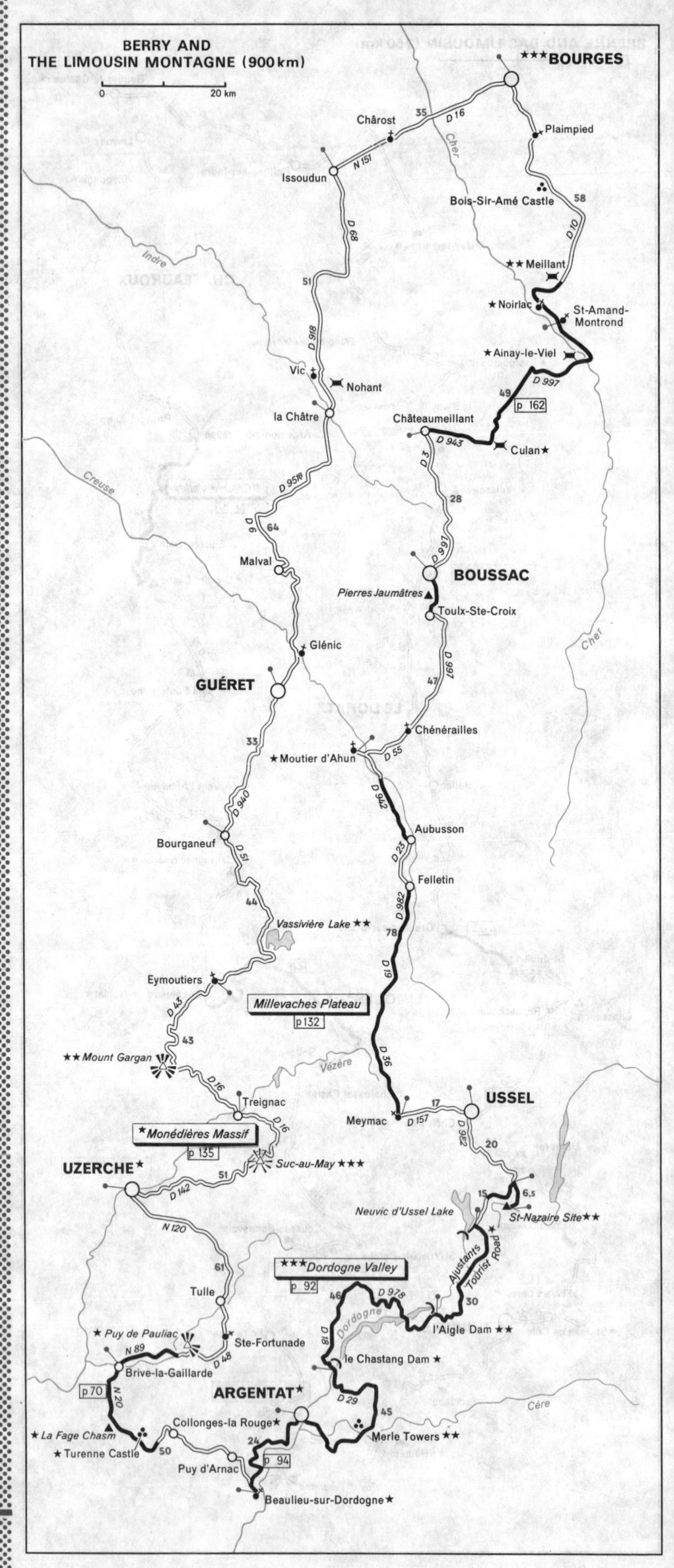
BERRY AND
THE LIMOUSIN MONTAGNE (900 km)
0
20 km
★★★BOURGES
Plaimpied
Chârost
Issoudun
Bois-Sir-Amé Castle
★★Meillant
★Noirlac
St-Amand-Montrond
★Ainay-le-Viel
Vic
Nohant
la Châtre
Châteaumeillant
p 162
Culan★
Malval
BOUSSAC
Pierres Jaumâtres
Toulx-Ste-Croix
Glénic
GUÉRET
Chénérailles
★Moutier d'Ahun
Aubusson
Bourganeuf
Felletin
Vassivière Lake ★★
Eymoutiers
Millevaches Plateau
p 132
★★Mount Gargan
Treignac
Meymac
USSEL
★Monédières Massif
p 135
Suc-au-May ★★★
UZERCHE★
Neuvic d'Ussel Lake
St-Nazaire Site★★
Ajustants
Tourist Road
★★★Dordogne Valley
p 92
Tulle
l'Aigle Dam ★★
★Puy de Pauliac
Ste-Fortunade
Brive-la-Gaillarde
le Chastang Dam ★
p 70
ARGENTAT★
Collonges-la-Rouge★
Merle Towers ★★
★La Fage Chasm
★Turenne Castle
Puy d'Arnac
p 94
Beaulieu-sur-Dordogne★
Indre
Creuse
Cher
Vézère
Dordogne
Cère

PRINCIPAL FESTIVALS

DATE	PLACE	PAGE	TYPE OF FESTIVAL
Easter to 15 October 9pm (10pm from July to September); 8.50F tickets sold in museums	**Rocamadour**	156	*Son et Lumière*
1 May and Sunday before	**Cluis**	145	*Lumas* (local word for snail) fair
Early June	**Chancelade**	154	Musical concerts in the Périgord
Whit Saturday, Sunday and Monday	**Vassivière Lake**	154	National Regatta
Mid-June to late July. Starting-time variable: ☎ (55) 28.24.35 or 28.21.86; 20F (10pm in August; 9pm first fortnight in September, 18F)	**Merle Towers**	132	*Son et Lumière:* Mediaeval pageant
Last two week-ends in June	**Nohant**	145	Musical, theatrical, literary folklore presentations recreating the Romantic period
Late June-early July	**Bellac**	54	National Drama, Music and Dance Festival
First week in July	**Montauban**	139	*Occitanie* Festival: theatre
First fortnight in July	**Brantôme**	69	Dance Festival
26 July	**Ste-Anne-St-Priest**	72 19	Pilgrimage to Ste-Anne
Late July-August	**Sarlat**	172	Drama Festival
July-August	**Bonaguil**	60	Musical evenings
July-August	**Gourdon**	108	Music, Dance and Drama Festival
13-15 August	**Pompadour**	155	Showjumping Competition
Sunday preceding the 15 August	**Étang de la Mer Rouge**	71	Pilgrimage to Notre-Dame de la Mer Rouge
15 August	**Brantôme**	69	National Showjumping Competition
Second and third weeks in August	**Montauban**	139	Summer Festival : Ballet
Late August to early September	**Gargilesse**	107	Harp concerts (in the church)
1st Sunday in August	**Pompadour**	155	Horse Trials
2nd Sunday in September	**Argenton-sur-Creuse**	49	Procession and pilgrimage
September	**Limoges**	117	International show for the Limousin breed of cattle
Last Sunday in September	**Aixe-sur-Vienne**	123	Pilgrimage to Notre-Dame d'Arliquet
2nd Sunday after the 6 November	**St-Léonard-de-Noblat**	169	Festival of the *Quintaine*

THE LIMOUSIN "OSTENSIONS"

Every seven years (1988) the Haute-Vienne and Creuse Departments honour their saints: St. Martial the Limousin, St. Valerie *(p 117)*, the "good St. Eligius" who was born at Chaptelat and founded the monastery at Solignac, St. Stephen of Muret and many others; also the hermits who lived in the Limousin and Marche Forests and St. Junien, St. Victurnien, and St. Leonard, founders of the monasteries scattered in the valleys. The Virgin Mary is sometimes included under such invocations as Our Lady of Arliquet or of the Relics as at Aixe-sur-Vienne.

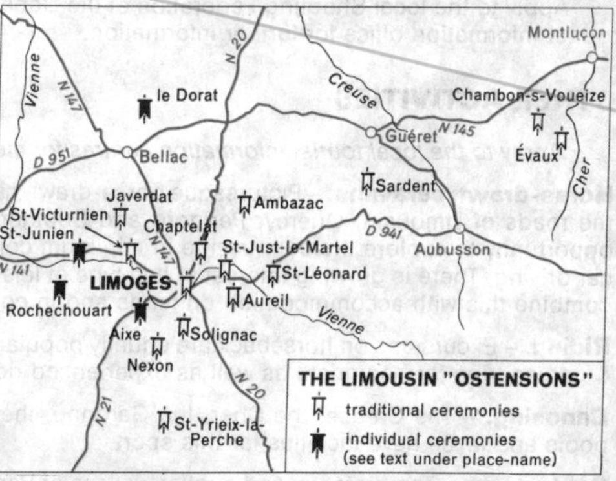

The *ostensions* or solemn exhibition of relics to the faithful go back to the 10C. One of the earliest of these festivals was held at Limoges when a terrible epidemic was raging. This was ergotism, or the burning fever, to combat which the relics of St. Martial were brought out. A visitation – whether in the form of a plague or an illustrious personage – became an occasion for holding these ceremonies which later came to be repeated at intervals.

Each town has a traditional ceremony of its own calling for religious festivals of the folklore type. The blessing of the flag which is solemnly hoisted to the belfry pinnacle marks the opening of the *ostension*. Once the festival has been opened on the Sunday after Easter, the relics are presented to the faithful for veneration in their shrines or reliquaries, which are, in some cases, masterpieces of the goldsmiths' and silversmiths' art. Picturesque processions march through bunting and flower-decked streets in towns and villages, accompanied by fanfares, drums and banners and escorted by guards of honour, occasionally in surprising costume, representatives of different craft guilds and other groups in rich finery. Neighbouring parishes, sometimes in great numbers, join in these manifestations of popular faith which is why fifty or more come to Le Dorat for the closing of the *ostensions*.

PLACES TO STAY

The mention facilities pp 38-39 *under the individual headings in the body of the guide refers to the information given on these pages.*

The map opposite indicates towns selected for the accommodation and leisure facilities which they offer to the holidaymaker. To help you plan your route and choose your hotel, restaurant or camping site consult the Michelin publications, the traveller's friends.

Accommodation

The Michelin Red Guide France of hotels and restaurants and the Michelin Guide Camping and Caravaning France are annual publications which present a selection of hotels, restaurants and camping sites. The final choice is based on regular on the spot enquiries and visits. Both the hotels and camping sites are classified according to the standard of comfort of their amenities. Establishments which are notable for their fortunate setting, decor, setting of peace and tranquility and their warm welcome are distinguished by special symbols.

Planning your route, sports and recreation

The Michelin Sectional Map Series at a scale of 1:200 000 covers the whole of France. For those concerning the region see the layout diagram on page 3. The maps are an essential complement to the tourist and annual guides, and all the publications are carefully cross-referenced. In addition to the wealth of road information, the touristic details include beaches, bathing spots, swimming pools, golf courses, race courses, panoramas and scenic routes.

OUTDOOR ACTIVITIES

FISHING

Perigord, Quercy and Berry and, above all, Limousin are particularly favoured by fisher-men. Rivers, brooks and lakes are filled with fish of every kind – trout, pike, perch, carp, tench, bream, roach, shad and black bass – and in the Indre, the Corrèze and the Aveyron, crayfish are multiplying rapidly.

Whatever fishing station he chooses the angler must observe the fishing regulations and should obtain particulars from the local angling associations, tourist offices or Water and Forestry Authorities.

SHOOTING

The region rich in game is a paradise for shooters. The Brenne is popular for wild fowling – ducks, teal, snipe – while the open forests of Berry abound with pheasants, deer and wild boar.

On the vast expanses of the Causses with their occasional copses the shooter can put up a hare, common grey or red legged partridge and quail. Woodcock are to be found in the combes in winter.

Membership of a private club or local Shooting syndicate is usually necessary. Some organisations issue one day permits.

Apply to the local Shooting Federation of the Department concerned or to the local tourist information office for further information.

OTHER ACTIVITIES

Apply to the local tourist information centres for more information on the following :

Horse-drawn caravans. – Picturesque horse-drawn caravans, a fairly common sight on the roads of Limousin, Quercy, Perigord and Southern Berry, give holidaymakers the opportunity to explore the countryside in minimum comfort and without the stresses of car driving. There is growing interest in this type of leisurely holiday and it is possible to combine this with accommodation on farms and in country hostels.

Riding. – Excursions on horseback are equally popular and most caravan hire firms also organise trips for beginners as well as experienced riders.

Canoeing. – The Creuse, the Cher, the Garonne, the Lot, the Tarn and the numerous pools and lakes have facilities for this sport.

Speleology. – The plateaux and sunken valleys of Perigord and Quercy are particularly rich in caves and chasms. Potholers should contact the local clubs or the Fédération Française de Spéléologie, 130, rue de Saint-Maur, 75011 Paris.

Rambling. – Many long-distance footpaths enable ramblers to discover the region covered by this guide. Topo Guides published by the Fédération Française de la Randonnée Pédestre, Comité Central de Grande Randonnée (92 rue de Clignancourt, 75883 Paris Cedex 18, ☎ 259 6040) give detailed itineraries and useful advice to ramblers.

The Michelin Sectional Map Series is revised regularly.
These maps make the perfect travelling companion.

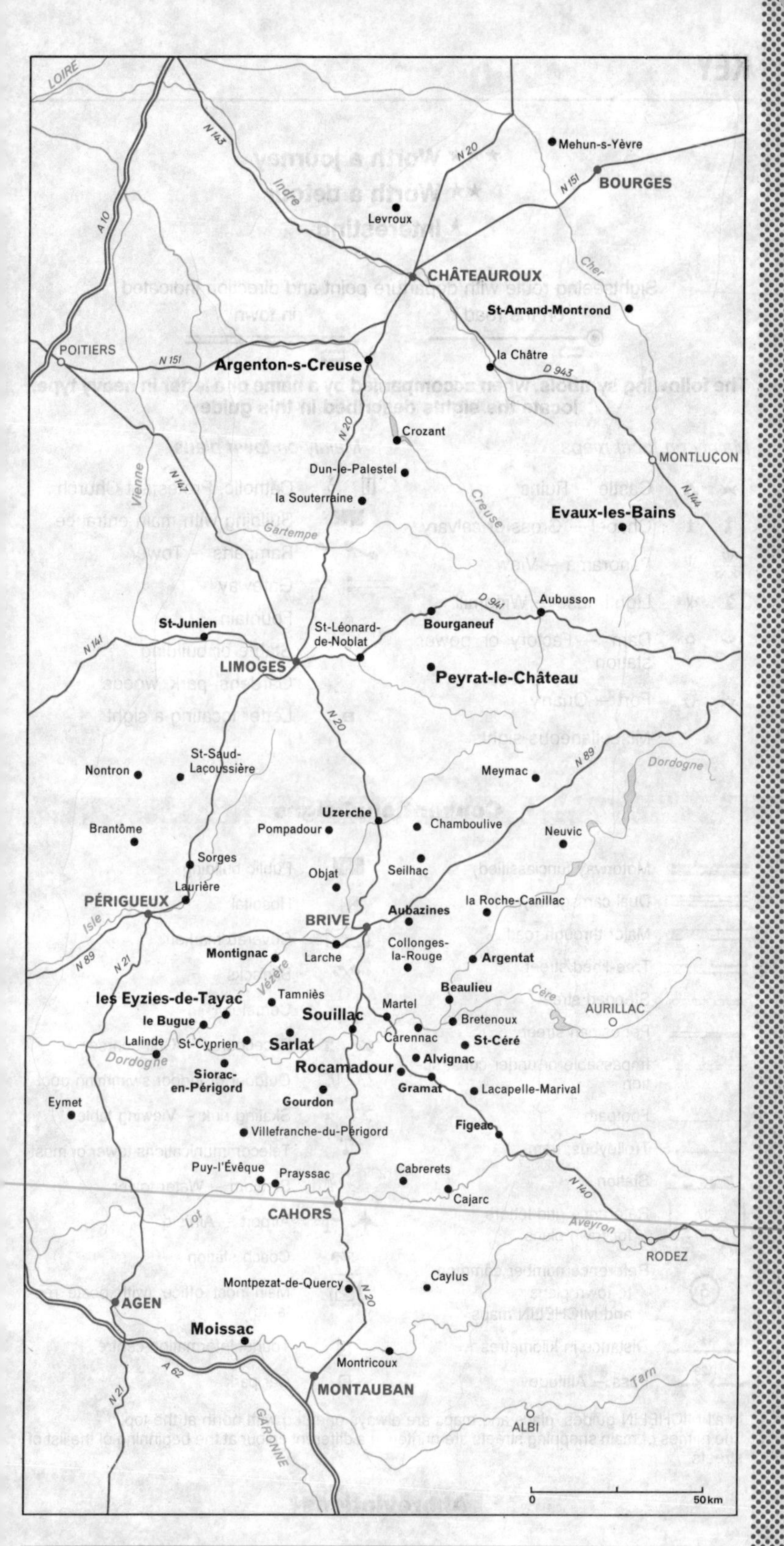
LOIRE
N 143
A 10
Indre
N 20
Mehun-s-Yèvre
N 151
BOURGES
Levroux
Cher
CHÂTEAUROUX
St-Amand-Montrond
POITIERS
N 151
Argenton-s-Creuse
la Châtre
D 943
N 20
Crozant
Dun-le-Palestel
MONTLUÇON
Vienne
N 147
la Souterraine
Creuse
N 144
Evaux-les-Bains
Gartempe
D 941
Aubusson
St-Junien
Bourganeuf
St-Léonard-de-Noblat
N 141
LIMOGES
Peyrat-le-Château
N 20
N 89
St-Saud-Lacoussière
Nontron
Meymac
Dordogne
Uzerche
Brantôme
Pompadour
Chamboulive
Neuvic
Sorges
Seilhac
Objat
Laurière
PÉRIGUEUX
Isle
BRIVE
Aubazines
la Roche-Canillac
N 89
N 21
Montignac
Larche
Collonges-la-Rouge
Argentat
Vézère
Beaulieu
les Eyzies-de-Tayac
Tamniès
Martel
Cère
AURILLAC
le Bugue
Souillac
Bretenoux
Lalinde
St-Cyprien
Sarlat
Carennac
St-Céré
Dordogne
Alvignac
Siorac-en-Périgord
Rocamadour
Gramat
Lacapelle-Marival
Eymet
Gourdon
Figeac
Villefranche-du-Périgord
Puy-l'Évêque
Prayssac
Cabrerets
Cajarc
N 140
Lot
CAHORS
Aveyron
RODEZ
Caylus
Montpezat-de-Quercy
N 20
AGEN
Moissac
Montricoux
A 62
Tarn
N 21
MONTAUBAN
GARONNE
ALBI
0
50 km

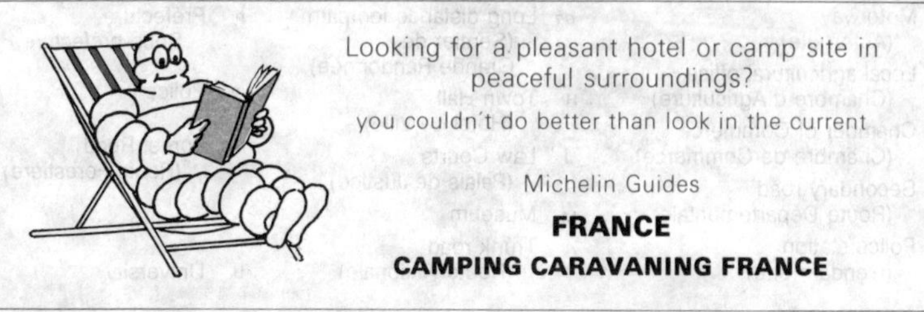
Looking for a pleasant hotel or camp site in peaceful surroundings?
you couldn't do better than look in the current
Michelin Guides
FRANCE
CAMPING CARAVANING FRANCE

KEY

★★★ **Worth a journey**

★★ **Worth a detour**

★ **Interesting**

Sightseeing route with departure point and direction indicated

on the road — in town

The following symbols, when accompanied by a name or a letter in heavy type, locate the sights described in this guide

Mainly on local maps

- Castle – Ruins
- Chapel – Cross or calvary
- Panorama – View
- Lighthouse – Windmill
- Dam – Factory or power station
- Fort – Quarry
- Miscellaneous sights

Mainly on town plans

- Catholic, Protestant Church
- Building with main entrance
- Ramparts – Tower
- Gateway
- Fountain
- Statue or building
- Gardens, park, woods
- B Letter locating a sight

Conventional signs

- Motorway (unclassified)
- Dual carriageway
- Major through road
- Tree-lined street
- Stepped street
- Pedestrian street
- Impassable or under construction
- Footpath
- Trolleybus, tram
- Station
- A B Reference grid letters for town plans
- 3 Reference number common to town plans and MICHELIN maps
- 12 Distance in kilometres
- 1429 Pass – Altitude

- Public building
- Hospital
- Covered market
- Barracks
- Cemetery
- Racecourse – Golf course
- Outdoor or indoor swimming pool
- Skating rink – Viewing table
- Telecommunications tower or mast
- Stadium – Water tower
- Airport – Airfield
- Coach station
- Main post office (with poste restante)
- Tourist information centre
- Car park

In all MICHELIN guides, plans and maps are always oriented with north at the top.
The names of main shopping streets are printed in a different colour at the beginning of the list of streets.

Abbreviations

- *A* Motorway (Autoroute)
- A Local agricultural office (Chambre d'Agriculture)
- C Chamber of Commerce (Chambre de Commerce)
- *D* Secondary road (Route Départementale)
- G Police station (Gendarmerie)
- *GR* Long distance footpath (Sentier de Grande Randonnée)
- H Town Hall (Hôtel de Ville)
- J Law Courts (Palais de Justice)
- M Museum
- *N* Trunk road (Route Nationale)
- P Préfecture Sous-préfecture
- POL. Police
- *R.F.* Forest Road (Route Forestière)
- T Theatre
- U University

TOWNS, SIGHTS AND TOURIST REGIONS

AGEN

Michelin map 79 fold 15 – Pop 32 893

Agen lies stretched out in the plain between the Garonne and the Ermitage hillside, in a fertile region. A market town for early vegetables and fruit (peaches, *chasselas*, a white table grape and plums) the name of Agen is linked with plums in the mind of every *gourmet*.

A spacious and modern looking town with wide avenues and the Gravier Esplanade, Agen is the focal-point for the central Garonne region between Bordeaux and Toulouse.

A group of Artists and Learned Men. – The Renaissance shone with particular brilliance at Agen. **Bandello** (1485-1561), banished from Milan, found a prosperous refuge on the banks of the Garonne. This monk, diplomat, soldier and writer of tales and romances aptly described the social intrigues at the time of the Renaissance and his main work *Novelle*, a series of 214 stories, was translated into English. It is said that the themes of several of Shakespeare's plays were based on Bandello's tales – *Romeo and Juliet, Much Ado About Nothing* and *Hamlet*. **Julius-Caesar Scaliger** (1484-1558), who was born in Padua, settled in Agen and brought his influence to bear on many men of letters; his son, Joseph-Juste Scaliger (1540-1609) was an eminent philologist.

Bernard Palissy (1510-1590), who was born near Monpazier and was the author of several technical and philosophic works, is best remembered as a glass-blower and potter. He bent himself to unending work and harsh sacrifices – it is said that he burnt the furniture to keep his kilns going – in his determination to rediscover the formula of a certain glaze. He invented a ware half-way between Italian and glazed earthenware and was most successful with "rustic" decorated bowls (coloured mouldings of animals such as snakes, lizards, fish and crayfish).

Fruit and Early Vegetables. – Agenais stretches over the hill and plateau area known as the **"pays des serres"**, which is bordered by the valleys of the Lot and the Garonne and derives its basic economic wealth from these two valleys. They form the natural corridors between the Atlantic and the Mediterranean and owe their fame to the market-garden produce and fruit which can be grown in their mild climate *(p 18)*.

■ SIGHTS *time: 1 1/2 hours*

Museum★★ (M). – *Open 10am to noon and 2 to 6pm; closed Tuesdays, 1 January, 1 May, 1 November and 25 December; 5F.*

The museum is in the elegant 16-17C Vaurs, Vergès, Estrade and Monluc mansions.

Ground floor. – Start the tour in the large gallery devoted to mediaeval archaelogy where the main exhibit is the **tomb of Etienne de Dufort** and his wife; the recumbent figures rest on a plinth decorated with carvings set in trilobar blind arcades. A 16C Brussels tapestry depicting the Month of March hangs on the wall.

The room reserved for Gallo-Roman archaeological finds in the Agenais region contains the museum's most beautiful exhibit, the **Venus of Le Mas,** a Greek marble statue discovered last century near the Mas d'Agenais. The statue is admirable for the beauty of its modelling, the line of its draperies and the perfection of its proportions.

The theme of an adjoining room adorned with a great Renaissance chimneypiece is hunting and war: ancient arms (note a 16C hunting dagger) and tapestries (The Hunter, 17C).

First floor. – Go up the spiral staircase in the Vaurs mansion (also on a spiral axis) to see the collections of 16-17C paintings of the French and foreign schools. A Portrait of a Man by Philippe de Champaigne and a Village Fair by Teniers the Younger are noteworthy.

Next to the reconstruction of the dispensary of Agen hospital is displayed a large ceramic collection including **earthenware** from France and other countries from the time of Bernard Palissy *(above)*. On the same floor there is an unusual collection of **paperweights** by Bourdon de Saint-Amans (1774-1856), a native of Agen, as well as unique specimens of fine china which he produced in an attempt to compete with English porcelain.

Note a portrait of the Countess du Barry in the passage leading to the rooms devoted to **17-18C French painters:** fine portraits like that of the Count of Toulouse by François de Troy, and works by Watteau, Nattier, Lancret, Hubert Robert, etc.

The next room contains a series of **paintings by Goya** which are among the most valuable possessions of the Agen Museum. They include a revealing self-portrait, the ascent of a balloon and a small canvas entitled *Caprichos*, a forerunner of surrealism. There are also works by other Spanish masters and a fine painting by Tiepolo.

The 19C is represented by a masterpiece by Corot, **L'Etang de Ville d'Avray,** and by Isabey, Courbet, Pre-Impressionist (several works by Boudin) and Impressionist (Lebourg, Caillebotte) collections. Note a Portrait of a Woman by the Romanian painter Grigoresko.

Second floor. – There are more 19C works displayed including fine Impressionist landscapes (Sisley, Guillaumin, Labasque). Among the 20C exhibits are an unusual canvas by Picabia, works by **Bissière** (a native of Lot-et-Garonne) displayed in a splendid room with paired windows, and paintings and drawings by Le Moal and Manessier.

From the tower *(viewing table)* there are fine views of the town and the hillsides of Gascony.

Basement. – The vaulted cellars of the Vaurs Mansion contain the **prehistoric collections** ranging from ancient flints to the more sophisticated specimens of the Neolithic Age found in Agenais.

St. Caprasius' Cathedral (St-Caprais) (B). – The former collegiate church of St-Caprais was founded in the 11C and raised to cathedral status in 1802. The most outstanding part of the church is the 12C chevet: apse flanked by three apsidal chapels lit by semicircular windows.

The interior, which was completely restored last century and decorated with frescoes depicting the titular saints of Agenais, is striking for the disproportion of the nave and the transept crossing. The nave is short, it has two bays only and is, doubtless, incomplete; the large transept crossing was originally intended to be covered by a dome.

Pont-Canal (D). – This aqueduct is 500 m - 550 yds long and has twenty-three arches; it was constructed to enable the Garonne lateral canal to cross the Garonne river. There is a good view of the whole scheme from the road N 113 *(leave by ⑦)*.

The foot-bridge to the Graviers esplanade also affords an interesting view of the aqueduct, the town and the Garonne.

AHUN

Michelin map 72 fold 10 – Pop 2 035

Ahun was built on a hill overlooking the Creuse half-way between Guéret and Aubusson, and was an important Gallo-Roman centre.

Church of St-Sylvain. – Outside, the decoration of the chevet is strikingly elegant: between the semicircular bays stand columns bearing beautiful capitals adorned with carved animals, birds and palm fronds.

Inside the late 17C woodwork in the chancel is outstanding: the carved panels and pillars, the statues of St. Giles and his hind and St. Silvanus, recall the woodwork of Le Moutier-d'Ahun *(p 145)*.

A gilded retable carved by Jean Pavillon, master sculptor from Guéret, a fine 12C baptismal font hewn in granite, and beneath the porch on the left, a multicoloured stone *pietà* dating from the 15C, complete the church furnishings.

Crypt. – *This is reached by an outside stairway, on the north side of the church.*

The crypt lies beneath the chevet and the south apsidal chapel, and consists of two chambers ending in a semicircle. The first chamber is divided into three aisles by six single columns which support groined vaulting.

The pre-Romanesque part of the crypt contains an ancient reliquary-tomb which was venerated in earlier times from the church above by means of small rectangular openings or *fenestella.*

AINAY-LE-VIEIL (Castle) ★

Michelin map 69 fold 11 – 9 km - 5 miles south of St-Amand-Montrond – *Local map p 160*

The first view of the castle is of a stark mediaeval pile in a charming verdant setting by the river. You may wander freely in the park.

The castle is open daily 10 to 11.40am and 2 to 6.40pm (sunset out of season); closed 1 December to 31 January; 12F.

Once through the postern there appears a graceful Renaissance building set at right angle on two sides of the octagonal mediaeval wall.

Go through the guardroom and make for the watch-path from which there is a pleasant view of the moat dotted with water-lilies and of the crenellated ramparts flanked by nine towers. There is a striking contrast between the mediaeval wall and the Renaissance main building which was completed early in the 16C by Gilbert de Chevenon, Marquis of Bigny. The building has a warm ochre patina and the decoration is concentrated in the hexagonal tower which is embellished with balusters and wreathed columns.

The chapel has a fine coffered ceiling. In the great drawing-room, an impressive chimneypiece bears the arms of Louis XII and Anne of Brittany.

Les AIX-D'ANGILLON

Michelin map 65 southeast of fold 11 – Pop 2 165

Located in the small Colin and Ouatier valleys and bordering the vast plain of the Berry-Champagne and the Sancerre Hills, Aix contains old houses and a Romanesque church, the transept crossing of which is framed by Berrichon passages *(p 29)* and is topped by a dome on squinches.

EXCURSION

Morogues; Maupas Château; Menetou-Salon Château. – *15 km - 9 miles; leave Aix north on the D 46, continue 5 km - 3 miles.*

Morogues. – Pop 376. An octagonal belfry-porch precedes the 14C **church**. Inside there is a magnificent canopy in wood from the Sainte-Chapelle in Bourges. The seats of the officiating priests were placed under the three delicate pierced pinnacles. In the chancel are two polychromed statues (14C): St. John the Baptist and the other statue is said to be St. Symphorian; in the north chapel is a Virgin and Child.

Leave Morogues west on the D 59.

Maupas Château. – *Open Palm Sunday to 15 October, 10am to noon and 2 to 7pm; closed mornings weekdays, Palm Sunday to 1 July and 8 September to 15 October; 12F.*

The château's two wings, with mullioned windows, are joined by a staircase turret on the courtyard side and a machicolated tower on the garden side. A **plate collection**★ (17-19C) decorates the main staircase; among the 887 plates on display note the Nevers, Moustiers and La Rochelle items. Two rooms contain memorabilia of the Duchess of Berry and the Count of Chambord. On the floor below is the old kitchen.

Continue along the D59 to Menetou-Salon.

Menetou-Salon Château. – *Open Palm Sunday to 2 November 10am to noon and 2 to 6pm, Sundays and holidays; the rest of the week, afternoons only; closed Tuesdays; 12F.*

Once the home of Jacques Cœur *(p 59)*, the château set amidst the vineyards was damaged during the Revolution. However, in the 19C the château was rebuilt and enlarged, incorporating the old part. The outbuildings house a collection of vintage cars – Turcat Mery and Panhard Levassor (1899). The adjacent room is a saddlery with its collection of harnesses. The château is decorated inside by beautiful 15C Flemish tapestries; note as well the saloon and two libraries.

ALLASSAC

Michelin map 75 fold 8 – Pop 3 560

Situated in undulating countryside near the Vézère, Allassac has a certain charm with its old houses and their slate roofs.

The Gothic **church**, built of black schist set off in places with red sandstone, is preceded by a machicolated belfry-porch. Near the church stand the only remains of the old fortifications, Caesar's Tower, built in drystone in the 9 and 12C.

EXCURSIONS

Donzenac. – Pop 1 947. *6 km - 4 miles to the southeast by the D 25.* This small town is built near the rich Brive Basin *(p 13)*. There are still some old houses near the church with its 14C bell tower.

Le Saillant; St-Bonnet-la-Rivière. – *17 km - 11 miles. Leave Allassac to the northwest by the D 134.*

Le Saillant. – This hamlet is in a pleasant setting at the mouth of the Vézère Gorges *(p 185)*. From the beautiful old bridge with pointed cutwaters spanning the Vézère you can see, on the right bank, surrounded by a moat, a 12C manorhouse.

Leave Le Saillant to the west by the D134 then bear left in the direction of Objat where you take the D901 to Juillac.

St-Bonnet-la-Rivière. – Pop 334. The village has a Romanesque church which is circular in shape and is flanked by a belfry-porch. Legend has it that a knight on his return from the Holy Land built a church to resemble the Holy Sepulchre.

AMBAZAC

Michelin map 72 fold 8 – *Local map p 122* – Pop 4 658

Ambazac, a small town surrounded by hills, some of which reach an altitude of 700 m - 2 300 ft *(p 123)*, commands the region between Marche and Limousin.

The economy of the Ambazac region, based as it was on arable farming and stock-rearing was largely transformed in 1948 with the discovery of important high-grade uranium deposits (pitchblende) near La Crouzille *(see map p 19)*. This deposit was the starting point for further prospection in the area and new deposits are now exploited by mining or opencast working. Uranium from the Limousin mines contributes largely to the fuel needs of the French nuclear industry.

The Treasure★★. – *In the church. Illumination: 1F.*

The remarkable treasure came from Grandmont Abbey *(p 123)*. It consists of the dalmatic of St. Stephen and the reliquary shrine, both of which are in a special case.

The Dalmatic. – This precious robe, dating from the 12C, is made of Mozarabic silk and has shiny gold motifs on a red background. Among the embroidered motifs may be seen the Byzantine eagle.

Reliquary Shrine. – The shrine is of beaten chased copper, ornamented with *champlevé* enamelling, polished faceted gems and filigreework; it is held to be the most beautiful example of 12C Limousin metal craftsmanship to have come down to us. It is sufficiently large to contain the relics of St. Stephen of Muret.

Ambazac Church – The reliquary shrine.

Terrace. – A view of Ambazac in its setting of hills can be gained from the terrace built near a hilltop Marian sanctuary to the southwest of the town, near the D 914.

EXCURSION

Taurion Valley. – *Round trip of 24 km - 15 miles, about 1 hour. Leave Ambazac to the southeast by the D 5 then take the D 56 to the right.* This road passes through pleasant countryside before crossing the Taurion.

St-Martin-Terressus. – Pop 439. This village overlooks the reservoir of the Chauvan Dam.

Turn left into the D 29. This winding and picturesque road affords several glimpses of the St-Marc Dam. *Take the D 5 to the left.* The road going down through pasture land gives fine views of the reservoir lake of the St-Marc Dam.

Pont du Dognon. – The bridge crosses the Taurion in a **site** with wooded and rocky cliff faces.

The road serpents upwards giving a last view of the bridge and dam before returning to Ambazac through rolling countryside.

ARGENTAT ★

Michelin map 75 fold 10 – *Local maps pp 93 and 94* – Pop 3 424 – *Facilities p 38*

The old houses of Argentat rise in the centre of the picturesque plateaux of the Bas-Limousin at the outlet of the upper valley of the Dordogne *(p 92)*.

First impressions★. – You discover the full beauty of the Argentat **setting★** when approaching from the south. You get a first glimpse from the D980 2 km – 1 mile from the town. From the bridge across the Dordogne you see the picturesque huddle of the **lauze** (roughly hewn slabs of stone of either schist or lava) and slate roofs of the old houses of the right bank with here and there a turret, a gable or pepper-pot tower. Upstream from the bridge, on the left bank, the houses of another old quarter crowd together, their wooden balconies jutting out over the river.

The Argentat Dam (Barrage d'Argentat). – This is one of five dams with a hydro-electric power station on the upper Dordogne *(p 92)*. It was built 2 km – 1 mile upstream from Argentat to utilise to the best advantage the waters of the Le Chastang Reservoir. It rises to a maximum height of 35 m – 115 ft and is 190 m – 623 ft long along the crest. Four sluices can empty 4 000 m^3 - 880 000 gallons a second. This power station has five hollow piles, three of which are equipped with hydro-electric generators.

EXCURSIONS

La Xaintrie. – *Round tour of 60 km - 37 miles – about 2 hours – Local map p 45. Leave Argentat to the southeast by the N 120, which follows the valley of the Maronne.*
At La Broquerie, within sight of the Hautefage dam, the road crosses the river and rises rapidly, making many turns above the rocky and wooded ravines. In Sexcles take to the left the D 136 which climbs amidst wooded slopes, up to the plateau from where there are fine views of the Maronne valley and the mountains of Auvergne. The road then skirts the

foot of the **château du Rieux** (13 and 16C) before passing through St-Bonnet-les-Tours, and clings to the side of the ravine. Then take to the left the D 13, providing many passing glimpses of the Merle Towers which you circle once having crossed the Maronne.

Merle Towers★★. – *Description p 131.*

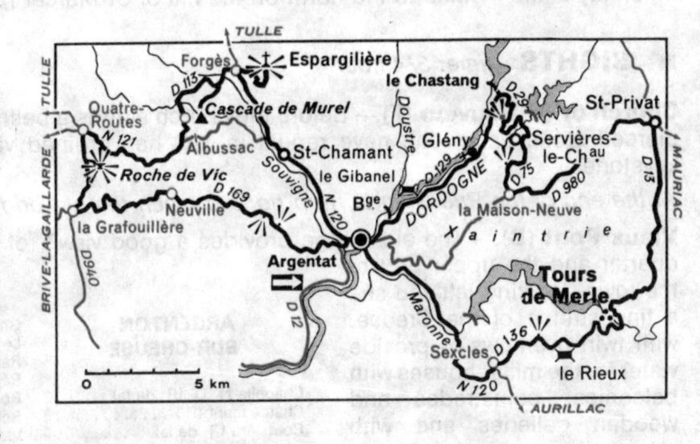

To reach St-Privat the D 13 crosses **Xaintrie** – a corruption of the word Saint-Trie. It consists of a granite plateau deeply cut by the gorges of the Dordogne, the Maronne and the Cère, and is an impoverished area where moorland and scrubland alternate with pine and silver birch woods. The contrast between the desolate aspect of the plateau and the gentler countryside of the enclosed valleys adds to the enjoyment of the excursion.

St-Privat. – Pop 1 167. The 13 and 16C church has a powerful square tower.

Take the D 980 to the left and at La Maison-Neuve turn right into the D 75 a picturesque road, from which one sees, for the first time, the setting of Servières-le-Château.

Servières-le-Château. – Pop 718. This former stronghold rises in a picturesque **setting★** overlooking the deep gorges of the Glane. With its stone-slate roofs, Servières stands encircled by jagged rocks and pine trees. The old castle, which once belonged to the Turenne family *(p. 181)*, was set on fire in 1916 by the German officers interned there. It has since been rebuilt and is now a nursing home.

Beyond Servières begins the descent into the valley of the Dordogne. As you descend you will notice the Le Chastang Dam and also a signpost marking the path to a belvedere from which there is a view over the whole dam and the reservoir stretching behind it.

Le Chastang Dam★. – *Description p 94.*

The D129 brings you back to Argentat. The road runs more or less parallel with the left bank of the Dordogne which flows at the foot of wooded hills, and is at times overlooked by cliffs.

Glény. – The chapel, all that remains of the former church, has an attractive chevet and a **bell gable** (a gable wall which is pierced by openings in which hang the bells).

Just before you reach the Argentat Dam you will see the elegant outline of **Le Gibanel Castle** which stands reflected in the reservoir.

Cascade de Murel★ (Murel Waterfall); Roche de Vic★ (Vic Rock). – *Round tour of 44 km - 27 miles – about 1 3/4 hours – local map above. Leave Argentat by the N 120 going in the direction of Tulle.* The road goes up the little Souvigne valley bordered on either side by wooded hills.

St-Chamant. – Pop 560. The church doorway, preceded by the belfry-porch with wooden hoardings, is interesting. Note the doorway capitals and the tympanum with its double register of carvings showing above the Twelve Apostles, Christ in benediction with an angel on either side.

Follow the N 120 as far as Forges and there, opposite a Cross, take a surfaced local road on the right to approach the hamlet of Espargilière. Leave the car at the first house.

Espargilière Calvary. – *1/4 hour Rtn. Take the path on the left up to the Calvary.* The view from the monument extends over meadows to the wooded hillsides of the surrounding valleys.

Leave Forgès in the direction of Albussac by the D 113. At Grandchamp take the road to the left (D 113 E) till you come to the car park.

Murel Waterfall★. – Walk along the bank of the Valeine with its clear waters to reach the waterfall which is situated in a delightful setting of greenery and rocks.

Return to Grandchamp. Take to the left D 113 which flanks the hillside and provides fine views of the Souvigne valley. On leaving Albussac follow the D 87 before turning right onto the N 121. This road crosses pretty little valleys interspersed with chestnut woods before reaching the moorland plateau. *At Les Quatre Routes turn left into the D 940 in the direction of Figeac, then left again (road signposted; car park).*

Vic Rock★. – *Description p 70.*

Continue along the D 940 to La Grafouillère where you turn left into D 169. 5 km - 3 miles beyond Neuville there is a view, on the right, of the Dordogne valley and shortly afterwards, on the left, of a wooded ravine. *You pick up the N 120 as you come into Argentat.*

Join us in our never ending task of keeping up to date.

Send us your comments and suggestions, please.

Michelin Tyre Public Limited Company
Tourism Department
81 Fulham Road, LONDON SW3 6RD.

ARGENTON-SUR-CREUSE

Michelin map 68 folds 17 and 18 – *Local map p 88* – Pop 6 141 – *Facilities p 38*

Argenton, today, is a pleasant little town with its picturesque old houses spread along the river banks of the Creuse; it replaces the Gallo-Roman city of Argentomagus which lay 2 km – 1 mile to the north on the hill of St-Marcel *(p 172)*.

■ SIGHTS *time: 3/4 hour*

Church of St-Sauveur (**F**). – Before the church stands a belfry-porch surmounted by a pierced stone spire. The nave rebuilt in 19C has groined vaulting with emblazoned keystones.

At the end of the Rue Grande, turn right to reach the old bridge.

Vieux Pont (**B**). – The old bridge provides a good **view**★ of the river Creuse, the old quarter and the upper part of the town. Looking left you see a fine stretch of the Creuse, with twin overflows to provide water for the mills; houses with balconies, balustrades and wooden galleries and with slate roofs, overlooking the river and others built along the cliff which is densely overgrown. The great gilded statue of Notre-Dame of Argenton dominates the Chapel of Notre-Dame des Bancs, on the right with the stone spire of St-Sauveur, and in the far distance the belfry of the Church of St-Marcel.

Beyond the bridge is an **old house** with a small Renaissance door.

ARGENTON-SUR-CREUSE

Chapelle-N.-D. (R. de la) 2
Châteauneuf (R.) 3
Coursière (R. de la) 4
Grande (Rue) 6
Ledru-Rollin (R.) 7
Raspail (R.) 9
République (Pl. de la) 12
Rochers-St-Jean (R. des) 13
Rousseau (R. Jean-J.) 15
Victor-Hugo (R.) 18

Turn left into the Rue Raspail. On the right, you will see the **former college**, known also as the old prison, built in the Renaissance style, crowned with a bell turret and with a sculptured doorway.

Chapel of St-Benoît (**D**). – This former Gothic collegiate chapel (15-16C) has been restored. Outside there is a fine doorway with wreathed columns; on the left stands a statue (1485) of the Virgin and Child.

Higher up and on the opposite side of the road to the chapel, take the Rue de la Coursière which rises steeply. As you go up the view of the town and its setting becomes more extensive.

Chapel of Notre-Dame des Bancs (**E**). – This pilgrimage chapel *(p 37)* is dominated by an enormous gilded statue of the Virgin Mary. All that remains of a fortress dismantled in 1632, it was erected in the 15C on the site of the ruins of a 2C sanctuary built by St. Ursinus, first Bishop of Berry. The small statue that stands above the high altar is venerated under the name of Good Lady of Argenton (Bonne Dame d'Argenton) and it is said she protected the town from the plague in 1632.

From the terrace you get a complete **view**★ of the town: the eye travels from the picturesque quays to the houses adorned with gables and turrets, roofs of slate or brown tiles, dwells briefly on the belfries of St-Sauveur's Church and St-Benoît's Chapel and follows the line of the valley of the Creuse as it circles the town in a hilly setting.

Return to the starting point Place de la République by way of the Rue Victor-Hugo and the Pont Neuf.

EXCURSIONS

St-Marcel. – *2 km - 1 mile to the north. Leave Argenton by ⑤, the D 927. Description p 172.*

Prunget; Mazières. – *10 km - 6 miles to the east. Leave Argenton by ①, the N 20 and after 8 km - 5 miles take the D 30 to the right.*

Prunget Keep (Donjon de Prunget). – This massive 14C tower rises from a wooded hilltop overlooking the smiling Bouzanne valley. The keep is still impressive with buttresses, battlements and corner towers. Of the castle there remain the postern and traces of the fortified walls.

Follow the D 30 and after 800 m - 1/2 mile turn left.

Mazières Keep (Donjon de Mazières). – Also overlooking the valley, this powerful tower adjoins a castle.

Go back to the D 30 and turn right. As the Prunget keep comes into view, turn left and left again. Return to the N 120 via the Bois des Sallerons.

ASSIER

Michelin map 75 southeast of fold 19 – Pop 485

This Quercy village, due to the generosity of **Galiot de Genouillac**, Grand Master of the Artillery of France under François I, possesses two remarkable Renaissance monuments: the church containing the tomb of this ostentatious captain and the castle of which only a part, and that much damaged, remains.

Church. – This was built between 1540 and 1549 and is the original structure. The decoration on the outside is a long panegyric of Galiot's exploits and titles to fame.

A **frieze**★ goes right round the church. The subjects depicted include: sieges, battles, knights, foot-soldiers and artillerymen, and will surprise the visitor who will hardly expect to see such warlike motifs ornamenting a religious building. The frieze is a useful document on 16C arms and costume.

The **doorway**★ already has a Classical air: on the tympanum two cherubim proffer to the Virgin Galiot's insignia, his sword as the master of the horse and St. Michael's collar. The portico formed by two columns surmounted by a triangular pediment supports a domed niche.

Inside, the first chapel on the left contains the great captain's **tomb**★: the recumbent figure in court dress lies on a marble sarcophagus; above in high relief, Galiot is shown surrounded by his military emblems and two gunners who would appear to be waiting on his orders to fire. The star **vaulting**★ of the chapel, which forms a dome supported on squinches, is outstanding and very unusual.

Castle. – *Guided tours 1 June to 30 September, 10am to noon and 2.30 to 6.30pm: the rest of the year, apply to the caretaker, ☎ 40 57 31; closed Tuesdays.*

"Although built in a very ugly setting, in rough, ugly and mountainous country, the Castle of Assier," Brantôme (historian and biographer, 1540-1614) maintained, "equals in splendour the palaces of the Loire valley." This was because it was the creation of a great lord, a man of war certainly but also an ambitious courtier who loved to display wealth and glory. Everywhere you see his motto with its double meaning either as: *J'aime fortune* – I love fortune; or *J'aime fort une* – I love one greatly.

Three wings of the castle fell to the picks of the demolition men in the 18C; the only part standing today is the wing containing the guardroom.

The outer face of this building still has its machicolations between the two round towers, giving it a severe appearance. No such severity is to be seen in the design of the **inner façade**★: the lines are pure, and friezes divided into sections run above each storey.

The many scenes from the legend of Hercules symbolise the captain's omnipotence; cannon-balls and cannon spurting flames recall his office of Grand Master of the Artillery.

A small lapidary museum housed in rooms with ogive vaulting, is open to the public. A fine staircase in the transitional Gothic-Renaissance style leads to the next floor where the ceiling has collapsed and the timber work can be seen.

AUBAZINES★

Michelin map 75 fold 9 – *Local map 70* – Pop 673 – *Facilities p 38*

Aubazines (formerly Obazine) is in a pleasant **setting** of wooded hills, facing the Coiroux Gorges. The village built on a promontory nestles around the church, which recalls the great Cistercian abbey that once stood there and of which only a few buildings remain.

The Founder. – St. Stephen, who was born in a hamlet in Corrèze in 1085, founded the Abbey of Aubazines as a hermitage in 1125. In 1142 the community adopted the rule of St. Benedict. St. Stephen was installed as abbot by the Bishop of Limoges and during his abbacy the community expanded rapidly. In 1147 the monks adopted the Cistercian Law becoming a sister house of Cîteaux.

In the nearby Coiroux Gorges once stood the only convent for nuns founded by St. Stephen in 1142. Only a chapel in ruins remains *(excavations in progress)*.

Church★. – This former abbey church which was built in the 12C, is a very fine example of the Cistercian style of architecture. The octagonal belfry, which is only one storey high, shows the Limousin influence.

The church was truncated in the 18C losing six bays and now has a nave with three bays with cradle vaulting and side aisles with groined vaulting. The transept crossing is roofed with an elegant dome on pendentives; three chapels with flat east walls open into each arm of the transept. The chancel is terminated by a five-sided apse.

The south transept contains a remarkable 12C oak cupboard embellished with blind arcades; this is one of the oldest pieces of religious furniture in France.

The 18C stalls whose misericords present a series of carved heads with widely differing expressions, a 15C *pietà* in multicoloured stone and four 12C patterned grey glass windows are all of interest but are totally eclipsed by the wonderful **tomb of St. Stephen**★★. This takes the form of a stone shrine which was placed over the tomb of the founder in the 13C. The canopy above the recumbent figure has two sloping sides and rests on arcades supported by small columns; the sloping sides are decorated with high reliefs; the Virgin with the Child Jesus on her knees, is shown greeting St. Stephen and his religious orders of monks and nuns twice, once on earth and once on the day of their resurrection. The richness of the decoration, the delicacy and truth of the facial expressions make this one of the most precious architectural specimens of Gothic times.

Former abbey. – *Guided tours 1 July to 14 September at 3.30 and 4.30pm; the rest of the year at 3 and 4pm; closed Mondays (Tuesday if Monday is a holiday), during Holy Week and 15 September to 1 November; 7F.*

Now occupied by a community of nuns of the Oriental church. The visitor sees the former chapterhouse with its groined vaulting resting on two round columns, the old heated common-room, the monolithic fountain and the fish breeding pool, fed by a long canal, dug by the Cistercians to bring water to the abbey and the village.

AUBUSSON

Michelin map 73 fold 1 – Pop 6 153 – *Facilities p 38*

Aubusson, built in the upper valley of the Creuse, still manufactures the tapestries and carpets that have won it renown over the last five centuries. A College of Decorative Arts opened in 1884 offers courses aimed at keeping up this tradition. The Jean Lurçat Cultural Centre has recently been set up to promote this craft.

A time-honoured craft. – It would appear that tapestry weaving was imported from Flanders in the 14C by Marie de Hainault who became Countess of Marche and it was only in the 15C that the tapestry weavers of Aubusson won wide fame. The Lady and the Unicorn, a 15C masterpiece now in the Cluny Museum in Paris, is believed to have been woven by the craftsmen of Aubusson. Their fame peaked in the 16 and 17C with *verdures* (flower and foliage designs in shades of green) as well as sacred, mythological and historical themes, and Colbert granted them the title of royal tapestry-makers.

With the departure abroad of many of the weavers, particularly to Germany, in 1685 at the Revocation of the Edict of Nantes, the industry faced ruin. It recovered only at the beginning of the 18C working closely with the painters of that time: Watteau, Lancret and Boucher. The 19C was a period of decline between the aftermath of the Revolution and competition from wallpaper. Nowadays the town takes pride in several factories weaving by methods that have been well tried for over a hundred years. The great speciality of Aubusson is *basse-lisse* tapestry where the looms are horizontal as in the weaving of Beauvais and Gobelins tapestries.

AUBUSSON

Chapitre (R. du)	2	Grande Rue	9
Chateaufavier	3	Îles (Quai des)	12
Dayras (Pl. M.)	4	Lurçat (Pl. J.)	13
Déportés (R. des)	5	Marché (Pl. du)	15
Espagne (Pl. Gén.)	6	République (Av.)	16
Fusillés (R. des)	7	St-Jean (R.)	18
		Sandeau (R. J.)	19
		Vieille (R.)	22

A fresh start. – At the beginning of the 20C inspiration was flagging. Although technically perfect the tapestries were mere copies of paintings in a variety of colours.

In the 1930s a fresh impetus was given thanks to a collector, Madame Cuttoli, who commissioned designs from the greatest contemporary painters. From 1939 **Jean Lurçat** (1892-1966) in collaboration with Gromaire, played a decisive part in the rebirth of the art of tapestry-weaving. A new generation of cartoon designers emerged with Prassinos, Tourlière, Saint-Saëns, Picart-le-Doux, Dom Robert and Wogensky among others. Whilst not neglecting traditional themes, Aubusson showed renewed creative originality and gained further international renown.

■ THE TAPESTRIES *time: 1 1/2 hours*

Several private galleries exhibit the wares of local workshops. Most of them are to be found in the town centre, in the Grande Rue and in the surrounding area.

Jean Lurçat Cultural Centre (F). – *Open 9am to 12.30pm (9.30am to noon out of season) and 2 to 6pm; closed Tuesdays; 7F.*

This severe, functional building is devoted to the art of tapestry weaving. There is a theatre, a gallery for large temporary exhibitions, a library and a reference section as well as a demonstration workshop.

In the **contemporary tapestry gallery★** (salle de tapisserie contemporaine) there is a permanent display of major works by Lurçat (Winter), Gromaire (Brittany), Saint-Saëns, Lagrange, Julien and Maingonnat (Autumnal Undergrowth).

Tapestry and Carpet Exhibition★ (H). – *Open 15 June to 30 September, 9.30am to noon and 2 to 6.30pm; 8F.*

The exhibition which is held in the town hall comprises tapestries worked to traditional and modern designs. There is a workshop where craftsmen demonstrate the various stages of tapestry weaving.

■ ADDITIONAL SIGHTS

The Old Tapestry Weaver's House (**Maison du Vieux Tapissier**) (E). – *Open 15 June to 30 September, 9.30am to noon and 2 to 6.30pm; 6F.*

In this 16C house you can see an old workshop, a display of tapestries and samplers of Aubusson stitchery, pieces of local furniture and documents describing the history of the town and how the *basse-lisse* tapestry weaving workshop came to be set up at Aubusson.

Old Town. – It stretches on both sides of the Grande Rue. Go along the **Rue Vieille** which is reserved for pedestrians and where the old houses have been completely renovated and turned into art galleries, craft and antique shops. The attractive Place de la Libération contains a 16C turreted house known as the Maison des Vallenet (**B**) and a fountain dating from 1718, adorned with heraldic devices.

There is a pleasant view from the old bridge, Pont de la Terrade, an interesting 16C construction with pointed cutwaters, of the houses rising in terraces on the left bank of the Creuse at the foot of some impressive sized rocks.

View. – From the terrace near the Church of Ste-Croix (which contains a fine tapestry made in 1770 of the Vision of Constantine), a steep path climbs rapidly to the summit of the hill and the Esplanade du Chapitre where the ruins of the castle of the counts of Aubusson still stand. From the castle there is a view of the whole town and its setting.

EXCURSION

Creuse Upper Valley. – *Round trip 26 km - 16 miles – about 3/4 hour.* Michelin maps 73 fold 1 and 72 fold 10. *Leave Aubusson by ⑥.* The D 942 passes at the foot of some rocks to reach a plateau. Beyond Combarioux bear left into the D 18A which crosses the Creuse by the Chambons Bridge and then runs parallel with the river bank. Take the D 18 to the left, the valley narrows before you reach La Rochette and its chapel which is close to a road bend.

Continue for 50 m – 55 yds to the left to reach the Romanesque chapel built in 1569 and later restored when a bell-tower sheathed in wooden scales was added. It stands in a charming setting of lush rolling meadows through which the Creuse meanders. On the way back to Aubusson the road climbs and, closely following the hillside contour, affords bird's-eye views of the valley.

AUVÉZÈRE Valley

Michelin map 75 folds 6 and 7

The valley of the Auvézère links the wooded farmlands of Limousin with the valleys of Périgord, offering scenes of agricultural husbandry and bare landscapes.

The Auvézère source rises on the Limousin plateau and flows first through a region of granite and schist. Often the roads that run near the valley of the Auvézère provide only occasional glimpses of the river. The best views are to be found between Savignac-Lédrier (fine La Forge Castle down below) and Tourtoirac.

- The road overlooks the wooded slopes dotted with rocks of the Auvézère Gorges continuously on the right from Savignac-Lédrier to St-Mesmin.
- The picturesque D 72E5 and D 72E4, offer remarkable glimpses of the gorges before dropping down first to the St-Mesmin Mill and then the Pervendoux Mill. These mills in picturesque settings at the foot of escarpments, use the strong current to turn their wheels. The villages are perched on hill slopes covered with oak and chesnut woods. Downstream from Génis, beyond the confluence with the Dalon, the waters are often tinged with a reddish colour when the river is in spate.
- The D 5, north of Cubas, is hemmed in by wooded hills on one side and, on the other, the river as it winds through the meadows. Then the valley opens out, meadows, market gardens and plantations of walnut trees carpet the alluvial floor of the valley.
- The valley at **Tourtoirac** *(p 179)* is particularly attractive, being bordered on both sides by wooded hills and cliffs.

Below Cubjac, the Auvézère describes wide loops, then narrows once more to flow between steep rock walls, before joining the River Isle.

AZAY-LE-FERRON ★

Michelin map 68 fold 6 – Pop 1 146

Azay-le-Ferron which stands on the boundaries of Touraine and Berry, bordering on Brenne and the Preuilly Forest, is dominated by the imposing outline of its château.

Château★. – *Open 10am to noon and 2 to 6pm (4.30pm in October and March; closed in January, on Tuesdays all the year round, and Wednesdays, Thursdays and Fridays out of season; time: 3/4 hour; 8F.*

You get a full view of the main façade from the French style gardens with their yews and clipped box-trees surrounded by tall trees. The château buildings offer a mixture of styles dating from the 15 to the 18C: a massive machicolated tower built in the late 15C is joined by a 17C building known as the Humières' Wing to the elegant Renaissance style main buildings, called the François I Pavilion; on the far right stands the Breteuil Pavilion completed in 1714.

Apartments. – The château contains much valuable **furniture★**, especially in the Empire style. On the first floor three rooms are furnished in the Empire and Restoration styles (early 19C): a sitting room with furniture in the so-called "Egyptian" style also contains an Aubusson carpet and drawings by Carle Vernet (1758-1836); a bedroom in Empire style contains a boat-shaped bed with posts in the form of swans' necks and pale maplewood furniture; a Restoration saloon has a wonderful parquet floor designed as a rosette.

In the library there is a fine 16C Flemish tapestry; the grand saloon and the banqueting hall contain a wide variety of precious objects, including four large decorative 17C paintings from the school of Genoa. These once hung in Richelieu Château in the Loire valley country. The château was destroyed not long after the Revolution.

There is a good overall view of the gardens and the court of honour from the circular path round the parapet of the great tower.

BEAULIEU-SUR-DORDOGNE ★

Michelin map 75 north of fold 19 – *Local map p 94* – Pop 1 603 – *Facilities p 38*

Beaulieu, built on the right bank of the Dordogne, owes its fame to the fine Romanesque church of the former Benedictine monastery.

Foundation and Growth of the Abbey. – Raoul, Archbishop of Bourges, visited this part of the country in 855 and, enchanted by the beauty of this particular site which he christened *bellus locus – beau lieu* - beautiful place – decided to found a community there. The monastery grew early to considerable importance in spite of the bloody struggles over its suzerainty by the lords of Turenne and Castelnau. The abbots then had to reckon with the city merchants who, gaining privilege after privilege, were soon practically independent.

The Benedictine Reformation. – The monks began to take liberties with the discipline of the order and at the onslaught of the Wars of Religion (1562-1598) deserted the abbey. In 1663 the Abbot of La Tour d'Auvergne called on the austere Benedictine Congregation of Maurists to undertake the necessary reforms and to repair the monastery buildings. The community was thus able to live serenely until the time of the Revolution which finally drove away the monks.

■ ST. PETER'S CHURCH★ (Église St-Pierre) *time: 1/2 hour*

The abbey church was built by monks of the Cluniac order in the 12C in the Limousin Romanesque style.

South Doorway★★. – The doorway was carved in 1125 and is one of the greatest masterpieces of Romanesque sculpture. The craftsmen who made it came from Toulouse and worked on the carvings at Moissac, Collonges, Souillac and Carennac.

The doorway is preceded by an open porch; the sculpture is remarkable for both composition and execution. The theme on the tympanum is the Last Judgment.

(1) In the centre, Christ in Majesty dominates all by His height and extends His arms in welcome to the chosen.

(2) On either side two angels sound trumpets, while above, four angels (3) hold the instruments of the Passion. The Apostles are grouped left and right (4) and below them (5) the dead rise from their graves.

Monsters line the upper part of the lintel (6). The lower part (7), as at Moissac *(p 134)*; is decorated with rosettes from which emerge chimera, serpents and monsters.

(8) Four prophets in clinging robes stand against the pier.

Two rounded arcades supported on small columns stand on either side before the door; they are badly multilated but behind them can be seen, on the left (9) Daniel in the lions' den and, on the right (10) the Temptation of Christ.

Make for the west face, opposite which stands a **Renaissance house** adorned with statues and medallions. Continue round the church, bearing left, passing swiftly through a street lined with old houses before taking, on the right, a covered alley that will bring you to the Place des Pères. The former monastery buildings in ruins can be seen on the right. Go round the chevet containing the apse and its crown of apsidal chapels with sculptured modillions. Rising above the chapels is the fine octagonal tower which covers the transept crossing. Return to the south door.

Interior. – The church was designed as a place of pilgrimage where crowds might circulate freely. The nave has cradle vaulting, no windows and wide side aisles which extend beyond the arms of the transept into an ambulatory with radial chapels. A tall asymmetrical dome on pendentives rises above the transept crossing from engaged columns. Dark galleries open off the nave through twin bays whose arches stand on two small squat columns. The same arrangement is to be found in the arms of the transept and the chancel which has oven vaulting and is lit by five rounded bays.

Treasure. – Placed in a strong cupboard in the north arm of the transept, this consists of a remarkable 12C seated **Virgin★** of silver gilt wood, a 10C silver reliquary, a 13C shrine of *champlevé* enamel, two 14C arm reliquaries and various silver gilt and pewter ornaments.

EXCURSION

Queyssac-les-Vignes; Curemonte; Puy-d'Arnac. – *Round tour of 34 km - 21 miles – about 2 hours. Leave Beaulieu to the south by the D 41 then take the D 12 to the right.*

Queyssac. – Pop 213. The village is built on a promontory against a background of vineyards, woods and fields. There is a viewing table at the top of the tower *(restored)* of the old castle which is reached through the courtyard of the hotel *Au Vin Paillé*. From the viewpoint there is a vast **panorama★** of the Dordogne valley, marked by Castelnau Castle, Carennac and the Montvalent amphitheatre running from the east across to the southwest; to the southeast can be seen the St-Laurent Towers dominating St-Céré and to the north and northwest lie Vic Rock and Turenne Castle.

Take the D 12 then the D 15^E to the right which meets up with the D 15 north of Végennes.

Curemonte. – *Description p 90.*

Continue along the D 15 which affords good views of Curemonte and at the church of St-Genest bear right on the D 106.

Puy-d'Arnac. – Pop 325. Puy-d'Arnac lies at the base of a hillock, crowned by a church. There is a steep road up which you can go by car, from the village to the terrace where the church stands. From there you get an extensive **panorama★** of the countryside of valleys, hills and fields, which is so characteristic of the Dordogne; to the northwest can be seen the rugged mountains of Meyssac and Turenne.

Return to Beaulieu on the D 940.

BEAUMONT

Michelin map 75 fold 15 – Pop 1 302

Beaumont was built as a strongly fortified *bastide* in 1272 by the seneschal of Guyenne in the name of Edward I, King of England and today retains only traces of the fortress as well as many arcaded houses.

Church of St-Front. – This church, built by the English in 1272, has four strong towers flanking the façade and chevet and a parapet walk, and was the last outpost of defence in time of war.

Restoration on a considerable scale was carried out last century and took away the military character of the building. On the west face capitals decorated with carved foliage carry the arches of a fine doorway which is surmounted by a gallery with a delicately ornate balustrade.

Rampart ruins. – A good view of the perimeter walls, the 13C fortified Luzier gate and the impressive outline of the Church of St-Front can be seen by going westwards, beyond the line of ramparts.

EXCURSION

Bannes Castle. – *5 km - 3 miles northwest by the D 660 then take the road to the left.* *Local map p 98.* This elegant 16C building perched on a rock spur is flanked by round towers with pepper-pot roofs.

BELLAC

Michelin map 72 fold 7 – Pop 5 465

Bellac rises up on a spur overlooking the valley of the Vincou which flows into the Gartempe – a picturesque setting in a green and undulating countryside on the borders of the Limousin plateaux and the Poitou plains.

Giraudoux' Native Soil. – Châteauroux *(p 83)* may claim the glory of having educated Jean Giraudoux at its lycée, but it was in Bellac that he was born in 1882 (d 1944). The countryside he knew as a child is depicted in *Suzanne et le Pacifique*. He described Bellac with the following words: "...a countryside of streams and hills, a patchwork of fields and chestnut woods... for it was a land with a long history, it was the region of Limousin."

Giraudoux created a new type of drama for the theatre, a drama containing irony, poetry and magic. *Siegfried, Amphytrion 38, Intermezzo, La Guerre de Troie n'aura pas lieu* (The Trojan War Shall Not Take Place), *Électre, Ondine* and *La Folle de Chaillot* (The Mad Woman of Chaillot), make him one of the greatest of contemporary dramatists. His style is sparkling, full of twists and innovations.

Every year in July a drama, music and dance festival dedicated to Giraudoux is held in Bellac.

■ SIGHTS *time: 1 1/2 hours*

The Setting. – Leave the car in the Place de la République near the Town Hall, a 16C mansion, and go up the Rue Lafayette. From a terrace about one hundred yards up the street you get a good view of the church, the Vincou flowing rapidly between rocky banks, the old stone bridge and the viaduct.

Church. – The church is built on a terrace overlooking the Vincou and shows a strange juxtaposition of the Romanesque and Gothic styles. A great square belfry surmounts the two naves, one 12C and Romanesque, the other 14C and Gothic. The two naves lead to the chancel which ends in a flat chevet.

To the left of the entrance, in a chest set into the wall *(to open introduce a 1 F piece)*, admirers of gold and silver plate may see a beautiful 12C **shrine** embellished with *cabochons* and medallions of *champlevé* enamel *(see minor arts, p 30)*. It is one of the oldest in Limousin.

Mementoes of Giraudoux. – A **monument** dedicated to Jean Giraudoux, the work of the sculptor Chauvenet, was erected in 1951 in a garden planted with great trees next to the town hall. On either side of the medallion bearing his portrait are depicted six heroines from his books and plays: Ondine and Alcmène, Judith and Bella, Isabelle and Suzanne.

Admirers of the poet may also visit the **house** where he was born in Rue Jean Jaurès. *Open 1 July to 31 August, 3 to 7pm.* There are documents relating to the author and his family: letters, photographs, models and theatre bills. His own room and his library which contains a valuable collection of his manuscripts, are open to the public.

EXCURSIONS

Basse-Marche★. – *Round tour of 55 km - 34 miles – about 3 hours. Leave Bellac by the N 145 to the east and take the D 1 on the right.*

Rancon. – Pop 652. This peaceful town in the Gartempe valley is built on a hillside. In the small square beside the town hall is a 12C lantern to the dead which is surmounted by a cross with five foils (cusps).

The 13C church in the transitional Romanesque-Gothic style, fortified in the 14C, was formerly part of the town's defensive perimeter. Note the machicolations on the chevet and the openings for the archers. The belfry, a 16C square tower, ends in an onion-shaped dome covered with shingles. In the chancel is a fine 13C wooden Christ and in the north aisle, a 17C Aubusson tapestry banner.

Follow the picturesque D 1 to Châteauponsac.

Châteauponsac. – *Description p 82.*

Leave Châteauponsac to the north by the D 45 which winds through pleasant, wooded scenery, then take the D 942.

Magnac-Laval. – Pop 2 512. This Limousin town is famous for a procession to St. Maximinus which wends its way through more than 50 km – 30 miles of the countryside on Whit Monday. The pilgrims wearing garlands of flowers round their necks leave after midnight mass and return after sunset the following day.
The 12C church has a flat chevet and a fine hexagonal belfry; it contains the relics of St. Maximinus.

Leave Magnac-Laval to the west by the D 942.

Le Dorat★. – *Description p 91.*

Return to Bellac by the D 675 which runs through the Gartempe valley.

Blond Hills★. – *Round tour of 60 km - 37 miles – about 2 1/2 hours. Leave Bellac to the south by the D 3 in the direction of Blond.*

Blond. – Pop 756. The church is late 12C. Traces of the fortifications (battlements) added in the 16C appear above the doorway which is framed by two huge buttresses.

Leave Blond to the southeast. Take the D 5, a picturesque little road through woodlands. *Turn right after 5 km – 3 miles.*

Vaulry viewing-table. – From this knoll the **view** extends as far as the Ambazac hills and the Limousin plateaux to the east and southeast.

Return to Blond.

Leave the D 5 on the outskirts of the village and take a small road to the left into the Blond Hills.

Blond Hills★. – This small granite yet wooded massif rises above the Limousin plateau. To the left of the road, the Puychaud rocks are a curious jumble of rocks worn by erosion. On the south side the road wends through a countryside dotted with lakes.

Just before Beaucartu, bear left into a road suitable for cars which is signposted.

Pierre Branlante. – Leave the car and continue for 50 m – 55 yds on foot. A rock pile, precariously balanced, lies hidden in the woods.

Return to the road and continue along it for a while, then turn right into the D 204 in the direction of Mortemart.

Peyrelade. – At the entrance to the hamlet, a road on the left which is suitable for cars leads to a rocky platform from which you can enjoy a good **view** of the Limousin mountains and of Nontronnais.

Mortemart. – Pop 161. This village was the home of the Mortemart family of which Madame de Montespan, favourite of Louis XIV, was a member. The old covered market, two former convents, curious old houses, together with the few towers that are all that remain of the castle buildings, make a picturesque architectural group. The chapel of the former Augustinian monastery now serves as the parish church. It has a curious onion-shaped belfry covered in slates; inside are interesting 15C carved stalls and a Baroque retable with a picture of the Assumption.

Take the D 4 in the direction of Mézières-sur-Issoire.

Fraisse Castle. – This elegant Renaissance building is complemented by fine outbuildings that stand at right angles to the main structure.

Take the D 4 and the D 951 which lead back to Bellac.

BELVÈS

Michelin map 75 fold 16 – *Local map p 97* – Pop 1 652

Belvès – the name means *belle vue* - fine view – is built in a picturesque hilltop setting overlooking the valley of the Nauze. Arrive from the southeast by the D 52 or from the south by the D 710, to get a view of the whole town at once, the old houses with their turrets and bell towers, the terraced gardens and shrubberies.

Place d'Armes (Square). – Still to be seen in the square in the centre of the town, are the old belfry and the covered market with its round tiled roof: note the pillory chain attached to one of the pillars. The former Dominican monastery surmounted by an octagonal clock tower is in the Place de la Croix-des-Frères. There are some fine Gothic and Renaissance houses between the two squares.

Rue des Filhols also starts from the Place d'Armes. Note on the left the Bontemps mansion, a fine Renaissance building which has been restored.

BÉNÉVENT-L'ABBAYE

Michelin map 72 folds 8 and 9 – Pop 1 203

The best view of Bénévent-l'Abbaye is from the north, from the D 912. To the southeast the town is dominated by the mass of the Puy de Goth. The monastery founded here in the 11C took on new life after receiving a relic of St. Bartholomew from the Italian town of Benevento. In deference it took the name of Bénévent.

Church. – The church was built in the 12C in the transitional Gothic style. A two storey belfry-porch ornamented with blind arcades, an impressive nave, an octagonal tower surmounted by a conical spire and a stone lantern compose this fine building which stands on the left of an esplanade planted with lime trees. The doorway has a multifoil pointed arch with small columns decorated with capitals supporting slender covings.

Go right round the church to admire the numerous carved modillions; facing the chevet are some of the buildings which used to form part of the abbey – one has a door carved in the Renaissance style.

Interior. – The broken barrel vaulting of the nave is upheld by great pillars separated by narrow passageways. Two chapels open off the transept, while the crossing itself is surmounted by a cupola corresponding to the octagonal tower seen from outside. Three more polygonal chapels open off the narrow ambulatory. The church is especially noteworthy for the 38 capitals carved with symbolic animals around the chancel and in the nave.

Puy de Goth★. – *Take a steep uphill road southeast of the town. Leave the car where three roads meet and take one on the left (1/2 hour on foot Rtn).* From the summit (541 m – 1 775 ft) there is a semicircular **view★**, southwest over the mountains of Marche and Limousin, southeast over the Auvergne mountains where, on a clear day you can single out the Puy de Dôme and the Puy de Sancy.

EXCURSION

Le Grand-Bourg. – Pop 1 422. *5 km - 3 miles to the north by the D 912.* Le Grand-Bourg church was built in the 13C by Canon Gérald de Salagnac whose tomb lies in the north transept. The church is preceded by a 17C bell-tower and flanked by massive buttresses. Note the capitals of the north door which are adorned by small figures. In the chancel a high relief carved in granite and probably dating from the 12C, depicts the Virgin and Child in a pose reminiscent of the style of Auvergne.

BERGERAC

Michelin map 75 folds 14 and 15 – *Local map p 98* – Pop 27 704

Bergerac lies spread out on both banks of the river in the Dordogne alluvial plain; it owes its association with the name of Cyrano (whose statue is on the Place de la Myrpe) to the literary fame of Edmond Rostand (1868-1918). Its avenues are lined with lovely crape myrtle (lagerstrœmia) trees. The Bergerac wines are well known, among the best is Monbazillac *(p 54)*.

Bergerac, as the most important town in southern Dordogne, is the local centre for agriculture, wine and industry. Tobacco *(p 17)* plays an important part in the economic life of the region and the only experimental Tobacco Institute in France is near Bergerac.

A state powder factory, producing nitro-cellulose for use in such industries as filmmaking, paint, varnish and plastics, further increases the prosperity of the town.

■ SIGHTS *time: 1 1/2 hours*

Tobacco Museum★ (Musée du Tabac). – *Open daily, 10 am to noon and 2 to 6pm; 2.30 to 6pm Sundays and holidays from Easter to 1 October only; closed Tuesday mornings; 7F.*

The museum is housed in the 17C Peyrarède mansion. It traces the extraordinary progress of a plant which, till the 15C, was known only to the American Indian tribes but is now used in every part of the globe.

The exhibition includes works of art, objects and documents outlining the history of tobacco, its influence on manners, habits and politics; the propagation of the plant,

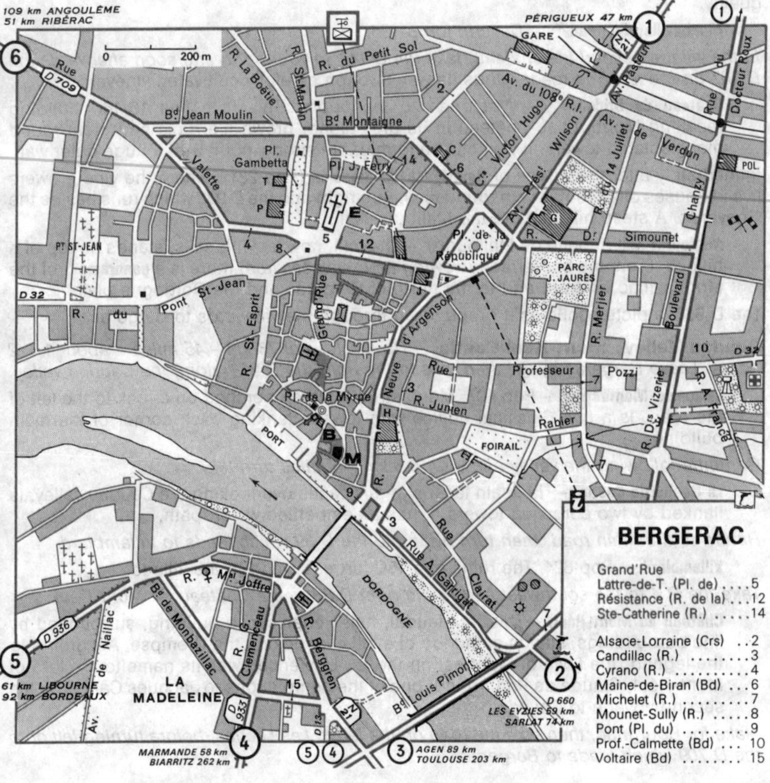

tobacco production and trade under the *Ancien Régime;* the different ways of enjoying tobacco and finally sales and consumption today.

A collection of snuff boxes and pipes from various countries, paintings, rare books, etchings and lithographs complete this interesting presentation.

Museum of Urban History (Musée d'Histoire urbaine) (M). – *Same opening times as for the Tobacco Museum.*

This is in a gallery in the same building. It contains prehistoric collections, canvases by Bergerac painters and an extensive department on regional history: recent archaeological finds.

Church of Notre-Dame (E). – Built in the Gothic style this 19C church has a slender bell tower. There are two fine paintings in the east chapel: an Adoration of the Magi attributed to Pordenone (1484-1539), a Venetian painter; and an Adoration of the Shepherds attributed to the Milanese Ferrari (*c* 1480-1546), student of Leonardo da Vinci. In the west transept is an immense Aubusson tapestry portraying the Bergerac coat of arms.

Monastery of the Recollects (Couvent des Récollets) or **Winemakers' Guild** (Maison du Vin) (**B**). – *Open 3.30 and 4.30pm; in July and August also 10.30 and 11.30am, 1.30, 2.30 and 5.30pm; closed Sundays, Mondays (out of season) and holidays; 6F.*

Built between the 12 and 17C the structure is of brick and stone. The inner courtyard, the former cloister, has a 14C and 16C gallery side by side; in one corner note the monk's oven. Some steps lead down to the wine cellar, a vast chamber with remarkable vaulting where the meetings of the *Consuls de la Vinée* are held. From the sumptuously decorated great hall on the first floor, there is a fine view of the Monbazillac vineyard.

EXCURSIONS

Monbazillac Vineyard. – *Round tour of 27 km - 17 miles – about 1 1/2 hours – Local map below.*

Go south out of Bergerac by the D 13. This road crosses a market garden area and then the meadowlands of the Dordogne alluvial plain before reaching the first slopes and the vineyards *(the vineyard area is marked on the map on the right).* The famous vineyard of Monbazillac has a reputation that goes back hundreds of years. There is a story that in the Middle Ages, when pilgrims from Bergerac were visiting Rome, the pope asked, "And where is Bergerac?" "Near Monbazillac", replied the chamberlain.

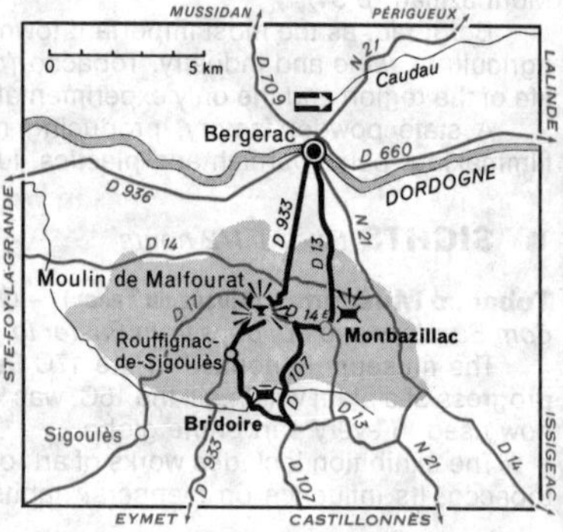

The white wine of Monbazillac is a sweet wine and is served with foie gras as well as dessert. The bunches are picked when they are very ripe and have reached the stage of "noble rot" – a guarantee of quality.

Monbazillac Château★. – *Description p 135.*

In the village beyond the château, take the D 14^{E} to your right, and soon afterwards the D 107 on the left. The roads winds its way through carefully cultivated vineyards.

Château de Bridoire★. – *Not open to the public.* This is a fine 15-16C building recalling Monbazillac Château in its grey stone, brown tile roofs and great round machicolated towers. It was once a formidable strong-point with a huge outer wall.

Immediately after the village of **Rouffignac-de-Sigoulès** (Pop 281), where the vine growers live in houses often roofed with round tiles, turn right into the D 933 which runs beside the vineyards. A steep hill leads to the Malfourat Mill.

Malfourat Mill (Moulin de Malfourat). – The mill, now lacking sails, stands on top of a hillock. From the bar terrace *(viewing table, access free)* there is a **panorama★** of the Monbazillac vineyard and to the north of Bergerac and the Dordogne plain.

The D 933 is picturesque as it drops down through the vineyards to Bergerac.

Caudau Valley; Mont-Réal Castle. – *Round tour of 73 km - 45 miles – about 1 1/2 hours. Leave Bergerac by ①, then take to the right the D 21^{E} along the Caudau valley.*

Lamonzie-Montastruc. – Pop 407. Montastruc Château perched on a rock to the left of the road, is a fine Classical edifice with towers flanking each corner of the main building.

Continue following the valley and after 8.5 km - 5 miles turn left.

La Gaubertie Castle. – The main façade of this castle overlooking the Caudau valley, is flanked by two corbelled towers. It has an embattled watch-path.

Return to the main road, then turn right into the D 39 which leads to Villamblard.

Villamblard. – Pop 824. The ruins of a 15C fortress stand in the village.

Take the D 4 to the southwest and to the right D 38 to the Château de Mont-Réal.

Château de Mont-Réal. – This half-feudal, half-Renaissance building, surrounded by fine outbuildings, stands at the top of a hill overlooking the Crempse. According to the legend, the town of Montreal on the St. Lawrence owes its name to the lord of Mont-Réal, Claude de Pontbriand, one of the companions to Jacques Cartier on his second voyage to Canada.

Make for Bourgnac, then take the road on the left to Les Lèches, before turning left onto the D 709 which leads to Bergerac.

BESSE

Michelin map 75 southwest of fold 17 – Pop 183

Standing in the centre of the forest that covers much of Quercy between the Lot and the Dordogne, is the little village of Besse with its interesting Romanesque church roofed with stone slates *(p 44)*.

The chevet ends in an apse with oven vaulting. The belfry-porch, which has an asymmetrical roof, protects a remarkable carved **doorway★**. On either side of the door are two capitals carved in archaic style and ornamented with simple figures; among the subjects depicted are the Seven Deadly Sins, scenes in the Garden of Eden, an angel with the paschal lamb, and hunting scenes.

EXCURSION

Villefranche-du-Périgord. – Pop 800. *Facilities p 38. 8 km - 5 miles to the south by the D 57.* This bastide *(p 32)* commanding the valley of the Lémance, still has a vast covered market and some of the arcades which once surrounded its main square.

BEYNAC-et-CAZENAC ★★

Michelin map 75 fold 17 – *Local map p 97* – Pop 460

Beynac Castle stands on a remarkable **site★★**, rising from the top of a rock; it commands the beautiful Dordogne valley as it winds between hills crowned with castles. It was here, in the village sheltering at the foot of the cliff face, that the artist responsible for the first drawing of Bibendum lived.

A Redoutable Stronghold. – In the Middle Ages Beynac, Biron, Bourdeilles and Mareuil were the four baronies of Périgord. When the Capetians and the Plantagenets were rivals, the castle, captured by Richard Lionheart, was used as a base by the sinister Mercadier, who banded his men to pillage the countryside on behalf of the King of England. In 1214 during the Albigensian Crusade *(p 25)*, Simon de Montfort seized the castle and dismantled it. The castle was later rebuilt as we see it today by a lord of Beynac. During the Hundred Years War (1337-1453), when the Dordogne marked the front between the English and the French, there were constant skirmishes and raids between the French, based at Beynac, and the English at Castelnaud.

Castle. – *To reach Beynac take the D 703 on leaving the village to the west (3 km – 1 1/2 miles).*

Open 1 March to 15 November, 10am to noon and 2.30 to 6pm; time: 3/4 hour; 9F.

The castle is in the form of an irregular quadrilateral extended on the south side to form a bastion. The keep, whose austerity is modified only by crenellations, dates from the 13C. A double perimeter wall protected the castle from attack from the plateau; on all the other sides there is a sheer drop of 150 m - 490 ft to the Dordogne. The main building dating from the 13 and 14C, is prolonged by the 15C seignorial manorhouse to which a bartizan was added in the 16C.

Interior. – *Restoration in progress.* The great Hall of State, where once the nobles of Périgord used to assemble, has fine barrel vaulting; the oratory is decorated with Gothic frescoes naïve in style with lively draughtsmanship depicting the Last Supper, a Christ of Pity at the foot of His Cross, such as He appeared to St. Gregory according to the mediaeval legend, and members of the Beynac family.

From the watch-path and the south bastion, which overlook the Dordogne and are reached by the main staircase (17C), there is a wonderful **panorama★★** of the valley and from left to right, of the Domme Barre and the Castles of Marqueyssac, Castelnaud and Fayrac.

Calvary. – This stands on the cliff edge 150 m - 164 yds to the east of the castle. A **panorama★★** as wide as the one from the castle watch-path can be seen from this point.

BIRON Castle ★

Michelin map 75 fold 16

Biron Castle, perched at the top of a puy, rears up the great mass of its towers and walls on the borders of Périgord and Agenais and commands a wide horizon.

From the Capitol to the Tarpeian Rock. – Among the many celebrated men of the Biron family, the fate of **Charles de Gontaut** should not be forgotten. Friend of Henry IV, he was appointed first Admiral and then Marshal of France. In 1598 the Barony of Biron was created and conferred as a dukedom on Charles de Gontaut who was next promoted to be Lieutenant-General of the French Army and then Governor of Burgundy. Even these honours did not satisfy him and in league with the

(After a photo by M. Foucault, Éd. Tel)

Biron – The castle.

Duke of Savoy and the Spanish Governor of the state of Milan, he laid a plot which would have led to the breaking up of the kingdom of France. Biron, his treason exposed, was pardoned. But the mercy of Henry IV did nothing to halt his ambitions. Once more he plotted against his Lord. Once again he was exposed and was taken before the King, who agreed to pardon him if he would confess his crime. The proud Biron refused. He was beheaded in the Bastille on 31 July 1602.

TOUR *time: 1 hour*

Open 1 February to 30 October, 9 to 11.30am and 2.30 to 6.30pm; the rest of the year, 10am to noon and 2 to 4.30 pm; closed Tuesdays, 15 December to 31 January; 8F.

Pass through the doorway to reach a vast court around which stand buildings varying greatly in appearance and architectural style. This monumental assemblage is the product of the fourteen generations of the Gontaut-Biron family who have owned the castle. The guards' tower, now the caretaker's lodge, is an elegant building in which are happily juxtaposed battlements. a watch-path and Renaissance decoration.

The **chapel**★ was built in the Renaissance style in the 16C. A pierced balustrade runs round the base of the roof. The lower chamber serves as a parish church for the village; the upper chamber or seignorial chapel, which opens directly on to the court has remarkable ogive vaulting. Note the recumbent figures of Pons de Gontaut-Biron who died in 1524 and that of his brother Armand who was Bishop of Sarlat.

From the terrace between the chapel and the Collector's Office, a large building divided by a turret where the peasants paid their dues, there is a bird's-eye view of the town.

It is worth while visiting the immense kitchens, paved with great stone slabs, the hall of state, going up the monumental staircases, walking in the delightful inner court with its colonnade and looking at the ramparts and terraces from which there are fine **views**★. The varied styles and unusual lay-out of the buildings add to the interest of the visit.

Le BLANC

Michelin map 68 fold 16 – *Local map p 68* – Pop 8 051
See town plan in the current Michelin Red Guide France.

Le Blanc, on the banks of the Creuse, lies between Brenne and Poitou. In the lower town, St-Génitour Church has a Romanesque belfry and a Gothic style nave. As it was built on the site of a former Romanesque priory, the chancel is not aligned with the nave.

Upper Town. – Cross the bridge over the Creuse and continue straight on to the Rue de la Poterne; follow this up the hill, noticing the old houses as you pass. Take the Rue du Docteur-Fardeau and the impasse St-Cyran, to reach the little esplanade next to the Romanesque Church of St-Cyran, now secularised. You are now near the 12C castle which once controlled the ford across the river Creuse and around which the town came to be built.

From the esplanade there is a wide view of the lower town dominated by the church belfry, the viaduct on the far left and the river lined with trees.

BONAGUIL Castle★★

Michelin map 79 fold 6 – *Local map p 124*

This majestic fortress, which stands on the borders of Périgord Noir and Quercy, is one of the most perfect examples of military architecture from the late 15 and 16C. Its uniqueness is that although it appears to be the traditional defensive stronghold able to hold off any attack its conception was also adapted to the use of firearms: loopholes...

A Strange Character. – It was a strange quirk of character that made **Béranger de Roquefeuil** enjoy proclaiming himself the "noble, magnificent and most powerful lord of the baronies of Roquefeuil, Blanquefort, Castelnau, Combret, Roquefère, Count of Naut". He was a brutal and vindictive man, and, in his determination to be obeyed, did not hesitate to use force. But extortion and outrage brought revolt; the better to crush this, Bérenger transformed Bonaguil Castle, which had been built in the 13C, into an impregnable fortress. It took him nearly forty years to build his fortified eagle's aerie, which looked an anachronism when compared with the châteaux being erected by his contemporaries for a life of ease at Montal, Assier and along the Loire. However, his castle was never attacked and was intact at the eve of the Revolution. Yet dismantled during the Revolution this colossus, in spite of its mutilations, still stands today as a challenge hurdled by the last of the feudal barons at the Renaissance. This masterpiece of military architecture, while still keeping the traditional defences against attack by escalade or sapping, was also designed to make use of artillery.

TOUR *time: 1 1/2 hour*

Lecture tours: in March (from Palm Sunday), April, May and September at 10.30am, 2.30, 3.30 and 4.30pm; 1 June to 31 August at 10, 11am, 3, 4, 5 and 6 pm; in October, November and February on Sundays and holidays only, at 3 and 4.30pm; 10F. Musical evenings (nuits musicales) see p 37.

After passing through the outer wall, the visitor comes to the barbican. This was an enormous bastion on its own with its own garrison, powder store, armouries and way of escape. The barbican formed part of the 350 m - 380 yds long first line of defence whose bastions, thanks to the embrasures, were able to cross-fire.

The second line of defence consisted of five towers of which one, known as the Grosse Tour is among the strongest round towers ever to have been built in France. The tower is 35 m - 115 ft high and is crowned with corbels; the upper storeys served as living quarters, the lower held the musket, culverin and harquebus.

The keep overlooked both lines of defences; it served, with its cant walls, not only as a watch-tower but also as a command-post. Shaped like a vessel with its prow, the most vulnerable point, turned towards the north, it was the last bastion of the defence.

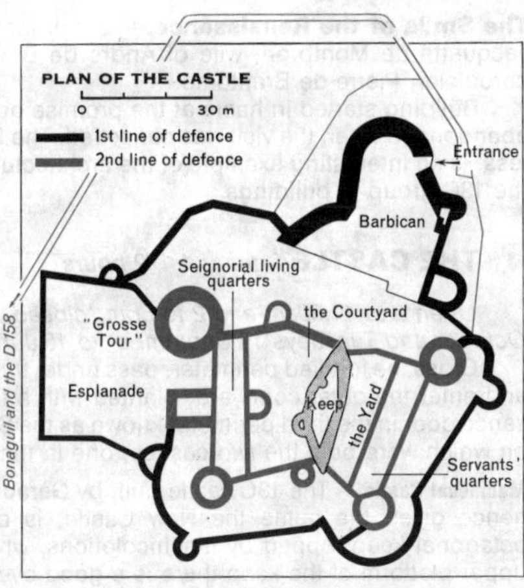

(After a document of Max Pons)

With a well sunk through the rock, outhouses where provisions could be stored, and heating and drainage systems, dry internal ditches and tunnels which enabled the troops to move about quickly, the castle garrison of about a hundred men could easily withstand a siege provided they were not betrayed or starved out.

Les BORIES Castle

Michelin map 75 fold 6 – 12 km – 7 miles northeast of Périgueux

The castle built in the 16C by the St-Astier family, stands in a pleasant site on the bank of the river Isle.

Guided tours 1 July to 30 September, 10 to 11.30am and 2 to 6.30pm.

The castle comprises the main building flanked by two round towers and a massive, square battlemented tower. Inside the **architecture**★ is outstanding.

A monumental stairway rises inside the square tower with a small room occupying the space in the centre on each floor; there was a Gothic chapel on the gound floor. The kitchen has pointed vaulting and is very ornate; it has two huge chimneypieces with surbased arches.

In the guardroom there is an unusual vault on squinches resting on ogive ribs starting from a central column.

The great hall contains Louis XIII furnishings, a fine Renaissance chimneypiece and a Flemish *verdure* (tapestry in shades of green).

BOUGES Château ★

Michelin map 68 fold 8 – 9.5 km – 6 miles northeast of Levroux

Set in the heart of Berry-Champagne *(p 12)* this château built in the 18C in the Italian style on the site of a former stronghold, closely resembles the Petit Trianon at Versailles by the arrangement of its pediments and façades.

Open 1 April to 30 June and in October, daily (except Tuesdays) 10am to noon and 2 to 6pm; 1 July to 30 September, daily 9am to noon and 2 to 6pm; 1 November to 30 March, Wednesdays 2 to 5pm, Saturdays and Sundays 10am to noon and 2 to 5pm; 11F (7F for the park only).

The outbuildings are vast edifices with tall mansard roofs and include fine stables with a **harness room** containing an important collection of saddles, harness and riding boots. In the wing set at right angles, there are several horse drawn carriages dating from the beginning of the century.

The château contains an interesting collection of 18C **furniture**★, particularly sofas and chairs – many of the pieces bear the marks of famous cabinet makers –, which was patiently assembled by the previous owners. Note in particular the small Louis XV salon, the games room with its fine furniture, the drawing-room with its marble chimneypiece and astronomical clock, and the charming Louis XVI bedroom.

French style gardens and a 80 ha – 198 acre **park**★ planted with a variety of fine trees and with a pond bring the visit to an end.

BOURDEILLES ★

Michelin map 75 fold 5 – Pop 728

The impressive Castle of Bourdeilles, with the village clustered at its foot, makes a delightful picture as it stands on the rocks that rise up sheer above the river Dronne. It was here in 1540 that Pierre de Brantôme *(p 66)* was born.

A Coveted Spot. – In 1259 Saint Louis ceded Périgord and Bourdeilles, his most important barony, to the English. This incredible desertion made the country rise in distress and divided the Bourdeille family: the elder branch supported the Plantagenets, the younger, the Maumonts, the Capetians. A little later, after plots and lawsuits and urged on by the king, Géraud de Maumont, Counsellor to Philip the Fair, seized the castle of his forbears. He turned it into a huge fortress. Philip the Fair then, to show his strength in Périgord, exchanged land in Auvergne for Bourdeilles and installed a strong garrison within the fief of his enemies, the English.

The Smile of the Renaissance. – Credit for the plans for the 16C castle must go to Jacquette de Montbron, wife of André de Bourdeille and sister-in-law of the famous chronicler, Pierre de Brantôme.

Building started in haste at the promise of a visit by Catherine de' Medici, and was abandonned when the visit was cancelled. The Renaissance part of the castle, nevertheless, is an interesting example of the architecture of that period and adds a light note to the 13C group of buildings.

■ THE CASTLE★ *time: 1 1/2 hours*

Open 9 to 11.30am and 2 to 6pm; closed 15 December to 1 February, first week in October and Tuesdays 15 September to 15 June; 8F.

Cross the fortified perimeter, pass under the watch-path to penetrate the second wall and enter the outer courtyard, planted with a fine cedar. Then pass through a Renaissance door in the third perimeter known as the Seneschals' door, to reach the esplanade, on which were built the two castles, one in the 13C, the other in the 16C.

Mediaeval Castle. – The 13C castle built by Géraud de Maumont on older foundations and hence given the name the New Castle, is an austere building surmounted by an octagonal keep topped by machicolations, whose walls are eight feet thick. From the upper platform of the keep there is a good overall view of the castle.

Renaissance buildings. – Sober and elegant in appearance these consist of a rectangular living block and a wing at right angles to it. The **furnishings**★★ are remarkable.

On the ground floor there is a series of wooden 15 and 16C chests and a splendid 16C sculpted panel from Burgundy portraying the Teaching of the Infant Jesus. In an adjoining room note the recumbent figure of Jean de Chabannes and a replica of the Holy Sepulchre, which came from Montgé Priory. The armour room with its fine old tiling, contains corsairs' sea chests and a magnificent Renaissance table.

On the first floor visit the dining hall with its 16C chimneypiece and the Gothic room which precedes the sumptuously decorated **gold room**. Note the original French style ceiling, woodwork and paintings by Ambroise Le Noble of the Fontainebleau School. Note the magnificent tapestry, after a cartoon by Laurent Guyot, showing François I and his falconers.

In three rooms on the second floor, amidst other pieces of furniture there are 15-16C Spanish paintings, cabinets with secret drawers, a 16C four-poster bed, armchairs in Cordova leather, a fine 17C octagonal table and especially the **bed of Emperor Charles V**, heavily gilded and sculpted.

From the watch-path at the end of the promontory overlooking the Dronne, there is a **view**★ of the castle and its setting: a Gothic bridge with cutwaters, an old mill in the shape of a boat roofed in round tiles and the green waters of the river flowing past the rocks below.

BOURGANEUF

Michelin map 72 fold 9 – Pop 4 030 – *Facilities p 38*

Bourganeuf is built on a spur overlooking the Taurion valley in a smiling countryside of wooded hills. There is a good overall view from the D 912, northwest of the town.

Prince Zizim. – This Muslim prince failing in his attempt to usurp his brother's throne, sought refuge with Pierre d'Aubusson, Grand Master of the Order of St. John of Jerusalem, who had him transferred to Bourganeuf in 1483. Here the Prince continued to live in his accustomed luxury, giving Bourganeuf an air of the Arabian Nights. In 1485 he was sent to Rome and he died some years later of poisoning, without have accomplished his dreams.

BOURGANEUF

Girardin (R. E.-de) 3
Kléber-Chapou (Av.) 4
Viviani (Av. R.) 5
Zizim (R.) 6

Zizim's Tower (Tour Zizim). – *Guided tours in April, May, June and September, Sundays and holidays only 2.30 to 6.30pm; 1 July to 31 August, daily 10.30 to 11.30am and 2.30 to 6.30pm; 5F.*

The tower was part of the former castle, seat of the great Auvergne priory of the Order of St. John of Jerusalem, and served as Prince Zizim's prison. There are remarkable **timberwork ceilings**★ of oak on three storeys. Finds excavated from local Gallo-Roman sites are exhibited.

From the top floor of the tower there are good views of the town and the surrounding countryside.

Town Hall (H). – *Open 8.30am to noon and 2 to 6.30pm; closed Saturdays, Sundays and holidays.*

There is a fine 18C **Aubusson tapestry**★ in the council chamber. The symbols of the *Ancien Régime* (pre-1789) – the sceptre and the hand of justice – and those of Liberty – the fasces of the lictors, the sword and scales of justice – surround a curious central motif: an eye set in a crown of oak leaves.

BOURGES ★★★

Michelin map 69 fold 1 – Pop 79 408

From whichever direction you approach the city you see, soaring above the Berry-Champagne countryside, the tall outline of St. Stephen's Cathedral. From afar it foretells the rich mediaeval past that the tourist will discover in the heart of this old city built on the slopes of the hill whose base is washed by the waters of the Yèvre and the Auron and a network of rivers and marshes. Bourges has kept dazzling souvenirs of its hours of glory and its incomparable artistic treasures will appeal to the art lover. As the commercial and industrial centre of Berry, the city has become the regional capital.

HISTORICAL NOTES

"Supremacy for the Bituriges". – This proud motto indicates well the important role played by the capital of these powerful Celts. Avaric, "the town that was rich in water", benefited from its site on a hill encircled by rivers in the flat and bare countryside of Champagne.

The name, latinised to Avaricum, recalls one of the momentous episodes in the Gallic wars when this city of about 40 000 inhabitants courageously resisted Caesar's legions but finally knew defeat and destruction.

The Roman occupation did not, however, prevent Avaricum retaining a certain autonomy both in politics and administration and even becoming, in the 4C, the capital of the old province of Aquitaine.

A Patron of the Arts: Jean de Berry. – The young Duke Jean de Berry, third son of King John the Good of France, made Bourges the capital of his duchy and a centre of the arts of utmost importance. From 1360 to 1416 the Duke, an inspired lover of the arts, spent a fortune as, with mad prodigality, he commissioned work from painters, illuminators such as Paul de Limbourg, the author of the *Très Riches Heures* (The Rich Hours), now to be seen in the Chantilly Museum, gold and silversmiths, potters, master glassworkers, sculptors such as André Beauneveu and architects.

"A vaillans cœurs, riens impossible". – "To a valiant heart, nothing is impossible" was the motto of **Jacques Cœur,** Master of the Mint to King Charles VII of France at a time when that kingdom was largely occupied by the English.

This man of humble origin, son of a furrier, had an extraordinary life: amazingly gifted in commerce and trade, he soon made a colossal fortune. He armed merchantmen with the idea of seizing the markets of the eastern Mediterranean from the traders of Genoa and Venice; he set up counting-houses in Marseilles and Montpellier, and bought houses and land; from being the man in charge of the finances of Bourges, he became, in 1427, Counsellor to Charles VII and principal emissary for the kingdom's expansion of trade; finally he built a magnificent palace at Bourges, though he was to see little of it. Hated by many courtiers who were jealous of his political and diplomatic offices, the honours he had bestowed upon him and the king's favour, he fell into disgrace, a victim to his own advancement. He was arrested in 1451 and condemned to perpetual banishment, confiscation of all his property and a heavy fine.

But this was not the end for Jacques Cœur: he escaped from Beaucaire Prison, sought refuge in Rome and was given command by the pope of a fleet of ships. It was while he was on the Ninth Crusade to liberate the Christian islands in the Greek archipelago, that he died in 1456 in Chios.

The University, Storm Centre of New Ideas. – The town of Bourges owes the foundation of its university in 1463 to Louis XI, who was born in Bourges Palace. Its influence spread far beyond the duchy for over a century. The law school under such masters as Alciat (1529-1533) and Cujas (1559-1566) attracted many students some even from abroad. It was thus that German students coming from Heidelberg brought with them the new doctrines of Luther: Calvin, at that time a student at Bourges, learnt these new theories and began to form the outlines of the principles he was later to publish in his *Institutes of the Christian Religion*. His ideas on reforming the Church found many adherents and, in spite of persecution, soon gained support in Bourges and throughout Berry.

The duchy was thus divided and became a battlefield during the period of the Wars of Religion; the prosperity of the city, which had been much reduced by a terrible fire in 1487 which destroyed two-thirds of the town, came to an end.

Economic Rebirth. – Not until the end of the 19C did Bourges regain its economic energy when the establishment of metallurgical, aeronautical and chemical industries and of a military garrison attracted a large work force to the town. A Michelin tyre factory stands on the north side of the town.

■ ST. STEPHEN'S CATHEDRAL★★★ (Cathédrale St-Étienne) (Z) *time: 1 hour*

The vigour of the architecture, the harmony of proportion and the richness of the decoration make one marvel before this cathedral.

The Founder: Henri de Sully. – It was in about 1185 that it was decided that a cathedral dedicated to St. Stephen should be built to take the place of a Romanesque basilica, that, in turn, had replaced a smaller church built in about the 3C.

Henri de Sully who was then Archbishop of Bourges was in close enough touch with the Paris diocese to know that a new style of architecture was being developed in the Ile-de-France. The groups of craftsmen who worked at Bourges no doubt had also worked at Soissons, Sens, Chartres or at Notre-Dame in Paris.

The crypt was completed by the end of the 12C; it corresponds exactly in line with the chevet above it. The construction of the Church proper began with the chevet and by the end of the 13C had reached the west face and the two towers. The doorways with all their carving were completed only at the beginning of the 14C. The building was consecrated by Archbishop Guillaume de Brosse in 1324.

Additions and Restorations. – The southern tower was consolidated during the 14C by a construction linked to the tower by a reinforced arcade known as the *pilier butant* – the buttress pile. Once this had been built it was possible to install the great window above the central door. The chapels between the buttresses were built in the 15C.

Misfortune came with the 16C; in 1506 the north tower collapsed and had to be entirely rebuilt; in 1562 a Protestant army pillaged the cathedral and destroyed the magnificent statues that adorned the west face; two hundred years later the canons decided to remove the rood screen and the eighteen stained glass windows in the chancel. Last century restoration was undertaken but much of it was unfortunate and balustrades, bell towers and pinnacles were added to the building.

Exterior. – *See diagram below.* The doorways of the west face are aligned by the pedestal formed by the fifteen steps up to the cathedral. Dignity and strength seem to emanate from this grouping of steps and doors framed by the two towers of unequal height. On the right, the Deaf Tower, never completed, is architecturally more sober in style than the Flamboyantly decorated Butter Tower on the left.

St. Stephen's Cathedral – The doors of the west face.

Five doorways beneath individual gables stand in a line beneath the great stained glass window, known as the *grand housteau* – the great western gable. The asymmetry of the doorways gives an impression of originality and great variety.

A frieze of 62 bas-reliefs (**1**) runs between two lines of niches from left to right and depicts the life of Christ: the Annunciation, the Nativity, the Adoration of the Magi, the Flight into Egypt, scenes from the Passion and episodes from the book of Genesis.

The five doorways of the west face, from right to left, are as follows:

St. Ursinus' Doorway. – The story of St. Ursinus, the first Bishop of Bourges, and of St. Justus is depicted on the tympanum (**2**). The two saints, having received their mission from the Pope St. Clement, leave for Berry; St. Justus dies on the way; St. Ursinus preaches at Bourges and consecrates a church there; he converts and baptises Léocade, the Governor of Aquitaine, and his son. Figures of angels, father-confessors and prophets adorn the covings (**3**); against the pier (**4**) stands a modern statue of the saint.

St. Stephen's Doorway. – The tympanum (**5**) is devoted to episodes in the life and the martyrdom of St. Stephen, patron of the cathedral. Angels and prophets are to be seen in the covings (**6**); a modern statue of St. Stephen stands before the pier (**7**).

Central Doorway. – Its theme is the Last Judgment. Great vitality and realism make the doorway one of the masterpieces of 13C Gothic sculpture. The lower part of the tympanum (**8**) depicts the Resurrection: the naked dead raise their tombstones and turn to look towards heaven; above them, the Archangel Michael with his scales proceeds to judgment, weighing souls: on his right, the chosen fly to the bosom of Abraham who symbolises heaven, on his left the damned are hurled into the burning cauldron of hell.

The upper part of the tympanum represents Christ surrounded by angels bearing the instruments of the Passion; to the left and right the Virgin and St. John ask for his blessing on their knees while above Him two angels hold the sun and the moon to mark the passage of time. Cherubim, angels, saints, martyrs, patriarchs and prophets are to be seen in the covings (**9**), a modern figure of Christ stands before the pier (**10**).

The Virgin's Doorway. – The doorway had to be partly rebuilt after the collapse of the north tower in the 16C. The Death, the Assumption and the Coronation of the Virgin are depicted on the tympanum (**11**).

St. William's Doorway. – On the tympanum (**12**) are episodes in the life of the saint who was Archbishop of Bourges at the beginning of the 13C; he is shown receiving offerings for the building of the cathedral, protecting the unfortunate, performing miraculous cures and exorcising a man while the devil flees, disguised as a wolf.

Go round the cathedral by the north.

The north face is embellished by a 12C doorway which was incorporated in the present cathedral. The lintel is adorned with a frieze of flowers and foliage. On the tympanum are scenes from the life of the Virgin.

The chevet is original in having little turrets above the radial chapels. The outline is harmonious and the double flying buttresses built above it add to its grace.

The south face is also adorned with a 12C doorway. Christ appears in majesty on the tympanum, surrounded by the symbols of the Evangelists; angels and the prophets and kings of the Old Testament crowd the covings. Biblical scenes decorate the capitals at the top of the statue-columns; before the pier stands a fine 13C Christ. The right panel of the door was given to the cathedral by Jacques Cœur and bears his monogram.

Go round the south tower and enter the cathedral by the Virgin's Doorway.

Interior. – St. Stephen's Cathedral, which is 124 m - 407 ft long, 41 m - 135 ft wide and 37 m - 121 ft high to the top of the inner vaulting, is one of the largest Gothic cathedrals in France (Gloucester Cathedral is 420 ft long and 144 ft wide). There are no transepts and this gives the nave with its four side aisles a feeling of greater majesty; the five aisles correspond to the five doorways.

The columns of the nave rise in a single thrust to a height of 17 m - 56 ft and they are encircled by groups of smaller columns, some of which reach the vaulting. To extend the perspective the architect increased slightly the distance between the pillars in the chancel.

The building is original in having double side aisles of different height with windows on two levels; the five bands of light and shade thus created within the cathedral considerably enhance the architectural effect *(see cross section)*.

A double ambulatory continues the line of the twin aisles. Five small radial chapels, each semicircular in shape, open on to the apse.

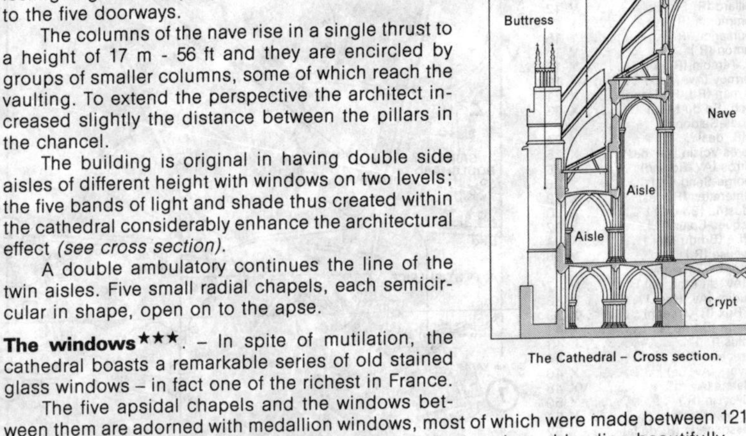

The Cathedral – Cross section.

The windows★★★. – In spite of mutilation, the cathedral boasts a remarkable series of old stained glass windows – in fact one of the richest in France.

The five apsidal chapels and the windows between them are adorned with medallion windows, most of which were made between 1215 and 1225. Blue and red predominate, their warm deep colours blending beautifully.

There are interesting 15 and 16C windows in the side chapels, but the most precious jewels are to be found in the chancel.

Entering the chancel by the outer south aisle you see:

1) Window on the life of Joseph: among the scenes depicted are Joseph's dream – first medallion at the bottom; Joseph in Egypt – second medallion; Pharaoh's dream and Joseph being recognised by his brothers – top medallion.
2) Chapel of St. Francis of Sales: episodes are shown in the lives of, left, St. James the Apostle, centre, John the Baptist and right, John the Evangelist.
3) St. Thomas' window: Thomas, a skilful architect, is shown summoned before Gondophares, King of India. The apostolate and martyrdom of St. Thomas.
4) Window of the Apocalypse: Christ sits on a rainbow in the central medallion surrounded by twenty-four old men.
5) Chapel of St. Philomena: the life and martyrdom of the chief three deacons of the early church, St. Lawrence, St. Stephen and St. Vincent.
6) Window of the Passion of Our Lord.
7) Window on the Last Judgment.
8) The Lady Chapel: the window is of 16C glass, the statues at the entrance are of Duke Jean de Berry and his wife Jeanne de Boulogne.
9) Window depicting Abraham, Isaac, Moses, David and Jonah *(has been removed)*.
10) Window of the Prodigal Son.
11) Chapel of Our Lady of Lourdes: the figures of St. Denis, St. Peter, St. Paul and St. Martin can be seen.
12) Window of the Good Samaritan.
13) Window giving the story of St. Stephen's relics.
14) Chapel of Sainte-Croix (Holy Cross): scenes depicted show St. Mary of Egypt, St. Nicholas and Mary Magdalene.
15) Window on the wicked rich man: the story of Lazarus whom the wicked Dives refused to help. Above, Lazarus is shown in triumph.

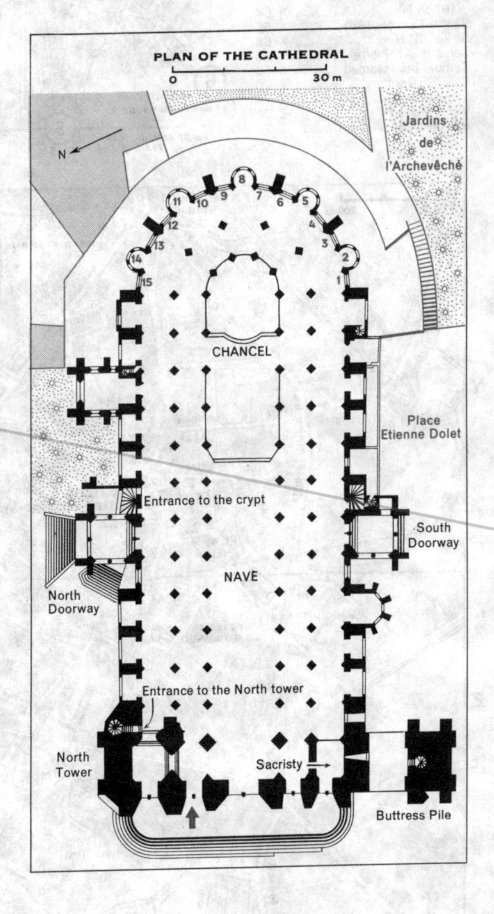

Ascent of the North Tower. – *Open 9am to noon and 2 to 6pm; closed Sunday mornings, 1 January, 1 and 8 May, 1 November and 25 December; 6 F.*

From the top of the tower there is an interesting view of the cathedral and the town.

BOURGES

Auron (R. d') .... Z
Jean-Jaurès (Av.) .... Y
Moyenne (R.) .... YZ

Armurier (R. des) .... Z 2
Baffier (R. Jean) .... X 3
Branly (R. Édouard) .... Y 4
Calvin (R.) .... Y 6
Cambournac (R.) .... Y 7
Chapelle (Rte de la) ...... X 8
Chappe (R. de la) .... Z 10
Coillard (R. François) ..... Y 12
Commerce (R. du) .... Y 13
Coursarlon (R.) .... Y 15
Danton (R.) .... V 16
Dr. Témoin (R. du) .... Y 17
Dormoy (Av. Marx) .... VY 19
Farman (Rd. Pt. Henri) ..... X 21
Foch (Bd du Mar.) .... X 23
Fonds-Gaidons
(R. des) .... X 24
Frères-Voisin (Av. des) .... X 25
Garros (Av. Roland) .... X 26
George-Sand (Pl.) .... Y 28
Hémerettes (R. des) .... Z 29
Industrie (Bd de l') .... X 30
Jacques-Cœur (R.) .... Y 32
Joffre (Bd du Mar.) .... X 34
Joyeuse (R.) .... Y 35
Lattre-de-Tassigny
(Av. du Mar. de) .... V 37
Laudier (Av. Henri) .... V 38
Le Brix (R. Joseph) .... X 39
Liberté (Bd de la) .... X 41
Malus (Pl.) .... Z 43
Mirebeau (R.) .... Y 44
Nevers (Av. de) .... X 46
Orléans (Av. d') .... VX 48
Pelvoysin (R.) .... Y 50
Pignoux (R. de) .... X 51
Poissonnerie (R. de la) .... Y 52
Près-le-Roi (Av. des) ...... X 53
Prinal (R. du) .... Y 55
Puits-Neuf (R. du) .... V 56
Pyrotechnie
(Pl. de la) .... X 57
St-Michel (Rte de) .... V 61
Salle-d'Armes
(R. de la) .... X 64
Santos-Dumont (Bd) .... X 65
Sellier (R. Henri) .... X 66
Sémard (Av. Pierre) .... X 68
Sembat (Av. Marcel) .... X 69
Tory (R. Geoffroy) .... Y 70
Vauvert (R. de) .... X 71
Victor-Hugo (R.) .... Z 73
95e de Ligne (Av. du) ..... Z 74

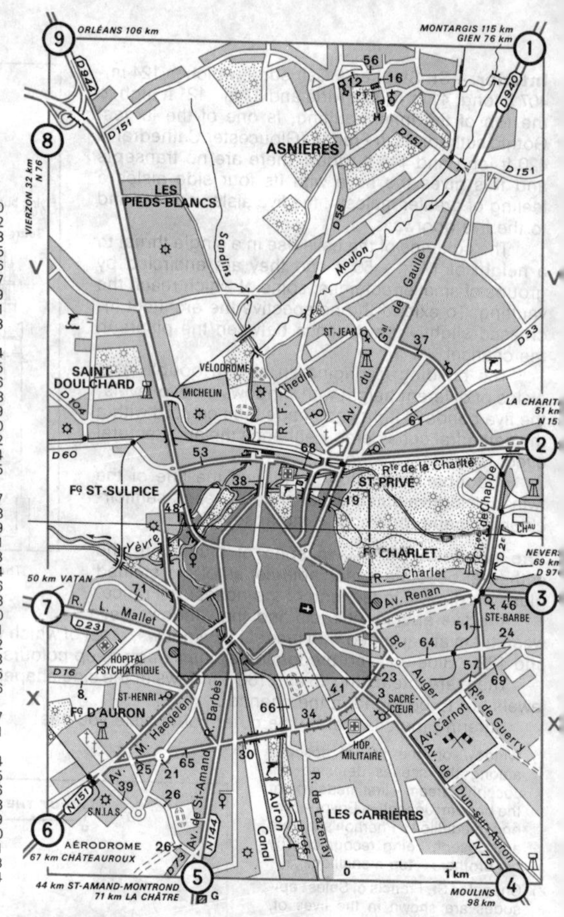

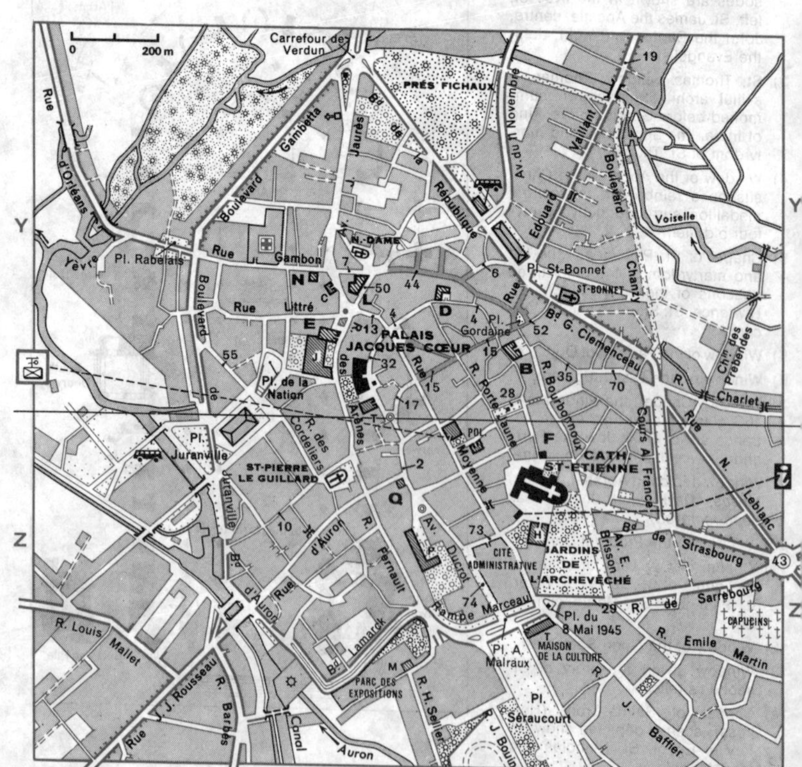

You will find an* index *at the end of the guide listing all subjects referred to in the text or illustrations (monuments, picturesque sites, points of interest, historical or geographical items, etc.).

Crypt★★. – *Same opening times as the North Tower.*

A long sloping gallery leads down to the vast late 12C crypt known as the Underground Church or the Church of St-Guillaume. Twelve large windows let in the light and reveal the architectural design of this sanctuary: six massive pillars support ogive vaulting of excellent proportions; these pillars and those separating the two aisles of the ambulatory are flanked by columns with crotcheted capitals.

The crypt contains the recumbent white marble figure of the Duke of Berry, the sole reminder of a grandiose tomb executed by Jean de Cambrai between 1422 and 1438. The tomb was originally placed in the Sainte-Chapelle at Bourges; this was destroyed in 1757. The 14C windows of the prophets *(under restoration)* also came from the Sainte-Chapelle. Fragments saved when the rood screen was destroyed in the 17C are on view. Resting against the Gallo-Roman outer wall is a 16C Placing in the Tomb.

Behind the sculpture, stairs lead to a little cradle vaulted gallery, the remains of a sanctuary built in the 10 and 11C.

The Archbishop's Gardens★ **(Jardins de l'Archevêché)** (Z). – Le Nôtre is credited with the designing of these gardens in the 17C; they were extended during the 18C. The gardens which contain beautiful flowerbeds and fine shaded alleys, provide a good view of St. Stephen's Cathedral, particularly of the great nave and chevet.

Tithe Barn (Grange aux Dîmes) (Z F). – Opposite the cathedral's north doorway at the corner of Rue Molière, this massive building with its buttresses and stairway designed as a half-timbered balcony, was used to store the dues paid to the church.

■ JACQUES CŒUR'S PALACE★★ (Palais Jacques Cœur) (Y) *time: 3/4 hour*

Guided tours Palm Sunday to 31 October, 9 to 11.10am and 2 to 5.10pm; the rest of the year, 10 to 11.10am and 2 to 4.10pm; closed Tuesdays, 1 January, 1 May, 1 November and 25 December; 5F.

The architectural elegance, the richness and variety of decoration, make this one of the most beautiful and sumptuous secular buildings of the Gothic age. This splendid mansion was commissioned in 1443 for Charles VII's famous Master of the Mint, and was intended no doubt, as the place to which he would retire. It was completed in less than ten years; the cost was 100 000 gold *écus*.

Jacques Cœur fell into disgrace in 1451 and so never enjoyed his completed palace. In 1457 it was restored to his heirs and from then on knew many changes of fortune. In 1679 it belonged to Colbert (statesman: 1619-1683); soon afterwards it was acquired by the city of Bourges. Since 1925, when it was bought by the State, it has been completely restored.

Exterior. – Jacques Cœur's Palace is in the form of an uneven quadrilateral consisting of four main buildings round a central court. While the west face, which may be seen from the Rue des Arènes, looks like the exterior of a fortress with massive towers and bare walls rising above the remains of the Gallo-Roman perimeter, the east face draws attention by the delicacy and richness of its decoration. This appears, in one instance, as a motif of hearts and shells – emblems from Jacques Cœur's coat of arms – adorning the mullioned windows of the top floor and the balustrade at the base of the eaves.

On either side of a balcony on which stood an equestrian statue of Charles VII until the time of the Revolution, there now stand, in the space of partly opened blind windows, the figures of a man and a woman, the master and mistress of the house.

To the left of this wing, at the base of the octagonal staircase tower, Jacques Cœur's motto may be seen inscribed: *A vaillans cœurs, riens impossible* (To a valiant heart, nothing is impossible).

As you enter the central court there is a striking difference to be seen between the sober appearance of the galleries – no doubt kept for business by the Master of the Mint – and the rich decoration of the main living quarters containing the banqueting and ceremonial halls and the private apartments. Three staircase towers divide the façade. The central tower, which is hexagonal, is carved with rare trees such as palms, oranges and dates to evoke the Orient where Jacques Cœur had voyaged, and bears another of the master's well known mottoes: *Dire, Faire, Taire* (Speak, Act, Be Silent).

Jacques Cœur's Palace – The central courtyard.

Interior. – A tour of the palace (22 of the 43 rooms) gives an idea of the luxury to which a wealthy burgher with a taste for beautiful things and practical sense could aspire. The taste for luxury produced the magnificence of the dining hall with its monumental chimneypiece where a 15C tapestry with a thistle motif now hangs; the practical sense comes out in the installation of running water, a boiler-room and bathroom and the planning of staircases and corridors so that those wishing to take a bath could do so without going outside to adjoining buildings. The same practical good sense made him install beneath the eaves a pigeon loft for the homing pigeons which kept him in close touch with his counting-houses. A gallery with wooden cradle vaulting in the shape of an inverted boat keel leads to the chapel. This has a remarkable painted ceiling: on a blue ground strewn with stars, angels bear streamers on which, in Gothic lettering, are passages from the *Gloria* and the *Song of Songs*. Two oratory chapels, which could be heated, are contained within the thickness of the north and south walls on either side of the altar and were probably used by Jacques Cœur and his wife.

In one of the private apartments a fine monochrome stained glass depicting a galley is noteworthy. Interesting architectural details may be seen in different parts of the buildings: armorial bearings, high and low reliefs and bosses such as those in the room known as The Treasury which has a heavy iron door closed with a secret lock. One of the bosses shows a scene from the romance of Tristan and Iseult: Queen Iseult goes to find Tristan in the garden; King Mark, forewarned of the meeting, hides in a tree, but Tristan seeing the reflection of the king's face in a pool, is careful to speak only commonplaces to Iseult.

■ ADDITIONAL SIGHTS

Hôtel Cujas★ **(Y E)**. – *Open 10 to 11.30am and 2 to 5.30pm; closed Tuesdays, 1 January, 1 May, 1 November and 25 December; 5.50F.*

This elegant building was designed in about 1515 by Guillaume Pelvoysin for Durando Salvi, a rich Florentine merchant who had settled in Bourges. The famous jurist Cujas bought the mansion and finally died there in 1590. Since 1877 it has been owned by the city which uses it to house the Berry Museum.

The main building is flanked at either end by two corbelled towers; the left one is round and has fine cresting along the roof top; the one on the right has right-angled walls and pilasters.

Berry Museum (Musée du Berry). – On the ground floor are **archaeological collections**★ dating from prehistory to the end of the Gallo-Roman period. Among the exhibits may be seen items from the various industries developed in Berry in pre-Roman times and different aspects of Gallo-Roman civilisation in the 2 and 3C from domestic life (building materials, utensils, cisterns, toilet articles, accessories and jewellery) and public life (coins, roads, theatres and amphitheatres and business items).

In one gallery 200 steles (funerary stones, laid out as in a cemetery) evoke vividly and often with great realism the life of both the rich and humble. They are often inscribed with religious symbols.

The rural life of Berry in the 18 and 19C is evoked on the first floor in an exhibition covering costumes, local crafts, the art of the La Borne potters, with many works by the Talbot family (amusing figurines and objects from the 18C to the present day).

Prés-Fischaux Gardens★ **(Y)**. – A beautiful garden has been laid out on marshland between the river and the close of St. Ambroise Abbey where the Protestants used to gather in the 16C to sing Marot's (poet: 1495-1544) psalms.

The designer has kept the avenue of plane trees and added a rose garden, French style flower-beds and ponds, to make a setting of pleasing perspectives through arches of clipped yew trees.

Hôtel Lallemant★ **(Y B)**. – *Open 10.15 and 11.15am, 2.15 and 3.15pm ; also 4.15 and 5.15pm Sundays and holidays; closed Mondays, 1 January, 1 May, 1 November and 25 December; 5.50F.*

This magnificent Renaissance mansion has retained the name of Jean Lallemant, the rich cloth merchant who had it built; it was altered in the 17C and has been converted into a museum of decorative art.

The site on which the mansion was built straddled the Roman wall of the town and different parts of the house are on different levels.

A sloping ramp, covered with cradle vaulting and used to lead horses in and out of the building, goes through to the **main courtyard** which is on two levels. The large main building shows the styles of different architectural periods: the mullioned windows and arcades are 15C, the doors to the corridors and the window-frames of the bays above the passageway are 16C and the entablature and round frontons bearing the arms of the Dorsannes who once owned the mansion, are 17C. Right round the courtyard at the level of the first floor is a kind of frieze of terracotta medallions portraying the heads of prominent personages of Antiquity.

Rooms on the ground floor with restored coffered ceilings contain 16-17C furniture, tapestries and paintings. There are several pieces of marquetry: chests, Louis XIV bureaux and a large incrusted ebony cabinet decorated about 1650.

The **chapel** has a curious coffered ceiling decorated with the symbols of alchemy and philosophy and heraldic devices among which are those of the Lallemant family. The symbols of the Evangelists painted in the four corners of the ceiling have contributed to make the decoration of the oratory one of the enigmas of 16C French art.

On the upper floors, there are several rooms hung with old tapestries where are displayed beautiful collections of ceramics, enamels and ivories and especially of furniture including an inlaid Henri IV chest, a Boulle table and chair, and a remarkable ebony cabinet dating from 1650 which is inlaid with ivory and arranged as a theatre on the inside.

The Guildhall (Hôtel des Échevins) (Y D). – There is a striking difference in architectural style between the two parts of the building:

– the living quarters at the far end of the courtyard date from 1488 and were built in the Renaissance style. A fine **octagonal tower**★ juts out from the façade and, rising to a height of three storeys, contains a circular staircase which gives access to each floor. This tower is richly decorated with accoladed arches embellished with foliated crotchets in a variety of leaf motifs which include thistle, oak, cabbage and tapering maple.

– the gallery on the left was built in 1624 in the Classical style.

Church of Notre-Dame (Y). – *Closed on Sunday afternoons.* The church was almost entirely gutted by the fire of 1487 which destroyed two-thirds of the town. The church was known as St-Pierre-le-Marché before being dedicated to Our Lady. When it was rebuilt many modifications were made to the original plan including the addition of side aisles and the square tower that rises at the north end of the west face. The church is therefore a mixture of styles: the nave has ogive vaulting with emblazoned keystones, the south door is Renaissance and adorned with a statue of the Virgin Mary. In the south aisle, opposite the door, a beautiful white marble font is adorned with lilies and a coat of arms and is said to have come from the Sainte-Chapelle at Bourges.

Old Houses (Y). – The whole town centre comes under a preservation and renovation scheme which aims at restoring the half-timbered houses (many date from the 15 and 16C) to their former glory. The results are particularly noticeable in the lively pedestrian area from Rue Mirebeau to Rue Coursalon via Place Gordaine.

Maison de Pelvoysin (Y L). – An interesting group of old, half-timbered houses stands at the corner of Pelvoysin and Cambournac Streets. Next to these is the house of Pelvoysin, the cathedral architect. It is built of stone and now houses the savings bank. The street was so narrow when it was being built, that the architect designed the front to stand at an angle to the street thus giving the house an appearance of greater width and dignity. Inside there is a fine chimneypiece. The courtyard can best be seen from the Rue Cambournac.

Maison de la Reine Blanche (Y N). – Standing at numbers 17-19 Rue Gambon this is the most interesting of the old houses because of the richness of its decoration. On the ground floor the capitals beneath the brackets are ornamented with religious scenes; from left to right these are: St. Martin sharing his cloak, the Saviour, the Annunciation and the Visitation. On the first floor every column is decorated with two small dancers, some of which have been damaged. Each window on the ground floor has above it an accoladed arcade with sculptured crotchets and finials in relief.

Birthplace of Jacques Cœur (Z Q). – A half-timbered, corbelled house, standing at the corner of the Rue d'Auron and the Rue des Armuriers, bears an inscription describing it as the house in which Jacques Cœur was born (*c* 1395-1456). In fact it was built early in the 16C on the site of a house which came to Jacques Cœur through his marriage.

Church of St-Pierre-le-Guillard (Z). – *Closed for restoration.* According to legend, funds for building the church were provided by the Jew, Zacharie Guillard, whose mule knelt before the Holy Sacrament as it was being carried by St. Antony of Padua through Bourges in about 1225.

A massive belfry-porch leads to the nave flanked by side aisles to which chapels were added in the 15C. The sexpartite vaulting rests on crotcheted capitals above slim columns. The two-storey nave is of a somewhat primitive Gothic design.

EXCURSION

Former Abbey of Plaimpied. – *10 km - 6 miles to the south of Bourges by the D 106. Description p 155.*

BOUSSAC

Michelin map 68 south of fold 20 – Pop 1 868

The former walled town of Boussac, built on the borders of Berry-Champagne and Marche, overlooks the Petite Creuse river from a promontory at the end of which stands the castle.

Castle. – *Open 9am to noon and 2 to 6pm (7pm Sundays and holidays in season); time 3/4 hour; 20F.*

The best view of the castle in its **setting**★ is from the bridge over the Petite Creuse. The castle appears as a sheer wall of brown stone divided by square towers with tiled roofs. The former drawbridge has been uncovered *(excavations in progress).*

Make for the vast, shaded esplanade, in front of the castle's principal façade. The stark main building was enlivened in appearance in the 15 and 16C by the addition of mullioned windows and turrets ornamented with armorial bearings and shields. Above the doorway may be seen the arms of Jean de Brosse, Lord of Boussac and companion to Joan of Arc.

There is an impressive chimneypiece in the guardroom where the famous Lady and the Unicorn series of 6 tapestries once hung from 1660 to 1882. The kitchens, George Sand's room on the first floor (her novel *Jeanne* is set in this castle) and on the second floor, Prince Zizim's room *(p 58)* may all be visited. These rooms and the 18C salon are embellished with fine old furniture and hung with tapestries.

EXCURSION

Pierres Jaumâtres; Toulx-Ste-Croix. – *27 km - 17 miles – about 1 hour – see local map p 66.* Michelin maps 68 south of fold 20 and 73 fold 1.

Leave Boussac to the south by the D 997, and soon afterwards bear right into a picturesque road which climbs steeply. Leave the car at the point where a path goes off to the right, leading to Pierres Jaumâtres.

Pierres Jaumâtres. – *1/2 hour Rtn on foot.* 595 m – 1 952 ft up on the top of Mount Barlot surrounded by heathland is a curious mass of granite blocks, described by George Sand in her novel *Jeanne*. From the top there is a good **view**★ to the north over Berry and Bourbonnais and south over the mountains of Marche and Limousin.

Continue on the D 67 then take the road to the right leading to Toulx-Ste-Croix.

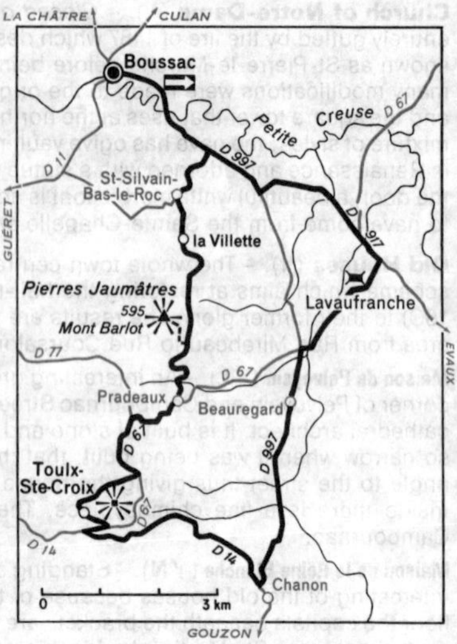

Toulx-Ste-Croix. – Pop 435. This village perched 655 m – 2 500 ft up on a granite hilltop, stands on the site of a former Gaulish encampment which eventually became a Gallo-Roman town. There is a curious Romanesque church built of granite with a separate belfry-porch containing sarcophagi.

A road, 200 m – 220 yds long, leads from the church to a tower *(to climb the tower, apply to the keeper)*. From the platform there is a remarkable **panorama**★★: in the foreground you see granite blocks scattered amidst ferns and heathers, woods, meadows and fields chequered by drystone walls, and in the distance Berry and Bourbonnais towards the north, the mountains of Marche and Limousin to the west and south, and in the south and southeast the Madeleine, Forez, Dômes and Dore Mountains.

Return to the D 67 then bear left into the D 14; on the outskirts of Chanon turn left into the D 997. 1 km – 1/2 mile beyond Beauregard bear right in the direction of Lavaufranche.

Lavaufranche Commandery. – *Open 1 July to 31 August, 2 to 6pm.* This 15C mansion with its 13C chapel and 14C keep, was the property of the Order of Malta until the Revolution. The chapel contains the carved tomb of Jehan Grimau (1480) as well as beautiful 13C **frescoes** including a Crucifixion, St. Catherine before Emperor Maximinus, and St. Peter.

An Art and Folk Museum housed in the outbuildings is also open to the public.

Return to Boussac by the D 997.

BRANTÔME ★★

Michelin map 75 fold 5 – Pop 2 101 – *Facilities p 38*

Brantôme lies in the smiling valley of the Dronne. Its old abbey and picturesque **setting**★ make it one of the pleasantest places in Périgord.

HISTORICAL NOTES

The Chronicler Brantôme. – The literary fame of **Pierre de Bourdeille**, better known as Brantôme, brought renown to the abbey of which he was commendatory abbot. Brantôme began life as a soldier of fortune and courtier, went with Mary Stuart to Scotland, travelled in Spain, Portugal, Italy and England and even to Africa. Wild ventures brought him into contact with the great in an era rich in scandal.

(After a photo by René Jacques)

Brantôme – The former Abbey and River Dronne.

After fighting at Jarnac in 1569, he withdrew to this abbey and began his famous chronicle. The Huguenots twice threatened to destroy the abbey during the Wars of Religion and he had to use all his diplomatic skill with Coligny, one the leaders of the Protestants, to save it from being pillaged. He left the abbey to return to court as chamberlain to Charles IX. In 1589 a fall from his horse crippled him and he left the restless and impetuous Valois court to retreat to his monastery and finish his chronicles.

Brantôme, whose posthumous fame lies in his *Vie des Grands Capitaines* – Lives of Great Men and *Dames Galantes* – Gay Ladies in which moral and historical facts are sometimes confused, was a lively, witty and sometimes cynical historian. He knew Ronsard the poet and other great writers of his time personally; he told a good tale well with piquant detail; his style was simple and therefore he has served as a model to many writers.

■ SIGHTS *time: 3/4 hour*

To get a full flavour of Brantôme, go and saunter on the banks of the Dronne, lined with weeping willows. The charm lies in the harmony, serenity and calm of the scene and the softness of the light. A 16C elbow bridge with asymmetrical arches, a Renaissance house with mullioned windows and the abbey make an attractive picture.

Former Abbey. – Brantôme, founded by Charlemagne in 769, was a Benedictine abbey: the relics which it contained of St. Sicaire attracted a multitude of pilgrims. It was sacked by the Normans and rebuilt in the 11C; in the 14C and again in the 18C the church and monastery buildings were considerably altered.

Abbey Church. – Angevin vaulting *(p 31)* replaced the two original cupolas in the 14C. The nave is plain and elegant; three tiers-point windows light the flat chevet.

The baptistry is adorned with a 14C low relief in stone of the Baptism of Christ. Another low relief, this time dating from the 13C and showing the Massacre of the Innocents, may be seen in the porch above the font which rests on a fine Romanesque capital decorated with strapwork.

Near the main doorway use one of the cloistral galleries from where you can get a glimpse of the former chapterhouse whose palm tree vaulting rests on a central column.

The **belfry**★★ was built apart from the church upon a sharp rock towering 12 m – 40 ft high, beneath which open great caves. It was erected in the 11C and is the oldest gabled Romanesque belfry in Limousin *(p 28)*. It has a roof of stone slates and has four storeys, each stepped back and slightly smaller than the one below. The ground level is roofed with an archaic dome; the upper storeys are pierced by round arches.

Monastery Buildings. – *Open at Christmas and 1 June to 15 September, 10am to noon and 2 to 6pm (4.30pm at Christmas); 2F.*

These buildings are occupied by the town hall, museum and local schools. The two wings are in pure 18C style as is the central part of the main building.

Inside, a beautiful monumental staircase dating from the 17C when the building was an abbey, leads to the monks' refectory and the dormitory which has a fine timber ceiling. The Renaissance style staircase to the town hall was built in the 19C.

The monks had installed service rooms in the caves behind the abbey including a bakery and a wine cellar. Huge carvings were made in the 16C of the Last Judgment and the Crucifixion in the living rock. The fountain of St. Sicaire plays nearby.

There is an annual exhibition of classical dance in the caves *(p 37)*.

Fernand Desmoulin Museum (Musée Fernand Desmoulin). – *Open Easter to 31 October, 10am to noon and 2 to 6pm; 2F.*

The museum, which is in the buildings of the former abbey, contains a **collection of prehistoric objects** found during local excavations including bone and silex tools.

Works by local artists are exhibited in other rooms. The end room is devoted to the strange pictures of the painter, Fernand Desmoulin (born in 1853 near Nontron), produced while he was under the influence of a medium.

EXCURSION

Château de Richemont. – *7 km - 4 miles to the northwest. Leave Brantôme by the D 939 and take to the right the road leading to St-Crépin-de-Richemont. After 1 km - 1/2 mile an avenue on the right leads to the château.*

Guided tours 15 July to 31 August, 10am to noon and 3 to 6pm; closed Fridays and 15 August; time: 1/2 hour; 5F.

This ungainly château composed of two main buildings at right angles was built in the late 16C by the chronicler Brantôme. On his death in 1614 he was interred in the chapel which is situated on the ground floor of the great square corner tower. In the entrance building, on the first floor is Brantôme's room, with fine woodwork.

BRENNE

Michelin map 68 folds 6, 7, 16 and 17

Brenne is an area of ponds and marshes, bordered to the north by the Claise, to the east by the Lancosme Forest and to the west and south by the valley of the Creuse.

Originally Brenne, which is more than 80 000 ha - 300 sq miles in extent, consisted of wastelands and oak forests. Today it appears as a succession of meadows scattered with heath and broom patches, and though still somewhat bleak, is not unattractive. In spite of efforts at reafforestation last century with pines, there are still many swamp areas marked by the presence of reeds and peat bogs. The monotony is broken by an occasional large farm. Nowadays the region is known particularly for its game and fish.

Tour starting from Le Blanc

79 km - 49 miles – about 2 1/2 hours – local map p 68

Leave Le Blanc (p 56) to the northeast by D 17, then follow the D 27.

Le Bouchet Castle. – *Guided tours 1 July to 15 September, 2.30 to 7pm; closed Tuesdays; apply to the caretaker; 10F.* This impressive mediaeval fortress, occupied by the English during the Hundred Years War, was restored in both the 15 and 17C. For three hundred years it belonged to the Rochechouart-Mortemart family and for a while served as the residence of the Marquise de Montespan who was born a Rochechouart-Mortemart and was the daughter and sister of the Lords of Le Bouchet. You may walk round the outside of the castle and visit the keep, terrace and part of the ground floor. From the keep and the terrace there is a view of the Brenne countryside and the Mer Rouge Pond.

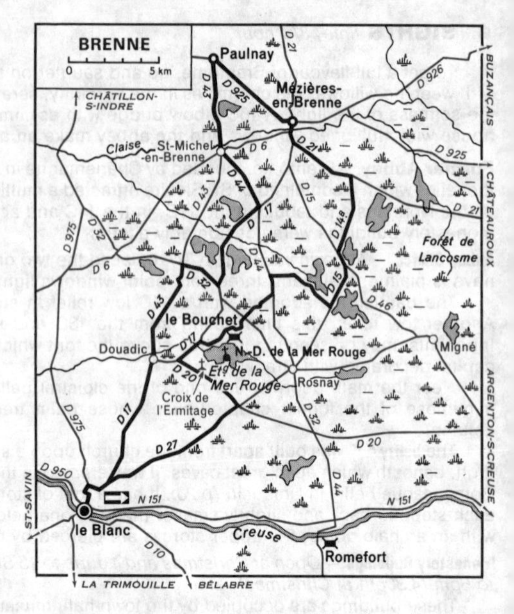

Étang de la Mer Rouge. – The Red Sea Pond is believed to have been given its name by a former owner, Aimery Sénébaud, on his return from the Holy Land, where he had been imprisoned beside the Red Sea. It is the biggest lake in Brenne and has an area of 445 acres. The Church of Notre-Dame de la Mer Rouge, rebuilt in 1854, stands on a headland to the south and is the site of a pilgrimage each year *(p 37)*. The statue of the Virgin, miraculously found in the hollow of an oak tree by Aimery in the 13C, was burned during the Wars of Religion. Replaced in 1650 the statue was stolen and later again replaced by a copy which is kept in the church at Rosnay and is brought out for the pilgrimage. As access to the chapel is difficult, the ceremonies are held at Croix de l'Ermitage in the forest near the pond.

Mézières-en-Brenne. – Pop 1 191. The most important town in Brenne is built on the banks of the Claise whose course is marked by a line of poplars. The church belfry, flanked by two stone turrets, has a porch ornamented with sculpture much of which was badly broken at the time of the Revolution. *Go in by the south aisle.* The nave has wooden vaulting with painted uprights and crossbeams. A Renaissance chapel was added to the south aisle by Nicolas of Anjou between 1543 and 1559. The stained glass **windows** date from the 14 and 16C. Some were restored in the 19C.

Paulnay. – Pop 440. The church dating from the 12 and 13C has an interesting Romanesque **doorway**★. Three rows of finely sculptured covings are supported on elegant capitals. Other capitals adorn the arcades surrounding the doorway. Inside the oven-vaulted chancel and the narrow bay are decorated by lovely ochre-coloured frescoes. The modern Stations of the Cross carved in wood and painted are the work of a monk from Fontgombault abbey *(p 106)*.

Tourists are advised to follow the route through the ponds indicated on the map to Le Blanc.

BRINAY

Michelin map 64 fold 20 – Pop 452

This calm, sheltered and attractive village is clustered on the left bank of the Cher.

Church of St. Aignan. – *Time: 1/2 hour.* The rectangular chancel of this modest Romanesque church has an interesting series of 12 **frescoes**★. Clearly influenced by the art of miniaturisation they have a strong sense of the decorative.

On the intrados of the chancel arch, frescoes represent the Work of the Months, while those in the chancel show scenes from the life of Christ. Going from left to right.

– North wall *(to the left)*. – Above are the Visitation, Nativity, the Annunciation and the Magi. Below the magi are shown before Herod and then returning home.

– East wall. – Above are scenes from the Massacre of the Innocents. Underneath are the Presentation in the Temple, Joseph's Dream and the Flight into Egypt. The last theme is continued on the lower part of the south wall and shows the fall of the Idols in the Temple of Hermopolis and the Flight of the Holy Family.

– South wall. – Above, the Baptism of Christ and the Marriage at Cana. Below the Temptation in the Desert, Christ banishing the devil and being served by angels.

– West wall. – The prophet Jeremiah can be distinguished and on a corner stone a curious figure represents a line from the Lamentations of Jeremiah, "He hath bent his bow, and set me as a mark for the arrow."

BRIVE-LA-GAILLARDE

Michelin 75 fold 8 – *Local map p 186* – Pop 54 032

Brive, which owes its suffix *La Gaillarde* – the bold – to the courage displayed by its citizens on the many occasions when it was besieged, is now a gay and welcoming town. It lies at the crossroads of Bas-Limousin, Périgord and Haut-Quercy.

A Brilliant Career. – **Guillaume Dubois** (1656-1723), the son of an apothecary from Brive, took Holy Orders, became tutor to Philip of Orleans and prime minister when Philip was appointed regent during the minority of Louis XV. Offices and honours were heaped upon him; he became Archbishop of Cambrai and became cardinal. He made an alliance with England and thus ensured a long period of peace in France.

BRIVE-LA-GAILLARDE

Faro (R. du Lt-Colonel) 3
Gambetta (R.)
Gaulle (Pl. Ch.-de) 5
Hôtel-de-Ville (R. de l') 6
Paris (Av. de)
République (R. de la)
Toulzac (R.)
Anatole-France (Bd) 2
Lattre-de-Tassigny (Pl. de) 8
Lyautey (Bd Mar.) 9
Raynal (R. Blaise) 18
Segeral-Verninac (R.) 19

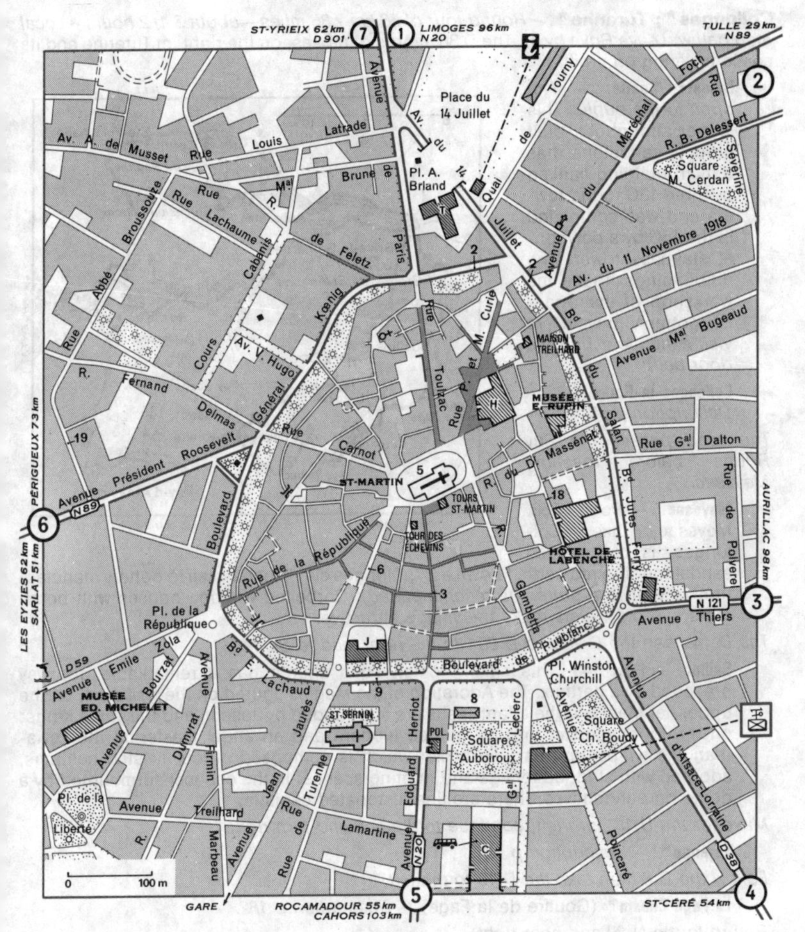

A Glorious Soldier. – **Brune** enlisted in the army in 1791 and rose to become general commanding the army in Italy in 1798. Following victories in the Netherlands and Italy he was appointed ambassador at Constantinople. He became the symbol of the Revolution and died, a victim of the White Terror, in 1815 at Avignon.

■ THE OLD TOWN *time: 1 1/2 hours*

Ernest Rupin Museum ★ (Musée Ernest-Rupin). – *Open 10am to noon and 2 to 6pm (5pm, 1 October to 31 March); closed Sundays and holidays; 3F.*

The museum is in an elegant Louis XIII mansion. On the ground floor it contains large collections on the prehistoric, Gallo-Roman, Romanesque and Gothic periods. In one room is exhibited a collection gifted by Lord Campbell, one of Napoleon's companions during his exile at Elba: Empire style furniture, Aubusson tapestries and memorabilia.

The first floor galleries house the painting, engraving and numismatic sections.

On the 2nd floor there are two fine galleries on ethnography and folklore, and military and religious art collections. The 3rd floor exhibits a section on natural history.

Hôtel de Labenche★. – This magnificent example of Renaissance architecture in the Toulouse style is the most remarkable secular building in the town. From the inner courtyard may be seen the great round arched arcades that support the L-shaped wings.

The almost yellow colour of the stone adds greatly to the beauty of the decoration which includes mullioned windows adorned with festoons, slender columns or caryatids. Above the windows are false openings from which project carved busts.

Church of St. Martin. – Only the transept, the apsidal chapels and a few capitals are Romanesque in this church. The aisles and the nave are 14C. The chancel was rebuilt in its original style by Cardinal Dubois in the 18C. Note the 13C baptismal font.

Old Houses. – A few old houses *(restoration in progress)* remain in the streets near St. Martin's. Several are ornamented with turrets and carvings: the town hall, the Treilhard house and the towers of St. Martin's. The most outstanding known as the Aldermens' Tower, was built in the 16C. It is flanked by a corbelled tower with windows placed between blind arcades surrounded by small twisted columns.

Edmond Michelet Museum. – *Open 10am to noon and 2 to 6pm; closed Sundays and holidays.*

The museum traces the history of the Resistance movement and of deportation with the help of paintings, photographs, posters and original documents relating to the camps, especially Dachau where E. Michelet was interned.

EXCURSIONS

Collonges★ ; Turenne★. – *Round tour of 56 km - 36 miles – about 3 1/2 hours – Local map below. Leave Brive by ④.* The D 38 affords glimpses, on the right, of Turenne and its castle towering on a hill.

Lacoste Castle. – *Not open to the public.* This former stronghold, built of local sandstone, has a main building flanked by three 13C round towers and was completed in the 15C by a polygonal staircase tower. The outbuildings house the workshop of the Spanish potter Vigreyos. *(To visit exhibition, ring the door bell).*

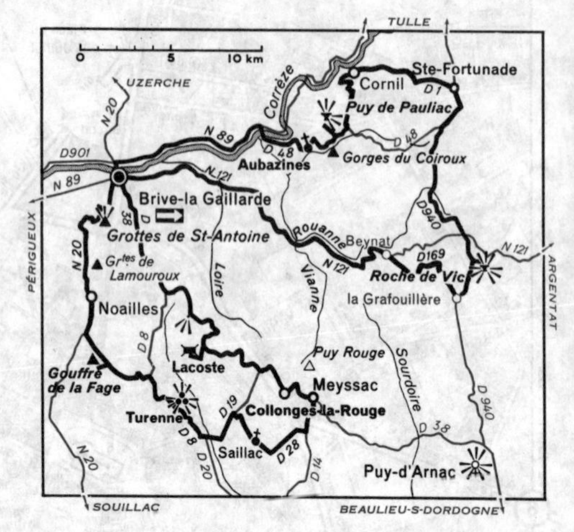

Collonges-la-Rouge★. – *Description p 86.*

The road passes the Puy Rouge before reaching Meyssac.

Meyssac. – Pop 1 255. Meyssac, like Collonges, is built of red sandstone. The red earth, known as "Collonges clay", lends itself to pottery manufacture *(a visit to a pottery is recommended).* Corbelled wooden houses with porch roofs and old towers make the village attractive.

The D 14, then the D 28 and D 28^E to the right lead to Saillac.

Saillac. – Pop 143. This small Romanesque church has a remarkable doorway preceded by a narthex. The Adoration of the Magi is figured on the **tympanum,** on the upper tier Mary and the Infant Jesus are surrounded by Joseph and the Three Kings: on the lower register are the winged leopard and an angel mastering the Leviathan.The tympanum rests on a pier which is composed of four twisted columns, adorned with studded foliage and hunting scenes. In the chancel surmounted by a dome on pendentives, there are fine historiated capitals.

Make for the D 19, turn left, continue to the D 8 and turn right.

Turenne★. – *Description p 181.*

Follow the D 8 then take the D 13 to the left.

La Fage Chasm★ (Gouffre de la Fage). – *Description p 182.*

Return to the N 20 and bear right.

Noailles. – Pop 515. Noailles lies in a pleasant setting of verdant hills. The church *(open 2 to 5pm in summer),* built on a hillside, is topped by a Limousin style bell gable. The chancel is Romanesque but the capitals have been carved in the archaic style. In the ogive vaulted nave are many memorial plaques to members of the Noailles family whose Renaissance château *(not open to the public)* may be seen from the church.

The picturesque N 20 winds down to the bottom of the Corrèze valley and provides a fine vista of Brive spread out in the centre of the valley. *Take a small road on the right which is signposted.*

Lamouroux Caves (Grottes de Lamouroux). – This picturesque group of caves arranged in five tiers, was used by man in times of danger.

St. Anthony Caves (Grottes de St-Antoine). – These caves hollowed out of the sandstone are arranged as chapels. The buildings house a small mission seminary under the direction of the Franciscan Fathers. Follow the Stations of the Cross to a terrace where there is a good view of Brive.

Return to Brive on the N 20.

Roche de Vic★ ; Puy de Pauliac★ ; Aubazines★. – *Round tour of 72 km - 45 miles – about 3 hours – Local map above. Leave Brive by ③.* The N 121 crosses the Loire, a small tributary of the Corrèze, before going up the valley of the Rouanne. With wide bends the road finally climbs to Beynat where you take the D 169, right, to Grafouillère and then D 940, left, for the Vic Rock.

Vic Rock★ (Roche de Vic). – *1/4 hour Rtn on foot.* Alt 636 m - 2 087 ft. The Vic Rock is a bare hill crowned with great granite blocks. A small chapel and a statue of the Virgin, both easily seen from the D 940, stand perched at the top. From here there is a **panorama★** of Bas-Limousin *(viewing-table);* in the foreground are hills and moorland; in the distance you see the Monédières Massif to the north and the plateaux of Quercy to the south.

The D 940 cuts across the plateau through a rolling countryside of woods and meadows.

Ste-Fortunade. – Pop 1 763. Near a much restored 15C castle stands a small Romanesque church containing on the left at the entrance to the south chapel, the **reliquary-head★** of St. Fortunade. This is a delightful 15C work in bronze.

Take the D 1 which drops down to the village of **Cornil** dominated by its Romanesque church and a ruined castle, and the river Corrèze, then the D 48^E, which climbs the plateau to join the D 48. Turn right; on the left there are lovely views of the Coiroux Gorges.

Puy de Pauliac★. – A surfaced road beginning to the right of the D 48 brings you close to the summit (alt 520 m - 1 706 ft) which is finally reached by a footpath *(1/4 hour Rtn on foot)* through the heather and chestnut groves. From the viewing table there is a wide **view**★: southeast lies the Vic Rock, and north the Monédières Massif.

Aubazines★. – *Description p 47.*

The N 89 runs beside the Corrèze all the way to Brive.

BRUNIQUEL★

Michelin map 79 fold 19 – *Local map 163* – Pop 446

Bruniquel, the bold outline of its castle set like a crown above the town, lies in a picturesque **setting**★ at the mouth of the great gorges that the Aveyron has cut through the Limogne Causse or limestone plateau.

According to Gregory of Tours (bishop, theologian and historian, 538-594), Bruniquel originated from the founding of a fortress on this spot by **Brunhilda**. The memory of this princess, who was the daughter of the king of the Visigoths and the wife of Sigebert, King of Austrasia, is kept alive by the tower that bears her name. Cruelties perpetrated on account of her rivalry with Fredegund, her sister-in-law, caused war between Austrasia and Neustria in the 6C. The death of the princess herself was so macabre that it has become famous: she was bound by her hair, an arm and a leg to the tail of an unbroken horse and smashed to pieces.

Old Town★. – Bruniquel is a pleasant place with its sloping alleys lined with old houses roofed with round tiles, the last of its fortifications, the town gateways and an old belfry.

Castle. – *Open 1 April to 30 September, 11am, 3, 4 and 5pm; (6pm in July and August); closed Tuesdays; 4F.*

The castle, built in yellow stone on foundations going back, it is said, to the 6C, has parts still standing that date from 12 to 15C. The barbican which defended the approaches to the castle from the village side, stands on the esplanade before the main building. If one is to believe the legend, Queen Brunhilda owned the castle whose massive square tower bears her name.

The Knight's Hall was built in the 12 and 13C and is decorated inside with small pillars and capitals.

There is a good view of the valley from a terrace near the chapel. Stairs lead to the first floor where a beautiful Renaissance chimneypiece may be seen in the guardroom.

In the seignorial part of the castle a Renaissance gallery looks straight down over the cliff to give a wide **view**★ of the river flowing below. Rock shelters have been hollowed out of the cliff-face.

EXCURSIONS

Montricoux. – Pop 754. *Facilities p 38. 6 km - 4 miles to the northwest.* Montricoux was built up on terraces above the right bank of the Aveyron river where it broadens out in a wide alluvial plain. The old perimeter walls are still standing, as is the square keep that formed part of a 13C castle that is no more. Certain alleys contain picturesque houses with mediaeval corbelling and timbering.

Puycelci; Forêt de Grésigne. – *Round tour of 40 km - 25 miles – about 2 hours. Leave Bruniquel south on the D 964; the road follows the Vère valley. Turn left onto the D 8.*

Puycelci. – Pop 442. On a rock platform, overlooking the green wooded valley of the Vère, stands the old fortified village of Puycelci, built in this picturesque **setting.** This former stronghold is still guarded by ramparts and flanked by 14 and 15C towers. Wandering around the streets you come across interesting houses and other buildings including the 15C castle of the Petit St-Roch flanked by two towers, the Féral Mansion which has a 15-16C façade pierced by doorways with pointed arches and the parish church with a Gothic nave and 18C belfry-porch.

Return to the D 964 and after 5 km – 3 miles take the D 87 on the left.

Grésigne Forest. – This forest covers 4 000 ha - 15 1/2 sq miles of an undulating massif lying on the left bank of the Aveyron on the borders of the Tarn Department. A Crown Forest in the 17 and 18C, it provided a valuable supply of seaworthy timber. Colbert made the forest protected property and instigated the making of roads to facilitate exploitation. The winding and picturesque D 87 runs through this forested massif where oak and hornbeam predominate.

The D 1 takes you back to Bruniquel.

BUSSIÈRE-BADIL

Michelin map 72 fold 15 – Pop 540

The Romanesque church at Bussière-Badil with its plain yet impressive appearance recalls the Cistercian church at Cadouin *(see p 72).*

The façade whose starkness is off set by the rose-coloured stone with which it is built is divided into three by buttresses. The doorway has a rounded arch and a triple line of sculptured covings supported by small columns adorned with beautiful capitals. A blind arcade on the left of the doorway has a carved tympanum. Above the vaults, built in the 15C, are two watch-turrets.

The dome above the transept crossing stands on pendentives which rest on small squinches. Capitals, some historiated, are the only ornament in this pleasantly proportioned building. Note the 16C statue of the Virgin and Child and a statue of Christ.

CADOUIN ★

Michelin map 75 fold 16 – *Local maps pp 97 and 98* – Pop 378

The Abbey of Cadouin founded in a narrow valley near the Bessède Forest in 1115 by Robert d'Arbrissel, was taken over by the Cistercians in 1119 and was extremely prosperous in the Middle Ages. The church and cloisters, restored after the Revolution, constitute an interesting architectural group.

The Holy Shroud of Cadouin. – As early as 1117 the new abbey became the possessor of a linen cloth adorned with bands of embroidery. This cloth had been brought from Antioch by a priest from Périgord and was believed to be the cloth that had been wrapped around Christ's head. The shroud became an object of deep veneration and attracted large pilgrimages, bringing great renown to Cadouin. Richard Lionheart, St. Louis and Charles V came to kneel before it in reverence. When the abbey was threatened by the English during the Hundred Years War, the Holy Shroud was entrusted to the care first of the monks at Toulouse and later those at Aubazines. It was only returned to Cadouin after endless lawsuits and the intervention of the pope and Louis XI.

In 1934 experts decided that the Holy Shroud of Cadouin was not genuine; the embroidered bands bore kufic inscriptions dating from the 11C.

Church★. – The building completed in 1154 is characteristic of the Saintonge area. The façade, which is powerful and massive and divided into three by great buttresses, is pierced above by three tall windows and below by a doorway with a round arch surmounted by a triple row of covings. The simplicity of the decoration – a double blind arcade on the lower left side with nine round arches on small columns above – brings out the golden yellow colour of the stone.

The church is well proportioned but differs from Cistercian architecture due to its plan which consists of a semicircular apse, with apsidal chapels and a more elaborate interior decoration: windows surrounded by mouldings, capitals with foliage and stylised animals; and in the two arms of the transept the elegant capitals are decorated with interlacing and palm fronds.

Access to the cloisters by the Place de l'Abbaye; enter by the Porte de la Tour next to the church; out of season go into the hall and ring at the second door on the right.

Cloisters★★. – *Guided tours 9 to 11.15am and 2 to 5.15pm; closed 15 December to 31 January and Tuesdays 15 October to 1 March; 8F.*

The liberality of Louis XI enabled the cloisters to be built at the end of the 15C in the Flamboyant Gothic style. The work, in fact, continued to the middle of the 16C as the Renaissance capitals of some of the columns bear witness. Despite the damage suffered during the Wars of Religion and the Revolution the cloisters remain a fine architectural monument.

At each corner there is a fine door: the royal door is adorned with the arms of France and Brittany, Anne of Brittany, who had married both Charles VIII and Louis XII, having been a benefactress to Cadouin. The ceiling bosses are carved into grimacing masks and amusing little scenes.

In the north gallery, facing the reader's lectern, may be seen the abbot's throne emblazoned with the abbey arms: the many scenes denoted on either side end in a large fresco of the Annunciation. The east gallery, commonly known as the Royal Gallery, contains pillars cast in the form of towers and decorated with themes from the Old and New Testaments.

EXCURSION

St-Avit-Sénieur; Ste-Croix. – *Round tour of 31 km - 19 miles – about 2 hours. Leave Cadouin to the west by the D 25 and take the D 27 to the right.*

Molières. – Pop 294. This unfinished English *bastide* has a Gothic church with a façade flanked by a tall square defensive tower of two tiers.

St-Avit-Sénieur. – Pop 385. *Works in progress.* Only partly ruined buildings remain of the Benedictine Abbey built in the 11C to the memory of St. Avitus, the soldier turned hermit. The church exterior is austere and rugged: in the 14C the building was fortified, as can be seen from the battlements crowning the porch, the tall and nearly blind walls of the nave and chevet and the towers, linked by a watch-path, on either side of the façade.

The nave is very spacious and has fine Angevin vaulting adorned with ribs or liernes and finely carved keystones. The building ends in a chancel with a flat chevet. The size of the arch bands leads one to believe that originally it was intended that the church should have a domed roof. A watch-path runs beneath the springing of the vaulting.

The only traces of the former abbey to be seen are a few cloistered arches and a part of the chapterhouse. Excavations have revealed the foundations of the monastic buildings and of a primitive Romanesque church. From the inner court there is a good overall view of the upper part of the nave of the church.

Follow the D 25 in the direction of Beaumont, before taking to the left the D 26, then a road to the right leading to Ste-Croix.

Ste-Croix. – Pop 84. This small village contains a charming Romanesque church and, nearby, the partly ruined buildings of an old priory. The 12C church is small but has pure lines. Contrasting with the small round tiles that roof the nave are the larger stone slates which cover the chevet and the apsidal chapels. The chevet is decorated with carved modillions. Above the façade stands a gabled bell tower. Inside, notice the square-based cupola and the Romanesque capitals.

Montferrand-du-Périgord. – Pop 185. Charming terraced village rising above the valley of the Couze. The covered market with its fine old pillars and the old houses and dovecotes make a picturesque scene.

The D 26 and the D 2 take you back to Cadouin.

CAHORS★★

Michelin map 79 fold 8 – *Local maps pp 108 and 125* – Pop 20 774

Cahors, enclosed by a bend in the river Lot and overlooked by rocky hills, was a flourishing commercial and university city in the Middle Ages and still retains precious items from its past. Formerly the capital of Quercy, it makes an excellent starting point for tours of the Célé and Lot valleys.

The Setting★. – If you approach the town from the north, we suggest you leave the N 20 3 km – 2 miles after St-Pierre-Lafeuille and take a local road (V 10) on the left. This pleasant road runs along the tops of the hills and affords good views of the surrounding hilly country and the valley of the Lot. It brings you suddenly before Cahors and you see it in its setting. The old town, stepped like an amphitheatre, bristles with belfries and battlemented towers, lines of fortifications and bridges.

HISTORICAL NOTES

The Sacred Spring. – A spring led to the founding of Divona Cadurcorum, later known as Cadurca and later still as Cahors. First the Gauls and then the Romans worshipped the source. The town grew rapidly in size: a forum, a theatre, temples, baths and ramparts were built. This spring still supplies the town with drinking water.

The Golden Age. – In the 13C Cahors became one of the great towns of France and knew a period of considerable economic prosperity due in no small part to the arrival of Lombard merchants and bankers. The Lombards were brilliant businessmen and bankers but also operated less worthily as usurers. The Templars, in turn, came to Cahors; gold fever spread to the townspeople and the place became the first banking city of Europe. Money was lent to the pope and to kings, and Cahors counting houses were everywhere.

The Loyal City and The Ungrateful King. – At the beginning of the Hundred Years War the English seized all the towns in Quercy: Cahors alone remained impregnable in spite of the black death which killed half the population. In 1360, under the Treaty of Brétigny, Cahors was ceded to the English, but the town, still unconquered, refused to be handed over. The King of France then ordered the keys of the city to be delivered up though the consuls protested with the words: "It is not we who are abandoning the King, but the King who is abandoning us to a foreign master." By 1450, when the English left Quercy, Cahors was a ruined city with many of its people gone.

Gambetta's Childhood. – Léon Gambetta has a special place even among the famous men of Cahors, who included Pope John XXII (1245-1334) and the poets Clément Marot (1496-1544) and Olivier de Magny (*c* 1529-*c* 1561). Born in 1838, the son of a grocer, young Gambetta often dreamed of sailing the seven seas. One day the young student went to watch a case at the assize court and became fascinated with the drama of the courtroom. The die had been cast, Léon Gambetta gave up all idea of going to sea to become an advocate.

In 1856 he left Cahors for Paris to enroll in the Law Faculty. His outstanding career as lawyer and statesman had begun.

■ VALENTRÉ BRIDGE★★ (Pont Valentré) *time: 1/2 hours*

The central tower is open from 1 July to 31 August, 9am to noon and 2 to 7pm; 6F.

The Valentré Bridge is a remarkable example of French mediaeval military architecture. The three towers with battlements and crenellated parapets and the pointed cutwaters breaking the line of the seven pointed arches, give it a proud bearing.

The best view of the Valentré Bridge and its towers, which rise 40 m - 130 ft, above the current, is from a little way upstream on the right bank of the Lot.

The Legend. – A legend in which the Devil plays an important part, though he loses in the end, is linked to the construction work which began in 1308 and went on for more than fifty years. The architect was in despair at the slow progress of the bridge and agreed to sign a pact with the Devil by which the Devil would bring all the materials necessary to the site and the architect, in his turn, would hand over his soul. The bridge rose quickly and work neared completion. The architect did not relish the idea of eternal torment and suddenly thought of commanding the Devil to bring him water in a sieve.

After a few vain attempts the Devil admitted himself beaten but in revenge, he broke off the topmost stone of the central tower, which has been known ever since as Devil's Tower. Every time the stone was replaced it fell off. When the bridge was restored, the architect had the stone firmly fixed and on the corner he had carved the little figure of a devil trying to dislodge it.

The Construction. – The original appearance of the Valentré Bridge was

(After a photo by Yan)

Cahors – The Valentré Bridge.

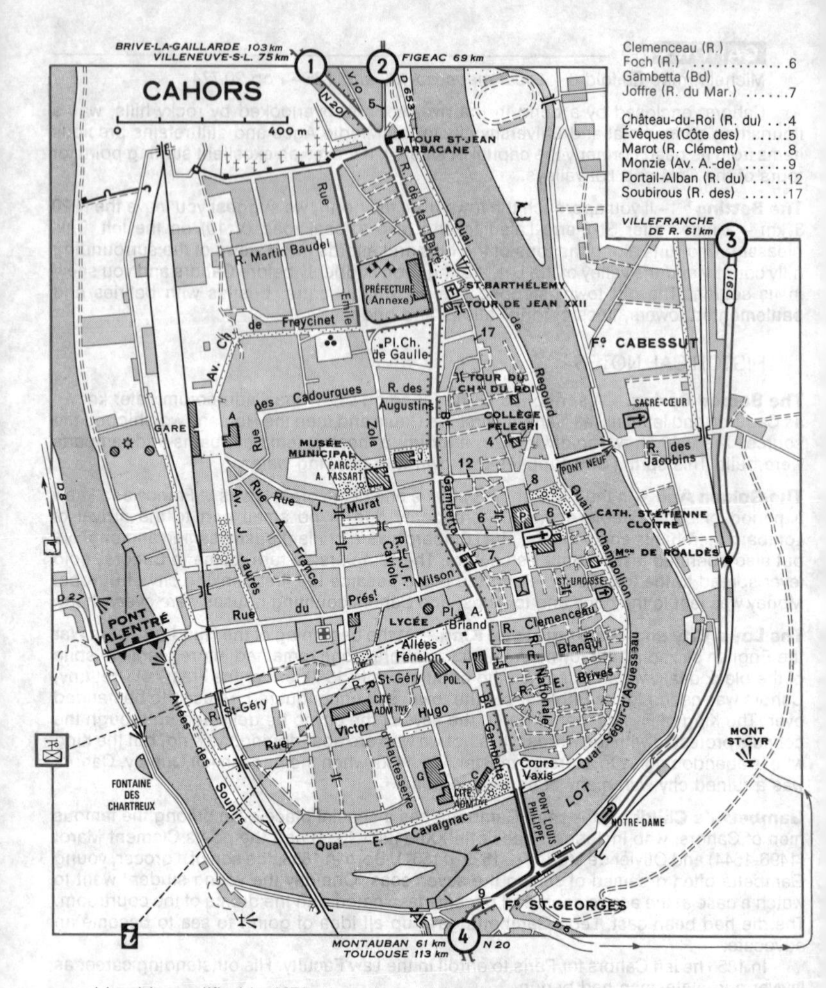

considerably modified in 1879 when the bridge was restored: the barbican, which reinforced the defences from the town side, was replaced by the present-day gate.

The bridge was originally an isolated fortress commanding the river; the central tower served as observation post, the outer towers were closed by gates and portcullises. A guardhouse and outwork on the left bank of the Lot provided additional protection.

The fortress defied the English during the Hundred Years War and also Henry of Navarre at the time of the siege of Cahors in 1580; it was never even attacked.

■ ST. STEPHEN'S CATHEDRAL* (Cathédrale St-Étienne) *time: 1/2 hour*

The clergy built this church as a fortress for reasons of safety in troubled times as well as of prestige. At the end of the 11C Bishop Géraud of Cardaillac began to build a church on the site of a former 6C church. Much of Bishop Géraud's church remains standing to this day. The trilobed south door dates from 1119. The north door is 12C, the restoration work on the original chevet dates from the 13C. The west face was built early in the 14C and the paintings within the domes and in the chancel were executed at the same time. The Flamboyant style cloisters and some of the outbuildings were commissioned at the beginning of the 16C by Bishop Antony of Luzech.

Exterior. – The west face is made up of three adjoining towers. The central one is topped by a belfry and opens with double doors. Above, on the first storey, the rose window is surrounded by blind arcades. Windows with twin bays complete the decoration which does not succeed in toning down the austere, military appearance of the façade.

North Door**. – This Romanesque door was once part of the main façade; it was transferred to the north side of the cathedral before the present wall was built. The **tympanum** *(diagram on the right)* depicts the Ascension. It was carved in about 1135 and from its style and technique belongs to the Languedoc school.

A mandorla or almond-shaped glory is the centrepiece of the composition: the haloed figure of Christ (**1**) stands with the right hand upraised and the left clasping a closed book. On either side an angel (**2**) explains the miracle to the apostles who are seen below in the trilobed blind arcades (**3**); beneath the central arch is the Virgin Mary (**4**) raising her hand to point at her Son. Above Christ four cherubim (**5**) fly out from the clouds to greet Him and take away His halo. On either side of Christ and the angels the sculptor has depicted scenes from the life of St. Stephen (**6**): his arrest by the Jews, his trial and the stoning, and the hand of God protecting the martyr.

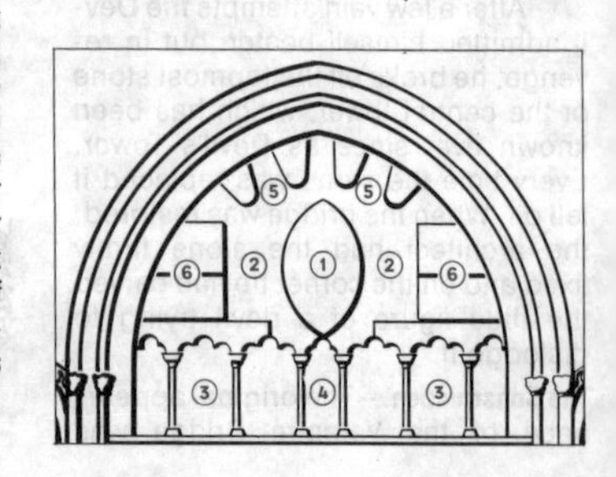

Follow the Rue du Maréchal-Foch to get a good view of the cathedral apse with two balustrades on the upper register; there are no buttresses and this adds to its massive appearance without destroying harmony.

Interior. – *Restoration work in progress.* Enter by the west door and cross the narthex which is slighty raised; the nave is roofed with two huge domes on pendentives. There is a striking contrast between the pale stone of the nave and the chancel adorned with stained glass and paintings. The frescoes of the west dome were uncovered in 1872; these show the stoning of St. Stephen in the central medallion, the saint's executioners round the frieze and eight giant-sized figures of prophets in the niches.

The chancel and the apse have Gothic vaulting and are decorated with mural paintings depicting the martyrdom of St. Stephen and St. Valerie in the chancel and the Coronation of the Virgin and the Adoration of the Magi at the end of the apse. The radial chapels, which were added in the 15C, are interesting on account of their carved decoration: one, the Chapel of St. Antony, opens on to the chancel through a beautiful Flamboyant Door.

Cloisters★. – Access to the cloisters is through a door on the right of the chancel. The cloisters are still rich in carved ornament in spite of considerable damage. The galleries are roofed with star vaulting – one keystone with pendant remains: it is above the northwest door and shows Jesus surrounded by angels. The engaged piers are decorated with niches which formerly contained statues. Near the chancel door you will see a spiral staircase and on the northwest corner pillar a graceful carving of the Virgin of the Annunciation.

In the chapel *(open 1 July to 31 August, 9am to noon and 2 to 6pm; closed Sundays and holidays; 3F)* there is a fresco of the Last Judgment and 16C paintings on the ceiling. The chapel also contains the treasure: church vestments; statues and portraits of 93 Bishops of Cahors from the 3 to the 19C.

You enter the inner court of the former arch-deaconry of St-Jean through the door in the northeast corner of the cloisters. Note the Renaissance decoration.

■ ADDITIONAL SIGHTS

Barbican and St. John's Tower★ (Barbacane et Tour St-Jean). – *Not open to the public.*

The ramparts constructed in the 14C completely cut off from the adjoining countryside the isthmus formed by the loop of the river Lot. Remains of these fortifications can still be seen and include a massive tower at the west end and the old doorway of St-Michel, which now serves as an entrance to the cemetery. It is on the east side, however, where the N 20 enters the town that the two most impressive fortified buildings remain: the barbican and St. John's Tower. The barbican is an elegant guardhouse which defended the Barre Gateway; St. John's Tower or the Tower of the Hanged Men, was built on a rock overlooking the river Lot.

Roaldès Mansion (Maison de Roaldès). – *Closed temporarily.*

The mansion is also known as Henry IV's Mansion because of an old story that the King of Navarre lived there during the siege of Cahors in 1580. The house dates from the end of the 15C and was restored in 1912. In the 17C it became the property of the Roaldès, a well-known Quercy family.

The south side, with its timberwork and balcony is crowned by a large round tower. The decoration of the north side – mullioned doors and windows, a rose window, Flamboyant suns – is characteristic of the Quercy school in about 1500.

Church of St-Barthélemy. – This church was built in the highest part of the town and was known until the 13C as *St-Étienne de Soubiroux, "Sancti Stephani de superioribus"* (St. Stephen of the Upper Quarter) in contrast to the cathedral built in the lower part of the town. The church was rebuilt over the centuries to its present design. It now contains a rectangular belfry-porch with three lines of bays in tiers-point one above the other; the belfry has no spire and is built almost entirely of brick. Its base dates from the 14C.

From the terrace near the church there is a good view of the Cabessut suburb and the Lot valley.

John XXII's Tower (Tour de Jean XXII). – This tower is the last part that is still standing of the palace of Pierre Duèze, brother of John XXII. It is 34 m - 112 ft high and was originally covered in round tiles; twin windows pierce the walls on five storeys.

Municipal Museum (Musée Municipal). – *Open 2 May to 31 October, 10am to noon and 2 to 6pm; closed Sundays and holidays; 5F.*

The museum is in the former episcopal palace. Several galleries evoke the Cahors of a bygone age and recall the lives of her well-known sons, Pope John XXII, Clément Marot and particulary Léon Gambetta, who is given pride of place with busts, drawings, signed letters and souvenirs. The former bishop's library contains an interesting ceramic collection. The chapel contains the original woodwork, a coffered ceiling and a floor which is a masterpiece in marquetry. For those interested in archaeology there is a sarcophagus and a mosaic dating from Roman times and some 15 and 16C sculpture.

Lycée Tower (Tour du Lycée). – From the Lycée Gambetta building which was once a Jesuit college, rises a graceful 17C octagonal tower built of rose-coloured brick.

Pelegri College Tower (Tour du Collège Pelegri). – The College was founded in 1368 and at first took in thirteen poor university students – the university had been established in 1332 at the instigation of Pope John XXII. Until the 18C, Pelegri College was one of the town's most important establishments. The fine hexagonal tower above the main building was constructed in the 15C.

Royal Castle Tower (Tour du Château du Roi). – Near Pelegri College stands what is today the prison and was once the governor's lodging. Of the two towers and two main buildings erected in the 14C, there remains the massive Royal Castle Tower.

EXCURSION

Mont St-Cyr. – *7 km - 4 miles by the Louis-Philippe Bridge to the south of the town and the D 6 which you leave after 1.5 km - 1 mile to reach the Mount, always bearing left.* From the top *(viewing table)* you get a good **view*** of Cahors: there is a marked contrast between the old and the new quarters of the town which are separated by the Boulevard Gambetta, Cahors' main artery. In the background can be seen the distinctive shape of the Valentré Bridge.

CAPDENAC

Michelin map 79 fold 10 – *Local map p 125* – Pop 1 033

Capdenac, perched on a rocky promontory encircled by a loop in the river Lot, still looks much as it did in former times. Due to its unique situation the town played a considerable role in mediaeval history. Today it owes its importance to Capdenac-Gare which is a busy railway junction.

Capdenac was considered, from the earliest of mediaeval times, to be one of the keypoints of Quercy. Some historians claim it as the site of the fortress of Uxellodunum – a bitterly controversial subject – the last site of Gaulish resistance to Caesar. What is certain is that at the beginning of the 8C King Pepin the Short seized a fortress built on this spot. Later, at the time of the Albigensian Crusade and during the Hundred Years War, Capdenac again became important strategically. At the beginning of the 16C, Galiot de Genouillac, seneschal of Quercy and Grand Master of Artillery to François I *(p 47)* acquired the castle, and during the Wars of Religion it became one of the main Protestant strongholds.

After the death of Henri IV, Sully, who now owned the property, came to live in it and stayed several years.

The Village. – *Time: 1/2 hour.* A road branching off the N 140 and climbing steeply brings you to the village which still has a definite character of its own with its narrow streets lined by corbelled wooden houses with pointed arches. It is also called Capdenac-le-Haut.

The remains of the ramparts and a stronghold are still to be seen. From a terrace near the entrance to this village, you can look out to the southeast over the Lot and the industrial, built-up area of Capdenac. From another terrace near the church you get a view, northwest, of one of the graceful meanders in the river Lot.

CARENNAC*

Michelin map 75 fold 19 – *Local map p 94* – Pop 376 – *Facilities p 38*

One of the most attractive sights to be found along the Dordogne is at Carennac where the picturesque houses with their brown tile roofs cluster round the old priory in which Fénelon once lived.

Fénelon at Carennac. – The priory-deanery at Carennac, which was founded in the 10C and attached to the famous abbey at Cluny in the following century, owes its fame to the long stay made there by François de Salignac de la Mothe-Fénelon before he became Archbishop of Cambrai.

While he was still a student at Cahors, Fénelon used to enjoy spending his vacations at the house of his uncle, senior prior of Carennac. In 1681 Fénelon's uncle died and the young abbot succeeded him, remaining at the priory for fifteen years. Fénelon was greatly revered at Carennac; he enjoyed describing the ceremonies and popular rejoicing that greeted his arrival by boat and his installation as commendatory prior.

Tradition has it that Fénelon wrote *Télémaque* while living at Carennac. The description of the adventures of Ulysses' son was at first only a literary exercise, but was subsequently turned into a tract for the edification of the Duke of Burgundy, Louis XIV's grandson, when Fénelon was appointed to be his tutor.

The Ile Barrade in the Dordogne was renamed Calypso's Island and the visitor will still be shown a tower in the village which is called Télémaque's Tower in which, it is maintained, Fénelon wrote his masterpiece.

■ THE VILLAGE *time: 1/2 hour*

The charming village where some of the houses still standing date from the 16C has changed little since Fénelon's day, but the deanery and its outbuildings suffered considerable damage at the time of the Revolution. The deanery was suppressed by order of the Royal Council in 1788 and put up for auction and sold in 1791.

Of the old ramparts there remain only a fortified gateway, and of the buildings, the castle and the priory tower. Go through the fortified gateway.

Church of St-Pierre. – In front of this Romanesque church, which is dedicated to St. Peter, stands a porch with a beautiful 12C carved **doorway***. It is well preserved and from its style would appear to belong to the same school as the tympana of Beaulieu, Moissac, Collonges and Cahors. In a mandorla (almond-shaped glory) in the centre of the composition, Christ is seen in Majesty, His right hand raised in blessing. He is surrounded by the symbols of the four Evangelists. On either side are the Apostles on two panels. The tympanum is framed with a foliated scroll in the Oriental style.

Inside, the archaic capitals in the nave are interesting for their ornament of fantastic animals, foliage and historiated scenes. The outstanding item in the church and one of the most interesting of the 16C is the **Placing in the Tomb**★: it stands in the false south transept. Christ lies in a shroud held by two disciples, Joseph of Arimathaea and Nicodemus; at the back two holy women support the Virgin and the Apostle John; to the right Mary Magdalene wipes away a tear.

Cloisters. – *These are reached through a door in the south aisle.*

The restored cloisters consist of a Romanesque gallery adjoining the church and three Flamboyant galleries.

Castle. – Temporary exhibitions are held in the castle which stands next to the church. A room on the first floor has a fine wooden ceiling which is decorated with Renaissance paintings.

CASTELNAU Castle★★

Michelin map 75 fold 19 – *Local maps pp 94 and 166*

On the northern border of Quercy stands the Castle of Castelnau with the village of Prudhomat lying at its foot. The great mass of the castle's red stone ramparts and the towers rise up from a spur commanding the confluence of the Cère and the Dordogne. The scale on which the castle defence was built makes it one of the finest examples of mediaeval military architecture.

More than three miles round, the castle, as Pierre Loti wrote, "is the beacon... the thing you cannot help looking at all the time from all angles: this cock's comb of blood-red stone rising from a tangle of trees, this ruin poised like a crown on a pedestal dressed with a beautiful greenery of chesnut and oak trees".

Turenne's Egg. – From the 11C onwards the barons of Castelnau were the strongest in Quercy; they paid homage only to the counts of Toulouse and styled themselves the Second Barons of Christendom. In 1184 Raymond of Toulouse gave the suzerainty of Castelnau to the Viscount of Turenne. The Baron of Castelnau refused to accept the insult and paid homage instead to Philip Augustus, King of France. Bitter warfare broke out between Turenne and Castelnau; King Louis VIII intervened and decided in favour of Turenne. Whether he liked it or not the baron had to accept the verdict. The fief, however, was only symbolic: Castelnau had to present his overlord with... an egg. Every year, with great pomp and ceremony a yoke of four oxen bore a newly laid egg to Turenne.

Castle★★. – *Guided tours 1 April to 30 September, 9 to 11.30am and 2 to 5.30pm; the rest of the year, 10 to 11.30am and 2 to 4.30pm; closed Tuesdays, 1 January, 1 May, 1 and 11 November, 25 December; time: 3/4 hour; 7F.*

Round the strong keep built in the 11C, there grew up during the Hundred Years War a huge fortress with a fortified perimeter wall. The castle was abandoned in the 18C and suffered depredations at the time of the Revolution. It caught fire in 1851 but was well restored between 1896 and 1932. The ground plan is that of an irregular triangle flanked at each corner by a round tower and with a tower partially projecting from each side. Three parallel perimeter walls still defend the approaches, but the former ramparts have been replaced by an avenue of trees.

As you follow the ramparts a **view**★ develops of the Cère and Dordogne valleys to the the north; northwest of Turenne Castle against the horizon; west the Montvalent Amphitheatre; southwest of Loubressac Castle and due south of the Autoire valley.

The main court, where stand the round keep and an impressive square tower 62 m - 203 ft high, known as the Saracen's Tower, gives one an idea of the vast scale of this fortress whose garrison numbered 1 500 men and 100 horses.

Interior. – In addition to the lapidary museum, many other galleries should be visited on account of their decoration and furnishings: the former Chamber of the Quercy States-General is lit by large Romanesque windows; the Pewter Hall and the Grand Salon contain Aubusson and Beauvais tapestries; the oratory has stained glass windows dating from the 15C and a 14C triptych of the Crucifixion and the life and martyrdom of St. Bartholomew.

Church. – *Not open to the public.* The former collegiate church of Castelnau lies below the castle. Like it, it is built of red ironstone.

CASTELNAUD Castle★

Michelin map 75 fold 17 – *Local map p 97*

The impressive ruins of Castelnaud Castle stand erect on a wonderful **site**★★ commanding the valleys of the Céou and the Dordogne. Right opposite stands Beynac Castle, Castelnaud's implacable rival throughout the conflicts of the Middle Ages.

In the 12C the castle *(restoration in progress)* belonged to the Cazenac family and at the time of the Albigensian Crusade (1209-1229) was occupied by Simon de Montfort (*c* 1165-1218, father of the English statesman and soldier). In the 14C alterations were made to provide it with battlemented keeps, bastions and casemates and make it a powerful fortress. Castelnaud was occupied for a considerable part of the Hundred Years War by the English, who were thus able to keep watch on Beynac which was loyal to the King of France.

From the tiltyard you get a view of the Céou valley to the south. From the east end of the terrace there is a remarkable **panorama**★★★ of one of the most lovely countrysides of the valley of the Dordogne: in the foreground the patchwork of fields with screens of poplars hemmed by a wide loop in the river, further lie Beynac with its castle, Marqueyssac Castle and, at the foot of the cliffs, La Roque-Gageac and in the far distance a line of wooded and rocky hills skirting the Dordogne Valley.

CAUSSADE

Michelin map 79 fold 18 – Pop 6 132

Caussade, at the southern edge of the Limogne Causse, was a Protestant stronghold during the Wars of Religion. At the beginning of the 20C it was a centre in the straw hat making industry, but fashions change, and today the factories turn out miscellaneous items.

Church. – The original church belfry, built in rose coloured bricks, can still be seen, graceful and eight-sided, rising three storeys high and topped by a crotcheted spire; the remainder of the building was rebuilt in 1882 in the Gothic style.

The old quarter near the church contains a few mediaeval houses.

EXCURSIONS

Négrepelisse. – Pop 2 871. *11 km - 7 miles to the south by the N 20 and soon after bear left on the D 64.* This small village in the Aveyron valley has a church topped by an octagonal belfry.

Notre-Dame des Misères. – *13 km - 8 miles to the southwest by the N 20 and from Réalville the D 40.* The chapel, founded in 1150 in a pleasant setting, is crowned by an eight-sided Romanesque belfry, two storeys high and with double blind arcades.

Puylaroque. – Pop 614. *14 km - 9 miles to the northeast by the D 17. Local map p 163*

Puylaroque was once a *bastide (p 32)* of Bas-Quercy; its flat roofed houses are packed on the top of a hill overlooking the valleys of the Cande and the Lère. A few corbelled houses with timbered walls can still be seen in the narrow streets near the church, which has a massive square belfry adjoining the main doorway. Views far over the rolling Quercy countryside and the plains of Caussade and Montauban can be obtained from several of the town's esplanades and especially from the one near the church.

CAYLUS

Michelin map 79 fold 19 – *Local map p 163* – Pop 1 520 – *Facilities p 38*

This little village of Bas-Quercy is set in a picturesque spot above the right bank of the Bonnette. The best view of the old town, closely grouped round the church with its tall belfry and overlooked by the ruins of the 14C fortress, is from the southwest along the D 926.

At the foot of the old town lies a small artificial lake.

■ SIGHTS *time: 1 hour*

Covered Market. – The great size of the market is evidence of Caylus's long-standing commercial importance. The old grain measures may still be seen cut into the stone.

Church. – This was once a fortified church as may be seen from the buttresses topped by machicolations. Inside, near the chancel, on the north side of the 14C nave, stands a gigantic figure of **Christ**★ carved in wood in 1954 by Zadkine, an artist born in Smolensk in 1890 and greatly influenced by the Cubist school and his friends Braque and Fernand Léger. The Crucifix is very striking and at the same time deeply moving. The 15C stained glass windows (restored) in the chancel are noteworthy.

Rue Droite. – In the Rue Droite starting from the church there are several mediaeval houses, in particular the 13C gable fronted house known as the **Wolves' Lair** (Maison des Loups) adorned with bosses and gargoyles in the form of wolves from which the house derives its names.

EXCURSIONS

Notre-Dame des Grâces; Lacapelle-Livron. – *Round tour of 10 km - 6 miles – about 1 hour.*

Leave Caylus to the north by the D 19. The road affords good views of the Bonnette river and soon passes, on the left, a path that leads to the Chapel of Notre-Dame de Livron, and becomes a picturesque *corniche*-style road overlooking the valley.

Notre-Dame des Grâces. – Built at the end of a promontory, this little pilgrimage chapel with its stone roof is Gothic in style with a fine sculptured doorway.

From nearby there is a wide view of the Bonnette Valley in its setting of hills dotted with woods and meadows.

Lacapelle-Livron. – Pop 157. This old village with its stone slated houses has a group of buildings, mostly in ruins, which were formerly a commandery of the Order of Knights Templars and after 1307 passed to the Knights of Malta until the Revolution. There remains a fortified manorhouse overlooking the Bonnette, with a central courtyard preserving the original layout of the commandery. To the south the Romanesque chapel stands opposite the former refectory which is now the guardroom.

Return to Caylus by the D 97 which follows the course of the Bonnette. There is the lovely St-Pierre-Livron waterfall on the right just outside Caylus.

Cornusson; Beaulieu-en-Rouergue★. – *10 km - 6 miles – about 3/4 hour. Take to the east the road leading to Cornusson.*

Cornusson Castle. – *Not open.* This castle for the most part rebuilt in the 16C, flanked by numerous towers, stands well placed on a hill commanding the Seye.

Take the D 33 to the south in the direction of Verfeil.

Former Abbey of Beaulieu-en-Rouergue★. – The Seye valley provides a splendid setting for the former Abbey of Beaulieu-en-Rouergue founded in 1144 as a dependency of Clairvaux. *Guided tours Palm Sunday to 30 September, 10am to noon and 2 to 6 pm; closed Tuesdays; combined tickets to the abbey and exhibition: 11F.*

The **abbey church** is a fine building which was built in the mid-13C. The ogive vaulted nave ends in an elegant apse of seven sides; a square chapel opens off each transept. Above the transept crossing rises an octagonal **lantern tower** on squinches. The chapterhouse, the oldest part of the abbey, and the Gothic storeroom are now open to the public. The former lay brothers dormitory above the storeroom is now an art gallery. *For information,* ☎ *(63) 30-76-84.*

CÉLÉ Valley★

Michelin map 79 folds 9 and 10 – *Local map p 125*

The Célé (from *celer* = rapid), which owes its name to its swiftness, is a delightful Quercy river which has cut a steep sided valley through the limestone plateau. The Célé valley, in addition to passing through beautiful country, contains important prehistoric sites and archaeological remains.

Valley of Paradise. – The Célé rises in the chestnut woods that grow on the granite soil of Cantal; it enters Quercy and makes directly for the river Lot, but within 5 km - 3 miles its course is blocked by the Capdenac Hill. The Célé gets round this obstacle by turning westwards and cutting through 40 km – 25 miles of limestone. This has resulted in a series of picturesque defiles where the river can be seen winding along, still undermining the bases of the steep and many-hued rock walls.

Adding to the beauty of the valley are the old mills built beside the river, and the archaic villages that stand perched on cliff ledges or half-hidden in the greenery: not for nothing was the former priory at Espagnac called the valley of Paradise.

The "Hébrardie". – Throughout the Middle Ages the greater part of the Célé valley was under the control of the Hébrard family of St-Sulpice, so that it virtually constituted a feudal benefice. The period when the influence of the Hébrards was so great, was known locally as the "Hébrardie". The family, which lived at St-Sulpice, enlarged or rebuilt the priories of Espagnac and Marcilhac and protected the local inhabitants, particularly at the time of the Hundred Years War. This great family numbered not only soldiers among its members – one was appointed seneschal of Quercy – but also eminent ecclesiastics such as Aymeric, Bishop of Coïmbra in Portugal and Anthony, Bishop of Cahors.

From Conduché to Figeac

57 km - 35 miles – about 1/2 day – local map p 125

The D 41 starts at Conduché, where the Célé flows into the Lot, and goes up the valley. The road is squeezed between the river bed and the cliff-face which rises at one side like a wall and at times even overhangs the route below. Many crops grow in the valley with maize tending to replace tobacco; the characteristic line of poplars marks the course of the river.

Cabrerets. – Pop 213. *Facilities p 38.* Cabrerets, set in a rocky amphitheatre, occupies a commanding position at the confluence of the Sagne and Célé rivers.

A good overall **view**★ of Cabrerets and its setting may be obtained from the left bank of the Célé, which is reached by crossing the bridge. On the far left is the impressive outline of Gontaut-Biron Castle, while opposite the ruins of the Devil's Castle (Château du Diable) cling to the formidable Rochecourbe cliff and seem about to fall and smash the village below. This eagle's aerie served as a base from which the English could pillage the countryside during the Hundred Years War.

The 14 and 15C **Gontaut-Biron Castle**★ *(not open to the public)* overlooks the valley. A big corner tower flanks the buildings that surround an inner courtyard. One of the mullioned windows of the façade opens on to the terrace with its ornamental balustrades which overhangs the road 25 m - 82 ft up.

The D 13 then the D 198 lead up the valley of the Sagne to the Pech-Merle Cave.

Pech-Merle Cave★★. – *Description p 149.*

Shortly after Cabrerets the road crosses the face of high grey coloured stone cliffs.

Pescalerie Fountain (Fontaine de la Pescalerie). – This is one of the most attractive sights of the Célé valley: a beautiful waterfall pours out of the rock wall quite near the road. It marks the surfacing of an underground river that has cut its way through the Gramat Causse; beside the waterfall an ivy-covered mill stands half-hidden by trees.

As the road emerges from a tunnel the cliffs are seen to overhang the right bank of the river. At this point the valley widens out.

Sauliac. – Pop 106. This old village clings to an awe-inspiring cliff of weird coloured rock. In the cliff-face can be seen the openings to the fortified caves used in time of war as refuges by the local inhabitants: the most agile climbed up by way of ladders; invalids and animals were hoisted up in great baskets.

Beyond Sauliac the valley bottom bears crops and pasture.

Marcilhac-sur-Célé. – *Description p 127.*

Bellevue Cave★. – *1.5 km - 1 mile beyond Marcilhac. Description p 127.*

Between Marcilhac and Brengues the contrast intensifies between the rocks with their sparse vegetation and the valley which is densely cultivated with pastures, vineyards and tobacco plantations with their drying grounds.

St-Sulpice. – Pop 116. The houses and gardens of this old village lie within the shadow of an overhanging cliff. The approach is guarded by a 12C castle which was rebuilt in the 14 and 15C. It is still the property of the Hébrard family of St-Sulpice.

Brengues. – Pop 150. This small village is in a pleasant setting, perched on a ledge overlooked by a vertiginous bluff.

As far as Boussac the valley widens and narrows by turns; rich farmhouses stand solidy, their dovecotes beside them. These dovecotes are often round with stone slated roofs, topped by a large flat stone.

Espagnac-Ste-Eulalie. – *Description p 99.*

Above Boussac the cliffs finally disappear and the countryside becomes one of wooded hills where the Célé spreads out into a wide alluvial bed.

Ceint d'Eau. – This 15-16C castle, flanked by massive battlemented towers, rises above the D 13 and overlooks the Célé valley.

Continue to Figeac (p 104).

CÈRE Gorges

Michelin map 75 north of fold 20 – *Local map p 94*

The Cère River rises in the Cantal Mountains, but its lower course runs through Quercy. Between Laroquebrou and Laval-de-Cère, the river flows through wild and picturesque gorges; once through these, the Cère continues past Bretenoux and the foot of a promontory on which stands Castelnau Castle, to join the Dordogne.

The railway follows the Cère Gorges from one end to the other, but no road has been built beside the river between Laroquebrou and Laval-de-Cère.

The valley may be enjoyed nevertheless from the following points:

– from the D 81, east of Camps: this winding road drops down to the bottom of the valley which is barred by a dam;

– from the **Rocher du Peintre**★, a terrace built to the south of Camps, there is a good **view**★ along the wooded ravines of the Cère;

– from the D 14 between Port de Gagnac and Laval-de-Cère the road winds its way between meadows and wooded hills and overlooks the Brugale Dam.

CHÂLUS

Michelin map 72 fold 16 – Pop 2 094 – *Facilities p 38*

The old city of Châlus, dominated by its keeps, recalls the memory of **Richard Lionheart's** tragic death. On every side are the solid granite masses, densely wooded, of the Châlus Hills, last buttresses of the Massif Central.

A Fatal Siege. – The tale is told of how in 1199 a serf belonging to Adhemar V, Viscount of Limoges, discovered a fabulous treasure trove of "ninepins and large balls, all in solid gold" (these items now figure in the arms of Châlus together with a long bow.) The Viscount of Limoges hid the treasure in his castle at Châlus. Nevertheless rumours of the find reached Richard Lionheart, King of England and Lord of Western France.

Richard demanded his share of the booty as overlord, and when his vassal refused to give it up, laid siege to Châlus. When he was directing the attack on the castle from far enough away, he thought, to be beyond the range of enemy arrows, he was struck on the shoulder by a quarrel from a cross-bow of a type never tried before and virtually, therefore, a "secret weapon". Richard refused to dress the wound which turned black, the poison went to his heart and the end came... So died, at forty-two, one of the greatest men of the Middle Ages.

The castle defenders paid dearly for the death of the king: all were hanged except the too skilled cross-bowman who was flayed alive.

Castle. – *Guided tours 1 July to 15 September, 10 to 11.30am and 3 to 6.30pm; 1 April to 30 June, Sundays and holidays only; closed 16 September to 31 March; time: 1/2 hour; 6F.*

The remains of a castle dating from the late 11C and known as **Châlus-Chabrol**, stand on rising ground in the upper part of the village. Still standing are the squat corner tower adjoining a 13C building and a tall keep with 3 m - 10 ft thick walls built of great granite blocks. It was from this tower that the fatal quarrel was aimed at King Richard.

From the upper platform *(access dangerous)* there is a **view** below of the old houses with their attractive brown tiled roofs dominated by the 13C tower of Châlus-Maulmont, the Tardoire valley, Puyconnieux and the wooded farmlands of Limousin.

EXCURSIONS

Montbrun; Brie. – *Round tour of 22 km - 14 miles – about 2 hours. Leave Châlus by the D 6 Bis.*

Dournazac. – Pop 851. The 12C St-Sulpice church, rebuilt in the 14C, has preserved in the apsidal chapels in its chancel and underneath the dome of the transept crossing interesting Romanesque capitals with carved motifs of foliage and figures.

Take the D 64 to the right.

Montbrun Castle. – *Guided tours 1 May to 2 November, 9 to 11.45am and 2 to 6.45pm; the rest of the year 10 to 11.45am and 2 to 4.45pm; 10F.* The castle *(illustration p 30)* overlooks a tree-shaded lake. The still visible moat bears witness to the military importance of this fortress which was besieged unsuccessfully by Richard Lionheart. First built in the 12C, the only part of the building from this period still standing is a tall square keep crowned with battlements.

The main building and defence walls, linked by round towers, one of which encircles the base of the keep, date from the 15C. The walls surround a courtyard onto which open two emblazoned doors. Although the castle was set on fire in 1917, the exterior is still intact. While touring the building you will see the crypt of an old chapel, a postern gate (once the castle entrance) and a Carolingian mote.

Follow to the right the D 213; 2 km - 1 mile further on a track on the right leads to Puyconnieux.

Puyconnieux. – From the top of this hill (alt 496 m - 1 627 ft) you will get extensive **views** of the rolling Châlus countryside and the Ambazac and Blond hills.

The D 213 and then the D 100 to the right lead to Brie Castle.

Brie Castle. – *Guided tours, 1 April to 30 September, Sundays and holidays only from 2 to 6pm; 8F.*

This 15C fortified manor has fine Louis XVI furnishings in the apartments. The keep has a spiral granite staircase.

Return to Châlus by the D 42.

CHAMBON-SUR-VOUEIZE

Michelin map 73 fold 2 – *Local map p 100* – Pop 1 288

Chambon has a pleasant setting at the confluence of the Voueize and the Tardes rivers in the green valleyed countryside of Combraille. Nearby are the picturesque ravines of the Voueize which you overlook as you travel along the D 917, north of the town.

St. Valerie's Church★ (Église Ste-Valérie). – *Time: 1/2 hour.* This is one of the biggest and most interesting churches in the Limousin Romanesque style. After a priory had been founded by the abbot of St. Martial of Limoges *(p 117)* to house the relics of St. Valerie, the building of a church was undertaken at the end of the 11C or early in the 12C. In the 15 and 16C the church was pillaged and mutilated; about 1850 it was restored and the nave covered with groined vaulting hiding the 15C timberwork.

Exterior. – The church is built of granite and is enormous: the overall length is 87 m - 285 ft, the width at the transept 38 m - 125 ft. A square belfry dating from the 13C and known as the Clock Tower rises above the porch. This has ogive vaulting and a Limousin doorway adorned with ovoli (convex quarter mouldings) and small columns whose capitals form a frieze. The chevet stands out well and is elegantly tiered; the bays of its five apsidal chapels are adorned with cable mouldings.

Interior. – This is noteworthy for its perfect proportions. The chancel is the most interesting part of the building; foliage and scrollwork adorn the capitals of its triumphal arch. Note the very fine woodwork.

CHANCELADE, Former Abbey (Ancienne Abbaye de CHANCELADE)

Michelin map 75 fold 5 – 7 km - 4 miles northwest of Périgueux

Founded in the 12C the great abbey which followed the rule of St. Augustine, was altered and restored in the 17C by the Venerable Alain de Solminihac and survived until the Revolution.

Church. – The tympanum of the Romanesque doorway is surmounted by elegant blind arcades. The massive square belfry which rises from the dome above the transept, consists of several tiers of blind arcades alternately built in the Romanesque and Gothic styles.

The chancel has fine 17C stalls with carved misericords and traces of 14C frescoes depicting St. Christopher and St. Thomas Becket.

Monastery buildings. – These include the former abbey house, now the presbytery, and the buildings round the courtyard and the garden.

Museum of Sacred Art. – *Open 1 June to 30 September, 2 to 6.30pm; 6F.*

The museum is housed in a room of the presbytery and in the two sacristies. Note an interesting collection of religious vestments, 17C statuettes, enamelled silver reliquaries and fine 17-18C furnishings.

Abbey house and outbuildings. – *Open 1 June to 30 September, 2 to 6pm; 7F.*

Grouped round the courtyard are the 15C laundry room with surbased cradle vaulting (now an art gallery), the stables, the workshops and a fortified mill.

Adjoining the courtyard is the garden overlooked on one side by the north façade of the abbey house with its two turrets, one of which is pierced by an attractively decorated late 15C doorway.

St-Jean Chapel. – This Romanesque chapel has a fine doorway with a rounded arch surmounted by a window framed with slender columns, and a graceful circular apse with flat buttresses.

CHÂTEAUMEILLANT

Michelin map 68 fold 20 – *Local map p 162* – Pop 2 187

This city, now known for the pale, light wines produced by the local hillside vineyards, was an important market and communication centre in Gallo-Roman times. It was converted in the 3C by St. Genesius who suffered martyrdom, it is said, on the present church site.

Church of St-Genès. – *Time: 1/2 hour.* The church, from its foundation, was under the aegis of the powerful Déols Abbey *(p 83)*; modifications were made to the structure after fires and the ravages of war. Built of fine grey and rose stone quarried at Saulzais-le-Potier *(16 km - 10 miles south of St-Amand-Montrond)*, the main façade, in the Berry style, is well proportioned and pleasing, with small columns surmounted by interesting sculptured capitals. Inside the church you will be struck by the height of the Romanesque nave where a timber roof has replaced the original cradle vaulting and the dome above the transept crossing.

Before the chevet, which is oven vaulted, is the **chancel**★ roofed with broken cradle vaulting upheld by beams and – a rare architectural feature – surrounded by six apsidal chapels, four of which open to the choir by twin rounded arches. Standing in one of the apsidal chapels, you get the impression of a forest of columns, many supporting historiated capitals. One of the capitals shows the Creation of Adam, the Temptation, Adam and Eve being banished and Cain killing Abel.

E. Chénon Museum (Musée E. Chénon). – *Open 15 June to 15 September, 10am to noon and 2 to 6pm; 6F.*

Installed in the 14-16C Hôtel de Marcillac the museum presents important Gallo-Roman and mediaeval collections, originating from local excavations: chipped flint tools, pottery, amphorae and coins.

CHÂTEAUNEUF-SUR-CHER

Michelin map 68 fold 10 – Pop 1 663

Châteauneuf is built up in steps from the River Cher to the foot of the castle walls.

Castle. – *Open 10 to 11.15am and 2 to 6.15pm (afternoons only 2 to 4.15pm, 1 November to 31 March); time: 3/4 hour; castle: 14F; wildlife park: 10F; combined ticket: 18F.*

This powerful fortress, which was built in the 11C on a terrace commanding the valley, was owned by the Culan family until the 15C. It was rebuilt in 1581 and altered in the 17 and 18C. From the terraces there are pleasant views of Châteauneuf and the Cher Valley.

Inside the castle the splendid decoration and **furnishings** create an intimate, lived-in atmosphere.

The former guardroom, through which one goes to reach the living quarters, contains a remarkable picture by Mignard (1612-95) of Claire Clémence de Maillé, wife of the Great Condé, Prince Louis II of Bourbon (military genius during the reign of Louis XIV).

The reception rooms with Louis XIV panelling contain interesting furniture (mainly 18C), Gobelins and Flemish tapestries, fine Dresden china and paintings by Isabey, the miniaturist.

The vast, well-lit kitchen has an impressive collection of utensils (200 pieces in shining copper) on display.

The inner courtyard, built at the end of the Renaissance period, is surrounded by stark looking buildings flanked by round towers.

Park. – In the castle park are aviaries with exotic birds and wild animals.

CHÂTEAUPONSAC

Michelin map 72 fold 7 – 21 km - 13 miles to the east of Bellac – Pop 2 653

The old part of the town, clustered round the Church of St-Thyrse, stands perched on a promontory overlooking an enclosed loop of the river Gartempe.

Church of St-Thyrse. – The building dates largely from the 12C though pointed vaulting was added in the narrow nave and aisles in the 15C. The tall transept crossing is crowned by a dome on pendentives. The chancel has fine round columns with capitals adorned with carvings.

Also of interest are a stone pulpit dating from 1642, a great 18C lectern and 16-17C coloured wooden statuettes.

View of the Gartempe. – Go round the church and walk to the end of the promontory. From there can be seen the valley of the Gartempe – sloping steeply on the left bank – an old Gothic bridge and, in the foreground, the Sous-le-Moustier Quarter (beneath the Abbey Quarter) – an interesting suburb crowded with picturesque 15C houses.

Museum. – *Open 1 July to 15 September, 2 to 6pm; the rest of the year, Sundays and holidays only; 7F.*

It is housed in a former Benedictine priory near the church. There is a fine collection of minerals and fossils in the prehistoric section; exhibits placed in about ten display cases trace the evolution of man and the tools used through the ages. Note a quartz **polishing tool** with 15 grooves (for flint and sandstone axes).

The archaeological section is particularly rich in Gallo-Roman chests and funerary urns, inscriptions, coins, pottery, statuettes (a bronze Mercury) and jewellery; most of these come from finds in the area.

In the section on traditional art and folklore, there is a very fine recreation of a **Limousin home setting** and a good collection of local costumes. Other rooms are devoted to various crafts (interesting oil press with stone furnishings) and to historical documents relating to Châteauponsac from the 15C to the present day.

CHÂTEAUROUX

Michelin map 68 fold 8 – Pop 53 967

Châteauroux, the capital of Bas-Berry is both a busy agricultural town and industrial centre with the production of cigarettes as the main product.

The Birth of Châteauroux. – Déols is now only a suburb of Châteauroux but in the Middle Ages it was the seat of one of the most powerful abbeys in the whole kingdom. This Benedictine Abbey was founded in 917 by Ebbes the Noble and had its privileges confirmed by thirty reigning popes. So great were its powers and its riches that it was called the "Breast of St. Peter." The castle of the Déols princes was built on an escarpment overlooking the Indre at the same time as the abbey; later it took the name of many of its overlords: *Chastel Raoul* (Raoul's Castle) or *Chasteau Raoulx* which, in time, became Châteauroux.

An Unfailing Friendship. – " Bertrand's name is joined to mine", Napoleon was wont to say, " he will live as long as I live". Henry Bertrand was born in 1773 at Châteauroux. Pursuing a military career he took part in the expedition to Egypt and in 1805 he became aide-de-camp to the Emperor. He distinguished himself at the battles of Austerlitz (1805), Jena (1806) and Wagram (1809) and was to become Palace Grand Marshal in 1813, replacing Duroc. He followed Napoleon to Elba and after Waterloo went, with his family, into voluntary exile on St. Helena. He was present at the death of Napoleon and, in 1840, was a member of the party that carried the Emperor's ashes to the Invalides where in 1847, three years after his own death, his mortal remains were also to be brought. His statue by Rude (1784-1855) stands in the Place Ste-Hélène.

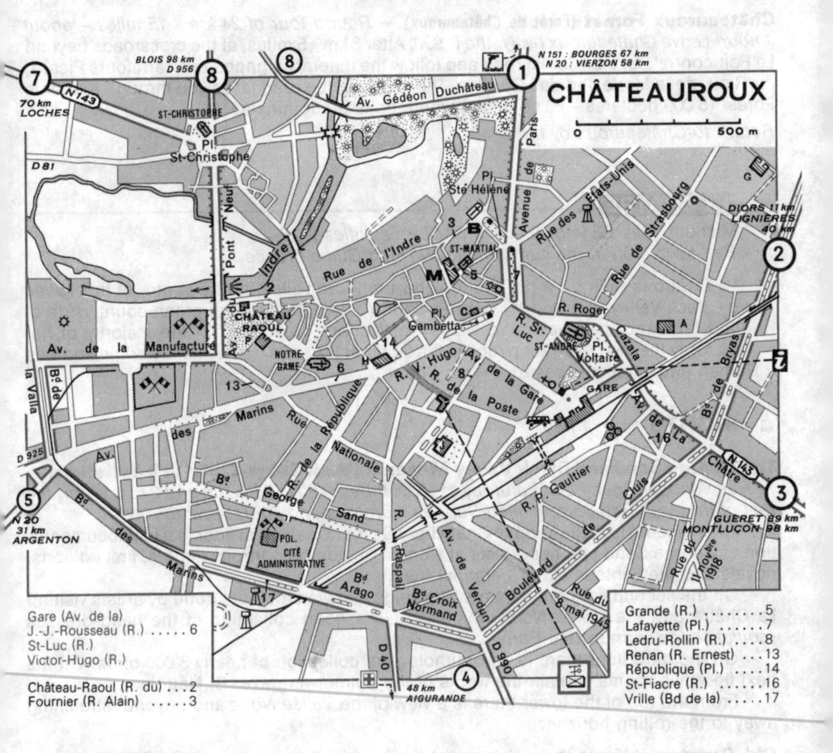

■ SIGHTS *time: 1 1/2 hours*

Bertrand Museum (Musée Bertrand) (M). – *Open 1 June to 30 September, 9.30am to noon and 2 to 6pm; the rest of the year, 2 to 5pm; closed on Mondays and 1 January, 1 May, 14 July, 1 and 11 November, 25 December.*

The museum is in an 18C mansion which once belonged to General Bertrand, and contains many mementoes of the General and the Napoleonic Era.

Ceramics, enamels, tapestries, paintings and the papers of men of letters connected with the Berry region – Maurice Rollinat (poet) and George Sand *(p 145)* – together with interesting sculpture taken from Déols Abbey make an attractive exhibition.

Other rooms are devoted to painting (Flemish, Dutch, French and Italian schools), the decorative arts, ancient and mediaeval archaeology and folk traditions.

Franciscan Church (Église des Cordeliers) (B). – This austere Gothic church (fully restored) contains remnants of 13C stained glass windows and traces of a 15C fresco. It is now an art gallery.

Raoul Castle (Château Raoul). – This castle was built in the 15C on the site of a 10C fortress. See the view of the castle and river from the Pont Neuf Bridge.

Former Déols Abbey. – *2 km - 1 mile to the north. Leave Châteauroux by ①.*

There are only a few traces now to be seen of the abbey church which was once a Romanesque masterpiece.

A single magnificent **belfry**★, built in beautiful grey stone, escaped destruction. At the tower base are historiated capitals among which can be discerned one that is remarkable, of Daniel in the lions' den; above are three tiers of blind arcades and a conical spire flanked by four bell turrets.

EXCURSIONS

Diors; Sassierges-St-Germain; Ardentes. – *Round tour of 40 km - 25 miles – about 1 1/2 hours. Leave Châteauroux by ②, the D 925.*

Diors. – Pop 546. Diors Castle, built in the 16C on the site of a former stronghold, was almost completely destroyed in an air-raid in August 1944. A museum has since been established in those outbuildings that could be saved: the **Museum of the Three Wars** (Musée des Trois Guerres) *(open 1 March to 31 December, 9am to noon and 2 to 6pm; closed Tuesdays and 1 January to 28 February; 12F).*

Foreign as well as French souvenirs of the 1870-1871, 1914-1918, 1939-1945, Indochina and Algerian wars have been collected: notices, letters, journals, autographs, uniforms, arms and commemorative plates, coins and stamps. Wax figures and dioramas complete the collections which are exhibited in chronological order.

The park with its wild animals is also open to the public.

On leaving Diors take the D 49 to the right, then the D 71.

Sassierges-St-Germain. – Pop 355. The Romanesque church is topped by a shingle covered belfry. The main doorway and the nave are adorned with interesting capitals.

The D 19 leads to Ardentes.

Ardentes. – Pop 3 287. The Romanesque church of St-Martin is decorated with primitive capitals and has interesting doorways.

To return to Châteauroux take the D 943.

Châteauroux Forest (Forêt de Châteauroux). – *Round tour of 24 km - 15 miles – about 1 hour. Leave Châteauroux by ④, the D 990.* After 8 km - 5 miles, at the crossroads beyond Le Poinçonnet, take the forest road and follow the itinerary signposted: carrefours Picard, du Riau, de la Motte and des Druides. This picturesque road takes you through the State Forest (5 000 hectares - 20 sq miles) where oaks predominate.

Return to Châteauroux by the D 40.

La CHÂTRE

Michelin map 68 fold 19 – Pop 5 142 – *Facilities p 38*

See town plan in the current Michelin Red Guide France

La Châtre is built on a hill overlooking the Indre valley, in the centre of the *Vallée Noire* (Black Valley) beloved by George Sand *(p 145)*. It is a dark green countryside of wooded farmland that the "good woman of Nohant" described in the majority of her novels. Only the old castle keep recalls the fact that the town had a military origin and was a Roman encampment (*castrum* = La Châtre).

■ SIGHTS *time: 1 hour*

The George Sand and Black Valley Museum (Musée George-Sand et de la Vallée Noire). – *71 Rue Venose. Open Palm Saturday to 15 October, 9.30 to 11.30am and 2 to 5.30pm; the rest of the year, 3 to 6pm; closed Sunday mornings and Thursdays; 5F.*

The museum is in the keep of Chauvigny Castle. On the first floor is a full documentation of George Sand and her guests at Nohant, including portraits, letters, first editions, novels and mementoes of her personal friends.

On the second floor are pictures, drawings and watercolours done by artists visiting La Châtre and the *Vallée Noire*. There is also a good collection of the head-dresses *(coiffes)* once worn in Bas-Berry.

On the third floor there is an ornithological collection of nearly 3 000 birds. On the next floor two rooms contain the works of the painter-engraver B. Naudin.

From the top of the tower there is a view of the *Vallée Noire* and beyond, stretching away to the rolling horizon.

Old Quarter. – From the old humpbacked bridges that cross the Indre there is a charming picture of old-style houses and former tanneries with porches and wooden balconies. More old houses may be seen in other parts of the town.

EXCURSIONS

Tour of the George Sand countryside. – *74 km - 46 miles – about 3 hours – local map p 85.* The tour enables the visitor to see where she lived and the countryside which served as a background to the novels which drew their inspiration from Berry folklore. Though the location of the *Mare au Diable* (Devil's Marsh) is no longer known and the *Moulin d'Angibault* (Angibault Mill) has lost most of its atmosphere other places retain the character they had last century. The countryside the novelist so enjoyed describing has not changed, "vivid and sombre in colour... the melancholy far distant views".

Leave La Châtre by the D 940. At Thevet-St-Julien take the D 69 to the left, before turning right onto the D 68.

La Berthenoux. – Pop 539. The vast 12C church *(closed Tuesdays)* is dominated by a square belfry crowning a fine dome resting on squinches. The capitals at the transept crossing are adorned with carved figures, animals and foliage.

The D 72 then the D 69 lead to St-Chartier.

St-Chartier. – Pop 561. Interesting small church and château (restored in the 19C).

Take the D 918 and the D 51ᴰ to return to Nohant.

Nohant Château. – *Description p 145.*

Vic. – *Description p 187.*

The D 69 and the D 38 then follow the course of the green valley of the Indre.
A forest clearing beside the D 38 was probably the site of the marsh known as the Mare au Diable, after which George Sand named one of her novels.

Turn round to cross the Indre and reach the D 19.

Lys-St-Georges. – Pop 171. The castle, whose towers rise straight up out of the moat, combines the architectural severity of a mediaeval fortress with the charm of the Renaissance. From the terrace *(visitors are allowed up to the postern but not across the moat)* you will see the 15C façade and the Gourdon valley.

Beyond Lys-St-Georges the D 74 goes through a countryside of wooded farmland.

Neuvy-St-Sépulcre. – *Description p 145.*

The D 51 wends through a green countryside.

Sarzay. – Pop 320. A proud feudal domain where the tall round towers have tiled roofs. Blanchemont Castle in George Sand's novel *Le Meunier d'Angibault* (The Angibault Miller) is based on Sarzay Castle. *Guided tours 1 April to 30 September, 10 to 11.20am and 2 to 6.20pm; closed Tuesdays; time: 1/2 hour; 8F.*

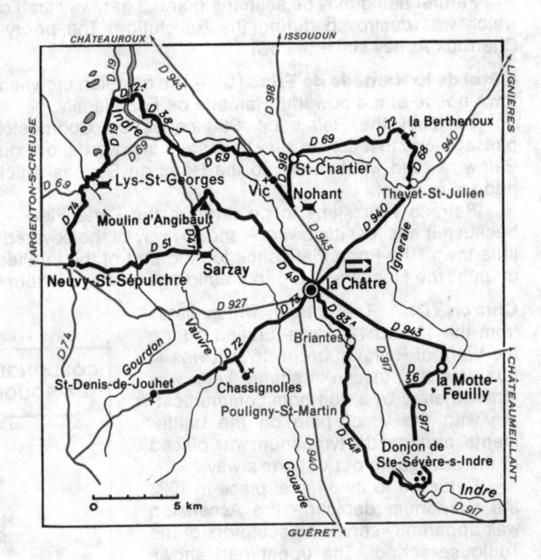

Beyond the now idle Angibault Mill (Moulin d'Angibault), which stands on the Vauvre (a tributary of the Indre), take the D 49 to return to La Châtre.

Ste-Sévère-sur-Indre. – *Round tour of 26 km - 16 miles – about 1 1/4 hours – local map opposite.*

Leave La Châtre by the D 83ᴬ. The country road first follows the Indre valley, then after Briantes, enters a countryside of green pastures.

Ste-Sévère-sur-Indre. – Pop 1 056. *Facilities p 38.* The ruins of the keep look down on the fertile valley of the Indre. In Market Square there is an old 17C covered market and a 15C fortified gateway.

Go north along the D 917 for 6 km – 3 miles then bear right into the D 36.

La Motte-Feuilly. – Pop 44. In the church is a mutilated tomb of Charlotte d'Albret, wife of Cesare Borgia. The 15C castle, like that of Briantes, is described by George Sand in her novel *Les Beaux Messieurs de Bois-Doré.*

Return to La Châtre by the D 943.

Chassignolles; St-Denis-de-Jouhet. – *16 km - 10 miles to the southwest – local map above. Leave La Châtre by the D 73 then take the D 41 to the left.*

Chassignolles. – Pop 567. The church is crowned by a large belfry-tower. A small Renaissance door with an emblazoned pediment, opens into the north transept.

Return to the D72 and turn left onto it.

St-Denis-de-Jouhet. – Pop 1 289. The Gothic church has a shingle covered steeple.

CHÉNÉRAILLES

Michelin map 73 fold 1 – Pop 701

An interesting early 14C **high relief★** on a tomb, said to be that of Barthélemy de la Place who founded the 13C church, may be seen in the third bay on the south side. The relief, carved in a hard white limestone consists of three friezes one above the other: on the lowest are funeral scenes, on the second the Virgin and Child and at the top, the Crucifixion.

EXCURSIONS

Villemonteix Castle. – *3 km - 2 miles to the west.* This 15-16C castle has pepper-pot roofs. *Not open to the public.*

Gouzon. – Pop 1 492. *10 km - 6 miles to the northeast by the D 997.* The church, topped by a curious small shingle covered belfry, has two beautiful doorways ornamented with mouldings and slender columns whose capitals form a frieze.

Gourmets...

The country's gastronomic specialities and fine wines are described on page 20.
Each year the Michelin Red Guide France proposes
a revised selection of establishments renowned for their cuisine.

COLLONGES-LA-ROUGE ★

Michelin map 75 south of fold 9 – 2 km - 1 mile northwest of Meyssac – *Local maps pp 70 and 94* – Pop 379 – *Facilities p 38*

Collonges "the red", built of red sandstone, has set its small manors, old houses and Romanesque church in a green countryside where vines and walnuts grow. The great officers of state of the Viscounty of Turenne relaxed in this city.

■ SIGHTS *time: 3/4 hour*

Leave the car near the old station (no cars allowed in the town between 1 June and 15 September) and follow the route marked on the plan below.

The Siren's House (Maison de la Sirène) (N). – This 16C corbelled house, with a porch and a beautiful stone roof, is adorned on the corner facing the Rue de la Barrière with the figure of a Siren holding a lute.

Farther along may be seen the pointed gateway arch of a former Benedictine priory, which was destroyed during the Revolution. The priory had been a dependency of Charroux Abbey since the 8C.

Hôtel de la Ramade de Friac (B). – The mansion crowned by two turrets was the former town house of the powerful Ramade de Friac family.

Go past the Relais de St-Jacques de Compostelle and through a covered passage-way to reach an alley and, soon afterwards, on your right, an old turreted house. Below, a road winds down to the Hôtel de Beuges which has a fortified turret with a pepper-pot roof.

Retrace your steps to go through the Porte Plate – the Flat Gateway, so called because it has lost its towers – and, by way of the covered markets, to the centre of this little town. The Porte Plate once formed part of the fortified perimeter wall guarding the church, the cloisters, the priory buildings and a few houses.

Church (D). – The church, which dates from the 11 and 12C, was fortified during the Wars of Religion in the 16C. It was at this time that the great square keep was strengthened by a gunroom communicating with the watch-path on the battlements, and that the tympanum was placed in the new gable out of harm's way.

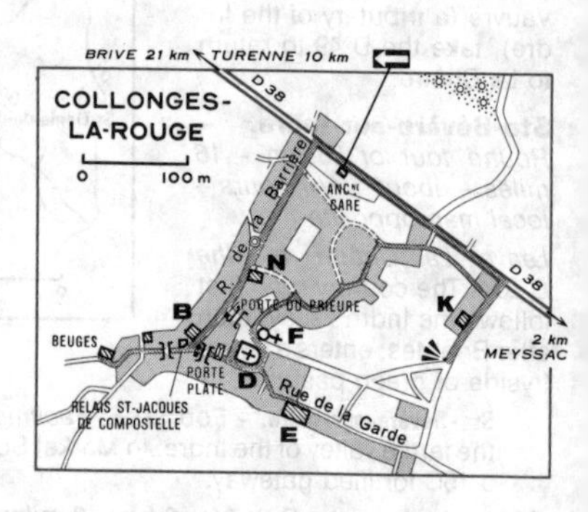

Returned to its original place in 1923 the tympanum depicting the Ascension was apparently carved by sculptors of the Toulouse school. The upper part shows the haloed figure of Christ holding the Gospels in one hand, the other raised in benediction. Christ is surrounded by angels.

The lower part of the tympanum shows, below graceful blind arcades, the Virgin and the Apostles.

The 12C belfry is in the Limousin style *(p 28)*: two lower square storeys pierced with round arched bays are surmounted by two storeys octagonal in shape and flanked by gables. The belfry covers the transept crossing where, inside, you can see four massive 11C columns. The nave covered with groined vaulting in the 14C has three 15C chapels off the north side and is adjoined to the south by a second nave in the Flamboyant style. The square chancel is 13C.

Vassignac Manorhouse (Castel de Vassignac) (E). – This elegant house was owned by Gédéon de Vassignac, lord of Collonges, captain-governor of the Viscounty of Turenne. Built as a manorhouse in 1583 it bristles with large towers and turrets with pepper-pot roofs and though it has many mullioned windows, its defensive role is obvious from its many loopholes and watch-towers.

Former Penitents' Chapel (Ancienne Chapelle des Pénitents) (F). – The chapel was built in the 15C and rearranged by the Maussac Family at the time of the Counter-Reformation in the 17C.

Go round the chapel to the left and shortly afterwards, bear right into a gently winding street through the oldest part of Collonges where you will see old houses ornamented with turrets and balconies and adorned with wisteria and climbing vines.

Maussac Manorhouse (Castel de Maussac) (K). – This building is embellished with turrets and a porch above the main door. A watch-tower projects from the square tower which is overlooked by a dormer window.

This manorhouse was the refuge before the Revolution of the last member of the Maussac family who then left for Italy and was to become the chaplain to Napoleon's sister, Princess Pauline Borghese.

Continue further south along the road to enjoy a pretty **view** of Collonges.

CORRÈZE Valley

Michelin map 75 folds 8 and 9 – *Local maps pp 70 and 181*

The Corrèze rises in the Monédières Massif and cuts a deep valley through the Limousin granite. It is the principal artery of the department which has taken its name and flows through the towns of Tulle and Brive before joining the Vézère.

Upstream from Tulle the D 23 enables the visitor to discover the characteristic scenery of the Corrèze valley, although here it is somewhat enclosed *(see p 181: Excursions from Tulle).*

From Tulle to Brive – *32 km - 20 miles – about 1 1/2 hours*

Leave Tulle (p 179) by ⑤, the N 89 which follows the right bank of the Corrèze.

As the road leaves the town it passes near the «Champ des martyrs» – the Martyrs' Field on which stands a memorial to the ninety-nine young men hanged at Tulle on the 8 and 9 June 1944. The valley soon narrows between high wooded slopes strewn with rocks; gneiss quarries are worked on the right bank of the river. Here and there the valley widens out again into flat meadowland. The road follows the course of the swiftly flowing river fairly closely. Beyond Pont-de-Cornil there is a view of the small church of Cornil and of its ruined castle on the left.

15 km - 9 miles from Tulle, cross the river and go through a tunnel to take the D 130 on the left to Aubazines.

Aubazines★. – *Description p 47.*

Take first the D 48 then the N 89.

Past the Aubazines station the valley slopes become less steep and the road leaves the river's edge on the approach to Brive *(p 68)* which is surrounded by large-scale industrial development.

COUSSAC-BONNEVAL Castle ★

Michelin map 72 folds 17 and 18 – 12 km - 8 miles east of St-Yrieix

The battlemented towers of Bonneval Castle rise on a height overlooking the village of Coussac in a typically Limousin countryside where fields divided by small streams alternate with quickset hedges and chestnut coppices. It is the native hearth of the Bonneval family.

Achmet-Pasha. – Claude-Alexandre was born in Bonneval Castle in 1675 and at an early age showed his desire to be a fighting man. He fought in the Italian Campaigns (1701-1706) then offered his services to the Austrian Emperor, becoming a general in the army. After a personal quarrel he again became a soldier of fortune, this time in the lands of the Ottoman Empire. He offered his talents to the Turkish ruler, reorganised the Turkish Army and led it in decisive victories against the Austrians. He was by this time a general in the artillery and took the title of Achmet-Pasha, "Pasha of the three tails", an honour which gave him precedence over ordinary pashas. But in spite of all his efforts he was never able to return to France and died in Constantinople at the age of seventy-two.

TOUR *time: 1/2 hour*

Guided tours from 2.30 to 6pm; 9F.

The castle was built in the middle of the 14C and was altered inside in the 18 and 19C. The plan is square with an inner courtyard: the corner towers are crowned with machicolations and topped with pepper-pot roofs; the keep and the Devil's Tower (Tour du Diable) adjoin another tower.

Inside the castle there are furnishings dating from the period of the Renaissance to the Directory (16C to the end of 18C). Remarkable tapestries and Louis XVI woodwork, portraits, engravings and contemporary documents recall the life of Bonneval-Pasha.

CREUSE Valley ★

Michelin map 68 fold 18

The Creuse, with the granite slopes of the Massif Central behind it, has cut a picturesque course between Fresselines and Argenton. The variation of agricultural and wild landscapes, the grandiose ruins that mark the river banks, the artistic and literary associations of the area add to the enjoyment of a stay in the valley.

The Creuse nearly always flows at the bottom of a ravine, hence its name (*creuser* = to dig). It derives from a great many streams that rise on the Millevaches Plateau 900 m - 2 952 ft up; the river, thus formed, flows through a succession of rocky gorges and narrow basins, describing a great circular sweep as its waters flow past the old cities of Felletin, Aubusson and Moutier-d'Ahun. At Fresselines the main stream is joined by the waters of the petite Creuse and begins the major part of its journey. For miles the river flows through the reservoir behind the Éguzon Dam, before being confined once more by a series of gorges until it reaches Argenton. Below the town the valley of the Creuse widens out and the river, now full and calm after its 240 km - 150 miles journey, flows into the Vienne.

Painters. – The rocks on the valley slopes, the attractive villages, the romantic ruins perched high above the river have long attracted artists. Crozant and Gargilesse were the favourite spots of a whole colony of painters, including such names as Théodore Rousseau and Claude Monet.

Writers. – To **George Sand** above all must go the credit of making the Creuse known. The valley was the setting for many of her novels: "The Creuse in April is perhaps the most beautiful river in the world", she wrote in *Laura*; in *Promenades autour d'un Village* she even found the beauties of mountain scenery in the hills beside the Creuse: "It is true that the beauty is not obvious and of small proportions, but there are great sweeps and views and the graceful and subtle folds in the landscape are infinitely satisfying..."

Maurice Rollinat the poet and Gabriel Nigond the local writer, have sung of the Creuse with its manorhouses and melancholy heaths fired by the broom and heather in flower.

From Argenton to Fresselines

73 km - 45 miles – about 3 hours – local map below

Leave Argenton (p 46) by ③, the D 913. Once outside the town, the road follows the course of the Creuse valley through an undulating region where farms stand alone surrounded by crops and meadows.

At La Prune bear left towards Céaulmont.

Céaulmont. – Pop 628. To the right of the road, in a meadow, a lovely little Romanesque church clings to the edge of a spur. Go round it from the south side to enjoy a fine **view★** of a loop made by the Creuse and in the distance of the Marche and Combraille plateaux.

Follow a small road which slopes down to the Creuse and cross the river on the first bridge you come to going in the direction of Le Menoux.

Take the D 48 to the right.

Follow the road as it winds uphill and bear right into a narrow road which runs close to the swift waters of the Creuse and leads to the small Roche-Bat-l'Aigue dam.

La Roche-Bat-l'Aigue. – A small dam, an overfall and a stretch of water are enclosed between rocks and high wooded slopes.

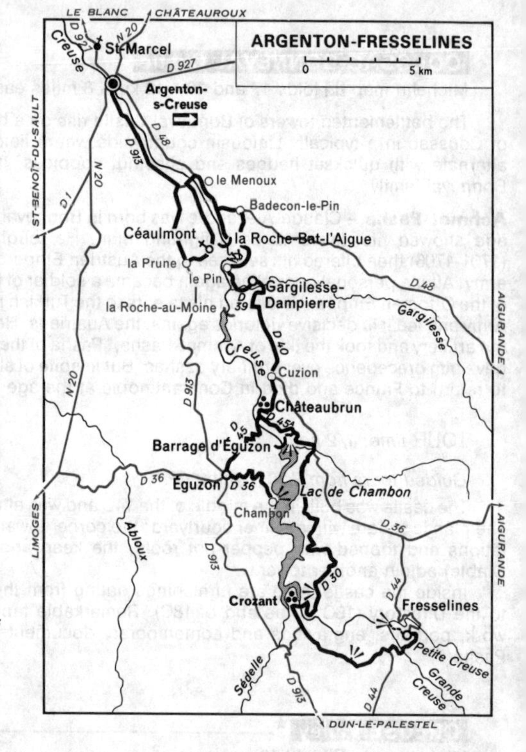

As you come out of Les Chocats you get a good **view★** of the **Le Pin meander**, a wide bend made by the Creuse in an amphitheatre of rocks and hills. In the foreground and within the bend is a chequer-board of fields and meadows outlined with quickset hedges. On the opposite side of the river, above a high promontory stands the Romanesque Church of Céaulmont.

After Le Pin the road, which is very beautiful, next drops down into the Creuse Gorges, follows the smiling Gargilesse valley and finally reaches Gargilesse-Dampierre.

Gargilesse-Dampierre. – *Description p 106.*

On leaving the village of Cuzion take the small road on the right.

Châteaubrun. – The massive towers of Châteaubrun, a fortress built in a picturesque setting overlooking the valley in the 12C by Hugues de Lusignan, inspired George Sand to describe this wild country in two of her novels. *Le Péché de Monsieur Antoine* and *Les Maupral.*

Return to the D 45 and cross the river at Pont-des-Piles.

Éguzon. – Pop 1 466. Éguzon was formerly a fortified town.

Chambon Lake (Lac de Chambon). – In a beautiful setting this great stretch of water contained by the Éguzon Dam makes a good water sports centre.

Return to Pont-des-Piles, cross the river and take D 45 A, which will bring you, after a power station, near the belvedere above the Éguzon Dam.

Éguzon Dam (Barrage d'Éguzon). – The dam came into service in 1926 and was one of the earliest of the really large dams to be built in Europe. It is 60 m - 197 ft high and 300 m - 984 ft long at the crest; the reservoir goes back (15 km - 9 miles) to the confluence of the Sédelle and the Creuse, where the two stretches of water reach out on either side of the ruins of Crozant Castle. The power station produces about 98 million kWh a year.

From a belvedere above the dam, reached from the D 45A on the right bank, there is a good view of the dam in its **setting★**, the reservoir receding into a landscape of hills and rocks and, downstream, of the valley of the Creuse.

The Creuse emerges from Chambon Lake and continues beside the road in the long climb to Crozant.

Crozant★. – *Description p 89.*

Beyond, a narrow winding road leads to Fresselines, situated not far from the confluence of the two Creuse rivers.

Fresselines. – Pop 846. Maurice Rollinat, the poet, worked and died in this town. A rocky path leads from the church to the confluence of the two Creuse rivers *(1/2 hour Rtn on foot)*, in picturesque surroundings.

CROCQ

Michelin map 73 north of fold 11 – *Local map p 132* – Pop 834

The little town of Crocq with its houses grouped on a hillside, lies at the centre of a pleasant region of woods, fields and pools. At the top of the bluff, looking down on the town is the solid outline of the towers, the last remains of a 12C fortress. It was in this market town in the **Franc Alleu Country**, former dependency of Auvergne, that the peasant revolt of the *Croquants* started in the 17C.

Church. – The church which is situated next to the towers contains, at the end of the north aisle near the narthex, a remarkable **triptych** of painted wood. Its seven panels depict the life of St. Eligius.

From the D 996 south of Crocq, there is a pretty **view** of the town and of the Monts Dore and the Monts Dômes in the distance on a clear day.

CROZANT ★

Michelin map 68 fold 18 – *Local map p 88* – Pop 732 – *Facilities p 38*

The massive Crozant Fortress, known as "the key to the Limousin", rises, still impressive though in ruins, from a rocky promontory commanding the confluence of the Creuse and the Sédelle.

Crozant which is said to have been founded in the 6C, was one of the most powerful and also one of the largest strongholds in the centre of France during the Middle Ages. It measured 450 m - 490 yds in length; the ramparts were more than half a mile round with ten towers to defend them, six facing the Creuse, four the Sédelle. Several thousand men formed the garrison for this citadel which belonged for a long period to the counts of Marche and played an important part in the Hundred Years War and the Wars of Religion.

The castle was already in ruins by the 17C when Richelieu ordered it to be dismantled.

Castle Ruins★★. – The most spectacular view of Crozant, the castle ruins and the Creuse valley with the river cutting its way through the ravines, is the one you come on suddenly as you approach from the east along the D 30. The view extends as you descend to the bridge.

Open Easter to 30 September, 9am to 7pm: time: 1/2 hour; 4F; tickets from the Hôtel des Ruines.

The towers which are still standing date from the 10 and 13C. The footpaths will bring you to all that remains of the two perimeter walls. The square keep served as the seignorial living quarters.

On the esplanade which was used as a parade ground, stands the base of the massive tower built by Isabel of Angoulême in the 13C. Other towers line the promontory to its end where only the ground floor of the Tour Colin remains.

Motor-boat trip. – Trip on the Éguzon Reservoir. *Regular services from 14 July to end of August at 2.45, 4 and 5.30pm – minimum 15 people – time: 1 1/2 hours; 21F. Apply to the Hôtel du Lac.*

CULAN ★

Michelin map 69 fold 11 – *Local map p 162* – Pop 1 055

The powerful mediaeval Fortress of Culan stands four square with its massive round towers topped by timber hoardings looking straight down into the Gorges of the Arnon. It was captured by Philip Augustus in 1188, reconstructed in the 13C and considerably altered in the 15C. The lords of Culant received Joan of Arc in the fortress after Orleans had been taken. Louis XI stayed here in May of 1465. The castle was later bought by Sully who subsequently sold it to the Prince of Condé; in the 17C it passed into the hands of Michel Le Tellier, father of the Minister Louvois.

The best view of the castle is from the D 943 coming from Montluçon where the bridge crosses the river: the stark façade, relieved only by its many mullioned windows, rises out of a tangled undergrowth and clings to the rock commanding both the ravine and the road.

Castle★. – *Open 9 to 11.30am and 2 to 6.30pm (5pm 1 October to 31 May; closed in February and on Wednesdays from 1 September to 31 May; time: 3/4 hour ; 12F.*

The apartments contain interesting furniture, fine 15C chimneypieces, old chests and remarkable **tapestries** including 15 and 16C Flemish ones and 17C Aubussons.

After the tour go to the end of the terrace where there is a good view of the Arnon valley.

EXCURSION

St-Désiré. – Pop 503. *11 km - 7 miles to the southeast.* This village on the borders of Bourbonnais, has a remarkable Romanesque **church**★, the remains of a priory built in the 11C.

The chevet has interesting carved brackets. Enter by the belfry porch which was added in the 19C during the restoration of the exterior.

Inside, the purity of the architectural style is striking. The nave, side aisles and arms of the transept are roofed with cradle vaulting while the transept crossing is covered by a dome on pendentives. The elongated chancel, slightly raised is flanked by two-storey high apsidal chapels which open onto the transept.

Stairs on both sides of the chancel, placed under the apsidal chapels lead to the crypt which is rectangular. This is the oldest part of the church; four single columns support the vault.

CUREMONTE

Michelin map 75 north of fold 19 – *Local map p 94* – Pop 231

Curemonte girt by ramparts and with its proud castles and noble mansions covered with flat tiled roofs clustering on a hilltop **site★** can be seen from afar. Its existence is recorded as early as the year 860AD but it is in the 11C that it gained fame coming under the sway of the lords of Turenne. This tranquil village is where the writer Colette lived during the war.

Tour of the Ramparts. – *Leave from the covered market near the church where you will find a plan of the village.* Opposite the market, note the calvary shaft which is adorned with twelve 16C bas-reliefs depicting the life of Jesus. Beyond stands a fine 18C turretted mansion.

The church has a bell gable and contains an 18C altar with a Baroque painted altarpiece.

Bear right behind the church. The perimeter wall in warm-coloured stone, flanked by bastions crowned with pepper-pot roofs, girts the Castle of Le Plas (round towers – 16C), the Castle of St-Hilaire (square battlemented tower – 15C). On the other side of the road stand 16-17C mansions.

In the Place du Château where are several old houses, turn left and walk along the ramparts to enjoy lovely views of the Martel plateau and of the Périgord Noir (Black Périgord).

Beyond the market, on the right, stands the 16C Castle of La Johannie.

DOMME★

Michelin map 75 fold 17 – *Local map p 97* – Pop 910 – *Facilities p 38*

Domme is remarkably situated on a rocky crag overlooking one of the most attractive countrysides of the Dordogne valley. The *bastide* is in the form of a trapezium and not in the more usual rectangle *(p 32)*. The surrounding fortifications have been adapted to the terrain. The houses built in a fine ochre stone, are ornamented with balconies and outside staircases covered with flowers or climbing vines. The remains of the fortifications of which three gateways remain, the panorama to be seen from the Barre Belvedere and the interest of the caves all go to make Domme a most attractive Périgord town.

HISTORICAL NOTES

Captain Vivans' Exploit. – When the struggles of the Reformation were inflaming France, Domme was resisting the Huguenots who were over-running Périgord; the town managed to hold out until 1588. A trick enabled the famous Protestant Captain **Geoffroi de Vivans** to take the town. Followed by thirty soldiers in the middle of the night, he climbed along the rocks that form the barre, a place so precipitous that it had not been thought necessary to fortify it. In silence the group entered the sleeping town. Suddenly, with drums beating and trumpets sounding, the Huguenots shouted and created an infernal row. In the middle of all the stupor and confusion, the attackers opened the tower doors to the waiting army. The inhabitants were not sufficiently wide awake to resist. Vivans became master of the town, installed a garrison, burnt down the church and the Cénac Priory *(p 96)* and established the Protestant faith. Joining the Catholics he sold them the place for 40 000 livres but was careful to dismantle the towers leaving ruins at the appointed hour (10 January 1592).

■ SIGHTS *time: 1 1/2 hours*

Leave from the Place de la Halle and follow the route marked on the plan below.

Pass in front of the church, which was rebuilt in the early 17C and make for the terrace overlooking the Dordogne.

Barre Belvedere (Belvédère de la Barre). – There is a wonderful **panorama★★** from the belvedere. From the foot of the steep rocks on which the town is built, develops a landscape that is typical of the Dordogne valley: the river, with poplars lining the banks, coils through the carefully cultivated plain while a dark line of hills stands out against the horizon. From west to east you notice the remarkable setting of Beynac and La Roque-Gageac, Vitrac Church perched on its rock and the Montfort and Giverzac Castles.

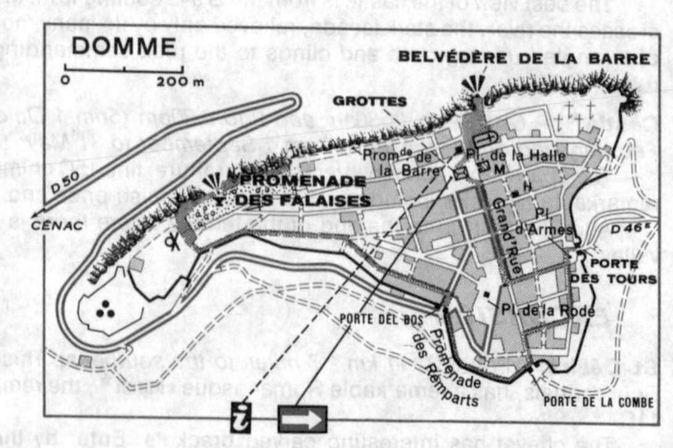

Caves★ (Grottes). – *Open 15 June to 15 September, 9am to noon and 2 to 7pm (6pm out of season); closed 31 October to 1 April; entrance below the covered market (halle); 8F.*

These caves served as refuges for the townspeople of Domme during the Hundred Years War and the Wars of Religion.

So far about 450 m - 490 yds of galleries have been cleared for the public to visit; the chambers are usually small and are sometimes separated by low passages. The ceilings in certain chambers are enriched with quantities of slender white stalactites. There are also places where stalactites and stalagmites join to form columns or piles. The Salle Rouge (Red Chamber) contains eccentrics *(p 16)*. Special lighting enhances the white and ochre colours of the concretions.

Bones of bison and rhinoceros, discovered when the caves were being opened, are displayed where they were found.

Cliff Walk★★ (Promenade des Falaises). – From a small terrace, as you leave the caves, you get a bird's-eye view of the Dordogne valley. At the top of the stairway take a path on the right leading into the public garden with its low wall hugging the cliff as far as a viewing table where you will enjoy an even wider **panorama★★★** than at the Barre Belvedere.

Leave the garden by the gateway and bear right towards the old mill. Go back by the grassy path with its quickset hedges which follows the line of the ramparts.

Rampart Walk (Promenade des Remparts). – When you come to the Porte del Bos, which has a pointed arch and was once closed with a portcullis, bear left to walk on the inner side of the ramparts. In spite of considerable damage the ramparts still have a proud air.

Opposite the Porte de la Combe, turn left towards the town where there are many fine houses to be seen. The beauty of the gold stone and the flat brown tiles is often enhanced by the addition of elegant wrought iron balconies and brightened by climbing vines and flower decked terraces.

Go through the late 13C **Porte des Tours,** the most impressive and best preserved of the town's gateways. *Guided tours: 1 June to 30 September at 11am and 5pm; 5F.* It was flanked on the outside by two massive semicircular bossaged towers. The gateway was defended by a watch-tower of which one can still see the battlements. The towers, now open to the sky, were built by Philip the Fair and originally served as guardrooms. They later held the Templars imprisoned between 1307 and 1318 and various English and French prisoners during the Hundred Years War.

Return by the Place de la Rode and the Grand'Rue to the Place de la Halle.

On the right stands the Governor's Mansion flanked by an attractive turret.

Le DORAT★

Michelin map 72 fold 7 – Pop 2 421

As the seat of the principal seneschalship of Basse-Marche from the 16C to the Revolution, Le Dorat prides itself on possessing one of the most remarkable buildings in Limousin, the Collegiate Church of St. Peter. Only the Porte Bergère, complete with its machicolations, remains of the fortifications built about 1420.

Every seven years the Le Dorat *ostensions (p 37)* give rise to unique ceremonies in which guards of honour take part – sappers and drummers in the uniforms of the First Empire (1804-1814).

■ SIGHTS *time: 3/4 hour*

Collegiate Church of St. Peter★★ (Collégiale St-Pierre). – In about 1100, on the site of a monastery built in the 10C and probably destroyed in the 11C, construction began simultaneously at the east and west ends of a church which after fifty years work bore the appearance we see today.

Exterior. – The collegiate church, which is built in fine grey granite, is striking in size and pleasing in proportion. The façade is surmounted by a squat belfry supported by two bell-turrets and opens with a wide, multifoil doorway showing a Mozarabic influence which was perhaps inspired by the pilgrims who had journeyed to Santiago de Compostela. The doorway's festooned covings bring a gay and original touch, lightening the starkness of the façade.

An elegant octagonal belfry of three tiers of unequal height surmounted by a soaring spire topped by a 13C copper gilt angel, rises above the transept.

From below the Place de l'Église at a former churchyard where the roads from Guéret and Bellac meet, there is a good overall view of the chevet, the arrangement in tiers of the apse, the apsidal chapels and the stone belfries. The central apsidal chapel supports a semicircular tower which formed part of the 15C town's defence system.

Interior. – *Go in by the west door.* From the first bay which has a round dome above, and is twelve steps above the level of the rest of the nave, one is struck immediately by the majesty of the building.

As you walk up the nave the plan of the church becomes apparent. It is in the form of a Latin cross with aisles that widen around the chancel, three apsidal chapels and a chapel branching off each arm of the transept.

The transept crossing, above which rises a tall dome on pendentives, is lit by Romanesque windows. The capitals in the chancel, which are decorated with palm fronds, are remarkable.

Crypt. – *Open weekdays, 8am to noon and 1.30 to 6.30pm (5.30pm, 1 November to 31 March); Sundays and holidays, 8 to 10am, 11am to noon and 1.30 to 5.30pm.*

The crypt is reached from the south arm of the transept. It extends the length of the chancel and resembles it in plan and proportion. This fine 11C sanctuary, dedicated to St. Anne, has columns whose primitive capitals are roughly hewn, one however is sculpted. The apsidal chapel contains fragments of 13C statues.

Sacristy. – This exhibits a multicoloured statue of St. Anne and a *pietà* dating from the 15C and a 13C reliquary cross with two crosspieces, which belonged to the treasure of the collegiate church.

Panorama. – At the Place de la Libération, the former rampart is now a belvedere which overlooks the public garden, Santillana del Mar, and gives a good view of the hills of Limousin beyond.

DORDOGNE Valley ★★★

Michelin map 76 folds 1 and 2 and 75 folds 9, 10, 15 to 19

The Dordogne is one of the longest rivers in France and is said to be the most beautiful. The variety and beauty of the countryside through which the river flows and the architectural glories that mark its banks make the valley a first class attraction for tourists.

A Lovely Journey. – The Dordogne begins where the Dore and the Dogne meet at the foot of the Sancy, the highest peak in the Massif Central. Swift flowing and speckled with foam, it crosses the Mont Dore and Bourboule Basins to leave the volcanic rocks of Auvergne for the granite of Limousin. Between Bort and Argentat, where once the river flowed between narrow ravines, there are now a series of reservoirs and great dams. The river quietens for a short time after Beaulieu, as it crosses the rich plain where it is joined by the river Cère which rises in Cantal. From this point the Dordogne is a great river, though it remains swift and temperamental; the limestone plateaux of Quercy bar its way and so with a pioneering spirit it pierced a passage through the Montvalent Amphitheatre. Once beyond Souillac and on the Périgord plateaux, the river begins to flow past great castles, washing the bases of the rocks on which they stand perched. Below Limeuil, where the river is joined by the Vézère, the valley widens out and after crossing rapids reaches Bergerac and then the Guyenne Plains with their vineyards. At the Ambès spit the Dordogne completes its 500 km - 310 mile journey; it joins the Garonne, which it nearly equals in size, and the two flow on together as the Gironde.

The Caprices of the Dordogne. – The Dordogne flows swiftly in the mountains and the plains, but its volume varies: winter rain storms, the melting of the snows on the Millevaches Plateau and in the Mountains of Auvergne bring floods almost every year which are sudden, violent and sometimes disastrous. Dam construction and other civil engineering projects in the upper valley have enabled the flow to be controlled.

The Days of the Sailing Barges. – For a long time there was river traffic on the Dordogne. A world of sailors and craft lived on the river in spite of the dangers and the stream's uneven flow. The boatmen used flat-bottomed boats known as *gabares* or *argentats* after the town with the largest boat-building yards. These big barges, sailing principally downstream, carried passengers and cargo, especially oak for cooperage, to Bordeaux. The journey was full of the unexpected and the bargees had to be skilled to get their boats through. When they arrived the boats were broken up and sold for timber. Today river traffic plies solely on the lower Dordogne; upstream the only boats to be seen are those of anglers or canoeists.

Water power. – Considerable economic importance has accrued to the river Dordogne with the harnessing of the current. The construction of dams and their dependent artificial lakes besides roads to the new hydro-electric stations has transformed the upper valley and has turned what was once an unknown and barely accessible area into a tourist region.

The harnessing of the upper Dordogne for hydro-electric power was favoured by the volume of the river, usually abundant, and by the impermeability of the granite rocks through which it has eroded a deep channel.

The great dams at Bort, Marèges, L'Aigle, Le Chastang and Argentat provide the energy for large power stations. Similar projects have been carried out on the Dordogne's principal tributaries, the Rhue, the Diège, the Triouzoune, the Danstre, the Maronne, and the Cère, in all there are some twenty-three undertakings within the basin of the upper Dordogne; they are capable of producing on average 2 900 million kWh a year or over 4 % of the electric power produced by all hydro-electric stations of France.

■ THE GREAT DAMS★★

From Bort-les-Orgues to Spontour

93 km - 58 miles – about 4 hours – local map p 93

Here the Dordogne used to flow through narrow gorges. The dams and reservoir lakes which now succeed one another down the valley, forming a gigantic water stairway 100 km - 60 miles long, have altered the appearance of the countryside, however they often fit remarkably well into the beautiful settings. All the same try to avoid the seasons when the waters are low and the lower, erosion-worn slopes are visible.

Bort-les-Orgues. – *See the Michelin Green Guide Auvergne (French edition only). Leave Bort-les-Orgues by the D 979 to the north.* 2 km - 1 mile from Bort, a belvedere has been built to the right of the road *(car park)*. From here there is a **view** of the dam, its lake and Val castle.

5 km - 3 miles from Bort turn left into the D 20 and soon afterwards the D 127.

In St-Julien turn left shortly before the church to the St-Nazaire site *(signposted)* on the edge of a sharp drop down to the Dordogne Gorges *(car park)*.

St-Nazaire Site★★ (Site de St-Nazaire). – *1/2 hour Rtn on foot.* After parking the car, bear right along the ridge of the slope and later follow a path of the Stations of the Cross. Pass a statue to St. Nazarius and make for the end of the promontory across the heather. A Calvary has been erected on the point from which there is a magnificent **view**★★ of the Dordogne and Diège Gorges. *Return to car park.*

Along the bottom of the valley stretches the lake controlled by the Marèges Dam.

Return to St-Julien and there turn left to take first the D 127 and then 2 km - 1 mile farther on the D 20, again on the left. The D 20 crosses the Diège, climbs wooded slopes and, as far as Roche-les-Peyroux provides views of the river.

After Liginiac take the D 42^E on your left then the D 42. From a terrace there is a bird's-eye view of the gorges and Marèges Dam below. The road continues to drop in hairpin bends (500 m - 547 yds further) – a belvedere affords a second view – down to the power station.

Marèges Dam. – The dam is impressive. The steep road ends at the power station. *Turn the car round and by way of the D 42, rejoin the D 20 and turn left.*

Puy de Manzagol. – *2 km - 1 mile.* 800 m - 900 yds from the junction of the D 42 and the D 20, a road on the right, the D 183, leads to the summit from where there is a vast **panorama** of the Neuvic-d'Ussel Dam and the Massif Central *(viewing table).*

Turn back and take the D 183 to the right.

Neuvic Lake. – The D 183 and then the D 982 on the left skirt the beautiful lake into which flow the waters of the Triouzoune, a tributary of the Dordogne from the north, contained by the Neuvic d'Ussel dam.

Neuvic. – Pop 2 274. *Facilities p 38.* This attractive village built on the hillside has a beach with a sailing school and a centre for water skiing.

Return to the D 20 and go up to the crest of Neuvic d'Ussel dam.

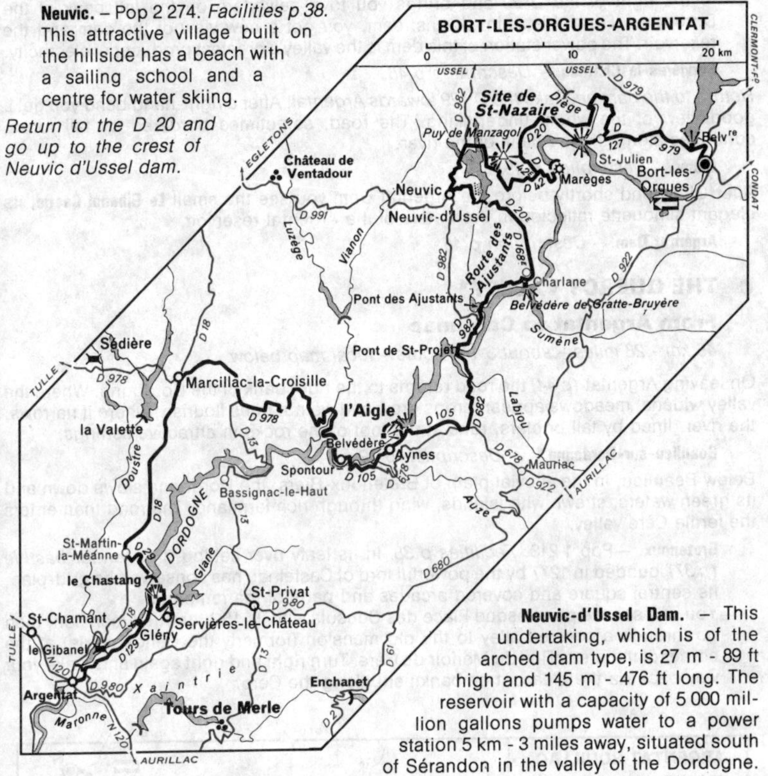

Neuvic-d'Ussel Dam. – This undertaking, which is of the arched dam type, is 27 m - 89 ft high and 145 m - 476 ft long. The reservoir with a capacity of 5 000 million gallons pumps water to a power station 5 km - 3 miles away, situated south of Sérandon in the valley of the Dordogne. After supplying the power station (annual output of about 45 millions kWh) the Triouzoune waters go to serve the L'Aigle Dam.

Return to the crossroads and turn right into the D 20 E. Shortly after Sérandon bear right into the D 168 E.

After Charlane the **Ajustants Tourist Road★** (Route Touristique des Ajustants) follows the Dordogne valley with its rock strewn and wooded slopes.

Gratte-Bruyère Belvedere. – *To the left below the road.* This is a magnificent point from which to see the Sumène flowing into the Dordogne.

The road, which has been cut out of the side of the rock, provides beautiful views of the L'Aigle reservoir. *Cross the reinforced concrete Pont des Ajustants (bridge) to reach the D 982 which you follow to the left.* At first the road looks down on the L'Aigle reservoir from high up but affords only intermittent views of it. The D 982 crosses to the far bank of the river by the graceful Pont de St-Projet (suspension bridge) which provides a good view of the reservoir, and then goes up the narrow wooded Labiou valley.

Take the D 678 on the right and then turn right again to reach the D 105, which, after Chalvignac, provides beautiful views of the L'Aigle reservoir with its indented shoreline.

L'Aigle Dam★★. – Leave the car opposite the l'Aigle Dam and go on foot up the D 16 to the belvedere built below the dam *(the path lies between two road tunnels).* From the belvedere there is a good view of the dam as a whole and the valley below it.

The dam impresses by its size and the boldness of concept. Two "ski-jump" flood control gates can let through 880 000 gallons a second.

Return to the left bank and the D 105 which is now laid out as a *corniche* road and provides views from different angles of the L'Aigle Dam.

Aynes. – The granite houses with their slate roofs are grouped round the chapel.

After going through Aynes and crossing a bridge over the Auze, bear right into the D 978 which runs beside the Le Chastang Dam reservoir as far the Pont de Spontour (bridge).

From Spontour to Argentat

60 km - 37 miles – about 2 1/2 hours – local map above

There is no road beyond Spontour that runs beside the river and a long detour has to be made before you rejoin the Dordogne at the Le Chastang Dam.

For a few miles after Spontour the D 978 runs beside the river as it bends in an enclosed part of the valley. This good but winding road then climbs up to the plateau. Branching off the D 978, the D 13, affords good views, between La Chapeloune and Bassignac-le-Haut and particularly from the suspension bridge, of the Le Chastang reservoir.

Marcillac-la-Croisille. – Pop 777. This small village on the granite plateau grew at the point where Roman roads met. It is situated near La Vallette Lake and Meyrignac with its recreation facilities.

Take the D 18 across the plateau, then at St-Martin-la-Méanne the D 29 which winds down into the valley again and skirts the steep cliffs towards Le Chastang dam.

Le Chastang Dam★. – This great dam is 85 m – 280 ft high and 300 m – 985 ft along the crest. Less than a mile beyond the dam a narrow winding path *(signposted)* leads off to the right of the D 29 and brings you to a belvedere on the left bank of the Dordogne. From this point downstream, you get a new view of the dam and the reservoir. The power station of this dam is the valley's greatest producer of electricity.

Servières-le-Château. – *Description p 45.*

Return to the dam and take the D 129 towards Argentat. After a right-hand bend you get a good view of the whole undertaking. The road, sometimes bordered by tall rocks, continues along the left bank of the river.

Glény. – *Description p 45.*

After Glény and shortly before the Argentat Dam you see the small **Le Gibanel Castle**, its elegant silhouette reflected in the waters of the Argentat reservoir.

Argentat Dam. – *Description p 45.*

THE QUERCY VALLEY★

From Argentat to Carennac

45 km - 28 miles – about 3 1/2 hours – local map below

On leaving Argentat *(p 44)* the road returns to the right bank of the Dordogne. Where the valley widens, meadows appear, crops grow and walnut trees flourish; where it narrows, the river, lined by tall poplars, runs at the foot of the rocks in attractive settings.

Beaulieu-sur-Dordogne★. – *Description p 49.*

Below Beaulieu, in the alluvial plain of Bretenoux-Biars, the Dordogne slows down and its green waters, strewn with islands, wind through rich farmland. The road then enters the fertile Cère valley.

Bretenoux. – Pop 1 213. *Facilities p 38.* In its leafy river setting, this former *bastide (p 37)* founded in 1277 by the powerful lord of Castelnau has conserved its grid-plan, its central square and covered arcades and parts of the ramparts.
You can see the picturesque Place des Consuls with its 15C turretted mansion, then go through a covered alley to the old mansion (formerly the Gendarmerie) at the corner of the pretty Rue du Manoir de Cère. Turn right and right again and make your way back via the pleasant embankment along the Cère.

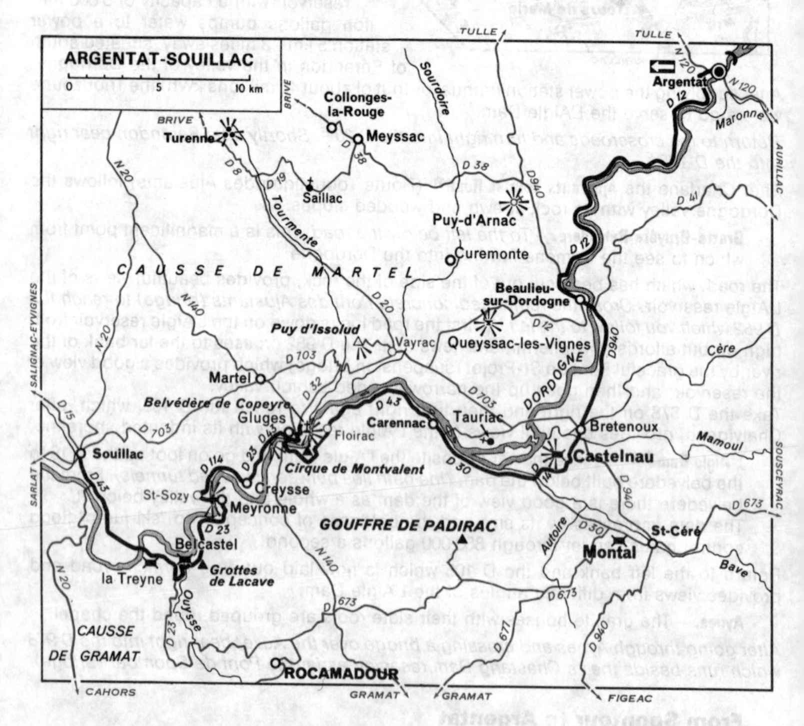

The river receives the waters of the Cère before passing within sight of the impressive mass of Castelnau Castle.

Castelnau Castle★★. – *Description p 77.*

Downstream from Castelnau the Bave tributary joins the Dordogne which divides into several streams flowing in a wide valley bounded to the south by the cliffs of the Causses or limestone plateaux.

Carennac★. – *Description p 76.*

From Carennac to Souillac

42 km - 26 miles – about 4 hours – local map p 94

Beyond Carennac the Dordogne cuts a channel between the Causses or limestone plateaux of Martel in the north and Gramat in the south and enters the beautiful area of the Montvalent Amphitheatre.

Montvalent Amphitheatre★ (Cirque de Montvalent). – The road is picturesque, running for the most part beside the river, though sometimes rising in a *corniche* above it. There are attractive views of the valley and the plateau cliffs.

Cross the Dordogne to reach the Copeyre Belvedere.

Copeyre Belvedere★. – There is a good **view**★ of the Dordogne and the Montvalent Amphitheatre from a rock on which stands a Calvary beside the D 32. The Dordogne can be seen at the foot of the cliffs describing a wide arc through pastures divided by lines of poplars; in the distance, on the left to one side of the river, is the Puy d'Issolud and on the right, on the other side, the village of Floirac.

Turn round and follow the right bank of the Dordogne.

Gluges. – This village lies along the river at the foot of the cliffs in a beautiful **setting**★. The former road crosses the village with its old houses.

The road then rises winding around a tall overhanging ochre-coloured cliff.

Creysse. – Pop 248. The charming village of Creysse with pleasant narrow streets, brown tiled roofs, houses approached by flights of steps and bedecked with climbing vines, lies at the foot of the rocky spur on which stands the pre-Romanesque church, the former chapel of the castle with its curious twin apses. You reach the church and the remains of the nearby castle by a stony alleyway which climbs sharply to a pleasant terrace. It is from a little square shaded by plane trees and near the war memorial that you get the best general view of the village.

Beyond Creysse the road follows the willow bordered bank as far as St-Sozy and then crosses the river by the suspension bridge at Meyronne.

Meyronne. – Pop 201. There is a pretty **view**★ of the river and the village picturesquely built into the cliffs, from the bridge over the Dordogne.

The road subsequently follows the course of the Dordogne through a beautiful countryside of rocks and cliffs, then crosses the river Ouysse near Lacave.

Lacave Caves★. – *Description p 114.*

Belcastel Castle. – A vertical cliff dropping down to the confluence of the Ouysse and the Dordogne is crowned by a castle standing proudly in a remarkable **setting**★. The eastern part of the main wing and the chapel only date from the Middle Ages; most of the other buildings were reconstructed last century. The chapel and terraces are open to the public. From the terraces there is a bird's eye view of the Ouysse and the Dordogne *(apply to the owner to visit in summer).*

Follow the D 43 to the next bridge.

La Treyne Château. – *Not open to the public.*
La Treyne Château stands perched on a cliff that rises perpendicularly above the left bank of the Dordogne.

The road then crosses the Dordogne, to run along the right bank to Souillac (p 177).

La Treyne – The Château and the Dordogne.

■ THE PERIGORD VALLEY★★★

From Souillac to Sarlat

29 km - 18 miles – about 1 1/2 hours – local map p 96

Leave Souillac (p 177) to the west by the D 703.

Subtle differences only distinguish the countryside of Quercy from that of Périgord Noir, through which the Dordogne flows below Souillac. The river is calmer and its meanders, separated only by narrow rock channels, form a series of rich basins. Peaks crowned with dark trees ring the horizon.
The road crosses the well cultivated alluvial plains, surrounded by wooded hills and follows the river bordered with poplars – a typical Périgord valley scenery.

At Rouffillac bear left, cross the Dordogne and at St-Julien-de-Lampon turn right towards Ste-Mondane.

Fénelon Castle. – *Guided tours 10 to 11.30am and 2 to 6.30pm (5.30 pm out of season); 12F; time: 1/2 hour.*
It was in this castle which belonged to the Salignac-Fénelon family from the 15C to the 18C, that Fénelon, the future Bishop of Cambrai, was born in 1651 and spent his childhood *(p 76).*

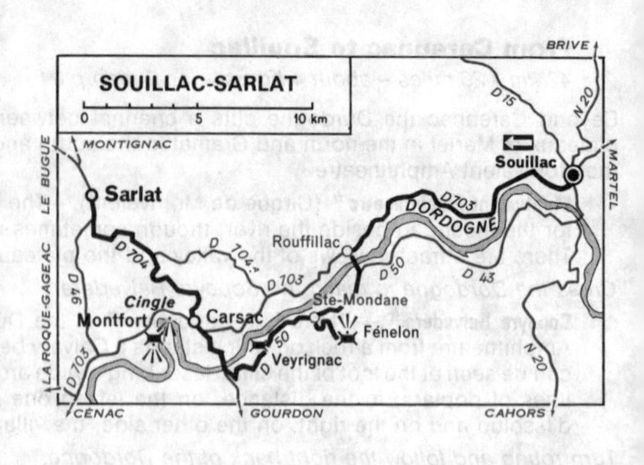

This noble edifice, built in the 13-15C has kept its military bearing – outer walls flanked with towers to protect the approach to the terrace on which the castle itself stands and from where there is a nice panorama. The entrance façade, modified in the 17C, has a horseshoe shaped flight of steps leading up to the cloisters and courtyard by the former drawbridge. You may visit the chapel and a room displaying memorabilia from Fenelon's era. There is also a collection of vintage cars. *(The apartments are not open to the public).*

Veyrignac Château. – *Guided tours 1 July to 15 September, 10 to 11.30am and 2 to 6.30pm; 13F; time 1/2 hour.*
This 17C château has been restored since it was burnt down by the Germans in 1944. From a terrace in the park there is a fine **view** of the Dordogne.

After Veyrignac, cross back to the right bank of the river.

Carsac. – Pop 950. The modest but delightful church of Carsac, built in a lovely golden stone, stands in a country setting not far from the Dordogne. The porch in the façade has five lines of covings resting on small columns. The massive Romanesque belfry and the apse are roofed with stone. The nave and the aisles have elegant keystones; the bay of the chancel has rounded barrel vaulting. A small dome on pendentives rises above the transept crossing; the chancel ends in a Romanesque apse with oven vaulting and is adorned with interesting archaic oriental-style capitals. Gothic chapels are situated on either side of the nave and at the entrance to the chancel. There are strikingly modern **stained glass windows** and a **Stations of the Cross** by Zack. The Stations are arresting for their primitive style and philosophical austerity; the texts are taken from the writings of Paul Claudel (diplomat and writer: 1868-1955).

At Carsac, join the D 704, which runs along the bottom of a valley to Sarlat (p 174).

From Sarlat to St-Cyprien

61 km - 38 miles – about 4 hours – local map p 97

This trip is the most attactive in Périgord. Great rocks rise up at every step, golden in colour and crowned with old castles and picturesque villages.

Carsac. – *Description above.*

From Carsac onwards the road, which follows the line of the right bank of the Dordogne, overlooks the fine bend of the river known as the Montfort Meander.

Montfort Meander★ (Cingle de Montfort). – There is a good **view**★ of the meander in the Dordogne from a turning *(car park)* in the D 703 which is itself, at this point, built into the rock. The course of the river below is outlined by poplars, while high up on top of the promontory, stands Montfort Castle.

Montfort Castle. – *Not open to the public.* Montfort Castle stands in a picturesque **setting**★. Its exceptional site roused the envy of those who wished to rule Périgord over the centuries and its history is made up of a long series of sieges and battles. In 1214 it was seized by the redoutable **Simon de Montfort** *(p 77)*, who razed it to the ground. It was rebuilt for the first time and then later destroyed three times – during the Hundred Years War (1337-1453), under Louis XI (1461-1483) and again by order of Henry IV (1562-1610). Each time it was destroyed it was rebuilt; the left wing was restored at the end of the 19C and the other buildings date from the 15 and 16C. Grouped at the foot of the castle is the village with its houses roofed with *lauze (p 44).*

Soon after Vitrac, Domme on its rocky promontory comes into view on the left.

Cénac. – Pop 900. The only remaining evidence of the large priory built in Cénac in the 11C is the small Romanesque church which stands outside the village. Even the church did not escape the Wars of Religion, and only the chevet did not suffer the depredations of the Protestants serving under Captain Vivans in 1589 *(p 90).* The short nave and transept were rebuilt in the 19C.
Go into the churchyard to get an overall view of the chevet with its fine stone roof and its column-buttresses topped by foliated capitals. A cornice, decorated with modillions bearing small carved figures, runs round the roof of each apsidal chapel.
Inside, in the chancel and the apse there is a series of interesting **historiated capitals,** which date from 1130. The scenes depicted include Daniel in the Lions' Den, Jonah and the Whale and a showman with his performing monkeys.

Domme★. – *Description p 90.*

There follows the most beautiful part of the whole valley: the Dordogne, lined with poplars, widens out considerably and flows through a mosaic of farmland and meadows. Next come the most extraordinary settings in which towns and castles could be built.

La Roque-Gageac★★. – *Description p 161.*

Castelnaud Castle★. – *Description p 77.*

A short section of road between Castelnaud and Milandes enables the visitor to pass at the foot of **Fayrac Castle,** a fine 15-16C manorhouse bristling with towers with pepper-pot roofs in a leafy setting on the left bank of the Dordogne facing Beynac-et-Cazenac.

Les Milandes Castle. – *Guided tours 1 June to 31 August, 9 to 11.30am and 2 to 6.30pm; Palm Sunday to 31 May and 1 September to early October, 9.30 to 11.30am and 2 to 6pm; 9F.* Built in 1489 by François de Caumont the castle remained the property of this family till the Revolution. More recently the castle was associated with the well known American singer, Josephine Baker or *La Perle Noire* as she was known in her Paris cabaret heyday in the 1920's and 30's. It was here that she achieved her dream of a "village of the world": gathering children of different races, religions and nationalities, bringing them up together to promote mutual understanding.
A spiral staircase gives access to the various floors. In addition to the possessions of the de Caumont family are furniture and effects belonging to Josephine Baker. The castle is surrounded by an attractively arranged garden. From the terrace there is a view of the park.

Return by the same road and cross the river by the Castelnaud bridge to join the D 703 on the right bank of the Dordogne.

Beynac-et-Cazenac★★. – *Description p 55.*

Beyond Beynac the valley does not widen out much before St-Cyprien *(p 168).*

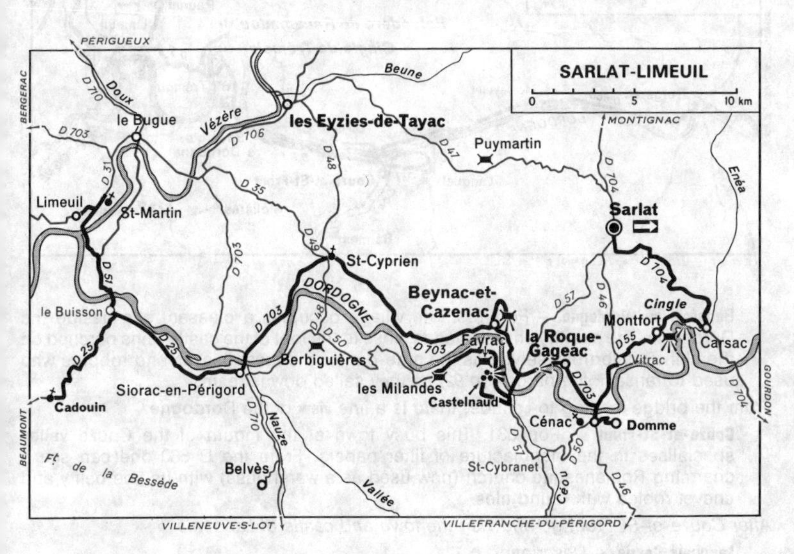

From St-Cyprien to Limeuil

34 km - 21 miles – about 1 1/2 hours – local map above

Below St-Cyprien *(p 168)* the Dordogne runs through an area where meadows and arable fields spread out to the cliffs and wooded slopes marking the edge of the valley.

Siorac-en-Périgord. – Pop 871. *Facilities p 38.* 17C castle and small Romanesque church.

From Buisson go by the D 25 to Cadouin.

Cadouin★. – *Description p 72.*

Return to Buisson from Cadouin and cross the Dordogne in the direction of Périgueux (D 51). On the right bank continue on the D 51 to the left to go to Limeuil. After crossing the Vézère, turn right.

Chapel of St. Martin. – This charming country church was built at the end of the 12C. It stands, encircled by cypresses, beside the D 31.

Turn round and take the road on the right for Limeuil.

Limeuil. – Pop 362. This old village stands in a pretty **setting**★ on a hill facing the confluence of the Dordogne and the Vézère.

From Limeuil to Bergerac

53 km - 33 miles – about 2 1/2 hours – local map p 98

Soon after the confluence of the Vézère and the Dordogne there is a belvedere at a spot known as the Roches Blanches, giving a fine view of the opposite bank.

Paunat. – Pop 217. *2.5 km - 1 1/2 miles from the D 31.* Paunat lies snugly in a small valley near the confluence of the Dordogne and the Vézère. It possesses an impressive Romanesque church *(closed for restoration)* built in fine ochre-coloured stone, which once formed part of a monastery attached to the powerful Abbey of St-Martial at Limoges *(p 117).* The exterior is austere with bare walls and high flat buttresses rising right to the eaves of the roof, which is covered in small tiles. The massive belfry-porch, with a domed chamber seen rarely in the Périgord leads to the vast main part of the church. Inside the long nave has ogive vaulting and the dome at the transept crossing rests on pointed arches.

Return to the D 31.

Trémolat. – Pop 543. This charming village contains a curious Romanesque church. Behind a massive belfry-porch stands the church, a veritable fortress with high bare walls. The interior is Périgord-Romanesque and consists of a single aisle, roofed by a series of domes on pendentives.

When you get to Trémolat follow the "Route du Cingle de Trémolat", the road northwards which rises high above the valley.

Racamadou Belvedere. – From the platform of the water tower there is an outstanding **panorama**★★ of the well-known meander, Cingle de Trémolat.

Tremolat Meander★★ (Cingle de Trémolat). – At the foot of a semicircle of high, bare, white cliffs coils the river, spanned by bridges of golden stone and lined with poplars. Beyond the wonderful stretch of water, which is often used for rowing regattas, lies a vast mosaic of arable fields and meadows; far away on the horizon, are the hills of Bergerac, Issigeac and Monpazier. The colours at sunset have to be seen to be believed.

Return to Trémolat and cross to the left bank of the Dordogne. The valley is dotted with tobacco drying yards.

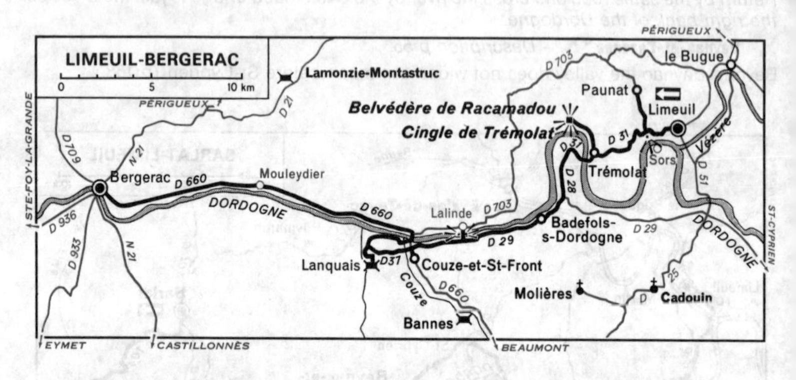

Badefols-sur-Dordogne. – Pop 150. The village occupies a pleasant site beside the Dordogne. The country church stands close to the foot of the castle ruins perched on the cliff. This fortress served as the hide-out for the local thieves and robbers who used to ransack the barges *(p 92)* as they sailed downstream.

From the bridge leading to Lalinde, there is a fine **view** of the Dordogne.

Couze-et-St-Front. – Pop 831. This busy town at the mouth of the Couze valley specialises in the manufacture of filter papers. From the D 660 one can see a charming Romanesque church (now used as a warehouse) with its fine belfry and chevet roofed with round tiles.

After Couze-et-St-Front go and visit the town and castle of Lanquais.

Lanquais Castle. – *Description p 114.*

Turn back, take the D 37 on the left and cross the Dordogne once more.

The D 660 follows the wide alluvial valley down to Bergerac *(p 53)*.

DUN-SUR-AURON

Michelin map 69 folds 1 and 2 – Pop 4 246

Dun, with the Auron river and the Berry Canal flowing on two sides, was once a fortified town. Even the castle has disappeared. It was from a castle window that Constable de Richemont and the Lord La Trémoille hurled Pierre de Giac, favourite of Charles VII, into the Auron.

Church of St-Étienne. – This former collegiate church which was built in the 12 and 13C, and altered in the 15C, stands near an attractive tree-shaded square. The Romanesque chevet shows a Poitou influence and its two radial chapels are supported by small clustered columns surmounted by capitals decorated with interlacing, foliage or scroll-work. The use of Berry limestone and red ironstone enhances the architectural decoration.

EXCURSIONS

Bois-Sir-Amé-Castle. – *10 km - 6 miles to the northwest. Leave Dun by the D 28 and soon after take the D 34 to the right.*

The impressive fortress of Bois-Sir-Amé was built between the valleys of the Cher and the Auron when Charles VII was only King of Bourges. There lived Agnès Sorel, his mistress. It is said, that in this flat countryside, fires lit at night brought news swiftly across the 30 km – 20 miles separating the fortress and Charles' castle at Mehun-sur-Yèvre. Only ruins remain of the fortress of Bois-Sir-Amé that was once quartered by massive towers and encircled by a moat.

Jussy-Champagne Castle. – *13 km - 8 miles to the northwest. Leave Dun by the D 36 and at Jussy turn right into the D 15. An avenue (signposted) leads to the castle.*

Guided tours 25 March to 15 November, 10 to 11.45am and 2 to 6.30pm; 12F.

The castle built of brick and stone, was started in the late 16C and completed in 1646. A covered gallery runs round the main courtyard.

The tour includes the kitchen with pointed vaulting, the chapel and an elegant dining-room with Louis XIV furniture. The drawing rooms are decorated with tapestries and paintings as well as furniture in the Louis XIII, Louis XIV and Regency styles. A canvas entitled "The Magician" by Michel Gobain (G. de la Tour's pupil) and a wall painting of "The Fine Arts" above a doorway from a cartoon by C. Vanloo are noteworthy.

Sagonne Castle. – *23 km - 14 miles to the east. Leave Dun on the D 34.*

Guided tours 1 July to 30 September, 2 to 6pm; closed Mondays; 8F.

This great 14C fortress reflected in the clear waters of a moat surrounding its perimeter wall retains a part of its defensive system. A large keep contains a chapel and a room adorned with mural paintings. Portraits, documents, arms and antique furniture are mementoes of Gabrielle d'Estrees and Mansart.

ENCHANET Dam ★ (Barrage d'ENCHANET)

Michelin map 76 south of fold 1 – *Local map p 93*

The Enchanet Dam describes its graceful curve in the wild setting of the Gorges of the Maronne, a tributary entering the Dordogne from the south.

The dam measures 230 m - 252 yds along the crest and is 68 m - 222 ft high; it is of the slim arched type, inclining downstream. The power station has an annual production of 58 million kWh.

The way down from Enchanet by the D 61 provides a bird's-eye view of the dam and the still waters of the reservoir which is more than 13 km - 8 miles long.

ESPAGNAC-STE-EULALIE

Michelin map 79 fold 9 – *Local map p 125* – Pop 77

In the delightful village built in the centre of a series of cliffs, the houses with their turrets and pointed roofs are grouped round the former priory known as Notre-Dame du «Val-Paradis».

Former Priory of Notre-Dame. – Founded in the 12C by the monk Bertrand de Grifeuille of the Augustinian Order it was attached to the Abbey of La Couronne (near Angoulême). In 1212 the priory became a convent for the Augustinian canonesses and expanded considerably under the ægis of Aymeric Hébrard *(p 79)*, Bishop of Coimbra. In 1283 the convent was moved to avoid flooding from the river Célé. During the Hundred Years War the convent suffered considerably, the cloisters were destroyed and the church was partly demolished. It was rebuilt in the 15C, however, and the community continued till the Revolution. The conventual buildings are occupied by the local school and the presbytery, decorated in the 18C style, occupies the former rooms of the abbess.

(After a photo by Arthaud, Grenoble)

Espagnac-Ste-Eulalie.

Church. – The present Flamboyant style church has replaced a 13C building of which there still remain the walls of the nave, a doorway and jutting out beyond the walls, the ruins of bays which were destroyed during a fire in the 15C. The exterior is peculiar in the pentagonal chevet being higher than the nave and, on the south side, in the belfry *(see illustration above)* being surmounted by a square chamber, built partly of brick and partly of timber, with above this, an octagonal roof of limestone tiles.

Inside, the three tombs with recumbent figures are those of Aymeric-Hébrard of St-Sulpice (d 1295) and of the Knight, Hugues de Cardaillac-Brengues (entombed here in 1342) and his wife. On the high altar, with a 17C gilded wood predella, stands an 18C retable framing a picture of the Assumption, after the painting of Simon Vouet.

ÉVAUX-LES-BAINS

Michelin map 73 fold 2 – Pop 1 906 – *Facilities p 38*

Évaux-les-Bains lies in the heart of Combraille and is a well-known spa, standing at 450 m - 1 500 ft, on a promontory jutting out between the Cher and the Tardes.

The Spa. – The ruins of the Roman baths indicate that the Romans knew the curative powers of the waters of the thirty-odd Évaux springs which pour out radioactive water at a temperature of 14-60 °C (57-140 °F). The thermal baths are now used to cure rheumatism and affections of the veins.

Church of St-Pierre-et-St-Paul. – This fine Romanesque building has an interesting 11-12C belfry-porch whose 13C top storey is octagonal in shape and bears a slim spire covered in shingles.

Pillaged and burnt in the 16C the church was rebuilt in the Gothic style, with the exception of the three arches at the entrance to the chancel, which remained untouched. Damaged in 1942, it has since been restored.

From the little square next to the church there is a good view of the chevet, the stepping of the nave and aisles and of the belfry-porch. The simplicity of line shows to full advantage the beauty of the stone which is a russet-yellow colour.

EXCURSIONS

Chambon-sur-Voueize; Rochebut. – *Round tour of 47 km - 29 miles – about 2 hours – local map below.* Leave Évaux by the D 915 which drops down into the Tardes valley and follows it through a landscape of hills often covered with broom.

Chambon-sur-Voueize. – Pop 1 288. *Description p 81.*

From Chambon go north for 2 km - 1 mile along the D 917.

Voueize Gorges. – The *corniche*-style road overlooks the river which runs between sharp rocks overgrown with trees, bracken and heather.

Turn round when the road leaves the ravines and return to Chambon. The D 993 overlooks the Tardes valley before rising to the plateau on the way to Budelière.

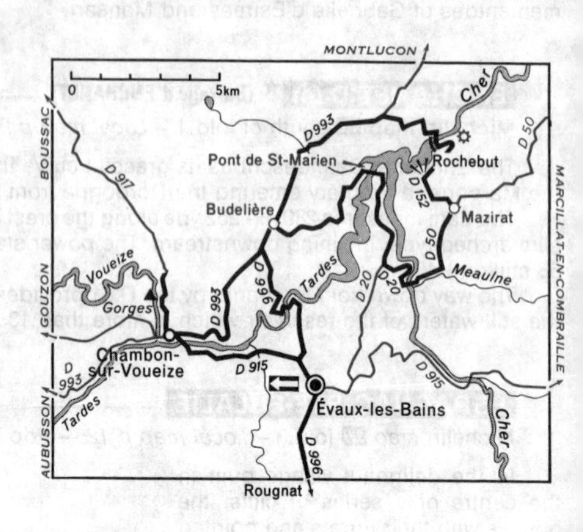

Rochebut Dam. – The dam stands in a pleasant setting of wooded hills. It is built on the Cher below its junction with the Tardes and serves a power station.

The D50 which is picturesque beyond Mazirat, drops down once more into the valley of the Cher. Once over the Cher the V 7 crosses the reservoir by the Pont de St-Marien (suspension bridge); continue by the V 1. After Budelière take to the left the D 996, a winding road which descends rapidly to the Tardes before climbing again to the plateau to reach Évaux.

Rougnat. – Pop 676. *14 km - 9 miles to the south by the D 996.* The church was built in the 12 and 13C. Inside note the fine woodwork and the paintings by the Italian, Giovanni Lombardi (1682-1752).

EXCIDEUIL

Michelin map 75 folds 6 and 7 – Pop 1 584

The last ruins of Excideuil Castle, recalling times when there were viscounts of Limoges and counts of Périgord, crown a hill overlooking the Loue valley.

Castle. – *Not open to the public.*

A curtain wall, one time façade of the feudal castle, links the two keeps, one built in the late 11C and one in the 12C and now practically dismantled. Beside the mediaeval fortress stands a Renaissance mansion complete with turrets and mullioned windows, which once belonged to the Talleyrand family for whom Louis XIII raised Excideuil to the title of marquisate in 1613.

A pleasant walk around the castle *(time: 1/2 hour)* is possible.

EYMOUTIERS

Michelin map 72 fold 19 – Pop 2 635

First a monastery was built on the granite hillock overlooking a bend in the Vienne, then a market village grew up around it. Of the monastery a collegiate church built between the 11 and 15C still remains.

Church. – The nave and belfry-porch are Romanesque. The belfry is square and decorated with blind arcades; the roof is covered with shingles. The contrast between the Romanesque part and the Gothic part – the chancel and the last bays of the nave – is best seen from inside. Enter by the south transept.

This elegant chancel is lit by fifteen clerestory windows containing remarkable stained glass made by the Limousin master glass-makers of the 15C and range in colour through blues and greens to gold and scarlet. There is a great rough-hewn statue of Christ opposite the pulpit.

The church also contains a late 13C reliquary cross, with two cross pieces, which is made up of ten small boxes with pierced hinges *(apply to the priest).*

Les EYZIES-DE-TAYAC ★★

Michelin map 75 fold 16 – *Local maps pp 97 and 186* – Pop 858 – *Facilities p 38*

The village of Les Eyzies stands attractively in a grandiose setting of steep cliffs crowned with evergreen oaks and junipers, at the confluence of the Vézère and the Beune.

The Vézère river, lined on either side by poplars, now winds between meadows and farmland, now narrows to flow beside walls of rock 50 to 80 m - 165 to 260 ft high. Shelters cut out of the bases of these limestone piles served as dwelling places for prehistoric man while the caves, which generally appear half-way up the cliffs, were used as temples in which to practise magic. The discovery within the last hundred years of these dwellings all within a limited distance of Les Eyzies has made the village the capital of prehistory.

THE CAPITAL OF PREHISTORY

The Lower Vézère and the Age of Cave Men. – During the Second Ice Age and in the era when the volcanoes of Auvergne were active, prehistoric man, in the wake of the animals he hunted for food, abandoned the northern plains, where the Acheulean and Abbevillian civilisations had already evolved, for warmer areas to the south. The lower Vézère, whose bed was then some ninety feet above its present level, attracted the migrants because of its forested massifs, its natural caves which were easily accessible, and overhanging rocks which faced the right way and could be hollowed out into shelters more easily than the friable and fissured limestone of the Dordogne valley.

Men lived in these cave dwellings for tens of thousands of years and left in them traces of their times and how they lived such as bones, ashes from their fires, tools, weapons, utensils, pottery and items of decoration. Their civilisation evolved simultaneously with the world around them. Animal species evolved into those we know today: after elephants and bears came bisons, aurochs, mammoths and later still musk-oxen, reindeers, antelopes, ibex, stags and horses.

When the climate grew warmer and rainfall more abundant at the end of the Magdalenian Period, man abandoned the caves for the hillside slopes facing the sun.

The Archaeologists' Paradise. – Methodical study of the deposits in the Les Eyzies region has considerably increased our knowledge of prehistory. In 1863 work began at the Laugerie and Madeleine sites; the discovery of objects such as flints, carved bones and ivory, tombs in which the skeletons had been coloured with ochre and were often buried lying east-west, greatly encouraged the early research workers. In 1868 workmen levelling the soil before laying the Périgueux-Agen railway track unearthed the Cro-Magnon Cave skeletons. Soon afterwards more thorough research in the Moustier and Madeleine Caves enabled two long periods of the Palaeolithic Age to be defined: the periods were called after the cave deposits – Mousterian and Magdalenian *(see text and diagrams pp 21-24)*. Discoveries proceeded apace in prehistoric sites and deposits: La Micoque, Laugerie-Haute, Laugerie-Basse, La Ferrassie (south of Savignac-de-Miremont) and Laussel; in shelters and caves containing hidden carvings and drawings: Cap Blanc, Le Poisson, La Mouthe, Les Combarelles, Bernifal and Commarque; and in caves containing coloured wall paintings: Font-de-Gaume and Lascaux.

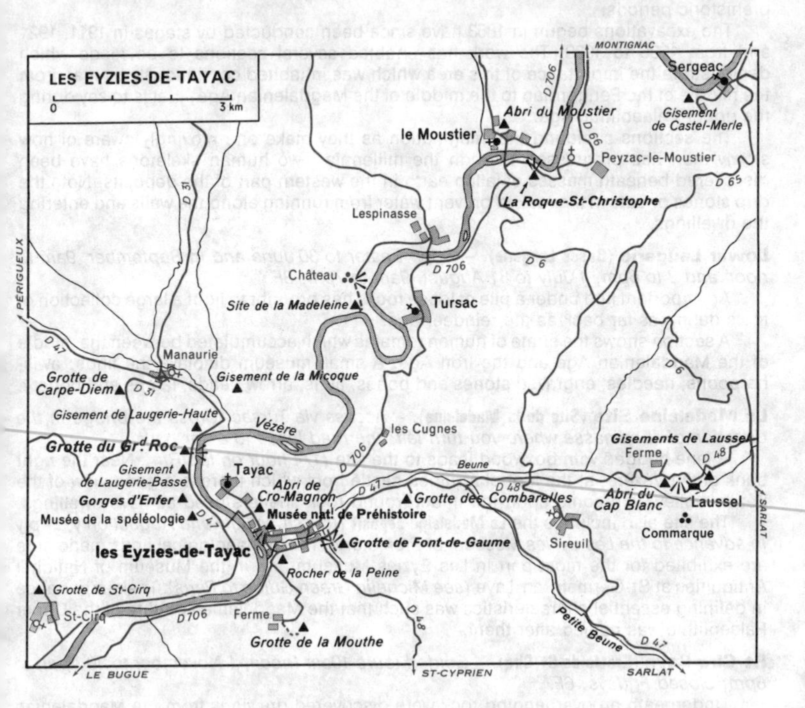

■ **SIGHTS** *local map above*

Prehistoric caves and rock shelters

The Font-de-Gaume Cave★ (Grotte de Font-de-Gaume). – *In season, tickets are sold in the morning only. Guided tours 1 April to 30 September, 9 to 11.15am and 2 to 5.15pm; the rest of the year, 10 to 11.15am and 2 to 3.15pm; closed Tuesdays, 1 January, 1 and 8 May, 1 and 11 November and 25 November to 25 December; 11F.*

Leave the car on the road to St-Cyprien (D 48) opposite a cliff-spur. A path takes you up 440 yds to the entrance to the cave which runs back in the form of a passage 130 yds long with chambers and other ramifications leading off it. The cave has been known for a considerable time, with the result that since the 18C, visitors have left their mark, not recognising the importance of the wall paintings. Detailed examination and study of the paintings date the frescoes as belonging to the Perigordian and Magdalenian Ages. Beyond a narrow passage, known as the *Rubicon*, are many multicoloured paintings, often superimposed on one another: all the drawings of horses, bison, mammoths, reindeer and other deer point to great artistic skill.

Cap-Blanc Rock Shelter (**Abri du Cap-Blanc**). – *Guided tours 1 July to 31 August, 9.30am to noon and 2 to 5pm; the rest of the year apply to the guide (Veyret) at the small village of Grèze; 4F.*

Excavation of a small Magdalenian deposit in 1909 led to the discovery of carvings in high relief on the walls of the rock shelter. Two bisons and particularly a frieze of horses were carved in such a way as to use to full advantage the relief and contour of the rock itself. At the foot of the frieze a human grave was discovered.

Les Combarelles Cave (**Grotte des Combarelles**). – *Guided tours (10 persons maximum) 9 to 11am and 2 to 5pm (3.15pm 1 October to 30 April); closed Tuesdays, 1 January, 1 and 8 May, 1 and 11 November and 25 November to 25 December; 7F; Sundays and holidays: 3.50F.*

A winding passage 275 yds long has on its walls for the last 130 yds of its length, many markings, some superimposed one upon another. The drawings include nearly 300 animals: horses, bison, bears, reindeer and mammoths can be seen at rest or at full gallop. This cave was discovered in 1901 and demonstrated the importance of Magdalenian art at a time when the learned were still sceptical about the worth of prehistoric studies. A second passage with similar cave drawings was the stage on which prehistoric man acted out his life as can be seen from the traces of domestic middens and the tools of Magdalenian men which have been discovered.

The Cro-Magnon Cave (**Abri de Cro-Magnon**). – This cave was discovered in 1868 and revealed in addition to flints and carved bones of the Aurignacian Age, three skeletons of adults which were studied by Paul Broca, the surgeon and anthropologist (1824-1880) who founded the School of Anthropology in France. The discoveries made in this cave were of prime importance in prehistoric studies, since they enabled the characteristics of the Cro-Magnon race to be defined *(p 22)*.

Upper Laugerie Deposit (**Gisement de Laugerie Haute**). – *Northwest of Les Eyzies to the left of the D 47. Guided tours 2 May to 31 October, 9 to 11.30am and 2 to 5.30pm; the rest of the year, 10 to 11.30am and 2 to 3.30pm; closed Tuesdays, holidays and 25 November to 25 December; 6F.*

Scientific excavations going on for nearly a century in a picturesque spot at the foot of high cliffs, have revealed examples of the work and art of the cave men and of other prehistoric periods.

The excavations begun in 1863 have since been conducted by stages in 1911, 1921 and from 1936 to 1939. The work has enabled several sections to be made which demonstrate the importance of this area which was inhabited continuously by man from the middle of the Perigordian to the middle of the Magdalenian Age; that is to say during the upper Palaeolithic Age.

The sections confound the imagination as they make one movingly aware of how slowly man has progressed through the millennia. Two human skeletons have been discovered beneath masses of fallen earth in the western part of the deposits. Note the drip stones or cuts in the rock to prevent water from running along the walls and entering the dwellings.

Lower Laugerie (**Basse Laugerie**). – *Open Easter to 30 June and in September, 9am to noon and 2 to 6pm; 1 July to 31 August, 9am to 7pm; 8F.*

An important find under a pile of loose rocks has brought to light a large collection of tools dating as far back as the reindeer age.

A section shows the strata of human remains which accumulated between the middle of the Magdalenian Age and the Iron Age. A small museum displays the finds: awls, harpoons, needles, engraved stones and bones, flints, arrow heads, lamps and pottery.

La Madeleine Site (**Site de la Madeleine**). – *Access via Tursac. Cross the bridge in the direction of l'Espinasse where you turn left; the road leads to a car park.*

A lane hedged with boxwood leads to the site *(1/4 hour on footRtn)*. Near the right bank of the Vézère, at the foot of a ruined castle from which there is a good view of the Vézère valley, you come upon the underground rock shelters used as cave dwellings.

The site also includes the **La Madeleine deposit** *(to visit, in July and August only, apply in advance to the Les Eyzies Museum of Prehistory)*. The archaeological finds made here are exhibited for the most part in Les Eyzies Museum and in the Museum of National Antiquities at St-Germain-en-Laye *(see Michelin Green Guide to Paris)*. Their importance in defining essential characteristics was such that the Magdalenian culture of the Upper Palaeolithic was named after them.

St-Cirq Cave (**Grotte de St-Cirq**). – *Guided tours 10am (noon, 1 November to 30 April) to 6pm; closed Fridays; 6F.*

Underneath an overhanging rock were discovered drawings from the Magdalenian Period, representing horses, bisons and ibex. However, the cave is best known for its drawing of a human figure. A small museum exhibits fossils and prehistoric tools.

La Micoque Deposit (**Gisement de la Micoque**). – This deposit revealed many items belonging to periods known as the Tayacian and Micoquian Ages which fall between the end of the Acheulean and the beginning of the Mousterian Ages. The finds are exhibited at Les Eyzies Museum.

Le Moustier. – This village contains a famous prehistoric shelter. *Guided tours 9am to noon and 2 to 6pm; closed Tuesdays and in winter; 4F; apply to Mme Guimbaud.* The prehistoric finds made at Le Moustier include a human skeleton and many flint implements. A Middle Palaeolithic Age has been named Mousterian after the finds.

An interesting 17C carved confessional may be seen in the village church.

La Mouthe Cave (**Grotte de la Mouthe**). – *Closed for restoration.*

This cave, which is in the form of a passage 274 yds long, was discovered by Rivière in 1895. It is a difficult cave to see as it is not lit by electricity, it is narrow and the floor is slippery in places. One hundred yards from the entrance are the line drawings, some highlighted with ochre. There are horses, bison, reindeer and other deer, but they are not easy for the amateur to decipher. A deposit from the Magdalenian Period was discovered at the mouth of the cave.

Castel-Merle. – *Open 10am to noon and 2 to 6pm (7pm in July and August); closed 1 October to 31 March; 8F.*

This site which is well known to the specialists, was for a long time closed to the public. Some of the finds are in Les Eyzies and Périgueux museums but a small local museum exhibits many interestings artefacts from the Mousterian Age to the Gallo-Roman era.

There are nine caves with wall sculptures (bison, horses) of the Magdalenian Age. In the fourth shelter a section shows the strata dating from the Aurignacian Age to the modern era. The sixth cave, the so-called English Fortress (Fort des Anglais) is a remarkable example of a cave dwelling.

Sites and natural phenomena

Grand Roc Cave★★ (Grotte du Grand Roc). – *Northwest of Les Eyzies to the left of the D 47. Guided tours 1 July to 15 September, 9am to 6pm; the rest of the year, 9 to 11.30am and 2 to 5.30pm; closed 2 November to Palm Sunday; 14F.*

There is a good **view★** of the Vézère valley from the stairs leading up to the cave and the platform at its mouth. The 40-50 yds of tunnel enables one to see, within chambers that are generally small in size, an extraordinary display of stalactites, stalagmites and eccentrics ressembling coral formations, as well as pendants and crystallisations.

Gorge of Hell★ (Gorges d'Enfer). – *Open 21 March to 14 November, 9am to 5.30pm (9am to 7pm, 1 May to 14 September); 13F.*

In the small valley of the Gorges d'Enfer there is a reserve where the animals portrayed in the prehistoric caves of the area can be seen in semi-liberty (tigers, bison, red deer, fallow deer, horses, wild boar and moufflons). You are free to wander along the forest trails within the reserve. The signposted path passing the pond leads to the imposing Gorges d'Enfer rock shelter.

The Carpe-Diem Cave (Grotte de Carpe-Diem). – *Guided tours 16 June to 14 September, 9.30am to noon and 2 to 6.30pm; 1 April to 15 June and 15 September to 30 October, 10am to noon and 2 to 5pm; 7F.*

Here and there in this 180 m - 200 yd long passage as it narrows and winds through the rock, you see stalagmites and variously coloured stalactites.

Rocher de la Peine. – This great rock, worn jagged by erosion, partially overhangs the road. A Magdalenian deposit was discovered within it but this has now been exhausted.

St-Christophe Cliff★ (La Roque St-Christophe). – *Guided tours 1 July to 15 September, 9.30am to noon and 2 to 6.30pm; Palm Sunday to 30 June and 16 September to 31 October, 10am to noon and 2 to 6pm; 10F.*

For half a mile this long and majestic cliff rises vertically (80 m - 262 ft) above the Vézère valley. It is like a huge hive with about a hundred caves hollowed out of the rock on five tiers. The traces of art and the tools show that it was inhabited 20 000 years ago: these finds are kept in Les Eyzies National Museum of Prehistory and in the museum of St-Germain-en-Laye. In the 10C the cliff terraces served as the foundation for a fortress used against the Normans and during the Hundred Years War and was subsequently destroyed during the Wars of Religion. From the **Pas du Miroir**, it was once possible to see one's reflection in the Vézère, for the river at one time flowed at the foot of the cliff (30 m - 99 ft).

The terrace affords a good bird's-eye **view★** of the valley.

Buildings and Museums

National Museum of Prehistory★ (Musée National de Préhistoire). – *In the village. Open 9.30am to noon and 2 to 6pm (5pm December to 28 February); closed Tuesdays; 6F weekdays; 3F Sundays and holidays; free on Wednesdays.*

The museum is in the castle of the former barons of Beynac. The fortress, which dates from the 11 and 12C and was restored in the 16C, was built beneath a rock overhang halfway up the cliff.

From the platform, on which stands a statue of primitive man by Dardé, there is a good view of Les Eyzies and the valleys of the Vézère and the Beune.

The display of rich collections of prehistoric objects and works of art discovered locally in the last eighty years is completed by diagrams showing the chronology of prehistoric eras, sections through the earth's strata and photographs.

A gallery on the first floor is devoted to different stone-chipping techniques and a synthesis of prehistory. Prehistoric art is represented by rock wall paintings and carvings as well as domestic objects.

The second floor gallery contains items from all the prehistoric periods. The Magdalenian tomb of a woman from St-Germain-la-Rivière, complete with its skeleton, has been reconstructed and may be seen in another building.

Museum of speleology (Musée de la spéléologie). – *Open 13 June to 15 September, 9am to noon and 2 to 6 pm; closed Saturdays; 5F.*

The museum is installed in the rock fortress of Tayac, which commands the Vézère valley. The four chambers, cut out of the living rock, contain a selection of items pertaining to speleology: pot holing equipment, exhibits describing the geological formation and natural life of the pot holes and various models.

Commarque Castle. – The impressive castle ruins on the south bank of the river Beune stand facing Laussel Château. Commarque was built as a stronghold in the 12 and 13C and played an important part in the Hundred Years War. Betrayed, it was occupied by the English and retaken by the seneschal of Périgord, who then handed it back to the baron of Beynac. Considerable parts of the fortifications are still standing. The keep, with its crown of battlements, the chapel and the various living quarters emerge from a mass of greenery to form a romantic setting.

Laussel Château. – *Not open to the public.* This 15 to 16C château is perched on a cliff, dropping straight down to the Beune valley. The building is small but elegant. A few hundred yards farther along the valley of the Beune a large prehistoric deposit was discovered which contained the famous Venus of Laussel, a fine low-relief dating from the Aurignacian Period which is now in the museum in Bordeaux *(illustration p 24).*

Tayac Church. – This fortified church is attractive for the warm golden tones of the stone with which it was built in the 11 and 12C and arresting in the severity of its architectural design. Two crenellated bell-towers with stone slated roofs frame the main part of the building which is lit only by narrow windows, single slits closely akin to loopholes. The main doorway is in the Limousin style.

Tursac. – Tursac church is dominated by a huge, stark bell-tower; a series of domes, characteristic of the Romanesque-Périgord style *(p 28)* covers the church.

FELLETIN

Michelin map 73 fold 1 – *Local map p 132* – Pop 3 130

Felletin is a small industrial town; the two main commercial activities are tapestry weaving – the craft was born here – and diamond cutting. The town, with the old quarter perched on a spur, lies in a pleasant hilly region of woods and meadows. The arc-shaped Building Trades School, built in 1954, overlooks the churchyard.

The tapestry *Christ in Glory*, designed by Graham Sutherland for the new Coventry Cathedral in England, was made by a firm of tapestry weavers in Felletin. The tapestry is the largest in the world and measures 74 ft 8 in high by 38 ft across.

Monastery Church (Église du Moûtier). – The church was built in the 12C by the monks of Chambon-sur-Voueize and dedicated to St. Valerie. In the mid-15C the church collapsed but was immediately rebuilt. The belfry dates from this time: it is a tall square tower of three storeys supported by buttresses with pointed tops.

Above the Gothic doorway on each storey are Flamboyant bays one above the other. The third or top storey is ornamented with gargoyles and statues at the four corners. The whole is surrounded by a pierced balustrade and surmounted by a lantern turret.

Church of Notre-Dame du Château. – A tapestry exhibition is held annually in this 15C church which has a shingle covered belfry crowned by a statue of the Virgin. *Open 26 June to 14 September, 10am to noon and 2 to 7pm; 6F.*

Tour of the Co-operative Diamond Works. – *Visits suspended temporarily.*

A Belgian businessman started the industry in the town in 1912 and it has since developed considerably. Diamond cutting depends on the skilled use of the naked eye and demands incredible precision on the part of the craftsmen who cut as many as 56 facets on minute stones.

EXCURSION

St-Georges-Nigremont. – Pop 200. *12 km - 7 1/2 miles to the southeast.* St-Georges Nigremont stands on the top of a hillock between the Limousin Montagne and the Millevaches Plateau. Near the 13-14C church, which has a massive square tower in front, is a terrace. This affords a view to the northeast of Crocq and beyond, to the Combraille hills and to the southeast as far as the mountains of Auvergne.

FIGEAC

Michelin map 79 fold 10 – *Local map p 125* – Pop 10 511 – *Facilities p 38*

The busy little town of Figeac, stretched out along the right bank of the Célé has grown up where Auvergne meets Haut-Quercy on the great pilgrimage route which ran from Le Puy to Conques, and to Santiago de Compostela.

Jean-François Champollion. – Champollion, the outstanding Orientalist whose brilliance enabled Egyptology to make such great strides, was born at Figeac in 1790. By the time he was 14 he had a command of Greek, Latin, Hebrew, Arabic, Chaldean and Syrian. After his studies in Paris, he lectured in history at Grenoble University. He undertook as did the English physicist, Thomas Young, the deciphering of a polished basalt tablet found by an expedition to the Nile Delta near Rosetta and known as the Rosetta Stone, now in the British Museum. The tablet bore three inscriptions: Egyptian hieroglyphics and cursive script and Greek. Champollion established that the texts were identical. He then discovered that the hieroglyphics denoted not only syllabic sounds but also ideas. Eager to prove his theory he went to Egypt and deciphered many texts. Unfortunately he died at the age of forty-two.

■ SIGHTS *time: 3/4 hour*

Church of St-Sauveur. – This former abbey church suffered greatly during the Wars of Religion and now, cheek by jowl with the 12 and 14C parts that still remain, are restorations of the 17 and late 19C. The huge building consists of a high nave encircled by a false triforium above which are clerestory windows. An ambulatory circles the long chancel. Two Romanesque capitals from the earlier doorway have been inverted and are used as holy water stoups. The former chapterhouse which prolongs the south arm of the transept has 17C wooden panels which were regilded and repainted in 1968.

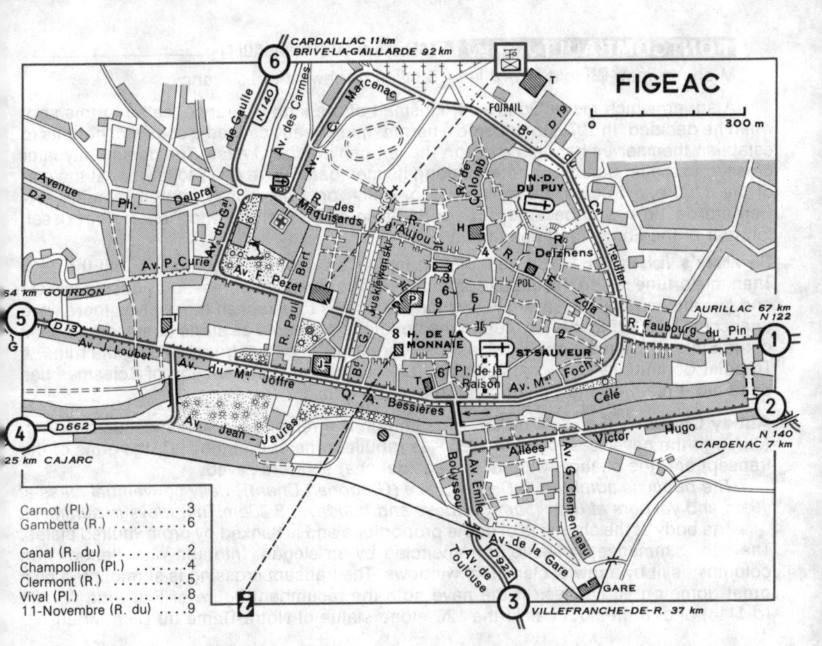

The Mint (Hôtel de la Monnaie). – The *oustal dé lo Mounédo* owes its name to a royal workshop housed in the mansion for more than 150 years when the town first became a royal bailiwick in the 13C. This restored Gothic building characteristic of local secular architecture has a *soleilho*, an open gallery on columns with a flat roof of fluted tiles. It has tiers-pointed windows placed either singly, paired or in groups.

The Hôtel de la Monnaie contains the tourist information centre and a **museum**. *Open 15 June to 15 September, 9.30am to noon and 2.30 to 7pm; closed Sundays and holidays; 5F.*

On the ground floor is the **Lapidary Museum** containing pieces of sculpture from religious and secular buildings, including the door of the former Sully Mansion.

On the first floor are displayed old coins and town seals of the time of the seven consuls and prehistoric collections. One of the rooms is given over to Champollion with a cast of the Rosetta Stone as the main exhibit.

Old Quarter. – This part of Figeac lies between the Hôtel de la Monnaie, and the Churches of St-Sauveur and Notre-Dame-du-Puy. Many of the old streets are lined with half-timbered houses decorated with balconies; in particular, the Rue Delzhens lined with old mansions. The Rue Gambetta has houses with fine 14 and 15C pointed arches.

Church of Notre-Dame-du-Puy. – This Romanesque building, greatly altered in the 14 and 17C, contains a late 17C retable carved in walnut.

The Needles of Figeac (Aiguilles de Figeac). – These are 12C obelisks nearly 15 m - 50 ft tall which it is believed, marked the boundaries of land over which the Benedictine abbey had jurisdiction: pursuit of one's enemies was not allowed within the boundary. Two of the four remain and the one which can be seen from the D 922 to the south of Figeac, is known as the **Côte de Cingle Needle** (Aiguille de la Côte de Cingle).

EXCURSION

Cardaillac. – Pop 453. *11 km - 7 miles to the northwest. Leave Figeac by ⑥, the N 140 and then take the D 15 to the right.* The old quarter, or Fort, stands on a rocky spur above the town. Of this triangular shaped fortification dating from the 12C there remain two square towers: the Clock or Baron's Tower and Sagnes Tower. *Only the latter is open.* The two tall rooms, with their vaulted ceilings are reached by a spiral staircase. From the platform there is a fine view ot the Drauzou valley and the surrounding countryside.

FOISSAC

Michelin map 79 fold 10 – *Local map 125* – Pop 320

This small rural village situated in the Villeneuve Causse is known for its caves discovered in 1958 about 1 km – 1/2 mile south of the village.

Caves★ (Grottes). – *Guided tours Easter to 31 May and in October, Sundays and holidays, 2 to 6pm; 1 June to 30 September, 10 to 11.30am and 2 to 6pm; time: 1 hour; 15F.*

An underground stream drains the caves. It is a tributary of the Lot into which it flows near Balaguier. During the visit of the 8 km - 5 miles of galleries note the gleaming white stalactites and the lovely formations in the Obelisk Chamber; the stalagmites and ivory-tower-like formations in the Michel Roques gallery. In one gallery there is a roof covered with round calcite mushroom formations, slightly slanted, thus proving that the stalactites were in the gallery well before earthquakes changed the aspect of the cave.

The bulbous stalactites known as "the onions" are also worth noting.

These caves were occupied by men during the Bronze Age and evidence of their daily existence is apparent throughout: their "hearth", bronze utensils and large curved shaped pottery. Also visible are skeletons of a man and woman and the imprint of a child's foot, fixed here in the clay 4 000 years ago...

FONTGOMBAULT Abbey ★ (Abbaye de FONTGOMBAULT)

Michelin map 68 fold 16 – 8 km - 5 miles northwest of Le Blanc

A spring which made Gombault, kinsman of the king of France, settle in this spot when he decided, in 1070, to become a hermit, had already caused a colony of hermits to establish themselves here in caves on the left bank of the Creuse. The community later crossed to the far bank. It counted among its members Pierre de l'Étoile who, at the end of the 11C, constructed the monastery of which only the abbey church remains, St-Bernard de Tiron who became prior of St-Savin-sur-Gartempe and Robert d'Arbrissel, founder of the Fontevraud community.

The Abbey's Vicissitudes. – The Benedictine monks stayed at Fontgombault until the 18C. Then misfortune fell on the abbey community of five: it was suppressed by decree in 1714 and two attempts by the Lazarists and the Sulpicians to establish themselves there were unsuccessful. During the Revolution the buildings were sold as stone quarries on behalf of the State. Only in the middle of last century was work begun on rebuilding the ruins. A Trappist Community was established in 1852; today the Congregation of Solesmes has once more restored the Benedictine rule to the house.

Abbey Church★ (Église abbatiale). – The church is a remarkable Romanesque building. Although the nave, destroyed in 1569 was rebuilt at the end of the 19C, the arms of the transept and the chancel with its five apsidal chapels were saved.

The public is admitted to Divine Office (Gregorian Chant); daily conventual mass at 10am and vespers at 6pm (5pm Sundays and holidays; 3.30pm Thursdays in summer).

The body of the church is of noble proportions and is flanked by groin vaulted aisles. The choir, immense, majestic and encircled by an elegant triforium with slender twin columns, is lit by a row of clerestory windows. The transept crossing is surmounted by a great dome on squinches. In the nave note the recumbent figure of Pierre de l'Étoile (d 1114) and in the south aisle the 12C stone statue of Notre-Dame du Bien-Mourir.

GARGILESSE-DAMPIERRE

Michelin map 68 fold 18 – *Local map p 88* – Pop 347

Gargilesse is one of the most attractive villages of the Creuse valley; it is in a pleasant leafy setting, has an interesting church, picturesque streets and old houses; it also has literary and artistic associations.

George Sand *(p 145)* lived there and chose it as the background against which to set several of her novels *Le Péché de Monsieur Antoine* and *Beaux Messieurs de Bois-Doré* (Monsieur Anthony's Sin and The Fine Gentlemen of Bois-Doré); she also wrote from there *Les Légendes Rustiques* and *Promenades autour d'un village* (Rustic Tales and Walks Round a Village). Artists such as Claude Monet, who painted autumn landscapes there, Théodore Rousseau, Osterlind and Henri Jamet came to settle in Gargilesse, attracted by the natural beauty of the area.

Church. – The Romanesque church (11-12C) stands within the walls of a mediaeval castle rebuilt in the 18C. The old keep and a door flanked by two towers are still standing.

The church and crypt are open daily during the season and on Saturdays and Sundays out of season; 1.50F; to visit apply to Mme Lopez, at the house opposite the path leading up to the church.

The church is well proportioned and has historiated capitals portraying the Twenty-four Old Men of the Apocalypse. The transept crossing is surmounted by a dome.

The crypt is enormous and is decorated with 12-15C **frescoes** of the instruments of the Passion, St. Gregory celebrating mass and the Apparition of Christ, the Crucifixion, the Assumption, the Resurrection of the Dead, the Visitation and the three Kings. A 12C Virgin and Child stands in the main chapel.

George Sand's Retreat, "Algira". – *Guided tours 1 April to 30 September, 9am to noon and 3 to 7pm; 4F; time: 1/2 hour. Apply to Mme Sand.*

Mementoes of the novelist, her son Maurice and her grand-daughter Aurore, are on display in this little house.

GIMEL-LES-CASCADES ★

Michelin map 75 fold 9 – *Local map p 181* – Pop 553

Gimel stands in a remarkable **setting★** – one of the most picturesque of Bas-Limousin – near Tulle and the valley of the Corrèze. The Montane flows amidst the rocks of a wild ravine and hurls itself down waterfalls 140 m - 460 ft high.

The Waterfalls★★ (Les Cascades). – *1 hour Rtn on foot. Tiring walk.* A path marked with arrows leads across Vuillier Park to the best places from which to see the falls. *Open Easter to 30 September, 9am to 7pm; 9F.* The first fall known as the *Grande Cascade* or *Grand Saut* (Great Fall or Leap) drops 45 m - 145 ft; immediately following is the *Redole* with a fall of 27 m - 90 ft. From this vantage point, the visitor gets a good view of the two cascades one above the other. The third waterfall is known as the *Queue de Cheval* (Horse's Tail) and appears suddenly, pouring from a little promontory amidst the rocks 60 m - 200 ft into impassable ravines known as the *Gouffre de l'Inferno* (Gulf of Hell).

Church. – *Time: 1/2 hour. Restoration in progress.* This contains an 18C pulpit, a 15C *pietà* and a remarkable treasure.

Treasure★. – The **shrine of St. Stephen★★** *(to visit apply at the presbytery)* is the chief treasure; it was made in the late 12C and is ornamented with Limoges enamels; the heads of the figures are in relief, their eyes are made of precious stones. The stoning of St. Stephen is depicted on it. There are, in addition, a 14C silver-gilt reliquary bust of St. Dumines, a soldier from Clovis' army who retreated into the Montane Ravines as a hermit, a very odd 18C "dish for souls" (plate for the host), a 14C *champlevé* enamel pyx and a 13C monstrance in gilded copper.

EXCURSIONS

Étang de Ruffaud. – *Round tour of 14 km - 9 miles.* The D 53 on leaving Gimel climbs to the small village of Touzac, before making for the Ruffaud Pool (bathing-place) which stands in a romantic setting of pine trees, birches and oaks. The D 26 takes the motorist on to the Brach Pool. The N 89 and then the D 53 will bring you back to Gimel.

La Valette; Sédière. – *Round tour of 43 km - 27 miles – about 1 1/2 hours – local maps pp 93 and 181. Leave Gimel to the south by the D 53^E, take the D 978 to the left, then D 26 to the right and finally to the left the D 61 in the direction of St-Pardoux-la-Croisille.*

La Valette Dam. – This dam stands on the Doustre, a tributary of the Dordogne. The slender arched type dam supplies the Marcillac power station which is equipped with two sets of generators of 33 000kW, with an annual capacity of 62 million kWh. From the road along the crest of the dam, there is a good view upstream of the reservoir in its attractive hill setting and downstream of the Doustre Gorges.

Return to the outskirts of St-Pardoux and take the D 131 to the right which affords a good view of Ferrier Pool, then beyond Clergoux, the D 135^E.

Sédière. – An elegant Renaissance château stands in a pleasant setting near a waterfall.

Return to Clergoux and take the D 978 to the right, then the D 53^E which lead back to Gimel.

GOURDON

Michelin map 75 fold 18 – *Local map p 108* – Pop 5 076 – *Facilities p 38*

Gourdon is the capital of a green undulating countryside called the Bouriane. The town, situated on the borders of Quercy and Périgord, rises in tiers up the flank of a rocky hillock upon which once stood the local lord's castle.

If you follow the circular route of the avenues which have replaced the old ramparts you will get pleasant views of the hills and valleys of Bouriane.

■ SIGHTS *time: 3/4 hour*

Rue du Majou. – The fortified Le Majou Gateway gives on to this narrow, picturesque street which is lined by the church of Notre-Dame du Majou and old corbelled houses. From a little beyond No 24 there is a good view, to the right, of the old fashioned Rue Zig-Zag. No 17, the former Anglars Mansion, has pretty mullioned windows.

Cardinal-Farinié (R.) . 2 — Cavaignac (Av.) . . . . . 3 — Dr-Cabanès (Bd) . . . . 4 — H.-de-Ville (Pl.) . . . . . 5 — Libération (Pl.) . . . . . 6 — République (Allées) . . 7

Church of St-Pierre (B). – The church was begun at the start of the 14C and was formerly a dependency of Le Vigan Abbey. The chancel is supported by massive buttresses. The door, in the west face, is decorated with elegant archivolts and is framed by two tall asymmetrical towers. The large rose window is protected by a line of battlements, a reminder of former fortifications.

The vast nave has ogive vaulting; wood panels of the 17C, carved, painted and gilded decorate the chancel and the south transept.

Go round the outside of the church from the left and go up the staircase and the ramp which leads to the esplanade where the castle once stood.

Esplanade. – There is a **panorama** to be seen from the terrace *(viewing table)*: beyond the town, whose roofs can be seen in tiers below the massive roof of St-Pierre's in the foreground, lie the plateaux stretching out from the valleys of the Dordogne and the Céou.

Return to the Place de l'Hôtel de Ville and go round the outside of the church starting from the right. There are some old houses opposite the east end including one with a fine early 17C doorway. Opposite the south door of the church take the Rue Cardinal Farinié which goes downhill and contains old houses with mullioned windows and flanking turrets. This will bring you back to the Place de la Libération.

Franciscan Church (Eglise des Cordeliers) (D). – *When closed, apply at the Tourist Centre (Syndicat d'Initiative) nearby.* The church of the former Franciscan monastery is worth a visit. It has a massive belfry-porch which was added in the 19C but the slender and pure lines of the nave are characteristic of early Gothic. The seven-sided apse is lit by stained glass windows dating from the 19C. At the entrance, in the middle of the nave stands a remarkable **font**★: Christ the King with the twelve apostles (14C) are depicted on the blind arcades on the outside.

EXCURSIONS

Cougnac Caves★ (Grottes de Cougnac). – *3 km - 2 miles to the north by the D 704. Guided tours Palm Sunday to 30 June and 1 October to 1 November, 9 to 11.30am and 2 to 6pm; 1 July to 30 September, 9am to 6.30pm; time: 1 hour; 12F.*

The Caves, consisting of two chasms about 200 m - 300 yds apart, spread their network of galleries beneath a limestone plateau on which a small oak wood grows.

The first cave consists of three small chambers with roofs apparently raining stalactites so closely are they packed. Many are very slender.

The second cave is bigger and has two remarkable chambers: the **Salle des Colonnes**★★ (the Pillar Chamber) is particularly striking for the views in perspective provided by columns reaching from the ceiling to the floor; the **Salle des Peintures Préhistoriques** (the Hall of Prehistoric Paintings) contains designs in ochre and black including deer, elephants and human figures.

Le Vigan. – Pop 836. *5 km - 3 miles to the east by the D 673. Restoration work in progress.* A Gothic church remains of an abbey founded in the 11C which became a chapter for canons regular in the 14C. The church chevet is overlooked by a tower rising from the transept crossing. There is fine ogive vaulting over the nave.

GRAMAT Causse★

Michelin maps 75 folds 18 and 19 and 79 folds 8 and 9

The Gramat Causse, which extends between the valley of the Dordogne in the north and those of the Lot and the Célé in the south, is the largest plateau in Quercy. It is a vast limestone plateau *(p 15)* lying at an average altitude of 350 m - 1 150 ft, containing many natural phenomena and unusual landscapes.

Autumn is the time to cross the plateau when the trees are turning and shed a golden light on the grey stones and rocks and the maples make a splash of deep red.

■ THE PLATEAU★

From Cahors to Souillac

111 km - 69 miles – about 1 day – local map below

Leave Cahors (p 73) by ②.

The D 653 runs beside the right bank of the Lot then goes up the charming valley of the Vers, which, at times, widens out into meadowland and at times narrows to pass between tall grey cliffs.

St-Martin-de-Vers. – Pop 112. The houses of this small village, with brown tiled roofs cluster round the church with its asymmetrical belfry-tower.

The road climbs up to the plateau where dry-stone walls and sparse vegetation stretch away as far as the eye can see.

Labastide-Murat. – *Description p 113.*

Beyond Labastide-Murat the D 677 crosses the east side of the plateau and then wends down to Gramat.

Just before Gramat station turn right and take the D 14 for 1 km – 1/2 mile.

Gramat Safari Park (Parc de vision de Gramat). – *Open in summer, 9am to 7.30pm; in winter, 10am to noon and 2 to 6pm; 17F.*

This park which extends over 40 ha – 99 acres, was acquired by the local authorities with a view to showing animals and plants in the open. A botanical park is being created. The animal park includes mainly European species living in semi-captivity in their natural environment. Follow the signposted itinerary over 3 km – 1 mile for a pleasant tour.

Make for the D 667 which leads to Gramat.

Gramat. – Pop 3 838. *Facilities p 38.* Capital of the limestone plateau that bears the same name, Gramat is also a great fair town (sheep, truffles and nuts). It is a good starting point for visits to Padirac, Rocamadour and the area that lies between the Lot and the Dordogne. It was here that the French Police Training Centre for Handlers and Dogs was established in 1945. *The kennels can be visited (handling demonstrations) from 15 June to 15 September on Thursdays except holidays from 3.30 to 5pm.*

Return to the D 677 and immediately after, take the D 39 to the right to the point where it joins the D 32 into which you turn right.

The D 32 goes to the edge of the plateau with fine **views** of Rocamadour and crosses the Alzou Canyon. Enter Rocamadour by the narrow ogive gateways.

Rocamadour★★★. – *Description p 157.*

Leave Rocamadour to the northeast by the D 32 and drive to L'Hospitalet (good **views** of Rocamadour); take the D 36 in the direction of Gramat. The Monkey Reserve is nearby on the right.

Monkey Reserve (Forêt des singes). – *Open 16 June to 31 August, 9am to 7pm; 1 April to 15 June and 1 September to 15 October, 10am to noon and 2 to 6pm; 10F.* Barbary apes are natives of the high plateaux of North Africa where they are an endangered species. There are 150 apes roaming freely in this woodland area (10 ha – 27 acres).

Return to L'Hospitalet where you join the D 673 to Calès.

This pretty road wends down the Ouysse Valley and affords views of the valley and the Gramat Causse to the left. After 9 km – 5 miles take a signposted road to the right.

Cougnaguet Mill (Moulin de Cougnaguet). – *Open 1 April to 30 June and in September, 10am to noon and 2 to 5.30pm; 1 July to 31 August, 9 to 11.30am and 2 to 6.30pm; 8F.* The rounded arches of this fortified mill span a loop in the Ouysse in a fresh green **setting**. It was built in the 15C at the foot of a sheer cliff on the site of a former mill to which the water rights were granted in 1279. There are four millstones which produced up to 4 tons of flour daily; one of them is still in working order and tourists are given a milling demonstration.

Continue along the little road which climbs to the D 247 into which you turn left. It affords splendid **views★** of the Dordogne Valley and of Belcastel castle at its best.

Lacave Caves★ (Grottes de Lacave). – *Description p 114.*

The D 43 which you join on the left passes at the foot of Belcastel castle.

Belcastel Castle. – *Description p 95.*

La Treyne Château. – *Description p 95.*

Beyond La Treyne Château the road cuts across a bend in the Dordogne before reaching Souillac.

■ THE N 20

From Souillac to Cahors

68 km - 42 miles – about 2 1/2 hours – local map p 108

Leave Souillac (p 177) by the N 20, going south. After crossing the Dordogne the road rises above the valley.

Lanzac Belvedere. – There is an extensive view from the left of the N 20 *(car park)* of the Dordogne valley, where the white shape of La Treyne Château can be seen standing out to the east and that of the dovecote of Le Bastit Castle to the southeast.

Beyond the Lanzac Belvedere the road crosses the limestone plateau and is pleasant and picturesque.
At St-Pierre-Lafeuille take the little road to the left and follow it for 1 km – 1/2 mile so as to see, from a distance, the impressive ruins of the Roussillon Fortress.

Roussillon Castle. – This mediaeval fortress *(restoration in progress)* is owned by the Gontaut-Biron family. Massive round towers rise above the valley.

Turn round and rejoin the N 20. 3 km - 2 miles after St-Pierre-Lafeuille turn left into the V 10, which runs along the hilltops and gives good views of the countryside, the hills and the valley of the Lot and brings you suddenly upon Cahors *(p 73)* in its **setting★**.

GUÉRET

Michelin map 72 fold 9 – Pop 16 621

Guéret, once capital of the county of Marche, is situated on a plateau lying alongside the wooded Chabrières Massif not far from the Creuse valley.

Municipal Museum (Musée Municipal) (M). – *Open 15 June to 15 September, 10am to noon and 2 to 6.30pm (5.30pm, the rest of the year); closed Tuesdays and certain holidays; 7.50F.*

The museum is in a fine 18C Classical building surrounded by a large flower garden. On the ground floor there is a collection of local archaeological finds and 19-early 20C sculptures. In the armoury swords and scimitars are to be found side by side with pistols and blunderbusses.

The walls of the staircase leading to the first floor have been hung with very fine 17C Aubusson tapestries which are best seen from the upper landing. Other tapestries hang on the first floor.

Two galleries on the first floor stand out for the interest and value of their contents:

The Gold and Silver Treasure Gallery★: a magnificent collection of Limousin *champlevé* enamel work from the 12 to 15C. Note in particular a processional cross, pyxes and the collection of shrines. The vivid colours of the enamels harmonise with the gilding and polished stones. Scenes depicted include the Crucifixion, the Adoration of the Magi, the Stoning of St. Stephen and the Martyrdom of St. Thomas Becket.

Amongst the painted enamel work dating from the 15 to 18C, several pieces can be attributed to some of the greatest masters of this art, namely Limosin, Laudin and Nouailher. The contents of this gallery are completed by 18C and 19C religious objects and a 13C embossed shrine.

The Ceramic Gallery: it contains china from Nevers, Moustiers, Rouen, Strasbourg and Delft as well as some Italian majolica and glassware. In the next room there are 140 pieces from China dating from Antiquity (Han dynasty) to the 17C (Ming dynasty).

The sculpture gallery displays 15-18C works.

In the picture section there are French, Flemish and Dutch paintings as well as more recent works by artists such as Guillaumin, S. Valadon and Marinot.

Finally the drawings gallery contains 19-20C exhibits.

The basement rooms house monumental sculptures of Gaulish deities and Gallo-Roman funerary steles.

A section devoted to the ethnography of the Creuse region is being set up.

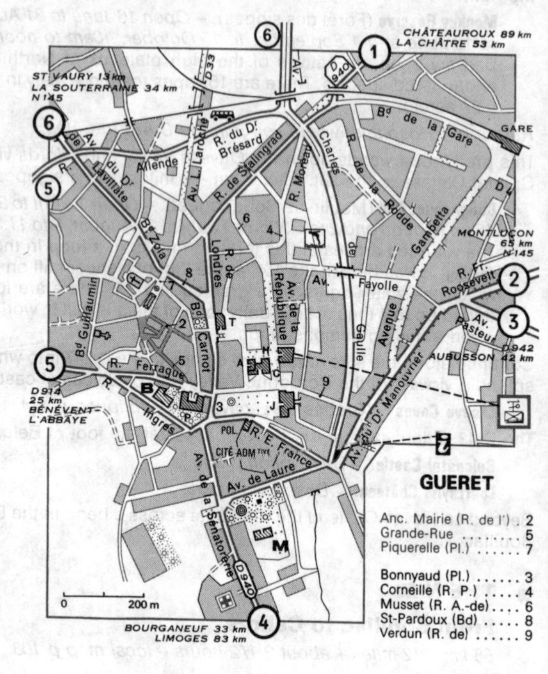

Hôtel des Moneyroux (B). – This late Gothic style building, contemporary with Jacques Cœur's Palace at Bourges *(p 63)* consists of two buildings joined by a corner turret.

The right wing was built after 1447 by Antoine Alard, Lord of Moneyroux and Treasurer of the Counts of Marche; his successor, Pierre Billon, had the other wing built at the beginning of the 16C. The façade is pierced by many mullioned windows and is topped by dormer windows ornamented with finials and pinnacles.

The two buildings are roofed with small brown tiles except for the turret pinnacle which is covered with shingles.

EXCURSIONS

Chabrières Forest. – *Round tour of 21 km - 13 miles – about 1 hour – local map below. Leave Guéret by ④.*

The D 940 soon enters Chabrières Forest, a tree covered massif where pines, oaks, beeches and birches grow and bracken forms a thick carpet underfoot. *Several walks are signposted.* A stonemason's workshop along the roadside indicates the importance of this craft in the past.

The hilly and picturesque D 940 brings you to the approach of La Chapelle-Taillefert from where you take the D 52 to the left. At St-Christophe turn left onto the forest road, then take the D 940 to Guéret.

Glénic. – Pop 581. *7.5 km - 4 1/2 miles. Leave Guéret by ①, the D 940.*

Glénic is built on a promontory overlooking the Creuse. Note the unusual fortified church whose 12C doorway is ornamented with crotcheted capitals.

St-Vaury; Roche. – *16 km - 10 miles. Leave Guéret by ⑥ on the N 145.*

St-Vaury. – Pop 2 524. The church contains, at the back of the altar, a 15C low-relief cut in limestone, depicting scenes from the Passion. There are also two small 13C enamelled reliquaries.

Return to the D 22 and turn left onto it.

Roche. – This hamlet is perched on a rocky plateau nearly 600 m - 2 000 ft up. From here there is an almost circular **panorama**★ from the valley of the Creuse in the northeast to the Ambazac Hills in the southwest; in the west foreground stands the mass of the Puy des Trois Cornes which rises to a height of 636 m - 2 087 ft.

HAUTEFORT★★

Michelin map 75 fold 7 – *Local map p 143*

Dating from the 17C and property of the Bastard family since 1929, Hautefort Château whose proud form dominates the skyline, resembles the royal palaces of the Loire valley rather than the Périgord fortresses. The château was seriously damaged by fire in 1968 but has subsequently been restored to its former appearance.

Bertrand the Troubadour. – The first Castle of Hautefort was built by the Limousin family of Las Tours and passed by marriage in the 12C to the house of Born of whom Bertrand mentioned by Dante in the Divine Comedy, is the best known member.

Bertrand de Born, the famous troubadour, became a warrior-knight when the need arose to defend the family castle against his brother Constantine. He obtained the support of Henri Court Mantel (Henry Shortcoat) and managed to remain master of Hautefort in spite of all Constantine's efforts and those of his ally Richard Lionheart. In 1186 his brother returned and razed Hautefort to the ground. Renouncing everything Bertrand retired to take monastic orders.

Marie de Hautefort. – The beautiful and virtuous Marie, daughter of the first Marquis of Hautefort, has remained famous for the deep admiration and Platonic love she inspired in Louis XIII (1601-43). She reigned over literary circles and the *Précieuses* drawing rooms.

■ THE CHÂTEAU★★

Part of the château (guided tours: 45 min), gardens and terraces can be visited from Palm Sunday to 1 November, 9 to 11.30am and 2 to 6.30pm; the rest of the year Sundays only 2 to 5pm; closed 25 December to 1 January; 10F.

Go through the beautiful park (30 ha - 74 acres) to the terraces, planted with flowers and boxwood, which overlook the village and offer views onto the park.

To reach the entrance to the château go to the end of the esplanade and cross the drawbridge over the moat, which is now decorated with flowers and boxwood. The court of honour is a vast square open on one side to the village, which clusters at the foot of the walls, while on the other three sides it is surrounded by the main living quarters.

To the south are two round towers topped with domes and turrets. Inside the southeast tower is a 17C chapel which contains the altar from the coronation of Charles X and 16C paintings on leather. The southwest tower has beautiful chestnut **timberwork**★★, the work of a guild: the Compagnons du Tour de France. It also contains the museum of Eugene Le Roy (1836-1907) who was born at Hautefort, in the château itself, and wrote *Jacquou le Croquant (p 161).* Another room contains objects saved from the fire.

The Renaissance gallery, the Tapestry Room, lined with tapestries from Flanders and Brussels, and the great staircase (17C) have also been restored.

■ CHURCH

Built on a vast square south of the château the church was the former chapel of an almshouse founded by the Hautefort. It has a fine dome topped by a lantern turret. Inside, the drum of the dome is held up by 18C statues of the Four Evangelists.

ISSIGEAC

Michelin map 75 fold 15 – Pop 686

The little town of Issigeac, lying in the Banège valley to the southeast of the great Monbazillac vineyard, possesses an interesting church and castle and picturesque timber work or corbelled houses.

Church. – The late Gothic church was built by Armand de Gontaut-Biron, Bishop of Sarlat, at the beginning of the 16C. A belfry-porch, supported by large buttresses, contains a doorway with a tympanum decorated with twisted covings.

The Bishops' Château (Château des Évêques). – The castle was built by another Bishop of Sarlat, François de Salignac, in the second half of the 17C. It now houses the town hall. The building is vast and is flanked by two square towers each with a corbelled turret of brick and stone on its north side.

EXCURSION

Bardou Château. – *7 km - 4 miles to the east by the D 25, after 5.5 km - 3 miles turn right in the direction of Bardou.* Built from the 15-17C, this interesting château, now restored, stands in a fine parkland setting.

ISSOUDUN

Michelin map 68 fold 9 – Pop 15 166

Issoudun goes back to Gaulish times and later, during the Middle Ages, was the stake in many a battle, the most famous being that between Philip Augustus and Richard Lionheart. The town was besieged several times, as well as set on fire.

The town keeps alive the memory of the pilgrimage to the castle abbey made by Louis XI, who had a special devotion to Our Lady. Every year on 8 September the Basilica of Notre-Dame-du-Sacré-Cœur is the centre of a great pilgrimage.

Balzac at Issoudun. – Honoré de Balzac (1799-1850) stayed at Frapesie Castle, near Issoudun. He wrote most of *César Birotteau* and also collected there the information he needed to write *La Rabouilleuse* (The Woman who Fished in Troubled Waters). Issoudun has retained the peculiar street names which appear in Balzac's works: La Rue du Boucher Gris (Drunken Butcher Street), La Rue à Chercher (Hard to Find Street).

ISSOUDUN

Casanova (R. Danièle) 6
Dormoy (Bd Marx) 12
République (R. de la) 23
10 Juin (Pl. du) 32
Avénier (R. de l') 2
Bons-Enfants (R. des) 3
Brossolette (R. Pierre) 4
Champion (Bd) 7
Croix-de-Pierre (Pl. de la) 9
Estienne-d'Orves (R. d') 13
Fossés-de-Villatte (R. des) 15
Gargolle (R. de la) 17
Ponts (R. des) 18
Poterie (R. de la) 19
Poulies (R. des) 20
Quatre-Vents (R. des) 21
Roosevelt (Bd du Prés.) 24
Sémard (R. Pierre) 25
Stalingrad (Bd de) 27
Trois-Places (R. des) 28
4 Août (R. du) 31

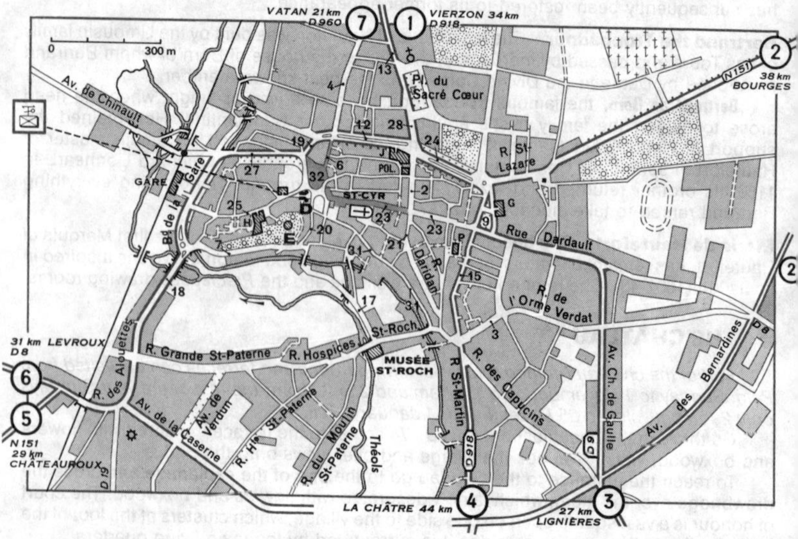

■ SIGHTS *time : 3/4 hour*

Church of St-Cyr. – There is a very fine 14-15C stained glass window in the chevet. It is divided into five vertical sections and in addition to depicting the Crucifixion contains medallions illustrating scenes from the lives of St. Cyran and St. Julitta. The choir and the Rosary Chapel contain fine sculptured stalls. Above the west door is a Descent from the Cross painted by Boucher of Bourges in 1625.

Belfry (Beffroi) (D). – The belfry, flanked by two round towers of unequal size, once served as a gateway through the castle wall to the town.

The White Tower (La Tour Blanche) (E). – The tower was built at the end of the 12C by Richard Lionheart. The inside is octagonal, the outside nearly circular; it is 33 m - 108 ft high and the walls are 4 m - 13 ft thick. *To visit, apply to the caretaker at the Town Hall.*

The three floors in the tower may be reached by the staircase of 145 steps. On the way you will see the fine ogive vaulted ceiling of the main hall. From the top platform there is a view over the town and the country that lies between the valleys of the Indre and the Cher.

St-Roch Museum. – *Guided tours 10am to noon and 2 to 7pm (afternoons only from 1 November to 30 March except Saturdays and Sundays); closed Tuesdays and some holidays; 6F.*

The museum is housed in the former hospital (Hôtel-Dieu) which is built on piles over the river Théols in a picturesque setting.

Lapidary Museum. – In the main ward is displayed a collection of Gallo-Roman remains. Statuettes and bronze swords in a display case are noteworthy.

Chapel. – The most outstanding items are two large carvings of the **Tree of Jesse**★; they were made at the end of the 15C and represent the genealogical tree of Christ, showing the ancestors of the Virgin and figures of the prophets, kings and knights. There are also interesting painted enamel plaques from Limoges including one by Limosin (16C) and many old statuettes (15-16C Madonnas). A charming small chapel with star vaulting contains two stained glass windows in the Flamboyant style.

Pharmacy★ (Apothicairerie). – Go through the rooms decorated with Aubusson tapestries and remarkable furnishings formerly used by the hospital officials, then through the kitchen to view a valuable pharmaceutical collection: 17-18C pharmacy (furniture, glassware and 400 Nevers porcelain jars), rare painted boxes and many unusual items.

EXCURSIONS

Forêts de Chœurs et de Bommiers. – *Round tour of 45 km - 28 miles – about 1 1/2 hours. Leave Issoudun by ③, the D 9, then take the D 16 to the right.*

Chezal-Benoît. – Pop 1 315. Sole reminder of a Benedictine abbey is the 12 and 13C church which stands in the grounds of the psychiatric hospital. The façade, which resembles those of Poitou is decorated with fine Romanesque capitals and fluted columns. The interior is pure Romanesque; the fine carved stalls in the chancel date from the 15C.

Take the D 65 ᴱ to the left out of Chezal-Benoît. This road runs alongside the forest, passing on the way a forester's lodge (Les Bindés), before reaching Pruniers.
In Pruniers take the D 925 to the right before forking right into the D 68 which takes you through the forest.

Chœurs and Bommiers Forests. – Extending over 5 000 ha - 19 sq miles these great forests are composed mainly of oaks while the undergrowth is mostly bracken and holly.
The D 68 leads back to Issoudun.

Tour of Font-Moreau Woods. – *47 km - 29 miles. Leave Issoudun by ②, the N 151.*

Chârost. – Pop 1 152. The south doorway of this Romanesque church which is built in iron limestone *(roussard)* is adorned with a figure of Christ surrounded by the symbols of the Evangelists.

Take the D 18 to the left in the direction of Poisieux then the D 114 to the right.

Ruins of Font-Moreau Castle. – The romantic ruins of the 15C Font-Moreau Castle, deep in the wood of the same name, comprise a small entrance fort, a perimeter wall with occasional round towers and now dry moats.

Drive to Bertigny and take the D 27 to the right and soon after turn right again into the D 16E.

Castelnau Castle. – *Not open to the public.* This magnificent Renaissance castle flanked by four corner turrets and girt by moats and pleasant gardens, has a square keep dating from the Middle Ages.

Continue along the same road as far as the N 151 which takes you back to Issoudun via Chârost.

JUMILHAC-LE-GRAND

Michelin map 72 fold 17 – 12 km - 7 miles southwest of St-Yrieix-la-Perche – Pop 1 454

Jumilhac Castle was built in a picturesque and romantic **setting★** on the tip of a rocky spur overlooking the Isle gorges. The church, formerly the castle chapel, has an octagonal belfry ornamented by two storeys of blind arcades.

Castle. – *Guided tours 1 July to 15 September, 10 to 11.30am and 2 to 6pm; out of season, Sundays and holidays only, 2 to 5.30pm; closed 15 November to 15 March; time: 1/2 hour; 6F.*

It was built in the 13C and altered during the Renaissance. It is an impressive building crowned with a multitude of pepper-pot roofs embellished with dormer windows, lantern towers and corbelled turrets. The slate roof is ornamented with fanciful 15C lead figurines, wreaths and birds along the crest.

The two side wings were built in the 17C. The wing on the right has a fine stone staircase with massive Louis XV balusters and the panelled great hall is adorned with a chimneypiece decorated with sculptures representing the four seasons by a Limousin craftsman. One room known as the "Spinner's" room has thick walls with naive decorations representing animals, angels and foliage. Louise de Hautefort is said to have been kept a prisoner here by her jealous husband.

LABASTIDE-MURAT

Michelin map 75 south of fold 18 – *Local map p 108* – Pop 732

Labastide-Murat, which stands at one of the highest points on the Gramat Causse was originally Labastide-Fortunière, but changed its name in honour of one of its most glorious sons.

The modest house in which Joachim Murat was born, on the southwest side of the town, and the château that he had built for his brother André, keep alive the memory of one of the most valiant soldiers of the French Empire (1804-1814).

The Fantastic Destiny of Joachim Murat. – Murat was born in 1767, the son of an innkeeper. He was destined for the Church, but at twenty-one decided instead to be a soldier. The campaigns in Italy and Egypt enabled him to gain rapid promotion under Napoleon, whose brother-in-law he became, and he was elevated to Marshal of the Empire, Grand Duke of Berg and of Cleves and king of Naples. The mad bravery he displayed on all the battlefields of Europe, his influence over his troops whom he did not hesitate to lead in battle, made him a legendary hero. His star declined like that of his master whom he abandoned in the dark days of the Empire. After the Bourbons had returned to Naples he tried to reconquer his kingdom, but he was taken prisoner and shot in 1815.

Murat Museum (Musée Murat). – *Guided tours 1 July to 31 August, 8am to noon and 2 to 6pm; closed Tuesdays; 5F.*

The museum is in the house where Murat was born (little street to the left of the church). You see the 18C kitchen, the inn saloon, a large genealogical tree and, on the first floor, mementoes of the king and of his mother.

EXCURSIONS

Soulomès. – Pop 128. *3 km - 2 miles to the southeast by the D 17.* There is a Gothic church with a square chevet and a belfry-porch which once formed part of a priory, in this small village on the Gramat Causse. Interesting 14C frescoes have been uncovered in the chancel. They illustrate episodes in the life of Christ. Scenes immediately recognisable include Jesus and Mary Magdalene, the Incredulity of St. Thomas, the Entombment and Christ Resurrected before a Knight of Malta.

Vaillac. – Pop 105. *5 km - 3 miles to the northwest by the D 17.* The outline of a massive feudal castle *(not open to the public)* looks down on this modest little village built on the Gramat Causse.

The castle was built in the 14 and 16C and consists of a huge main building flanked by five towers and of a keep.

Europe on a single sheet: Michelin Map nº 920.

LACAPELLE-MARIVAL

Michelin map 75 folds 19 and 20 – Pop 1 337 – *Facilities p 42*

The town has kept many buildings that bear testimony to its age and importance as the fief of Lacapelle-Marival which was held from the 12 to 18C by the Cardaillac family.

Castle. – The massive square machicolated keep flanked by watch-towers at each corner was built in the 13C. The living quarters, abutting on one side and divided by massive round towers, were added in the 15C.

The Gothic church, an old town gateway and the 15C covered market supported on stone piles and roofed with round tiles, make a charming group with the castle.

EXCURSION

Le Bourg; Rudelle; Aynac. – *Round tour of 27 km - 17 miles – about 1 hour. Leave Lacapelle-Marival by the D 940 to the south.*

Le Bourg. – Pop 222. The church is the only building to remain of a former priory. The transept and chancel are adorned with Romanesque blind arcades and fine capitals.

Turn right into the N 140.

Rudelle. – Pop 155. The **church** *(illustration p 31)* founded in the 13C by Bertrand de Cardaillac, the lord of Lacapelle-Marival, looks like a feudal keep crowned by a terrace with a crenellated parapet. From the churchyard *(access by an alleyway to the right of the church)* there is a view of the chevet and the building as a whole.

At ground-level an ogive vaulted hall is used as the parish church. The upper storey is reached by a wooden staircase climbing to the gallery, a ladder, a trap-door and finally a stone staircase. This refuge, which now contains the bells, is lit by narrow loopholes. To reach the terrace which also provided refuge, another ladder and stone staircase have to be climbed. From the machicolated watchpath there is a fine view of the village.

Follow the N 140 to Thémines, then take to the right the D 40.

Aynac. – Pop 689. Aynac castle stands in a countryside of woods and fields, its crenellated corner towers topped by domes crowding close to the keep.

The D 940 returns to Lacapelle-Marival.

LACAVE Caves ★ (Grottes de LACAVE)

Michelin map 75 fold 18 – *Local maps pp 94 and 108*

Near the valley of the Dordogne which makes a deep cut through the Gramat Causse, a series of caves at the foot of the cliffs beside the river was discovered in 1902 by Armand Viré, a student of E.A. Martel.

Guided tours 1 June to 31 July, 9am to noon and 2 to 6.30pm (6pm, 1 April to 31 May and 1 September to 14 October); in August 9am to 7pm; 19 F, children 11 F; time: 1 hour. A small railway and a lift bring you to the underground platform from which the visit proper begins.

The galleries visited by tourists are a mile long *(on foot Rtn)* and divide into two groups, visited one after the other. The shapes of the concretions in the caves look like people, animals, buildings and even whole cities.

The first group contains stalagmites and stalactites. Through the second group underground rivers run from crag to crag and flood out into pools.

In the lake Chamber (Salle du Lac) the fluorescent nature of the concretions makes the parts that are still growing, glow in the dark.

The Hall of Wonders (Salle des Merveilles) contains beautiful eccentrics.

Prehistoric tools and weapons made of bone and horn, and flints were discovered when the caves were being arranged for visitors.

LANQUAIS Castle

Michelin map 75 centre of fold 15 – 20 km - 13 miles east of Bergerac

Open 1 April to 31 October, 9.30 to 11am and 2.30 to 7pm; closed Tuesdays; time: 1/2 hour; 5F.

The castle was built over a long period in many different architectural styles.

Abutting on the mediaeval wing flanked by a polygonal tower with a spiral staircase, is a Renaissance structure. A group of workmen came from the Louvre to build this wing, which was in fact, only part of a larger plan that was never completed. It is a well-proportioned building. The windows are surmounted by triangular pediments.

You may reach the round tower, which is the oldest part of the castle, by way of the watchpath with its cross-shaped loopholes and battlements. From the tower platform you will see the park and Lanquais village clustered round its small Romanesque church. The Renaissance wing contains interesting furniture mostly of the Louis XIII period (1601-1643), beautiful chimneypieces and French ceilings. Particularly outstanding is the dining hall with its Toile de Jouy wall hangings.

LAROQUEBROU

Michelin map 76 fold 11 – Pop 1 070

This is a pleasant little town lying at the mouth of the Cère Gorges. Standing above the town on a lone rock are a statue of the Virgin and the ruins of the castle.

Castle. – From the terrace there is a good view. This was the residence of the lords of Montal. One of these, the Seneschal of Guyenne, was killed in Paris in 1631. His funeral at Laroquebrou brought such crowds to the town that when the time came to dispense alms, seventeen were smothered underfoot.

Church. – This ornate church is late Gothic in style.

St-Etienne-Cantalès Dam★. – *4.5 km - 3 miles to the southeast.* This dam is of the heavy arched type and is 70 m - 230 ft high, 270 m - 300 yds along the crest and 35 m - 115 ft thick at the base. The reservoir has a capacity of just under 30 000 million gallons. Flood waters are controlled by a "ski-jump" overfall which passes above the power station. The station itself is equipped with three generators capable of producing annually 85 million kWh.

Islands, headlands and an indented shoreline make this an attractive reservoir.

LARROQUE-TOIRAC Castle

Michelin map 79 fold 10 – 14 km - 9 miles southwest of Figeac

The castle clinging to a high cliff-face overlooks the village and the valley of the Lot. The large fortress was built in the 12C and was owned for a long time by the Cardaillac family, who championed Quercy resistance to the English during the Hundred Years War. The castle after being taken and retaken by the English was finally burnt down at the end of the 14C, but was raised again from the ruins during Louis XI's reign.

Guided tours from early July to early September, 11am to noon and 2 to 6pm; time: 1/2 hour; 10F.

A path starting from the church square *(car park)* leads to a round tower built at the beginning of the Hundred Years War as defence against attack by artillery. It leads to the part of the castle which was once used as servants' quarters and then through to the courtyard. The huge keep which once stood 30 m – 98 ft high but was razed to only 8 m – 26 ft in 1793, is pentagonal the better to resist the force of rocks hurled down at it from the cliffs above. A spiral staircase in a Romanesque tower abutting on the main building leads to the different storeys. The guardroom has a fine Romanesque chimneypiece, the main hall a Gothic one; the upper floors contain furniture and furnishings from the time of Louis XIII to the Directoire period (early 17C to late 18C).

LAUZERTE

Michelin map 79 fold 17 – Pop 1 697

Lauzerte has a picturesque **setting**★ and can be seen from afar in the undulating country of Bas-Quercy where the limestone hills are separated by fertile plains.

Lauzerte, which was once a *bastide* *(p 32)* built on a bluff in 1241 by the Count of Toulouse, was occupied by the English.

Upper Town. – The greystone houses with their almost flat roofs are clustered round the church of St-Barthélemy and the Place de la Halle.

This square with its covered arcades contains a half-timbered house. There are several old houses mainly in Rue du Château, some have timber walls, some are Gothic in style with twin windows and others are Renaissance with mullioned windows. Views of the gentle, rolling countryside of hills and small valleys.

EXCURSIONS

Tour in Quercy Blanc (White Quercy). – *24 km - 15 miles – about 3/4 hour – Local map opposite.*

Southeast of Lauzerte take the D 81 which branches off the D 953. The route indicated provides many views of the town of Lauzerte and takes the motorist through this picturesque hilly region. There is a marked contrast between the somewhat poor plateau, where lines of cypresses and houses with flat roofs covered with pale pink round tiles give a southern aspect to the countryside, and the valleys and hillsides richly covered in crops. The different types of soil enable the peasant farmer to grow a variety of crops and to achieve true economic independence within his own holding. In the valleys also there is a contrast: the valley bottoms contain rich meadows and are hemmed by lines of poplars; on the hillsides small parcels of land are diligently cultivated, especially those bearing vines, *Chasselas de Moissac*, tobacco or fruit trees.

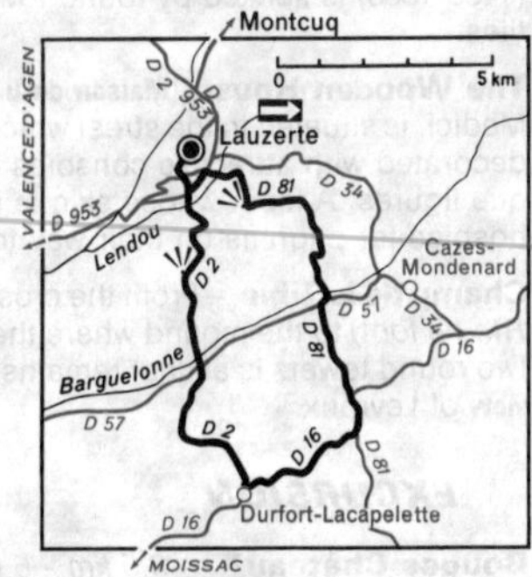

Montcuq. – Pop 1 082. *13 km - 8 miles to the northeast by the D 953.*

This village was once fortified. A tall tower, once the castle keep and now all that remains of the stronghold, stands on a hillock overlooking the Petite Barguelonne river. The **view** from the foot of the tower extends over the surrounding hills and valleys. The village also contains picturesque old houses with timber walls near the town hall.

LAUZUN

Michelin map 79 fold 4 – Pop 776

The former barony of Lauzun was raised to a duchy to honour the marshal of Lauzun.

Lauzun (1633-1723). – Lauzun was an officer cadet; he was witty, adored by women and was one of the most scintillating men at the court of Louis XIV, whose favourite he rapidly became. His hectic life abounded in romantic episodes of which the most famous was his proposed marriage to La Grande Mademoiselle, Duchess of Montpensier and cousin to the king. This was a subject that preoccupied the chroniclers of the day.

Château. – *Open Whitsun to 30 September, 11am to noon and 2.30 to 6pm; 8F.* This 16C château has a beautiful façade looking on to a courtyard; it can be seen on entering the park. The main building dating from the 15C has an octagonal turret and is joined to the Renaissance part by a domed pavilion which was started in the 17C in Lauzun but only terminated in the 19C.

Church. – This Gothic building contains a carved wood retable and pulpit in the Baroque style, and a 12C Virgin in the left apsidal chapel.

EXCURSION

Castillonnès. – Pop 1 409. *12 km - 7 miles to the northeast by the D 1 and then the N 21 to the right.* This former *bastide (p 32)*, founded in 1259 by Alphonse de Poitiers, is built on a hill commanding the Dropt valley. The central square is surrounded by covered arcades.

LESTERPS

Michelin map 72 fold 6 – 9 km - 6 miles east of Confolens – Pop 559

The Church of St-Pierre of Lesterps (pronounced Laitair) is all that remains of an abbey founded at the beginning of the 11C. It is preceded by an impressive **belfry-porch**★ in grey granite. Above the porch with its three bays adorned with rough hewn capitals rises a massive belfry 43 m - 141 ft high, whose top tier is pierced on each side with a triple arcade.

The interior is plain in style: a wide nave with cradle vaulting, flanked by narrow aisles, ends in an oven-vaulted apse built in the 19C. In the nave one can see parts of the former chancel, 12C capitals, one of which portrays the Holy Women at the tomb. Above the latter, medallions depict Christ in Benediction, the Virgin and Child and a knight, thought to be St. Gaultier of l'Esterps.

LEVROUX

Michelin map 68 fold 8 – Pop 3 126 – *Facilities p 38*

The pointed tiles of this small town cluster together in a hollow. Levroux renowned for its goat's cheese of the same name, retains an activity which goes back to the Middle Ages – the art of parchment making.

Collegiate Church of St. Silvanus (Collégiale St-Sylvain). – The building rests on older foundations, the remains of the Roman Governors' palaces. The tympanum of the main doorway portrays a Resurrection of the Dead and a Last Judgment. Statues of saints adorn the niches of the covings.

On entering the north aisle, note two fine multicoloured statues of wood and a Trinity.

The transitional Romanesque-Gothic chancel is supported by ribs which descend onto statue-columns. The late 15C **stalls** form a fine ensemble with cheek-pieces maliciously portraying the heads of clerics and laymen. The organ case (restored) also dates from the 15C.

Champagne Gateway (Porte de Champagne). – Situated near the church, the gateway (1435-1506) is flanked by round towers and its roof is covered with dark brown coloured tiles.

The Wooden House (Maison de bois). – This house, built in the 15C for Catherine de' Medici, is situated in the street which opens onto the façade of the Collegiate Church. It is decorated with attractive consoles representing angels' faces; at the corner are grotesque figures. A leper whose skin is scaling off reminds us that the house was formerly a hospice for pilgrims on their way to Santiago de Compostela in Spain.

Champ de la Tibie. – From the crossroads of the D 956 and the D 2 a path leads *(1/4 hour Rtn on foot)* to the mound where the Gallo-Roman city once stood. A gateway flanked by two round towers is all that remains of a ruined castle dating from the 15C. There is a fine **view** of Levroux.

EXCURSION

Bouges Château★. – *9.5 km - 6 miles to the northeast by the D 2. Description p 57.*

LIGNIÈRES

Michelin map 68 south of fold 10 – *Local map p 162* – Pop 1 867

Lignières lies in the heart of a region of family farms where stock is raised and lush meadows are divided by quickset hedges. When Calvin was a student at Bourges University this was an important centre of Calvinism where he established many reformed churches.

An interesting château built in the Classical style stands beside the Arnon.

Château. – *Only the outside may be visited from 9am to 6pm; closed Wednesdays; 3F.*

Jérôme de Nouveau acquired the Lignières land in 1653 and commissioned the building of the noble pile we see today on the site of a mediaeval fortress which had been transformed at the time of the Renaissance. To supervise the château's construction he called on François le Vau, brother of the well-known Louis le Vau, architect of the Louvre, of Vaux-le-Vicomte and Versailles. The building gives an impression at once of nobility and austerity.

As you walk round the castle there are pretty views of the park. A bridge across the moat, which was designed as an ornamental stretch of water, leads to the court of honour. This is surrounded on two sides by main living quarters and a great wing, linked by a gallery with tall windows. Small triangular pediments, supported on pilasters in the Louis XIV style, surmount the bay windows.

Church. – This was built near the Arnon in the 12C and still contains a doorway adorned with Romanesque capitals. In the chancel is the oratory where St. Jeanne de France, daughter of Louis XI, who lived for fifteen years at Lignières, used to worship.

LIMOGES ★

Michelin map 72 fold 17 – *Local map p 122* – Pop 144 082

A ford across the Vienne and two stepped plateaux that could be put to defensive use are the reason for Limoges' existence. In the Gallo-Roman period when the town was known as Augustoritum, it spread out in an amphitheatre along the right bank of the river. In the Middle Ages two separate and rival townships developed: the City grouped round its cathedral built on a low shelf overlooking the Vienne, and the Château, the busy commercial town on the opposite slope in the shadow of the powerful abbey of St-Martial.

The town today spreads out widely north of the Vienne; its industrial rise is largely due to its porcelain and enamel works and shoe factories. The modernisation brought about by the conversion to natural gas from the town of Lacq in the Landes, now places the Limoges porcelain industry technically to the forefront in world production.

HISTORICAL NOTES

The Limousin Apostle. – In about the year AD 250, **Martial** came to convert the people of Limousin to Christianity. The country was hostile and the missionary, pursued by the priests of the God Mercury, owed his safety to the protection granted him by a brave woman. The zealous Martial soon converted his hostess' daughter, **Valerie**, who broke off her engagement with the Roman Governor Stephen. Valerie was then condemned to death but Stephen found her death so moving that, in turn, he too was converted.

Sometime later Martial burst into a theatre, interrupted a bawdy scene and preached the Word of God. The actors seized him and, in front of the crowd, beat him before dragging him off to jail. A supernatural light began to glow within the prison and the people, crying out that a miracle had occurred, delivered Martial from captivity. He went immediately to the temple where he broke the false gods and consecrated the church to St. Stephen. From that time onwards Limousin became the "land of the saints".

The memory of St. Martial was perpetuated by building within the city itself, an abbey in which the saint's relics could be kept. The monastery soon became an important pilgrimage centre and a staging point on one of the routes to Santiago de Compostela. It was destroyed in 1791 *(see p 121)*.

Famous Citizens of Limoges. – Many of the sons of Limoges have gained fame. Among the artists are **Leonard Limosin** (1505-1576) "enameller and painter in ordinary to the king's royal chamber", who won favour with four monarchs. By his skill in engraving, painting and decoration he became one of the leaders of the great school of enamellers of the 16C whose fame, through the Laudin dynasty, lasted until the 18C. The painter **Auguste Renoir** (1841-1919), one of the masters of the Impressionist School, worked for some time at the beginning of his career as a painter of porcelain.

Among statesmen, **Pierre Vergniaud** (1753-1793) was the most famous orator of the Girondin Group in the Convention; there was also **Sadi Carnot** (1737-1894) who became President of the Republic.

Military prowess is brilliantly represented by Marshal **Jourdan** (1762-1833) commander-in-chief of the army of the Convention at the age of thirty-one, then of the glorious Sambre-et-Meuse army which he led to victory at Fleurus and on to the further successes in the conquest of Belgium, the victory of Aldenhoven and the occupation of Coblenz. The name of Marshal **Bugeaud** (1784-1849) is linked with the conquest of Algeria and the victorious war against Abd-el-Kader; his bravery and chivalry endowed him with immense prestige not only with his own men but also with the Berbers.

ENAMEL WORK AND PORCELAIN

Enamels. – *See p 30: Minor Arts.* Enamels are made from glass with a lead base in colours which have countless vivid variations of tone owing to metal oxides being added when they are compounded. The glass and colours are formed into hard, thin wafers which are powdered before being spread with a spatula over a flat backing of gold, silver or copper. Successive firings give the enamel the appearance of solid crystal, Enamel work has been known from ancient times but it was not until the 12C that Limoges acquired exceptional skill in its manufacture. Lead silicates and rare metal oxides such as gold, silver, uranium, cobalt, manganese, tungsten and copper are all found in the locality due to the presence of Primary Era faults.

Cloisonné and *champlevé* enamels (in which the colours are kept apart by thin outline plates and in which the colours are fitted into hollows made in the surface, respectively) came into their own in the Middle Ages. **Cloisonné** is obtained by soldering fine metal strips along the outlines of the design already laid on the metal object to be decorated; **champlevé**, which since the 12C is the only type to be produced at Limoges, is executed on a copper base sufficiently thick to be hollowed out with a graving tool. One or more coats of enamel are spread in the hollows; this produces glass pictures of monochrome on a dark background, gold camaïeu on a black or blue background, clear or opaque multicolour patterns, the tints frequently made even more vivid by the addition of gold or silver sequins inserted between two coats of enamel. The parts of the copper base not hollowed out, are usually gilded.

The Limousin workshops excelled in the *champlevé* technique until the 14C when **painted enamels** came in. In this, the design was outlined with a paintbrush on enamel coated over copper leaf. **Painted enamelling** is still practised today in Limoges, the enamellers having gone back to this method. The enamel, as in the 16C, is spread with a spatula and the original designs are outlined on the bases with an etching needle. Firing takes place as each colour is applied, at temperatures of from 1 100-800 °C (2 300-1 700 °F.), decreasing each time so as not to injure the tints beneath the latest one to be applied and fired.

A visit to a workshop helps one to understand the techniques employed. Most of the enamel workshop are prepared to let visitors see round during working hours. There are several workshops in Limoges, in particular around Place Wilson. At least go and look at their window displays.

Porcelain. – Among the industries for which Limoges is famous, porcelain, started at the end of the 18C, has been outstandingly successful.

Kaolin of remarkable purity was discovered at Saint-Yrieix in 1768 *(p 173)*. After encouraging experiments had been carried out at the Royal Factory at Sèvres, Turgot, who was then General Intendant of Limousin, set up a porcelain works in 1771. This was under the patronage of the Count of Artois and marked the beginning, for Limousin ceramics, of an era of prosperity which was hardly interrupted even by the troubled years of the Revolution. After 1815 the industry became concentrated round Limoges which, because of its position on the Vienne, could land the wood for the kilns from lumber rafts floated down river.

Nowadays, more than 50 % of all the porcelain made in France comes from Limoges. Approximately 3 500 workmen are employed in the factories and the ware is world famous.

Production is chiefly of tableware though the tradition of luxury articles continues, their high quality and finish denoting the great care with which the old standards are maintained.

Porcelain, the luxury chinaware. – China is made by firing a paste made basically from clay. The difference between different types of ceramic ware – bricks, stoneware, earthenware and porcelain – arises from the clay used, the appearance of the article and the temperature of the firing. There are two categories, depending on the type of clay: porous china – earthenware, glazed pottery, bricks and faïence (the latter is obtained from a porous paste which is white and fine grained, is fired at a temperature of about 950 °C - 1 740 °F and coated with a transparent glaze) and non-porous china – stoneware and porcelain – which owe their properties to the smoothness and vitrification of the clay at a high temperature.

For a long time porcelain imported from the Orient was the only kind known in Europe. Before 1700 attempts by French potters led to the production of **soft-paste porcelain.** Non-malleable this new material was difficult to work and did not tolerate very high temperatures. It was however of this soft-paste that the very fine pre-1771 Sèvres porcelain, was made.

With the discovery of kaolin at St-Yrieix in Limousin, the production of **hard-paste porcelain** made from a kaolin and sand base, became possible. The kaolin is first reduced to a liquid and homogeneous paste. The potters and turners cast it to the required shape; then the pots are lifted and finished. The articles are next given a preliminary firing at a temperature of 950 °C (1 650 °F); this is a partial firing and is known as the biscuit-baking. After glazing the ware is given a complete firing at 1 400 °C (2 550 °F) in kilns lit for each firing; this produces hard-paste porcelain. The ware is sometimes decorated at the "biscuit" stage (before glazing), but usually after glazing in which case a final firing at 800 °C (1 470 °F) is necessary to fix the decoration. Throughout the entire manufacturing process a single piece of porcelain is subjected to 30 different operations, manual or mechanical, each of which is followed by a strict control.

■ THE CATHEDRAL AND MUSEUMS *time: 2 1/2 hours*

St. Stephen's Cathedral★ (Cathédrale St-Étienne) (BZ). – St. Stephen's Cathedral is the most outstanding building in Limoges and the only one in all Limousin to be built completely in the Gothic style. It bears such resemblance in its design to the Cathedral of Clermont-Ferrand and Narbonne that it is thought all three must have been planned by the same architect, Jean Deschamps.

St. Stephen's was successor to a Romanesque church of which only a part of the crypt and the lower storeys of the belfry remain. The Gothic cathedral was begun in 1273; the chancel was completed at the beginning of the next century, and the first two bays of the nave had been constructed by the end of the 15C. Jean de Langeac undertook the completion of the cathedral in 1537, but died in 1541. Mgr. Dusquesnay completed the church between 1876 and 1888.

Exterior. – The **St. John Doorway★** is really the cathedral's main entrance. It is of very fine grained granite and was constructed between 1516 and 1530 when the Flamboyant style was at its peak. Two pierced galleries divide the façade into three tiers. A statue of Christ

(After a photo by Arthaud, Grenoble)

Cathedral – St. John's Doorway.

stands at the pier; the entire tympanum is adorned with a background of blind arcades filled in with richly coloured mosaics. An elongated gable frames the archivolt and rises to the base of the large rose window. The two Renaissance wooden doors are carved to show scenes from the lives of St. Martial and St. Stephen.

There is a good overall view of the chevet from the Rue Porte-Panet on the east side.

The belfry is square and just over 62 m - 203 ft high. The lower three storeys are Romanesque, but the lowest has been submerged in stonework added to support the tower. The next four storeys are Gothic, of which the three uppermost are octagonal, a design often found in Limousin architecture. The spire that crowned this tower was struck by lightning and destroyed in 1571. The belfry stood apart from the nave until last century when a modern narthex and three bays were added.

Interior. – The porch contains several memorial stones. The nave gives an impression of unity of style even though it took 600 years to build. The boldness and elegance of line of the roof vaulting are wonderful; the triforium is constructed to act as a base for the tall windows.

The **rood screen**★ (at the end of the nave under the organ-loft), built for Jean de Langeac by artists from Touraine between 1533 and 1534, once separated the chancel from the nave. This limestone screen is topped by a gallery with pendants decorated with statues of the Six Virtues, the work of Jean Arnaud. A large bay opens up the back wall. The niches, to either side of the door are framed by columns and pilasters. The ensemble is decorated in a rich Italian style. The low reliefs at the base depict mythological scenes – note Hercules' labours.

The three **tombs**★ that stand round the chancel are of considerable decorative interest. Walking round the chancel from the south you will see consecutively:

- the tomb of Raynaud de la Porte (14C), Bishop of Limoges and later Archbishop of Bourges and cardinal. He asked that he might be buried in the cathedral he had helped to build.
- the tomb of Jean de Langeac. This mausoleum was built in 1544 and is an example of the Renaissance style at its most delicate. Fourteen carved panels depict scenes in the life of St. John as described in the Book of Revelation. It is in effect an adaptation of the little Passion by Dürer, translated to stone with exceptional spirit and feeling for movement.
- the tomb of Bernard Brun who was, in turn, Bishop of Le Puy, Noyon and Auxerre. This monument, in the pure 14C French style, is adorned with four low relief panels: the upper panels show, on one side, the Coronation of the Virgin, on the other, Jesus Christ, the Virgin and St. John; the lower panels, the martyrdom of St. Valerie and the Crucifixion.

Municipal Museum★ **(Musée Municipal)** (**BZ M**). – *Open 10 to 11.45am and 2 to 6pm (5pm 1 October to 31 May); closed Tuesdays from 1 October to 30 June and 1 January, 1 and 8 May, 1 and 11 November, 25 December.*

The museum is housed in the former archbishop's palace. This elegant 18C building in grey granite near the cathedral was designed by two Limousin architects, the brothers Brousseaud.

The museum has some 300 **Limousin enamels**★★ dating from the 12C to the present day, most of which are on display in the main hall on the ground floor. Among the collection of painted enamels note two plaques by Monvaerni (15C), several pieces by Leonard Limosin and a ewer by Jean III Pénicaud (16C), and works by the Laudin family (17 and 18C).

The large department of Egyptology has a particularly rich collection of terracotta figurines. The section devoted to French painting includes 17-18C works (Nattier) and canvasses by Renoir, Guillaumin, Pascin, S. Valadon and Dufy.

In a large room on the first floor are displayed geological specimens found in Limousin while other rooms are devoted to Gallo-Roman finds; note in particular an early 2C fresco.

The fine vaulted cellars which were formerly the bishop's palace kitchens complete with chimneys, ovens and well, make a good setting for the ancient and mediaeval exhibits of the lapidary museum. These include cippi, sarcophagi, tombs, capitals, corbels and keystones.

Bishop's Palace Gardens (Jardins de l'Évêché) (**BZ**). – These pleasant gardens rise in terraces above the Vienne and provide a good view of the cathedral and the palace. There is also a botanical garden.

Adrien-Dubouché National Museum★★ **(Musée National Adrien-Dubouché)** (**AY**). – *Open 10am to noon and 1.30 to 5pm; closed Tuesdays; 9F weekdays; 4.50F Sundays and holidays.*

The museum was founded in 1867, became a national museum in 1881 and is named after the director Adrien Dubouché, who provided it with the foundation of its collections. Some 10 000 items, dating from the pottery of ancient times to porcelain from factories in production at Limoges today, show the evolution of chinaware in France and throughout the world.

We suggest that you start the visit on the first floor.

First floor. – The history of ceramic manufacture from the 8 to 18C is traced in the right wing: excellent specimens from the Middle East, Hispano-Moorish porcelain, historiated Italian faiences and chinaware from Spain and Holland (Delft). Other rooms show the development of French manufacture as seen from ware produced by centres such as Moustiers, Nevers, Rouen, Sèvres, etc.

The main hall contains precious Chinese porcelain. The items dating from the 7 to 13C are glazed. Next comes white porcelain; this is followed by blue and white china under the Ming dynasty (14-17C). During the same period a wide variety of coloured ware was also produced: "five colours", *famille verte* and *famille rose*.

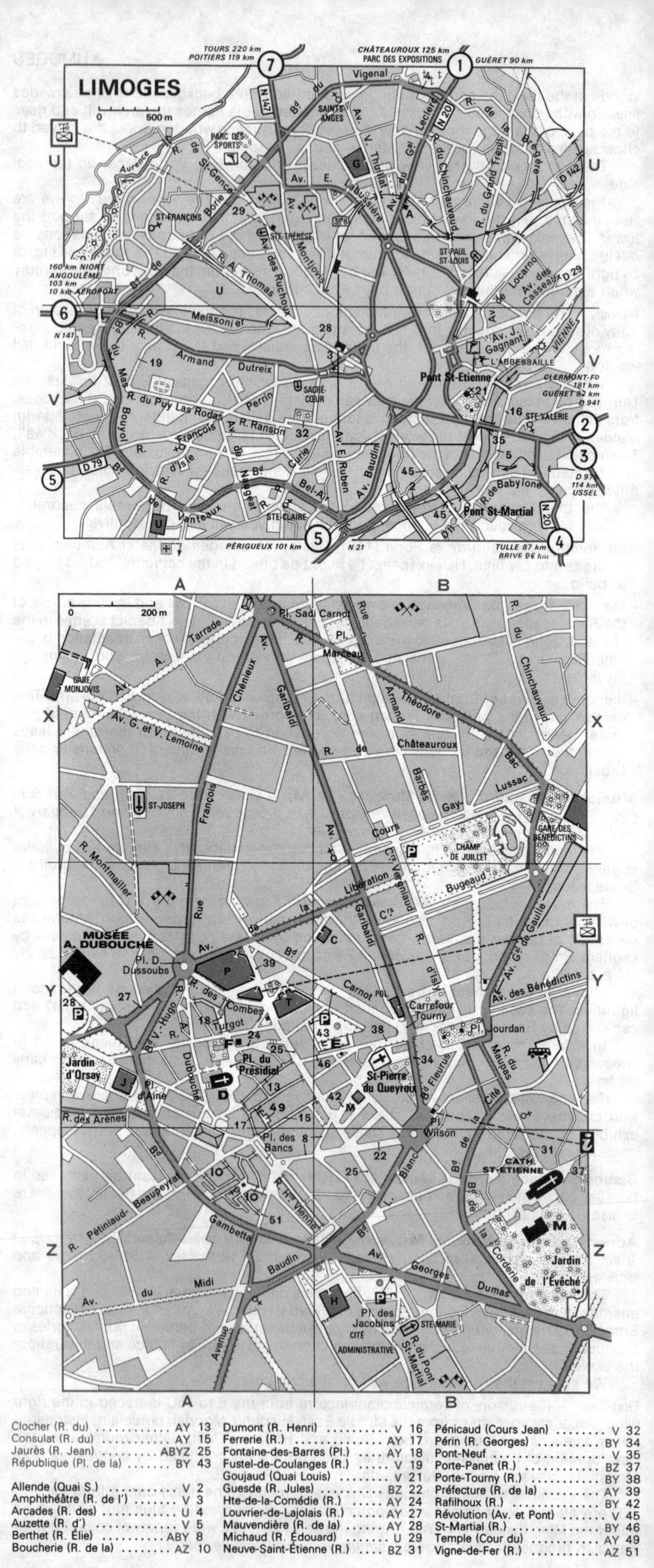

Clocher (R. du)	AY	13	Dumont (R. Henri)	V	16	Pénicaud (Cours Jean)	V	32
Consulat (R. du)	AY	15	Ferrerie (R.)	AY	17	Périn (R. Georges)	BY	34
Jaurès (R. Jean)	ABYZ	25	Fontaine-des-Barres (Pl.)	AY	18	Pont-Neuf	V	35
République (Pl. de la)	BY	43	Fustel-de-Coulanges (R.)	V	19	Porte-Panet (R.)	BZ	37
			Goujaud (Quai Louis)	V	21	Porte-Tourny (R.)	BY	38
Allende (Quai S.)	V	2	Guesde (R. Jules)	BZ	22	Préfecture (R. de la)	AY	39
Amphithéâtre (R. de l')	V	3	Hte-de-la-Comédie (R.)	AY	24	Rafilhoux (R.)	BY	42
Arcades (R. des)	U	4	Louvrier-de-Lajolais (R.)	AY	27	Révolution (Av. et Pont)	V	45
Auzette (R. d')	V	5	Mauvendière (R. de la)	AY	28	St-Martial (R.)	BY	46
Berthet (R. Élie)	ABY	8	Michaud (R. Édouard)	U	29	Temple (Cour du)	AY	49
Boucherie (R. de la)	AZ	10	Neuve-Saint-Étienne (R.)	BZ	31	Vigne-de-Fer (R.)	AZ	51

The left wing is devoted to research and development of ceramic manufacture in Europe in the 18C: soft-paste porcelain from St-Cloud where blue and white tones predominate, Chantilly porcelain with its brilliant colours, gold and blue Sèvres pieces as well as specimens from other European countries of the same period. There is also hard-paste porcelain from Germany (Meissen etc) and the first articles to be produced in the Sèvres, Limoges and Paris factories. In a small room are exhibited the works of Italian, French, German and Arab glass-blowers of the 14 to 18C.

Ground floor. – 19-20C porcelain from Europe but mainly from France with a large collection from Limoges.

■ ADDITIONAL SIGHTS

Church of St-Michel-des-Lions★ (**AY D**). – Construction began in 1364 and continued during the 15C when the north doorway was built and the 16C when a west bay was added. The plan is rectangular, characteristic of the hall-church.

Outside near the belfry door on the south side can be seen the two lions carved in granite which have given the church its name. It is believed that in the Middle Ages these lions served to mark the limits of jurisdiction of the abbots of St-Martial and the viscounts of Limoges. The upper octagonal tiers of the tower are braced by four walled turrets; a tall spire, topped by a pierced copper ball, rises to a height of 68 m - 223 ft. The north doorway is delicately ornamented.

Three parts of equal height resting on slender columns (some are offset on the outside) make up the interior. On either side of the chancel, at the end of the aisles, lovely 15C windows show the life of the Virgin Mary and that of John the Baptist. Behind the high altar, a monumental altar of carved stone supports a 19C gilded wood reliquary shrine which contains relics of St. Martial including the saint's head.

Church of St-Pierre-du-Queyroix (**BY**). – The façade dates from 1534 and is in the pointed Flamboyant style. The 13C belfry is well proportioned and served as a model for the church of St-Michel and St. Stephen's Cathedral in Limoges.

The interior, in the shape of a vast, irregular rectangle, is striking on account of its size; partly 12C, it still has the enormous round pillars of that period, adorned with flattened capitals, decorated with palm fronds. On the south side of the chancel a beautiful, vivid stained glass window depicts the Death and the Coronation of the Virgin. It was made in 1510 by Jean Pénicaud but has been restored.

The Christ carved in wood at the end of the 13C which is full of feeling (on the high altar) and at the end of the second aisle, a 17C retable of gilded wood are noteworthy.

Remains of the Abbey of St-Martial (**BY E**). – *Guided tours 1 July to 30 September, 9.30am to noon and 2.30 to 7pm; 2F.*

Place de la République stands over the site of a Gallo-Roman necropolis where was buried St. Martial *(p 117)*. His sarcophagus decorated with an early Christian mosaic may be seen in a crypt; opposite is the tomb of St. Valérie, and to the west is the great 4C sarcophagus (known as the "tomb of Tène-le-Duc") which is probably that of the Roman Governor Stephen *(p 117)*.

The church of St-Pierre-du-Sépulcre of which only the lower level remains, was built in the 6C over the crypt and its extension.

To the south of this structure stood the Abbey of St-Martial which was a religious, artistic and cultural centre in the Middle Ages but later declined. The buildings fell into ruin and the stones were recycled. There were no traces left after the Revolution. Walls have been excavated and stone fragments dating back to Antiquity and the Middle Ages have been brought to light.

Old Limoges. – The old town, once fortified, comprised the "City" and the "Château", and the banks of the Vienne.

St-Martial Bridge (**V**). – Built to replace a Roman bridge of which it retains three piles, it was destroyed in 1182 and later rebuilt; by 1215 it gave access to the "Château". This irregular structure has seven pointed arches and a pronounced hump back.

St-Etienne Bridge (**V**). – It was built in 1210 to provide access from the "City". This hump-back bridge has eight pointed arches, piers with cutwaters and stone posts on the inside of the parapet.

Cathedral Precinct. – Between St-Etienne bridge and the cathedral chevet is the Abbessaille Quarter (**V**) with its picturesque streets sloping down to the Vienne and lined with old houses. To the northwest of the cathedral are Rue des Allois and Rue Haute-Cité with restored half-timbered houses.

Place des Bancs (**AZ**). – To the southwest of this bustling square (market) the Quartier de la Boucherie was inhabited by butchers from the Middle Ages. St. Aurelian was the patron saint of this powerful guild.

In the picturesque **Rue de la Boucherie** (**AZ 10**) there are still some of the 80 butchers' shops recorded in the 13C. These and most of the tall wooden houses have been restored. At the entrance to the St-Aurélien Chapel stands a fine 15C monolithic cross.

On the other side of the square there are several pleasant streets reserved for pedestrians. Between Rue du Temple and Rue du Consulat, the **Cour du Temple** (**AY 49**) which is lined with half-timbered houses and arcaded galleries, is adorned by a lovely Renaissance staircase.

Place du Présidial (**AY**). – The north doorway of the church of St-Michel-des-Lions opens on to this square where the 17-18C royal administrative buildings remain standing. Note at the corner of Rue Haute-de-la-Comédie, the former **Maledent mansion** (**AY F**) which dates back to 1639. It has been fully restored and now houses the offices of the Ministry of Culture.

Orsay Garden (**AY**). – The ruins of vast arena dating from the Gallo-Roman period have been uncovered in this pleasant public garden.

EXCURSIONS

Solignac★; Chalusset★; St-Léonard-de-Noblat★. – *Round tour of 89 km - 55 miles – about 2 1/2 hours – local map below. Leave Limoges by ⑤, the N 21 which runs along the right bank of the Vienne. Turn left after 7 km - 5 miles into the D 32 which crosses the river.* This road is picturesque and goes up the valley of the Briance, winding its way through meadows. At Pont-Rompu hamlet, there is a view on the right of a picturesque old bridge with pointed cutwaters on which passed the ancient Roman way from Limoges to Bordeaux.

Solignac★. – *Description p 177.*

Follow the D 32 to Le Vigen. Its Romanesque church has a severe two-storeyed wall-belfry. Continue on the D 32 which affords a good view of Chalusset Castle. *Turn right into the D 32^A. Leave the car when you come to a bridge over the Briance.*

Chalusset Castle★. – The impressive ruins of Chalusset Castle are a perfect example of mediaeval military architecture in their plan and their position on a rock promontory, which juts forward to the point where the Briance and Ligoure rivers meet. The castle was built in the 12C and in 1577 it fell into the hands of the Huguenots who used it as a base for their battles against Limoges. The troops of Limoges took the notorious castle by force and dismantled it.

Only traces remain of the three outer walls, the square towers, the keep and the ramparts, but these traces, in spite of the overgrowth and the accumulation of earth and stones are still impressive in scale. *The ruins can only be reached (1/2 hour Rtn on foot) by a steep path. Take great care.* The keep and side-walls are of amazing size; broken-off ogive vaulting can be seen in several halls; a few capitals remain in the chapel.

Return to the D 32 and bear right until you come to St-Hilaire-Bonneval where you turn left; take the D 19 to join the D 979. Turn right and drive to Le Chatenet.

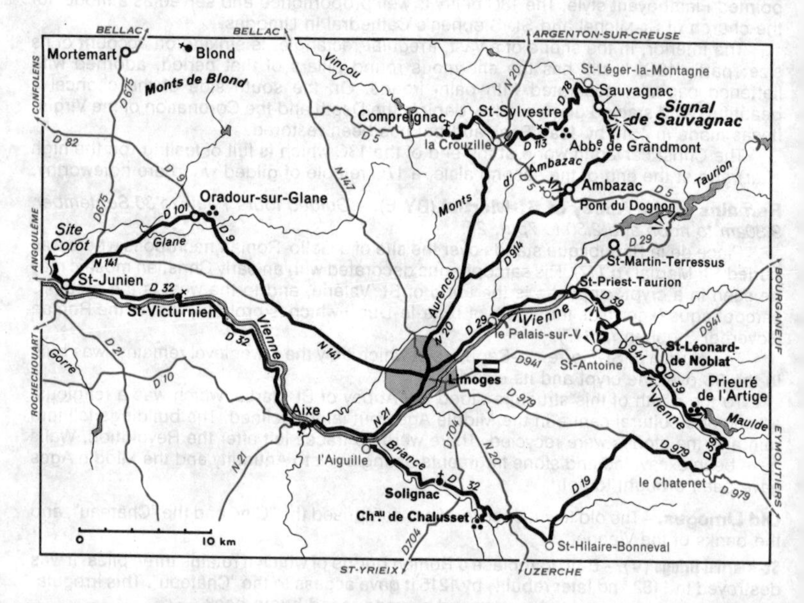

At Le Chatenet, take the D 39 on the left (direction St-Leonard-de-Noblat). The road crosses the Vienne and later the Maulde *(p 171)* near its confluence with the Vienne. *Immediately after the bridge over the Maulde, take on the right the road marked "Circuit Monts et Barrages" (Tour of Hills and Dams); opposite Artige Dam a metalled road on the left leads to the ruins of Artige Priory.*

Former Artige Priory (Ancien Prieuré de l'Artige). – *Description p 171.*

The road runs beside the Vienne beneath overhanging rocks before rising above the river.

St-Léonard-de-Noblat★. – *Description p 170.*

Cross the Vienne by the D 941 which follows the valley before climbing up to the plateau. At St-Antoine take the D 124, from which there is a fine panorama of the Ambazac Hills, before turning left into the picturesque D 39.

St-Priest-Taurion. – Pop 2 268. This village lies in a pleasant setting at the confluence of the Taurion, whose uncultivated valley is cut by dams, and the Vienne, which here widens out into a fine stretch of water flowing through a hilly countryside.

After Le Palais the D 29 follows the valley of the Vienne and for more than 2 km - 1 mile runs along the bank of the Palais Dam reservoir before reaching Limoges.

Oradour-sur-Glane; St-Junien. – *Round tour of 81 km - 50 miles – about 3 hours – local map above. Leave Limoges by ⑥, the N 141 and after 14 km - 9 miles, take the D 9 on the right.*

Oradour-sur-Glane. – *Description p 147.*

Return to the Vienne valley by way of the D 101 and the N 141.

St-Junien. – *Description p 169.*

Corot's View (Site Corot). – *Description p 170.*

The D 32 goes up the valley of the Vienne, following the right bank as far as St-Victurnien.

St-Victurnien. – Pop 1 271. The church with a double nave and ogive vaulting, has a 14C retable ornamented with paintings of the Passion and Resurrection. The retable adorns the altar which contains the relics of St. Victurnien. Notice the two holes in the back of the altar, which allowed the simple minded to put their heads in, to ask for a complete recovery. Note the 13C reliquary shrine in *champlevé* enamel.

The winding road goes up the left bank, overlooks the valley and provides good views of the river.

Aixe-sur-Vienne. – Pop 5 650. The *ostensions (p 37)* of Aixe provide, once every seven years, the unique spectacle of twenty reliquaries being carried in procession by members of the craft guilds, to the Chapel of Notre-Dame d'Arliquet and being brought back in torchlight procession.

Ambazac Hills. – *Round tour of 72 km - 45 miles – about 3 1/2 hours – local map p 122. Leave Limoges by ①, the N 20, then after 8.5 km - 5 miles take the D 914 on the right going towards Ambazac.* You cross a hilly region where woods and fields appear by turn and where steep valleys are often inundated by reservoirs.

Ambazac. – *Description p 44.*

Leave Ambazac to the northeast by the D 914, then after 6 km – 4 miles bear left into the D 28 A. This is a picturesque road running through a countryside of many valleys.

Sauvagnac. – This tiny village originated as a cell of Grandmont Abbey *(below)*. The chapel remodelled many times at different periods retains its severe 12C nave with pointed cradle vaulting and massive pillars; note a 15C *Pietà* to the right of the chancel. It is a pilgrimage centre to Our Lady whose richly clad statue crowns the high altar.
From the chapel a path *(signposted in red)* through the woods leads, near Sauvagnac Beacon (alt 701 m – 2 300 ft), to a pile of huge granite rocks known as Pierre Branlante (the Rocking Stone). From this point you can enjoy a wide **view**★★, southwest as far as Ambazac, east and southeast to Mount Gargan, the Monédières Massif and the Auvergne Mountains (Puy de Dôme and Puy de Sancy).

In this hilly region, you get views of the Ambazac Hills from the D 28A and the D 78.

Grandmont. – The only traces of Grandmont Abbey, the seat of an important order founded by St. Stephen of Muret (1046-1124), are the foundations and some dressed stone on the edge of the village. The abbey became very powerful in France and in other countries through numerous cells which later became priories. After the glory, decadence set in and the order was disbanded by the Pope in 1772. At the beginning of the 19C, the ruined abbey was acquired and demolished by a local businessman. A small pilgrimage chapel is a memento of the monastery and next to it is displayed a plan of the former buildings.

St-Sylvestre. – Pop 660. The church *(key at the Café-tabac nearby)* contains a remarkable **reliquary bust**★ of St. Stephen of Muret *(left of the chancel; illumination: 1F)*. This 15C shrine is of chased silver and along with the 13C reliquary of St-Junien on display, it originally came from Grandmont Abbey which stood at nearby Grandmont *(see above)*.

Take the D 113, then the D 5 which passes near the now unworked La Crouzille and the Margnac uranium mines *(p 19)* before reaching Compreignac.

Compreignac. – Pop 1 130. The fortified church built in the Limousin style, is crowned by battlements. One of the buttresses is topped by a watch-tower.

Return to Limoges by a road which joins the N 20. The N 20 is a good road, affording many views of the Ambazac Hills.

LOC DIEU, Former Abbey (Ancienne Abbaye de LOC DIEU)

Michelin map 79 north of fold 20 – 9 km - 6 miles west of Villefranche-de-Rouergue

On the borders of Rouergue and Quercy a castle half-feudal and half-Renaissance in appearance, was converted in the 19C within the remains of the Cistercian Abbey of Loc Dieu *(lieu divin:* divine spot).

The cloisters, chapterhouse and former abbey church can be visited. Open 1 July to 9 September, 10am to noon and 2 to 6pm; closed Tuesdays; 8F.

Only three of the 15C cloister galleries remain and these were restored in the 19C. The chapterhouse, also 15C, is supported by two elegant octagonal columns with fine mouldings.

Church★. – The church was built between 1159 and 1189 using stone of many shades, but with ochre and gold predominating; the completed building is a wonderful example of the Cistercian style, simple and unadorned, well proportioned and pure of line.

The nave, which is more than 20 m - 66 ft high, is flanked by narrow aisles. Most Cistercian churches end in a flat chevet, but this one has five apsidal chapels, four of them opening off the transept arms. The first chapel in the south arm of the transept contains a precious 15C **triptych**★ in carved and painted wood depicting scenes from the life of the Virgin framing a Madonna and Child. The transept crossing is roofed over with a square lantern tower. The church has quadripartite vaulting but its elevation remains Romanesque in character.

EXCURSION

Laramière. – Pop 240. *6 km - 4 miles to the west by the D 115.* A few of the buildings of the former priory founded in the 12C, may still be seen near the church. The chapterhouse is remarkable with its delicate ogive vaulting and capitals bearing effigies of St. Louis and Blanche de Castille. The walls and the vault are partly decorated with geometrical motifs.

LOT, Lower Valley ★★

Michelin map 79 folds 5 to 10

The River Lot is most beautiful where it cuts across the Quercy limestone plateaux. The river flows at the foot of promontories on which perch old villages; elsewhere the waters flow in great loops round picturesque towns and cities.

From the Cévennes Mountains to the Agenais. – The Lot is a tributary of the Garonne. It rises in the Cévennes on the slopes of Mount Le Goulet at an altitude of 1 400 m - 4 600 ft and flows right across the southern part of the Massif Central.

The winding course is an uninterrupted series of meanders or loops, circling tongues of land, some only a couple of hundred yards across. As it flows between the tall limestone cliffs of the Quercy plateaux its thousand curves provide splendid and constantly changing views. The valley is always picturesque, sometimes wild and bare, sometimes smiling and fertile. The Lot leaves Quercy at Libos and, after flowing a further 480 km - 300 miles, enters the Garonne in the Agenais plain.

Scenes from the Past. – Before the railway came, the Lot was an important navigational route. The river was first improved by Colbert and was later equipped with dams and even canals to cut across the promontories of the wider bends, as at Luzech *(p 126)*.

A fleet of barges, known as *sapines* or *gabares (p 92)*, sailed on the Lot, bringing cheeses from Auvergne, coal from Decazeville and wine from Cahors to Bordeaux.

The Lot Vineyards. – The slopes of the valley of the Olt – the old name for the Lot which is still found in such place names as St-Vincent-Rive-d'Olt and Balaguier-d'Olt – have long been famous for their vineyards. Quercy wines, with their high alcoholic content, have played a great part in making Cahors and the Olt valley famous.

In the 1C AD the Roman Emperor Domitian punished Cahors for rising in revolt by destroying its vineyards; after two centuries of teetotalism, Probus revoked the sentence. Despite the boycott on Bordeaux, through which the wine was shipped, wines from the Lot valley were preferred by the English for many centuries: Eleanor of Aquitaine brought Quercy to the King of England as part of her dowry, in 1287 letters patent were granted by the King in favour of these wines. The wine was exported to Poland, to Russia – where only the wine of Cahors could entice the Tsar Peter the Great away from vodka – and even to Italy. Legend has it that popes insisted on serving this wine at mass.

Two men of Quercy, Clément Marot the poet and Galiot de Genouillac, Grand Master of the Artillery of France, gave the wine to François I to taste, and the king's palate delighted in its velvet smoothness. Later, vines from the Lot hillsides were transported at great cost to Fontainebleau to create the Royal Vine Arbour. This famous vineyard was nearly wiped out by phylloxera soon after 1870, but care is restoring its quality.

■ CLIFFS ★★

From Figeac to Cahors – *114 km - 71 – about 1 day – local map p 125*

As it crosses Quercy, the Lot flows at the foot of hillside slopes, often strewn with rocks. Leaving Rouergue, the river hurls itself against the spur on which stands the old town of Capdenac, and then pushes its way between the cliff walls of the limestone plateau. From the top of these cliffs there are fine views of the valley.

Leave Figeac (p 104) by ②, the N 140, then after 5 km - 3 miles, take the D 208 a steep road on the left to Capdenac.

Capdenac. – *Description p 76.*

Return to the N 140, which you follow on the left to reach Capdenac-Gare. After Capdenac-Gare, take the D 86, which runs along the left bank of the river and soon provides pretty views of Capdenac. The river makes a wide bend in the centre of an alluvial plain on which crops are grown. Beyond St-Julien and after a climb, this picturesque road provides a good view of the Capdenac amphitheatre. After the Madeleine Bridge the road runs beside the Lot through a countryside of rocks and undergrowth. *Shortly after Balaguier-d'Olt, cross over to the right bank to reach St-Pierre-Toirac.*

St-Pierre-Toirac. – Pop 161. This small village, on the right bank of the Lot, possesses an interesting fortified church built between the 11 and 14C. The Romanesque apse alone belies the fortified appearance of this building which served as a defence point with its massive crenellated keep and upper floor *(no access)*. The short nave has cradle vaulting and interesting capitals. The chancel has trilobed arches; saw-toothed arches surround the stained glass windows of the apse.

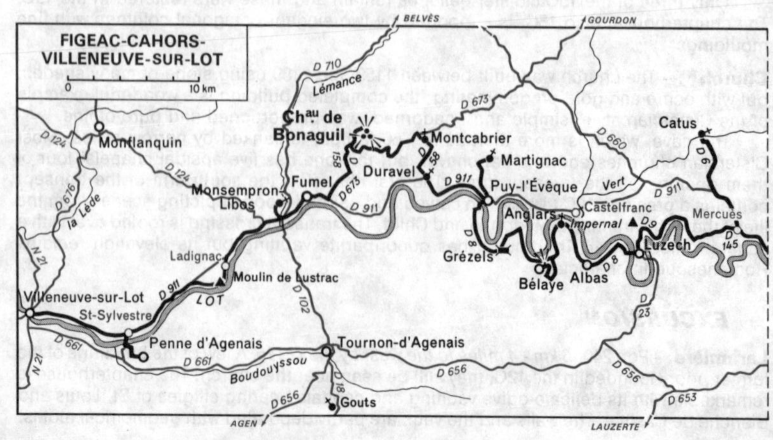

Larroque-Toirac Castle. – *Description p 115.*

Many delightful villages are to be seen on the right bank which is dominated by high rocks and vertical cliffs; as the valley widens the Lot spreads out into a great sheet of water.

Montbrun. – Pop 61. The village of Montbrun rises in tiers on a rocky promontory encircled by steep cliffs. It looks down on the Lot and faces the Saut de la Mounine. Towering above the village are the ruins of a fortress that once belonged to the powerful Cardaillac family.

Cajarc. – Pop 1 184. *Facilities p 38.* A picturesque small village.

Cross the river at Cajarc and follow the D 127 up the left bank as far as the Saut de la Mounine. The road overhangs the Lot to start with and immediately after Saujac rises and winds round to overlook a wooded gorge before reaching the top of the plateau.

La Mounine's Leap★ (Saut de la Mounine). – There is a good **view**★ of the valley from the top of this steep cliff and from the end of the spur you can see out over a wide bend in the river Lot as it circles a mosaic of arable fields. Over on the left, on the far bank, stands Montbrun Castle. The curious name, *Saut de la Mounine* – the little monkey's leap – comes from a strange legend. The lord of Montbrun was determined to punish his daughter for her love of another lord's son and ordered her to be hurled from the top of the cliff; a hermit, appalled at this cruel idea, disguised a small blind monkey *(mounine)* in women's clothes and hurled it into space. The father saw the object hurtling down and regretted his cruel action; on seeing his daughter alive and well his joy was so great that he forgave her.

Return to Cajarc and take the right bank once more. Soon after the town the road climbs and passes near a chapel built in the 12 and 13C, known as the *capellette* (the little chapel) and of which only the apse remains. From this spot there is a wide view of the valley.

At Larnagol cross the Lot in the direction of Calvignac.

Calvignac★. – Pop 203. This old village, where a few traces of its fortress may still be seen, is perched on a spur on the left bank of the Lot.

Staying on the same bank take the D 8 which leads to Cénevières.

Cénevières Castle. – *Guided tours from Easter to All Saints' Day, 10am to noon and 2 to 7pm; 10F.* This imposing castle clings to the vertical rock face. The 13C keep known as the Tour de Gourdon, altered in the 16C, has great vaulted rooms and secret dungeons *(oubliettes)*. A stone staircase leads to a Renaissance gallery, with Tuscan columns, which is surmounted by dormer windows with pierced pinnacles. The dining and main halls have coffered ceilings decorated with flowers and are hung with 15 and 16C Flemish and Aubusson tapestries.
In the small "alchemy room" there are 16C frescoes on mythological themes. From the terraces there is a far reaching **view** over the Lot valley.

Return to the D 662. At Tour de Faure take a left turn onto the D 181 and cross the river to reach St-Cirq-Lapopie in its remarkable setting, clinging to a cliff on the left bank of the Lot.

St-Cirq-Lapopie★★. – *Description p 167.*

Beyond St-Cirq-Lapopie the D 40, which is built into the cliff and cuts through small oak woods, has been designed as a tourist route. There is a good **view**★ of the confluence of the Lot and the Célé from a small belvedere. From the same spot a wide bend of the Lot can be seen curving between white and yellow cliffs.

Immediately after Bouziès, cross the Lot and again take the D 662. This runs close beside the river in a picturesque cliff setting. In several places the road has been cut out of the living rock which rises sheer above it and even overhangs at certain spots. Past Vers the valley broadens out, cliffs are replaced by wooded hills and the alluvial soil is given over to arable farming.

Notre-Dame de Vêles. – This small pilgrimage chapel was built in the 12C and has a fine square belfry and a Romanesque apse.

Laroque-des-Arcs. – Pop 379. Its name is a reminder of the aqueduct which, on a three-tiered bridge, crossed the Francoulès valley and took water to Cahors *(p 73)*. An old tower perched on a rock beside the Lot enabled guards to watch the river traffic and exact tolls.

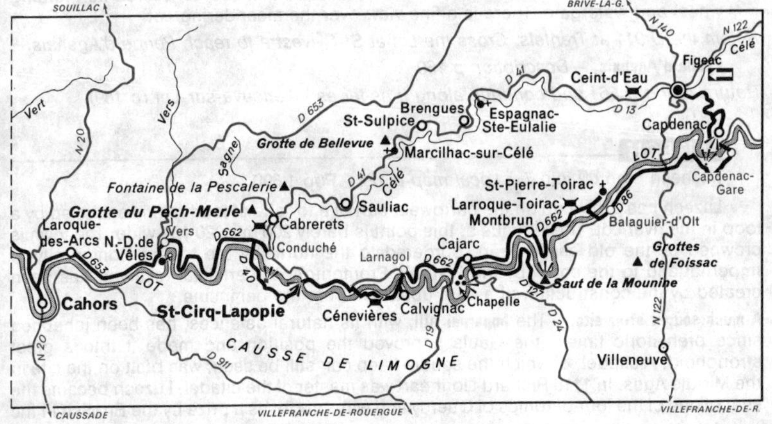

■ THE RIVER MEANDERS

From Cahors to Villeneuve-sur-Lot

120 km - 75 miles – about 1 day – local map p 124

The bed of the Lot winds in a series of meanders – *cingles* – as the river crosses the plateaux of Quercy between Cahors and Puy-l'Évêque. Beyond the valley broadens out.

Leave Cahors (p 73) by ①, the D 911 which overlooks the Lot.

Catus. – Pop 775. *8.5 km - 6 miles from Mercuès.* The chapterhouse, which adjoins the church and was once part of a former priory, contains beautiful Romanesque capitals and sculptured remains.

Beyond Mercuès, which is dominated by its castle, take the D 145 which leaves the valley for a short distance to cross a flourishing countryside of vineyards and orchards; then the road returns to the river and follows its every curve.

Luzech. – *Description below.*

Follow the left bank, there are good views along the valley.

Albas. – Pop 545. This village has narrow streets lined with old houses.

Anglars. – Pop 182. A Crucifixion adorns the main doorway of the Renaissance church.

Bélaye. – Pop 204. Bélaye, once the fief of the bishops of Cahors, stands on top of a hill. An extensive **view**★ of the Lot valley may be gained from the top of the spur and from the upper square of this little village.

Grézels. – Pop 263. The ruins of a feudal castle that has been destroyed and rebuilt many times, dominate the village. The oldest parts of the castle are the perimeter walls and corner towers. *Not open to the public.*

Puy-l'Évêque. – *Description p 157.*

To get to Martignac from Puy-l'Évêque, take first the D 28, which rises rapidly above the valley, then a local road.

Martignac. – This little village has a rustic church built in a beautiful golden stone and crowned by a tall, asymmetrical belfry with wooden walls. The nave and chancel are decorated with 15C **frescoes.** Yellow and ochre tones predominate. Although the drawing is stilted, the facial expressions and the composition of the frescoes make them extremely interesting. In the nave: a nobleman sitting on a man's back illustrates sloth, another carrying a ham in his arms is gluttony, while a woman riding a goat signifies lust. Facing this fresco is another showing the Coronation of the Virgin and the Elect being guided to Paradise by St. Michael and being received at the Gates by St. Peter. A Placing in the Tomb, angels and, on the vault, a Christ in Majesty the hand raised in benediction, may be seen from the chancel.

Beyond Puy-l'Évêque the terraces and hillsides are covered with vines, while the wide alluvial valley is carpeted with fields.

Duravel. – Pop 875. The 11C church has historiated capitals decorating the chancel. There is an archaic crypt supported by columns ornamented with rough-hewn capitals. The bodies of Saints Hilarion, Poémon and Agathon (*ostension* held every five years) lie buried at the back of the apse.

Take the D 58 to reach Montcabrier.

Montcabrier. – Pop 352. The church was partially rebuilt in the 14C. The restored Flamboyant doorway is surmounted by an attractive pierced belfry.

Follow the D 58 then the D 673 to the left and at St-Martin-le-Redon turn right into a local road called the Bonaguil Tourist Road (route touristique de Bonaguil), *finally branch right onto the D 158 which leads to Bonaguil Castle.*

Bonaguil Castle★★. – *Description p 56.*

Fumel. – Pop 6 659. This industrial town on the right bank of the Lot has blast furnaces, foundries, workshops, etc.

In Libos turn right for the D 276 which will bring you to the Romanesque church of Monsempron-Libos. On first seeing the village in its hilltop site you will be able to pick out the fine church chevet rising above the other buildings.

Monsempron-Libos. – *Description p 138.*

Before the railway bridge take a small road to the left leading to Ladignac.

Lustrac Mill (Moulin de Lustrac). – This 13C fortified mill has conserved its grinding wheel and watergate. There is a fine view over the meandering Lot.

Rejoin the D 911 at Trentels. Cross the Lot at St-Sylvestre to reach Penne d'Agenais.

Penne d'Agenais. – *Description p 150.*

Return to the D 661 and continue along it as far as Villeneuve-sur-Lot (p 189).

LUZECH

Michelin map 79 fold 7 – *Local map p 124* – Pop 1 690

Luzech has grown up on the narrowest part of a tongue of land nearly encircled by a loop in the river Lot. The isthmus at this point is barely 200 m - 220 yds wide. The town is crowned by the old castle keep, bordered to the north by the former Roman city of Impernal and to the south by the Pistoule Promontory. An artificial reservoir has been created by the construction of a dam upstream from the peninsula.

A much sought after site. – The **Impernal** hill, with its natural defences, has been inhabited since prehistoric times; the Gauls improved the position and made it into a great stronghold. A citadel, of which the square keep can still be seen, was built on the site in the Middle Ages. In 1118 Richard Lionheart was master of the citadel. Luzech became the seat of one of the four baronies of Quercy and was sought as a prize by the English in the

Hundred Years War. But the town resisted all attacks and became an important strongpoint. During the Wars of Religion it remained a faithful bastion of Catholicism under the bishops of Cahors.

Excavations of the Impernal site have revealed walls and traces of buildings dating from the Roman and Gaulish periods.

Old Town. – Near the 12C Penitents' Chapel there are a few old-looking alleys, but the most picturesque houses are to be found in the former Barry quarter on the opposite side of the Place du Canal. They are grouped in alleys running into the Rue du Barry-del-Valat, such as the Rue du Port, the Rue Antoine-de-Luzech where there is a 14C window and the Rue des Balcons where the dwellings are out of the ordinary.

Keep. – This 13C keep *(no admittance to the upper platform)* looks down upon the town with its brown roofs and the fertile valley.

MALVAL

Michelin map 68 fold 19 – Pop 53

In this small village in the smiling valley of the Petite Creuse, stand the ruins of a fortified castle. Du Guesclin, one of France's greatest warriors, who campaigned mostly against the English, once stayed here.

Church. – Only this partly Romanesque building remains of the Priory which depended in former times on the Abbey of Chambon-sur-Voueize. Built of granite the church has a chevet which is decorated with a cornice supported by corbels. The doorway is embellished by covings, small columns, torus and capitals. Inside there is a 12C reliquary shrine of St. Stephen in *champlevé* enamel.

EXCURSION

Le Bourg-d'Hem. – Pop 290. *14 km - 9 miles to the southwest.* Downstream from the Anzème Gorges, this village occupies a picturesque site on a mound overlooking the Creuse.

MARCILHAC-SUR-CÉLÉ

Michelin map 79 fold 9 – *Local map p 125* – Pop 240

Marcilhac is picturesquely built in the centre of an amphitheatre of cliffs in the Célé valley. Interesting old houses surround the ruins of a Benedictine abbey.

The Legal Jungle. – In the 11C Marcilhac Abbey controlled but let run to ruin the modest sanctuary of Rocamadour; noticing this abandonment some monks from Tulle installed themselves in the sanctuary. But in 1166 the discovery of the body of St. Amadour *(p 158)* turned the Sanctuary into a rich and famous place of pilgrimage. Marcilhac recalled its rights and expelled the monks from Tulle. Soon afterwards the Abbot of Tulle threw out the Marcilhac men and again occupied Rocamadour; then the lawsuits began. The case was acrimonious and the Bishop of Cahors, the papal legate, the Archbishop of Bourges, the pope even, were all called on to give judgment, but none gave an answer; finally after a hundred years of squabbling Marcilhac accepted an indemnity of 3 000 *sols* and gave up its claim to Rocamadour.

Marcilhac Abbey enjoyed remarkable prosperity until the 14C, but during the Hundred Years War it was virtually destroyed by marauding bands of Englishmen and the mercenary troops of France. After the Reformation the abbey, now only a ghost of its former self, fell into the hands of the Hébrards of St-Sulpice *(p 80)*. It finally disappeared during the Revolution.

■ **SIGHTS** *time: 1 1/2 hours*

Former Abbey. – The ensemble is made of two very distinct parts.

The Romanesque Part. – The west porch and the first three bays of the nave are open to the sky. They are flanked by a tall square tower which was probably fortified in the 14C. A rounded door on the south side is topped by sculpture forming a tympanum and depicting the Last Judgment: Christ in Majesty with figures on either side representing, it is believed, the sun and the moon, appears above two angels and St. Peter and St. Paul. These carvings are archaic in style and would appear to date from the 10C. Go through this doorway and enter the church to the right.

The Gothic Part. – This part of the church dating back to the 15C and only open to the fourth bay on the west side is built in the Flamboyant style. The chancel has star vaulting and is circled by an ambulatory. The chapel on the right is adorned with wood carvings of episodes in the life of Christ; the one on the left has 16C frescoes: Christ in Benediction with the twelve Apostles.

Take a path in the second bay on the north side to go to the former chapterhouse, which has delicately carved Romanesque capitals decorating the bays.

Make for an esplanade shaded by plane trees; a round tower marks the site of the abbot's house. Turn right and walk beside the Célé, following the ruins of the abbey ramparts. Go through the postern and round the church to return to the starting-point.

Bellevue Cave★ (Grotte de Bellevue). – *1.5 km - 1 mile to the northwest.* The route leading up to the cave is a *corniche*-style road overlooking the Célé valley and giving fine **glimpses** of the village and abbey. After a series of four steeply rising hairpin bends branch off to the left in the direction of the hamlet of Pailhès. *The car park is on the left 200 yards further on.*

Guided tours from Spring holidays to 30 September, 9am to noon and 2 to 7pm; in October on Sundays only, same opening times; 14F.

Discovered in 1964 this cave was opened to the public 2 years later. The chamber has coral-like concretions which are either dark red due to the presence of iron oxide or of shining white calcite. The stalactites hanging from the roof bristle with eccentrics defying the laws of gravity and very slender macaronis. The particularly delicate stalagmites resemble slim church candles. Hercules' Column, reaching from floor to ceiling is striking for its regularity. It is 4 m - 13 ft high with a circumference of 3.50 m - 11 ft and the upper part is made up of a disc at an angle of 45° to the top of the column.

MAREUIL

Michelin map 72 southeast of fold 14 – Pop 1 215

This former barony of Périgord has retained its 15C castle.

Castle. – *Open Easter to 31 October, 2 to 5.45pm; the rest of the year Sundays only, 2 to 4.45pm; closed Wednesdays; 7F.*

This castle lying in the open plain has been gradually rebuilt since 1965. Of the defensive system which formerly protected the fortress, there remain the perimeter walls and towers and only a section of the moat fed by the Belle.

A ramp leads to the entrance fort defended by two machicolated towers, in one of which is a late Gothic style chapel; although damaged during the Revolution note the chapel's attractive ribbed vaulting.

The main buildings are roofed with pink coloured tiles. They form a right angle and are joined at the corner by an oblong shaped keep. The whole opens onto a garden terrace.

The underground prisons and the living quarters are open to the public. In the main salon there are paintings by Nattier, Rigaud, Horace Vernet and fine Louis XV furniture. One room displays mementoes of Marshal Lannes: letters, sword, and portraits.

EXCURSION

Vieux-Mareuil; Cercles; La Tour-Blanche. – *Round tour of 30 km - 19 miles – about 3/4 hour.* Michelin map 75 folds 4 and 5. *Leave Mareuil to the southeast by the D 939.*

Vieux-Mareuil. – Pop 395. The church, although built in the 13C has all the characteristics of the Périgord Romanesque style, the nave is covered with three domes on pendentives, the two bay-long chancel is roofed with broken barrel vaulting and terminated by a flat chevet. The crenellations added in the 14C give the church a military aspect.

Take the D 93 to the south then turn right onto the D 84. When you come to a wayside cross or Calvary turn left.

Cercles. – Pop 187. The church was once part of a Romanesque priory. The beautiful west door is adorned with remarkable capitals.

La Tour-Blanche. – Pop 441. In the village there are old houses, of which one is in a delightful Renaissance style. West of the village, near a stream and a tree nursery, stands the last trace of a 13C fortress, a massive keep on top of a mound.

The D 2 and then the D 708 lead back to Mareuil.

MARTEL

Michelin map 75 fold 18 – *Local map p 94* – Pop 1 441 – *Facilities p 38*

Martel, built on the Quercy Causse or limestone plateau to which it has given its name, is known as the "town of the seven towers". It still possesses many mediaeval buildings. Today it is a busy centre for truffle marketing, the nut trade and canning.

The Three Hammers. – After stopping the Saracens at Poitiers in 732, **Charles Martel** pursued them into Aquitaine. Some years later he struck again and wiped them out. To commemorate this victory over the infidels and to give thanks to God, Charles Martel had a church built on the spot; soon a town grew up round the church. It was given the name of Martel in memory of its founder and took as its crest three hammers which were the favourite weapon of the saviour of Christianity.

The Rebellious Son. – Martel was the scene, at the end of the 12C, of a tragic series of events which brought into conflict **Henry Plantagenet,** King of England and Lord of all Western France, his wife Eleanor of Aquitaine and their four sons. The royal household was a royal hell. Henry could no longer stand the sight of Eleanor, who had previously been repudiated by the King of France, and shut her up in a tower. The sons thereupon took up arms against their father, and the eldest, **Henri Court-Mantel,** pillaged the viscounty of Turenne and also Quercy. To punish him, Henry Plantagenet gave his lands to his third son Richard Lionheart and stopped the allowance paid to his eldest son.

Henri Court-Mantel found himself without riches, surrounded and in an altogether desperate situation: to pay his foot-soldiers he plundered the treasure houses of the provincial abbeys. He took from Rocamadour the shrine and the precious stones of St. Amadour whose body was profaned; he sold Roland's famous sword "Durandal" to a Jew. But as he was leaving Rocamadour after this sacrilegious action, the bell miraculously began to toll: it was a sign from God.

Henri fled to Martel, where he arrived in a fever; he felt death to be upon him and was stricken with remorse. He confessed his crimes while Henry II was sought to come and forgive his son on his death bed; Henry was at the siege of Limoges and sent a messenger with his pardon. The messenger on his arrival found Henri Court-Mantel lying in agony on a bed of cinders, a cross at his breast. Soon afterwards he died.

■ SIGHTS *time: 1 hour*

Former Perimeter Walls. – Boulevards – the Fossé des Cordeliers and the Fossé des Capitani – have been built on the site of the old ramparts. The **Tournemire Tower** crowned with battlements, the Prison Tower, the Souillac and Brive Gateways recall the time when Martel was a fortified town well protected by double perimeter walls.

Leave the car in the car park along the north wall. Pass between the Post Office and the Tournemire Tower to enter the old town. In the square take Rue du Four Bas to the left.

Church of St-Maur. – This Gothic building has interesting defence features: two watch-towers rise from the ends of the flat chevet and the main bay is surmounted by a line of battlements. The belfry, which is 48 m - 157 ft high and is flanked at its base by stalwart buttresses, has narrow loopholes and is a veritable castle keep.

Beneath the porch is a fine historiated Romanesque **tympanum** depicting the Last Judgment. It shows Christ seated, His head adorned with a cruciform halo, His arms stretched wide to show His wounds; two angels hold the Instruments of the Passion while two others sound the trumpets. The nave is wide and the chancel with its flat chevet and star vaulting is lit by **windows** with 16C stained glass showing God the Father, the four Evangelists and scenes from the Passion.

Take the Rue Droite which is lined with old mansions to Place des Consuls.

Place des Consuls★. – In the centre is the 18C **covered market.** The wooden structure rests on massive stone pillars. On one side may be seen the former Martel measures.

Hôtel de la Raymondie.– This fine building was begun in about 1280 by the Viscount of Turenne and was completed in 1330. A crenellated belfry dominates the mansion which is flanked by a tower at each corner. The courtyard is adorned with elegant four-lobed rose windows. The mansion, formerly the law courts, is now the town hall.

In the rooms on the first floor note the two sculptured wooden chimneypieces and the Renaissance bas-relief. In the upper room of the keep a small local **museum** contains items found at the Puy d'Issolud excavations *(see below)*.

Maison Fabri. – This old mansion flanked by a round tower to the south of the square, is also known as the Mansion of Henri Court-Mantel. He died within its walls in 1183.

Hôtel de Chauffour. – On the west side of the square stands this 16-17C mansion, formerly a magistrates' residence.

Rue Tournemire. – This picturesque small street to the left of the Hôtel de la Raymondie runs along the 13C Hôtel de la Monnaie and other old houses and leads back to the starting point.

EXCURSION

Puy d'Issolud★. – *14 km - 9 miles. Leave Martel to the east by the D 703. At Vayrac take the D 119 to the left, which leads to the puy.* The plateau near Vayrac, of which the highest point is Puy d'Issolud with an altitude of 311 m - 1 020 ft is bordered by steep cliffs which fall away to little streams flowing into the Dordogne.

Puy d'Issolud was surrounded, in the time of the Gauls, by such solid earthworks and dry-stone defences that it was one of the most redoubtable *oppida* (towns) of Quercy, and is said to have been the former Uxellodunum, site of the last Gaulish resistance to Caesar after Alesia. The battle was waged with unbelievable ferocity and, after a stream had been diverted through underground caverns, ended with another defeat for the Gauls. Caesar, angered at the resistance put up by the besieged Gauls, ordered the right hands of all prisoners to be cut off.

Items discovered during excavations are on display in the museum of the Hôtel de la Raymondie in Martel *(see above)*.

From the plateau there is an extensive, although interrupted **view★** of the Dordogne.

MASSERET

Michelin map 72 fold 18 – Pop 731

Masseret village stands in a part of the Limousin countryside which is mostly woodland. The N 20 runs right through the village.

In the centre of Masseret stands a modern tower with a viewing table at its top *(104 steps)*. There is a beautiful circular **panorama★**: to the north can be seen the Ambazac Hills, to the east the Millevaches Plateau, the Monédières Massif and on a clear day the Mountains of Auvergne.

EXCURSION

St-Germain-les-Belles; Mont Gargan★★. – *30 km - 19 miles. Leave Masseret to the north by the N 20 then take the D 7 BIS to the right.*

St-Germain-les-Belles. – Pop 1 271. This building dating from the 14C is a fine example of a fortified church. The façade and chevet are protected by machicolations. Inside, to the right of the chancel, a spiral staircase gives access to the lookout points high above the tall pointed vaulting, and the watch-path.

Continue along the same road before taking the D 16 to the right and then the D 31, again to the right and the D 12. At Surdoux turn left on to the D 39.

Mount Gargan★★ (Mont Gargan). – Altitude 731 m - 2 398 ft. A road which climbs steeply to begin with, leads to the summit, crowned by the ruins of a chapel. As you go round the chapel, you see a vast **panorama★★**, southeast over the Monédières Massif, north over the hills of Marche and west to the Limousin Mountains.

MEHUN-SUR-YÈVRE ★

Michelin map 64 fold 20 – Pop 7 178 – *Facilities p 38*

This charming old town on the banks of the river Yèvre and the Berry canal, is important for its porcelain industry. The town's four factories *(open to the public)* produce about 20% of France's total tableware production.

Mehun's Golden Age. – The third son of King John the Good, **Duke Jean de Berry** (1340-1416) was a lavish patron of the arts and admirer of the art of manuscript illumination *(p 59)*. He rebuilt Mehun Castle in 1386 and it was here amidst a brilliant court that he welcomed writers such as Froissart, miniaturists like the Limbourg brothers and André Beauneveu. The latter who was also a sculptor and architect, worked for a lengthy period at the castle. The Duke was on friendly terms with them all and often invited them to visit his menagerie or his luxurious bath pavilion. Duke Jean de Berry left the castle to his grand-nephew Charles VII, who received Joan of Arc here in the winter of 1429 and 1430. The Dauphin, the future Louis XI spent his childhood at the castle and conspired against his father, Charles VII, who died here in 1461.

■ SIGHTS *time: 3/4 hour*

Porte de l'Horloge. – A 14C gateway (restored) at the top of Rue Jeanne d'Arc.

Rue Jeanne-d'Arc. – This street leads down towards the Yèvre between old houses which sometimes have wells in front of them. No 87, the house where Joan of Arc stayed, has elegant bays with trilobed arches; to the left is the esplanade leading to the castle. Further on the street crosses the Yèvre, giving fine views of the public washing boards and a watermill. A shaded promenade running alongside the Berry canal affords views of the castle and church.

Castle. – Of this marvellous fairy tale castle, visited and admired by Claus Sluter and Holbein, sculptor and painter respectively, there remain two round towers, one of which is namod after Charles VII (extensively restored). Vaulting springers and some of the chimneypieces can still be seen. The original plan of the castle is still visible – note the position of the bastion jutting out like a spur towards the river. A miniature of the Duke of Berry's *Très Riches Heures* (The Rich Hours) now in the Condé museum of Chantilly (north of Paris), executed by the Limbourg brothers, shows the castle as it existed in the 15C. Dismantled in the 17C the castle slowly fell into ruins. Excavations have revealed a Gallo-Roman foundation.

Collegiate Church of Our Lady (Collégiale Notre-Dame). – The construction of this building, Romanesque in style with the exception of the chapel added in the 15C, was started with the chancel (11C) which has a horse-shoe shape. The façade is preceded by a belfry-porch ornamented on the north side by a cross with interlacing, in the centre of which is the Holy Lamb.

At the entrance to the nave, on the left beside the baptismal font, is a 15C relics cupboard, which was fitted in the 17C with a carved wooden door representing the Education of the Virgin. In the south aisle is a Crucifixion painted by Jean Boucher from Bourges, the master of Mignard. There are also modern sculptured stations of the cross.

EXCURSION

Allogny Forest. – *Round tour of 40 km - 25 miles to the north by the D 79 in the direction of Neuvy-sur-Barangeon.*

Allouis Transmitting Station (Centre émetteur d'Allouis). – Note to the right of the road, *La Pierre de Lu* a great conglomerate made up of flint nodules. Situated on an open plateau, the Allouis Transmitting Station for Radio France, broadcasts the programmes of "France Inter", with its 308 m - 1 010 ft – high radio mast.

Take a small road on the right which runs along a cemetery; turn left into the D 20 in the direction of Allogny.

Allogny Forest (Forêt d'Allogny). – This wooded massif, a dark mass on the plateau which acts as a watershed, dominates the Cher and Barangeon valleys. This densely forested area is mainly composed of oaks with isolated clumps of Norwegian pines, hornbeams, birch and beech.

The D 56 between Allogny and St-Martin d'Auxigny traverses the forest. From the slope reaching down to St-Martin there is a fine view of the smiling and fertile Moulon valley, a welcome contrast to the forest.

The D 68 to the right and then the N 76 lead back to Mehun.

MEILLANT Château ★★

Michelin map 69 fold 1 – *Local map p 162*

Meillant Château, half-hidden by trees in its park, reveals the beauties of its architecture only a little at a time; the plain front seems, by contrast, to enhance the elegance and rich decoration of the east façade which is adorned with all the beauty of line of the late Gothic period graced by Italian influence.

The Amboise Family. – Charles I of Amboise obtained the Meillant lands by his marriage in 1464 and wished, immediately, to modernise the castle which was a massive structure flanked by high towers. But death came and it was to his son, Charles II, that the honour fell of completing the work on the château. Charles II was to become grand-master, marshal and admiral of France. As Governor of Milan, Charles II made such gains in Italy that he was able to complete the work planned for Meillant and also that for Chaumont in the Loire valley.

TOUR *time: 3/4 hour*

Open 9 to 11.30am and 2 to 6.30pm (4.30pm, 15 November to 15 February); 12F.

Exterior. – The feudal character of the château can now only be seen in the southern front. The towers, though stripped of their watch-paths, still stand guard with narrow loopholes.

The east façade is very different and approaches the château of the Loire in the richness of its decoration: two staircase turrets jut out from the main building and seem to have concentrated in them all the exuberance of the last blaze of the "flowering Gothic style": the pierced balustrade running at the base of the eaves, the carved dormer windows, the chimneys ornamented with flamboyantly decorated balustrades are all overshadowed by the incredibly intricate decoration of the Lion's Tower.

This tower, which owes its name to the lion, cast in lead, on its topmost lantern turret, strikes the onlooker by the close juxtaposition of contrasting carvings: twisted small columns, hearts entwined, monograms and crests with interlaced C's – the initials of Charles of Amboise – mountains on fire, the emblem of the château of Chaumont *(chaud mont* = hot mountain*)*, and figures looking out of false windows as at Jacques Cœur's Palace in Bourges *(p 63)*. A pretty 16C well and an elegant chapel of the same period, with buttresses topped by pinnacles, complete this harmonious group of buildings.

(After a photo by M. Foucault, Éd. Tel)

Meillant Château – The Lion Tower.

Interior. – Among the rooms containing remarkable furniture and furnishings are: the main dining hall, where the walls are covered in Cordova leather; the great salon, where a beautiful chimneypiece is surmounted by a balcony once used as a musicians' gallery. Note the 16C tapestries brought from Bruges and a portrait of Charles VII by Clouet; the bedroom of Cardinal d'Amboise; the library with its attractive view of the well and chapel; the armoury, decorated with Aubusson tapestries; and the Louis XII room with its chimneypiece and Aubusson tapestry.

The chapel contains interesting 16C stained glass; above the altar is a 15C altarpiece of the Rhenish School on painted and gilded wood, depicting scenes from the Passion.

MERLE Towers ★★ (Tours de MERLE)

Michelin map 75 fold 10 – *Local maps pp 45 and 93*

The remains of this feudal fortress *("Son et Lumière", p 37)* stand on a spur surrounded by the waters of the Maronne river flowing in a narrow bend.

An Impregnable Lair. – The Lords of Merle were the most feared in the region in the Middle Ages and the family jealously guarded this the surest of strongholds.

Alongside the 11C castle rose the castles of the younger sons until by the 14C the Merle domain was divided into seven. During the Hundred Years War the hill proved impregnable to the English who had made themselves master of all the strongholds of Auvergne and Bas-Limousin. Only the advent of artillery changed the fortune of this fortress which could be bombarded from neighbouring heights – now vulnerable, it was abandoned.

A Glance at the Ruins★★. – As you drive along the D 13 from the south you come suddenly on the Towers of Merle. The road crosses the Maronne by a suspension bridge and climbs the opposite hillside. Leave the car in a park in a right-hand bend some 700 m - 800 yds beyond the bridge. You get a breathtaking bird's-eye view of the ruins. Picturesque houses cluster at the foot of the castle walls.

MILLEVACHES Plateau

Michelin maps 73 fold 11 and 72 fold 20

The Millevaches Plateau, which lies between the upper valleys of the Vienne and Vézère, reaches an altitude of 977 m - 3 205 ft at Mont Bessou and Puy Pendu, northwest of Meymac. The name Millevaches does not come from the flocks which are none too numerous on the plateau, but from the countless springs – *batz* in Celtic means spring – which cut across the vast granite block rising here and there in wide, low undulations. The Creuse, Corrèze, Vienne and Vézère rivers rise on this plateau.

The Rooftop of Limousin. – The Millevaches Plateau, a sort of «high tableland», one of the oldest outcrops in Limousin, impresses by its very monotony. Bracken and heather serve only to increase the impression of solitude and poverty.

Such life as there is, is sparse and widely scattered, grouped in the hollows where pasture and crops can be grown; the density of the population, in fact, does not exceed 18 to the square mile and migration is justified on the grounds of the traditional poverty of the plateau.

Considerable efforts have been made to improve this vast area where the rigors of the climate exclude the growing of fruit trees and even chestnut trees. Reclamation began in about 1860 with the development of the railway. The indigenous forest, burnt down in 1575 during the Wars of Religion, had never been replanted; today thousands of acres have been planted with conifers which can resist the cold and whose cultivation provides an economic resource for the area, as can be seen by the many saw-mills. The dark patches of the forests alternate with the lighter ones of the heaths with their occasional granite outcrops. On the plateau itself the low granite crests seem as though they would roll on for ever, though the outline of the Auvergne Mountains stands out on the horizon. Here and there a herd of cattle or a flock of sheep graze, serving as a reminder of what the inhabitants once had to depend on for their livelihood in an area where the soil is so poor that it was decided the best use for it was to establish on it the vast military camp of La Courtine.

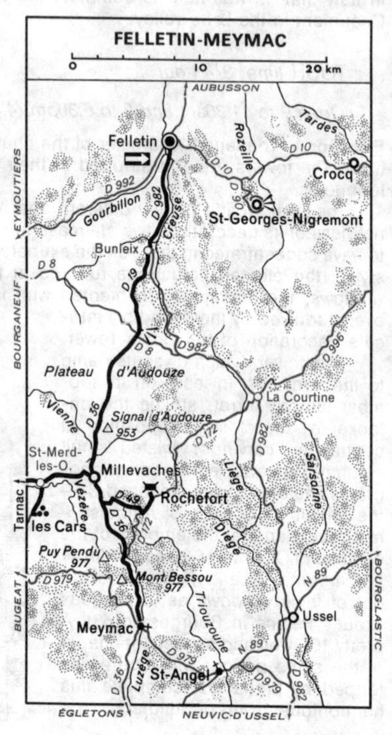

From Felletin to Meymac

46 km - 29 miles – about 2 hours – local map above

Leave Felletin (p 104) by the D 982, going south. The road goes up the valley of the Creuse and winds through a countryside of wooded hills and meadows. Turn right at Bunleix on to the D 19 which becomes D 36 and soon you see rising above the valley, the outline of the Millevaches Plateau. The road climbs steeply, ascending wooded slopes and providing wide views of the valley. As soon as you reach the plateau the contrast is breathtaking: wide expanses of gorse, bracken and heather are broken by conifer plantations.

Audouze Plateau★★ (Plateau d'Audouze). – The streams that run down from the western and northern slopes of the Plateau of the Audouze provide the waters for the river Vienne; the streams from the eastern and southern slopes those for the Diège, an important tributary of the Dordogne. The Ardouze Beacon (Signal d'Ardouze) which is out of bounds *(military area)* towers over the plateau.

Millevaches. – Pop 79. This little village, in the centre of the plateau to which it has given its name, still contains thatched cottages on the west side of the church.

Tarnac. – Pop 472. *16 km - 10 miles from Millevaches.* The church is half-Romanesque, half-Gothic. The north doorway is adorned with covings and medallions carved with figures among which can be seen St. George on the right and St. Giles on the left. In front of the church stands a tree known as Sully's oak. The pretty St-Georges Fountain is noteworthy.

Les Cars. – *9 km - 6 miles from Millevaches.* Visit the remains of an early Christian basilica and Gallo-Roman buildings.

Beyond Millevaches the road crosses a more fertile but hillier country.

Rochefort Castle. – *8 km - 5 miles from the D 36.* This old fortress, embellished by a wing added in the 17C, was built on a rock commanding a picturesque valley.

The descent into Meymac, overlooking the Luzège valley, has picturesque stretches.

Meymac. – Pop 2 783. *Facilities p 38.* Meymac clusters its many pointed slate-covered roofs round a Romanesque church. The **church** was once part of a Benedictine abbey founded in the 11C. The belfry-porch contains a Limousin style, multilobed doorway, flanked by two arches. The porch is adorned with Romanesque capitals carved in the archaic style. The nave has ogive vaulting and continues into a chancel which is equally wide. Note a 12C black Virgin on the pillar to the left of the chancel. To the right of the church stand the rebuilt buildings of the former Abbey of St-André. To the left stands the old covered market, with its wooden frame resting on granite pillars.

MOISSAC★★

Michelin map 79 folds 16 and 17 – Pop 11 408 – *Facilities p 38*

Moissac, encircling its old abbey on the right bank of the Tarn and both sides of the Garonne Lateral Canal, is surrounded by hills covered with fruit trees and vines which produce a well-known dessert grape.

The Golden Grape. – The hillsides of Bas-Quercy and Agenais which run down to the right bank of the Tarn and the Garonne between Montauban and Agen, produce, on average, 18 000 tons each year of a first class golden dessert grape, which is dispatched principally to Paris. The *Moissac* comes in the form of fine, long bunches of round, well-separated grapes with a golden tinge and a pearly bloom. The grape, which is sweet and scented, is known for its flavour.

HISTORICAL NOTES

The Abbey's Golden Age. – Moissac Abbey knew its greatest glory in the 11C. It appears to have been founded in the 7C by a Benedictine monk from the Norman Abbey of St-Wandrille. The abbey was pillaged and plundered by successive invasions of Arabs, Normans and Hungarians, and had only with much difficulty begun to recover when, in 1047, its whole destiny was changed. St. Odilon, the famous Abbot of Cluny who had just established the rule for the monastery at Carennac and was therefore passing through Quercy, attached Moissac Abbey to Cluny. This was the beginning of an era of prosperity. Thanks to the support of Cluny and the administration of influential abbots, Moissac Abbey established priories everywhere and its influence spread as far as Catalonia.

A Series of Misfortunes. – The Hundred Years War, during which Moissac was twice occupied by the English, then the Wars of Religion, brought down harsh blows upon the abbey. It was secularised in 1628 and was suppressed altogether during the Revolution. In 1793 the art treasures were pillaged and many of the sculptures mutilated.

In the middle of last century, the abbey only just escaped even further destruction since it was proposed to knock down the buildings to make way for the Bordeaux-Sète railway line. The Fine Arts Department intervened, however, and saved the abbey from final ruin.

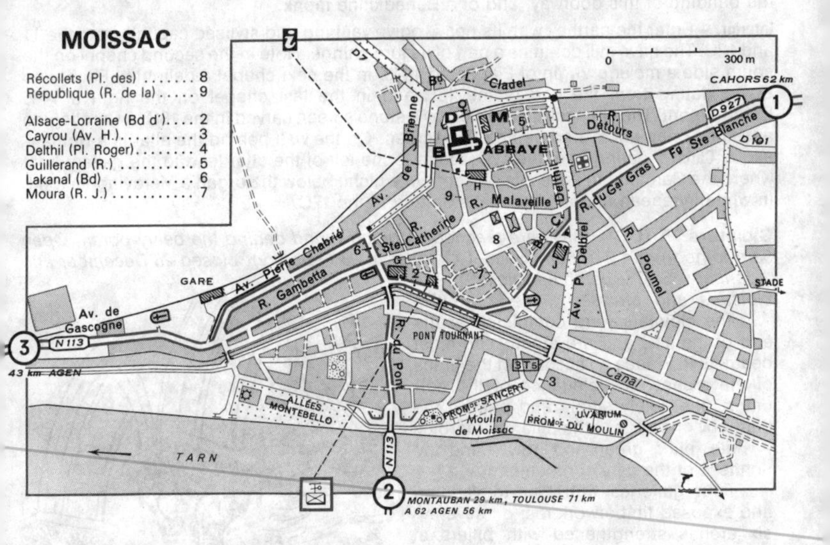

■ THE ABBEY *time: 1 hour*

Church of St-Pierre★ **(B).** – This is the former abbey church. The only part of the 11C building still standing is the massive belfry-porch, a sort of keep complete with watch-path built for defence purposes. The top storey was only added at the end of the Gothic period.

The two very different periods in which the nave was built, can be seen clearly from outside: the part in stone is Romanesque, the other in brick is Gothic. The Romanesque part can be seen in the foundations to the walls of the nave and in the rounded windows in the lower parts of the walls. The rest was erected in the 15C in the southern Gothic style.

South doorway★★★. – *Diagram p 134.* The tympanum over this doorway was carved between 1100 and 1130 and is generally accepted as a masterpiece of Romanesque sculpture. The majesty of composition, the scope of the scenes depicted, the harmony of proportion between the figures are so compelling and beautiful that a certain clumsiness of gesture and rigidity of stance in a few cases make no difference.

The theme is the Vision of the Apocalypse according to St. John. Christ (**1**) sits enthroned in the centre dominating all other figures by His size; crowned and haloed, He holds the Book of Life in His left hand and raises His right in benediction. The features are well defined, the eyes brilliant, the beard and hair are separated into symmetrical locks that add to the severity of expression and increase the impression of strength and majesty which emanate from the figure. The four Evangelists surround Him, each in symbolic form: St. Matthew as a winged young man (**2**), St. Mark as a lion (**3**), St. Luke as a bull (**4**) and St. John as an eagle (**5**). Two tall seraphim (**6**) frame this magnificent scene.

The remainder of the tympanum is filled with the figures of the 24 Old Men of the Apocalypse (**7**) ranged in three rows one above the other. All are turned towards Christ their expressions show at once amazement and fear at such an apparition. The sculpture has a rare dramatic intensity: the whole composition centres on the principal character towards whom everyone is looking. The beauty and grace of the figures, the perfection of the modelling, the attention to detail and the facial expressions are noteworthy.

The carving rests on a remarkable lintel (**8**). It is decorated with eight carved roses encircled by a cable which comes out of the mouth of a monster at one end and disappears into that of another at the other end.

The pier (**9**) is a magnificent single block of stone vigorously carved with three pairs of lions one above the other, their bodies crossed to form an X. A similar theme is to be found at Souillac *(p 178)*.

Completing the decoration of the central pier are two striking figures of old men (**10**), carved on the sides. On the engaged piers are St. Peter (**11**), patron saint of the Abbey, and the prophet Isaiah (**12**). The scalloped engaged piers and some of the decorative features would seem to recall Spanish-Moorish influence which could be explained by the fact that Moissac lies on one of the most frequented routes to Santiago de Compostela.

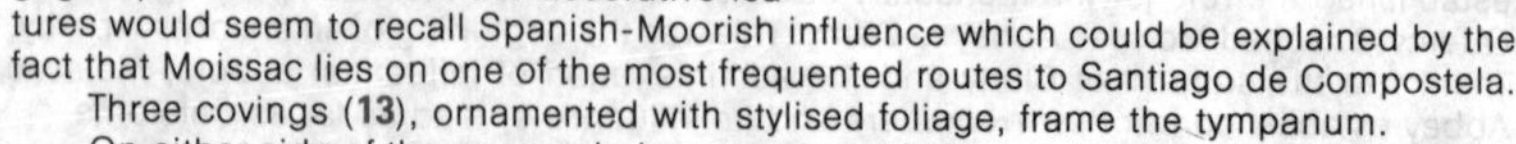

Three covings (**13**), ornamented with stylised foliage, frame the tympanum.

On either side of the engaged piers are carved historiated scenes: on the right (**14**) reading from the bottom to the top are the Annunciation, the Visitation, the Adoration of the Magi, the Presentation of Jesus in the Temple and the Flight into Egypt; on the left (**15**) are scenes of damnation: the miser and the adultress being tortured by demons, the story of the wicked rich man feasting without thinking of Lazarus, the poor man dying of hunger whose soul is being borne away by an angel so that it may be received in the bosom of Abraham.

The archivolt and pillars of the doorway are intricately decorated: on either side, on the columns flanking the door, may be seen the statues of Abbot Roger, who completed the building of this doorway, and of a Benedictine monk.

Interior. – Enter the narthex with its heavy ogive vaulting and stylised capitals from the 11 and 12C. The nave still contains a part of its furnishings. Note in the second chapel on the south side a moving Virgin of Pity dated 1476, in the next chapel a delightful Flight into Egypt dating from the end of the 15C and in the last chapel on the right a 1485 Entombment. The chancel is encircled by a stone screen carved in the 16C. A Carolingian apse has been uncovered behind this screen. On the wall behind the altar is a Romanesque **Christ**★ dating from the 12C; stairs to the left of the altar lead to the gallery from where the Carolingian apse can be seen. In a niche below the organ a Merovingian tomb in white Pyrenean marble. The stalls date from the 17C.

Cloisters★★ (D). – *These are reached by going round behind the belfry-porch. Open 9am to noon and 2 to 6pm (5pm, 1 October to 28 February); closed 25 December and 1 January; 6.60F; combined ticket to the cloisters and Moissac Museum: 8.80F.*

The cloisters were completed at the end of the 11C and are among the most beautiful in France on account of the grace of the arches, the elegance of the columns, alternately single and paired, the harmony of colour of the different marbles – white, pink, green and grey – and the richness of the carved ornament.

Four galleries with lean-to vaulting and exposed timberwork rest on seventy-six arches strengthened with pillars at each corner and in the centre of each side. These pillars are faced with blocks of carved marble bas-reliefs taken from old tombs. The figures of nine apostles can be made out and, on the pillar in the centre of the gallery, facing the entrance, is the portrait of Abbot Durand de Bredon, Bishop of Toulouse and Abbot of Moissac, who played a major role in the development of the abbey. The carving was made only fifteen years after his death and gives the impression of being a true portrait, so realistic is the execution.

(After a photo by Arthaud, Grenoble)

Moissac – The cloisters.

The capitals shows a variety of decoration: animals, foliage, geometrical motifs, historiated scenes and are treated with skill. Subjects from the Old and New Testaments include scenes from the life of Christ, the miracles performed by Christ, the parables and the Apocalypse. Other themes include events in the life of saints commemorated in the abbey.

A large cedar stands in the close. To the right of the entrance to the cloisters, a stairway leads to the first floor of the narthex: view of the cloisters.

The **cloistral museum** is in the four chapels off the east cloister gallery. There are the lapidary collection (11-13C), a collection of photographs illustrating the diffusion of the Moissac style of sculpture throughout Quercy *(see p 28: Romanesque sculpture)* and finally a section dealing with 17-19C religious furnishings and liturgical objects.

■ ADDITIONAL SIGHT

Moissac Museum (Musée Moissagais) (M). – *Open 9.30am to noon and 2.30 to 6pm (5.30pm, 1 November to 28 February); closed Sunday mornings, Tuesdays, 1 May and 1 December to 15 January; 3.30F; combined ticket to museum and cloisters: 8.80F.*

The museum is in the former abbot's lodging, a large building flanked by a 13C crenellated tower built of brick, which was dismantled during the Revolution. At the entrance two diagrams indicate the abbey's importance during the Middle Ages and its influence throughout the southwest. The great well of the 17C staircase provides the setting for an exhibition of historical and religious objects.

The rooms are devoted to folklore collections, including regional pottery, furniture, Moissac *coiffes* (head-dresses), a 19C kitchen from Bas-Quercy, varied crafts, coins and local costumes.

There is an extensive view from the top of the tower of the town, whose old quarters cluster around the abbey, and beyond to the valley of the Tarn and the Moissac hills.

EXCURSION

Boudou. – Pop 489. *7 km - 4 miles to the west. Leave Moissac by ③, the N 113, then take the road on your right after the St-Nicolas suspension bridge to the village of Boudou.* From a promontory *(viewing table)* south of the church a wide **panorama**★ of the valley of the Garonne unfolds. The right bank sweeps the foot of hills partly covered with vineyards, while the land stretching beyond the left bank is dead flat and carpeted with fields under crops divided by lines of poplars. On the left can be seen the confluence of the Garonne and the Tarn and the St-Nicolas-de-la-Grave reservoir.

MONBAZILLAC Château★

Michelin map 75 folds 14 and 15 – *Local map p 54*

Monbazillac Chateau rises proudly amidst the vineyard *(p 54)* on the edge of a limestone plateau overlooking the valley of the Dordogne. It is owned by the Monbazillac Wine Cooperative and has been restored and refurbished.

TOUR *time: 3/4 hour*

Open 1 March to 30 November, 9am to noon and 2 to 6pm; the rest of the year, 9.30am to noon and 2 to 5pm; 9F.

Exterior. – Built in 1550 this small chateau surrounded by a dry moat attracts the eye with its elegant silhouette in an architectural style half way between the military and the Renaissance. A crenellated watch-path and battlements surmount the main building which is flanked at each corner by a massive round tower. The façade is pierced by a double row of mullioned windows and a doorway ornamented in the Renaissance style. Two tiers of dormer windows rise above the machicolations. The grey patina of the stone tones in well with the brown tiled roofs of the towers and the pavilions. From the north terrace there is a good view of the vineyard and beyond, of Bergerac spread out in the valley of the Dordogne.

Interior. – The **Great Hall** with its French style ceiling decorated with gilt foliated scrolls has a monumental Renaissance chimneypiece, two fine 17C Flemish tapestries and 17C furniture. In an adjoining room are displayed rustic furniture from the Perigord region. There are also interesting documents tracing the history of Protestantism in France in another room.

Several rooms are open on the first floor; note in particular the **room** of the Viscountess of Monbazillac furnished in Louis XIII style.

The former castle cellars house a small museum displaying harvesting and wine making equipment used in the past.

MONÉDIÈRES Massif★

Michelin map 72 south of fold 19

Adjoining the Millevaches Plateau, the Monédières Massif stretching between the upper valley of the Vézère and the river Corrèze, forms the southern bastion of the Limousin Montagne *(p 13)*. This relatively low massif – the tallest peak is the Puy de la Monédière with an altitude of 919 m - 3 015 ft – is a highly eroded mass of crystalline rocks.

Although the region is open to considerable oceanic influences, brought by the Westerlies, the climate is essentially a mountainous one with arduous snowy winters and short hot summers.

The Forest in Flames. – At the time of the Roman conquest, the massif was covered by a forest which provided refuge for the druids who organised resistance to the invaders. Caesar became irritated and ordered the forest to be burned, the fire lasted for many months.

Patiently the mediaeval monks of Treignac set about replanting the Monédières. In the 16C, while his powerful neighbours sided with the Protestants, **Louis de Pompadour,** Baron of Treignac, remained a Catholic. His enemies sacked his domains. Returning to the tactics used by Caesar, Pompadour set fire to the forest; the fire spread over an area of 30 sq.miles, destroying castles, villages and crops. Louis was ruined, but the Huguenots fled.

In spite of many subsequent attempts, reafforestation has never been completed. Recently replanting has increased and thousands of conifers cover hillsides already crossed by a network of forest roads.

Heather and Bilberries. – In late summer the slopes are covered with a carpet of pink heather. Slowly but gradually bilberries are replacing the heather above 700 m - 2 300 ft, creating a new source of income and activity especially at the bilberry gathering time. Picked with an adroit movement of the hand the fragile berries are then dispatched to the canning factories and pharmaceutical laboratories. Nearly 200 tons are gathered annually and sent to the Puy de Dôme Department.

Tour starting from Chaumeil

29 km - 18 miles – about 1 hour – see local map below

Chaumeil. – Pop 218. This attractive village, capital of the Monédières, with its sturdy granite houses roofed with slates or stones, is clustered round the church adorned with a fine 16C porch. Inside the church, on the left of the chancel, there are a polychrome naive *Pietà* (16C) in wood in a display case (lighting), a Madonna and child and a reliquary.

An artificial stretch of water has been created a little to the north of the village.

Take the D 121, a narrow road which descends slightly.

Freysselines. – This small hamlet lies huddled into an amphitheatre of the same name.

The road winds along the south facing slope where arable crops alternate with rough grazing and chestnut groves.

At Chauzeix, take the road which climbs to the right, then right again onto the D 128 which rises amidst meadows and conifers. Note to the left the long ridge of the Puy Pantout (770 m - 2 526 ft).

The road skirts the Puy de Chauzeix with its wooded slopes and leaves the Puy de la Monédière to the left.

At the pass, Col du Bos, take the D 128 E to the right which leads to Suc-au-May.

Suc-au-May★★★. – *1/4 hour Rtn on foot.* Altitude 908 m - 2 979 ft. From the viewing table there is a **panorama★★★** of the Limousin countryside and the Millevaches Plateau to the northeast; the Monts Dore and Monts Dômes to the east and the Cantal Mountains to the southeast. The Monédières Massif in the foreground has an undulating severely eroded surface.

Return to the D 128 and at the pass, Col des Géants, take the D 32 to the right, which goes downhill amidst conifers. There are fine glimpses of the Puy Messou (907 m - 2 976 ft) to the left and the Suc-au-May to the right.

Le Mas Michel. – At the crossroads take the narrow road leading to this hamlet, which lies at the foot of the Puy Charrin. Old cottages built of dry stone make it worth a visit.

Return to the D 32 which leads back to Chaumeil.

MONFLANQUIN

Michelin map 79 5 – *Local map p 124* – Pop 2 356

This former *bastide (p 32)*, which was founded in the 13C by Alphonse de Poitiers, is built on a hill. Houses with round tiles – several have been carefully restored – cluster on the slope which is crowned by the tall outline of the church.

Small, picturesque streets climb steeply to the fine **Place des Arcades,** a square completely surrounded by covered arcades. The church is massive in the southern Gothic style with brick vaulting. The 15C fortified façade has been considerably restored.

From the street encircling the upper town, you can see wide **expanses★** of the neighbouring countryside through which flows the river Lède, a tributary of the Lot. There is a good view of Biron Castle *(p 55)* on the crestline to the northeast.

EXCURSION

Gavaudun; Biron★; Villeréal. – *Round tour of 48 km - 30 miles – about 2 hours. Leave Monflanquin to the east by the D 150.* The pleasant road cuts through rich agricultural land.

Gavaudun. – Pop 269. Gavaudun lies in a picturesque setting in the narrow, winding valley of the Lède. A massive 12-14C crenellated keep rises from the top of a rock spur overlooking the river and the village. The base is reached by a staircase cut out of the rock.

Leave the village to the east and take a small road in the direction of Laurenque.

St-Sardos-de-Laurenque. – The 12C church has a carved doorway with capitals adorned with animals and human figures and a frieze decorated with fishes. Note the outstanding capitals in the Romanesque nave.

Return to the D 150 and continue in the direction of Lacapelle-Biron. The road skirts the base of **St-Avit,** the hamlet where Bernard Palissy *(p 41)* was born.

Biron Castle★. – *Description p 55.*

Continue along the D 53 then take to the left the D 2 and the D 104.

Villeréal. – Pop 1 340. Villeréal, like so many other *bastides (p 32)* in Périgord, was founded in 1269 by Alphonse de Poitiers, the brother of St. Louis. He sought to build a group of fortified towns that would stem the advance of the English in the southwest. However, during the Hundred Years War the town was English, its original town plan has been preserved and it has many corbelled houses with overhanging roofs. The tall outline of the fortified church, built in the 13 and 14C, dominates the *bastide.* Charm and severity are combined on the exterior. The tall façade is framed by two towers topped by pointed bell-turrets and linked by a gallery. The tower on the left is pierced with loopholes. The covered market is supported by oak pillars.

The D 676 to the south returns to Monflanquin.

MONPAZIER★

Michelin map 75 fold 16 – Pop 533 – *Facilities p 38*

Monpazier was one of the *bastides* built to command the roads going from Agenais to the banks of the Dordogne. The square surrounded by arcades, the old houses, the church and the ruined fortifications make it the best preserved of the Périgord *bastides (p 32).*

A Difficult Start. – The *bastide* of Monpazier was founded on 7 January 1284 by **Edward I**, King of England and Duke of Aquitaine. This latest *bastide* was designed to complete the defences and control of Périgord begun in 1267 with the founding of Lalinde and continued with the construction of Beaumont, Molières and Roquépine. To this end he allied himself with Pierre de Gontaut, Lord of Biron. But difficulties soon arose: delays occured in the building, there were disagreements between the King of England and Philip the Fair. The situation soon became complicated with the result that during the Hundred Years War the *bastide* was assaulted and pillaged as often by the English as by the French.

The Reformation with Marshal de Biron as a leading figure, brought an era of violence. On 12 June 1574 the town was betrayed and captured by the famous Huguenot leader Geoffroi de Vivans who later took Domme *(p 90)* by trickery.

Buffarot the Rebel. – After the Wars of Religion were over, the peasants rose in a new revolt. The rebels, who were known as the Croquants, held a great gathering at Monpazier in 1594. The revolt flared up again in 1637: led by Buffarot, a weaver from the neighbouring town of Capdrot, 8 000 peasants tore through the length and breadth of the countryside plundering the castles.

The soldiers of the Duke of Épernon pursued them and after some difficulty, captured Buffarot. He was brought back to Monpazier, and as leader of the revolt, broken on the wheel in the main square.

■ SIGHTS *time: 3/4 hour*

The general layout of the *bastide (p 32)* can still be seen together with those of three of the original six fortified gateways. Several houses have kept their ancient appearance.

The town is in the shape of an oblong, the longer sides run from north to south and have a length of 400 m - 440 yds, the shorter of 220 m - 240 yds. Streets run from one end to the other, parallel with the longer sides, four cross-roads running east to west divide the town into rectangular blocks. Originally all the houses had the unique characteristic of being of equal size and separated from each other by narrow spaces or *andrones*, intended to prevent the spread of fire.

(After a photo by M. Foucault, Éd. Tel)

Monpazier – The main square.

Place Centrale★. – The picturesque main square is an oblong like the *bastide* itself. On the south side stands a covered market containing the old measures. Round the perimeter the arcades or covered galleries supported on arches which are sometimes pointed *(see illustration above)* have kept their *cornières*.

Church of St-Dominique. – The church façade has been restored at different times: the doorway was adorned with archivolts, the rose window and the gable rebuilt in about 1550. The single aisle is wide, has ogive vaulting and is extended to form a polygonal chevet.

Chapter House (Maison du Chapitre). – This 13C house stands near the church at the corner of the square and was used as a tithe barn. It is lit by paired windows on the upper floor.

MONSEMPRON-LIBOS

Michelin map 75 fold 6 – *Local map p 124* – Pop 2 736

The Romanesque church of Monsempron stands on a small hill overlooking the right bank of the river Lot. Above the chancel, fortifications, which remain from their construction during the Wars of Religion, can be seen.

Church★. – The church has a fine buttressed chevet with carved modillions and friezes, and a square belfry with a flat roof crowning the transept crossing.

The interior is remarkable for the juxtaposition of different architectural styles: the three Romanesque naves, altered in the 16C, have cradle vaulting supported on great round pillars whose capitals are so reduced that they form only an ornamental frieze decorated with carvings in the archaic manner. The transept and chancel, built over the crypt, are raised above the level of the nave: the transept is of a later Romanesque style than the nave and is adorned with beautiful historiated capitals; the deep Gothic chancel is ornamented with star vaulting. A kind of double transept covered by small oblong domes has been built before two apsidal chapels decorated with Romanesque capitals.

EXCURSIONS

Tournon-d'Agenais; Gouts. – *16 km - 10 miles to the south by the D 102.*

Tournon-d'Agenais. – Pop 921. Tournon stands in a picturesque **setting**★ on the crest of a hill near the valley of the Lot. The farther you go into the village, the better you are able to distinguish the line of the former ramparts by the houses which have been built along the top of the old walls. From the village there is a view of the valley with lines of trees screening the vineyards and maize fields. The village was once a *bastide (p 32)* and still retains the classic pattern of narrow streets intersecting at right angles. The main square has lost most of its covered arcades. From the small public garden there is a good **view** of Quercy to the south.

Gouts. – The Romanesque church, built in grey stone has a great unity of style. Together with the old cemetery shaded by cypress trees it makes a pretty setting.

MONTAL Castle ★★

Michelin map 75 fold 19 – 3 km - 2 miles west of St-Céré – *Local maps pp 94 and 166*

Montal Castle groups the harmonious mass of its buildings with their pepper-pot roofs on a wooded mound on a hillside near the smiling valley of the Bave.

The Miracle of Mother Love. – **Jeanne de Balsac d'Entraygues**, widow of Amaury de Montal, Governor of Haute Auvergne, had built for her eldest son, Robert, who was away warring in Italy for François I, a country mansion on the site a feudal stronghold. The chatelaine had the best artists and workmen brought from the banks of the Loire to Quercy and by 1634 there could be seen the masterpiece begotten of a mother's tender pride.

"Hope No More". – Everything was ready to receive the proud knight. Alas only Robert's body returned to the castle. The dream crumbled. Jeanne had the high window from which she had watched for her son blocked up and beneath it she had carved the despairing cry "Hope No More". Jeanne's second son, Dordé was absolved by the pope from his ecclesiastical duties in order that he might continue the line.

Death and Resurrection. – Montal was declared a national asset but became uninhabitable as a result of the depredations made during the Revolution; finally in 1879 it fell into the hands of a certain Macaire. This adventurer, permanently short of cash, made a bargain with a demolition group and divided the palace into lots: 120 tons of carved stones were parcelled up and sent to Paris. The masterpieces of Montal were then auctioned and dispersed. In 1908 Montal rose from the ruins: the new and devoted owner, M. Fenaille, set about finding and buying back at ransom prices all the Montal treasures, until he had refurnished the palace. Then he gave it to the nation in 1913.

TOUR *time: 3/4 hour*

Guided tours Palm Sunday to 31 October, 9.30 to 11.25am and 2.30 to 5.25pm (in August 3 to 6pm only); closed Saturdays except in July and August; 8F.

Exterior. – Steep stone roofs and massive round towers with loopholes give the castle the appearance of a fortress. But this fierce exterior makes the contrast all the greater with the inner courtyard, designed with all the graceful charm of the Renaissance.

Montal consists of two main wings linked at the corner by a square tower containing the staircase. A two-storey gallery to complete the square was planned for the other two sides of the courtyard but was never erected. The façade of the main building, in all its rich decoration, is one of the castle's chief glories.

The frieze. – Above the ground floor windows and doors runs a frieze 32 m - 100 ft long. It is a marvel of decorative diversity: cupids, birds, fantasies appear beside shields and a huge human head. There are also initials of the founder and her sons: J (Jeanne), R (Robert) and D (Dordé).

The busts. – On the first floor the mullioned windows alternate with false bays with intricately carved pediments which contain seven busts in full relief. Each statue is a likeness of a member of the Montal family; from left to right they are: Amaury; Jeanne his wife; Robert, the eldest son; Dordé, the second son; Robert de Balsac and Antoinette de Castelnau, Jeanne's parents, and Dordé de Beduer, who was abbot of Vézelay.

The windows. – They recall, in their decoration, those of Chambord: the dormer gables have small supporting figures on either side and the niches contain statues.

Interior. – You enter at the corner, where the wings meet, by a door flanked by pillars and topped by a lintel supporting several niches.

Renaissance staircase★★. – The staircase is built in the fine light stone of Carennac and is magnificently proportionned and decorated. Admire the fine carving beneath the stairs: ornamented foliage, shells, fantastic birds, initials, little figures go to make a ceiling whose decoration completes that of the key vaulting of the vestibules.

The Apartments. – The guardroom, which has a lovely chimneypiece, the Stag Room (Salle du Cerf) and the other rooms in which are to be found old pieces of furniture (mainly in the Renaissance and Louis XIII styles), retables, paintings and plates attributed to Bernard Palissy, and Flemish and Tours tapestries form an admirable group.

MONTAUBAN★

Michelin map 79 folds 17 and 18 – Pop 53 147

Montauban, on the border between the hills of Bas-Quercy and the rich alluvial plains of the Garonne and the Tarn, is an important road junction and busy market town, responsible for selling all the market garden produce and fruit grown in the region.

The use of pink brick for building, gives the town the particular character which is also found in most of the towns and villages of Bas-Quercy and in Toulouse.

HISTORICAL NOTES

A Formidable Bastide. – From the 8C onwards communities established themselves, on a hill overlooking the Tescou, the site now occupied by the suburb of Le Moustier. Later on a Benedictine Monastery established itself on the same hill and a township which took the name of Montauriol was quick to grow up round it. The people felt themselves to be the victims of abuses inflicted on them by the Abbot and the local lords and they sought the protection of the Count of Toulouse. The count founded a *bastide* in 1144 on the right bank of the Tarn. The inhabitants of Montauriol drawn by the advantages granted hastened to the new town "Mons albanus" now known as Montauban.

A Protestant Citadel. – By 1561 a large part of the town had gone over to the ideas of the Reformation; the two consuls were Calvinists and encouraged the people to pillage churches and monasteries. By the time the peace treaty of St-Germain was signed in 1570, Montauban had come to be known as a sure Protestant stronghold. Henry of Navarre reinforced the fortifications and it was in this town that three separate congresses of all the reformed churches of France were held.

But when Louis XIII became king the hour had struck for the « Catholic reconquest »: in 1621 Montauban was besieged by an army of 20 000. The town's resistance was heroic and three assaults were repulsed; after three months, the Catholic troops raised the siege. After La Rochelle had been taken in 1628, Montauban the last bastion of Protestantism, saw the armies of Louis XIII approach once more. This time the town showed no resistance and acclaimed the king and Cardinal Richelieu. The fortifications were destroyed; the Huguenots were granted a royal pardon.

A Great Draughtsman. – **Ingres** was born in Montauban in 1780, the son of a craftsman decorator. In Paris he became the student of David. At twenty-one he won the *Grand Prix de Rome* – a French award for study in Rome. After nearly twenty years stay in Italy he returned to Paris, where he opened a studio and founded a school. His talent showed best in his drawings; purity of line and exactness of detail reached perfection. He also showed great perception in his many portraits and pencil sketches. The painter bequeathed to his native town a major part of his works now in the Ingres Museum.

A Great Sculptor. – **Bourdelle** (1861-1929), also born at Montauban, owes much to his master Rodin. In his work – busts or sculptured groups – he knew how to combine virility of stance, simplicity of line and noble sentiments. One of his greatest works, *Hercules Drawing his Bow*, is exhibited in the Bourdelle Museum in Paris.

■ THE INGRES MUSEUM★★ AND PLACE NATIONALE★

Ingres Museum★★ **(Musée Ingres).** – *Open 10 am to noon and 2 to 6pm; closed Sunday mornings out of season, Mondays, 1 January, 1 and 8 May, 14 July, 1 and 11 November and 25 December. 8F.*

The episcopal palace was built in 1664 on a site that had been occupied by two successive castles. The first castle, known as the Lower Castle, was built in the 12C by the Count of Toulouse to command the Tarn valley; it was dismantled in 1229 and replaced on the orders of the Black Prince, a century later during the Hundred Years War, by another fortress. A few of the rooms of this castle still exist.

The present palace was bought by the township at the time of the suppression of the diocese early in the Revolution and was converted into a museum in 1843. This is a plain impressive edifice in red brick. The main building is flanked by two wings.

First floor. – This is the focal-point of the museum as it provides the setting for Ingres' works. French ceilings and marquetry floors are a perfect background to the collections.

The gallery devoted to Ingres' Classical style contains his remarkable composition, *Christ and the Doctors*, painted when the artist was eighty-two. A second large gallery has sketches, drawings from the nude, **portraits** and the *Dream of Ossian*, a vast canvas painted in 1812 which was intended for Napoleon's bedroom in Rome, in addition to works by the painters David (1748-1825), Chassériau (1819-1856), Géricault (1791-1824) and Delacroix (1798-1863). Note also the mementoes of Ingres – his painting materials and legendary violin – and finally a selection of his 4 000 **drawings** *(shown in rotation)*.

Second floor. – There are excellent Primitives and paintings from the 14 to 18C, most of which were donated by Ingres. A display case in Room I contains remarkable 15C Italian works; in Room III is exhibited a rich collection of 17C paintings of the Flemish, Dutch and Spanish schools. Interesting Louis XV and Louis XVI furnishings are also displayed. There is a bird's eye view of the Tarn and the Pont Vieux.

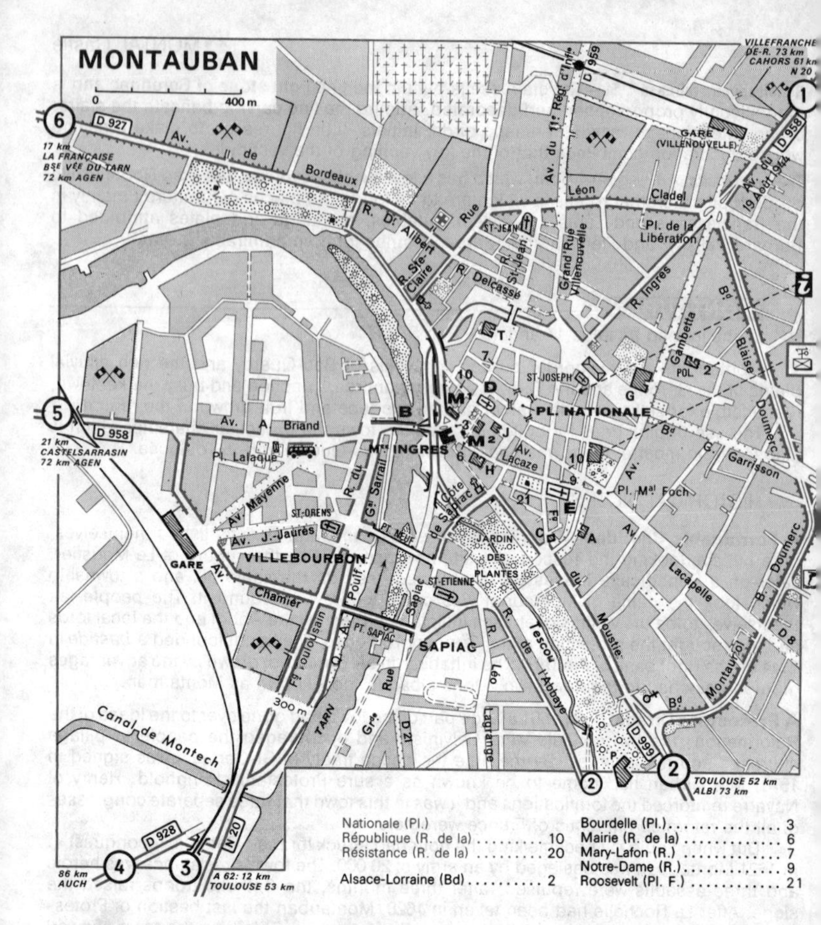

Ground floor. – A large gallery traces the artistic development of the great sculptor **Bourdelle.** Note "Hercules Drawing his Bow" in patinated plasterwork, one of his greatest works. The busts of Beethoven, Rodin, Leon Cladel, Ingres, and other bronzes such as "Night" and "Rembrandt as an Old Man" are outstanding.

The **Desnoyer gallery** displays the main works of the Montauban painter Desnoyer (1894-1972) and paintings by other local artists.

Basement. – In the 14C part of the castle, seven galleries on two levels with remarkable vaulted ceilings are devoted to local archaeology and history, applied arts and to temporary exhibitions.

The former guardroom known as the Black Prince's Chamber (14C) contains mediaeval lapidary collections and two fine chimneypieces adorned with the Cahors coat of arms. In the Jean Chandos Room are bronzes, terracottas and a 4C Gallo-Roman **mosaic** discovered at Labastide-du-Temple, northwest of Montauban.

A large collection of **local pottery** (Montauban, Auvillar) has also been assembled from donations to the museum.

Place Nationale★. – The arcades round the square were built in brick in the 17C, following two fires in 1614 and 1649 which destroyed the wood "covers". Roofed over with broken barrel or rounded vaulting, they provide the square with double galleries.

The variation in the vaulting and the warm tones of the brick do not detract from the overall architectural unity of the square but alleviate any impression of severity. The houses surrounding this fine square *(now a car park)*, also built of pink brick, are linked at the corners by porticoes set at an angle. In the mornings a colourful market is held.

■ ADDITIONAL SIGHTS

Pont Vieux (B). – As you cross the Pont-Vieux from the left bank, you see the outline of the former episcopal palace and, beyond many 17C houses, the tower of the Church of St-Jacques.

The bridge was constructed at the beginning of the 14C on the orders of Philip the Fair. It is entirely built of brick and is 205 m - 673 ft long, spanning the Tarn with seven arches which rest on piles protected by cutwaters. The arches are divided by smaller arches which allow more water to flow through when the river is in flood. The bridge was built at the same time as the Valentré Bridge at Cahors and, like it, was once fortified.

Two masterpieces by Bourdelle. – On Quai Montmurat near the Pont Vieux stands the **1870 War Memorial** which shows the artist's architectural sense. The admirable bronze of the **Last Dying Centaur★** opposite the Ingres Museum by the General Picquart square is a powerful, concentrated composition dating from 1914.

Church of St-Jacques (D). – *To visit, apply at the Syndicat d'Initiative.*

This fortified church which dominates the town is dedicated to St. James. After the Catholics had regained the town *(p 144)* the church was raised to the status of cathedral in 1629, a prerogative maintained until 1739.

The **belfry** stands on a square battlemented tower and was built of dull red brick on an octagonal plan at the end of the 13C. It is lit by three tiers of windows. The nave, flanked by chapels, was rebuilt in the 15C and given ogive vaulting in the 18C.

Cathedral of Notre-Dame (E). – *Closed on Sunday afternoons.* This is a Classical edifice of vast proportions. The west front, framed by two square towers, opens with an impressive peristyle adorned with four colossal figures of the Evangelists which are copies of those inside the cathedral. The chancel is long; the transept crossing is crowned by a dome on pendentives adorned with the Theological Virtues.

In the north transept may be seen the well-known picture by Ingres, the **Vow of Louis XIII:** in the foreground, the king turns towards the Virgin holding the Infant Jesus in her arms, and offers her his kingdom, symbolised by the sceptre and crown.

Former Board of Excise (Ancienne Cour des Aides) (M[1]). – This fine 17C mansion houses two museums.

Folk Museum (Musée du Terroir). – *Open 1 April to 30 October, 10am to noon and 2 to 6pm; closed Sundays, Mondays and holidays; 4F.*

On the ground floor, the Escolo Carsinolo, a Provençal association, presents life in the Bas-Quercy. Most of the ancient crafts are represented with tools, instruments and models. In one room there is a reconstruction of a 19C country household.

Natural History Museum (Musée d'Histoire Naturelle). – *Open 10am to noon and 2 to 6pm; closed Mondays, Sunday mornings and holidays; 4F.*

On the second floor, several rooms are devoted to a varied zoological collection including a large ornithological section of 4 000 birds, a number of which come from the tropics (parakeets, humming-birds, birds of paradise). There is also a paleontological section with many specimens from the Tertiary Period.

Prehistory Museum (M[2]). – *To visit, apply to the National History Museum.*

This annex to the Natural History Museum is housed in a fine mansion nearby. Most of the artefacts come from the region: Acheulean objects from the Tarn area, Mousterian flint tools from the Aveyron district; Perigordian and Magdalenian finds from the Bruniquel excavations. Tools and jewellery from the Neolithic Era and the Bronze and Iron Ages are from the Montauban region.

EXCURSION

Lower Valley of the Tarn. – The only part of the Tarn included in the area covered by this guide is the lower section of its course, from Bondigoux to where it joins the Garonne below Moissac. In this region of Bas-Quercy, where the Aveyron, the Tarn and the Garonne join, the most marked characteristic is the great width of the valleys. The alluvial plain spreads wide, limited only by two hilly regions; a great variety of crops flourish on this rich soil : wheat, maize, tobacco, early vegetables, fruit trees and vines.

Upstream from Montauban

33 km - 21 miles. Michelin maps 79 fold 18 and 82 fold 8. *Leave Montauban to the south by the D 21.*

Beyond Villebrumier, a former *bastide,* the D 87 rises to the crest of the hillside before reaching Villemur.

Villemur-sur-Tarn. – Pop 4 456. The Vieux-Moulin Saracen tower, the only remains of the town's fortifications, dominates this former fortress.

Between Villemur and Bondigoux the D 22 follows the right bank of the Tarn.

Downstream from Montauban

38 km - 24 miles. Michelin map 79 folds 16 and 17. *Leave Montauban by ⑥, the D 927.* The road crosses the Aveyron at its confluence with the Tarn.

Lafrançaise. – Pop 2 630. There is a wide view from the terrace near the church, of the river flowing between long lines of willows and poplars and of the vast alluvial plain.

Moissac★★. – *Description p 133.*

Beyond Moissac the N 113 follows the right bank of the river, rising slightly above it.

Boudou. – *Description p 135.*

MONTIGNAC

Michelin map 75 south of fold 7 – *Local map p 142* – Pop 3 165 – *Facilities p 38*

Montignac, built on the banks of the Vézère *(p 185)*, is dominated by a tower, a last reminder of the fortress which once belonged to the counts of Périgord.

■ LASCAUX CAVE (Grotte de LASCAUX)

Not open to the public. In season there are daily commentated slide shows near the former entrance pavilion to the cave.

'Lascaux 2', a reproduction of the Bull Chamber (Salle des Taureaux) and of a recess of the original cave, opened to the public in July 1983.

The Lascaux Cave is one of the greatest prehistoric finds in Europe, for the number and lifelike quality of the paintings. The cave was discovered on 12 September 1940 by four boys looking for their dog, which had disappeared down a hole.

A Treasure Worthy of Safekeeping. – The fact that the paintings were in such perfect condition raised great controversy as to their authenticity: this point has now been scientifically established beyond all possible doubt. The extraordinary freshness of the paintings can be explained by the presence, on the cave ceiling of very fine-grained chalk, of an impermeable layer which prevented water penetrating and forming stalactites, and on the walls of a fine layer of whitish calcite (carbonate of lime) which served as a ground for the frescoes and helped to "fix" them.

This impregnation of the walls continued after the drawings had been made and superimposed itself on them, protecting them and authenticating their date. For thousands of years the paintings were cut off from the outside air and were kept at a constant temperature. Deterioration set in when the cave was organised as a tourist attraction – the paintings were exposed to carbon dioxide breathed out by crowds of visitors and to the different temperature and humidity levels of the outside air.

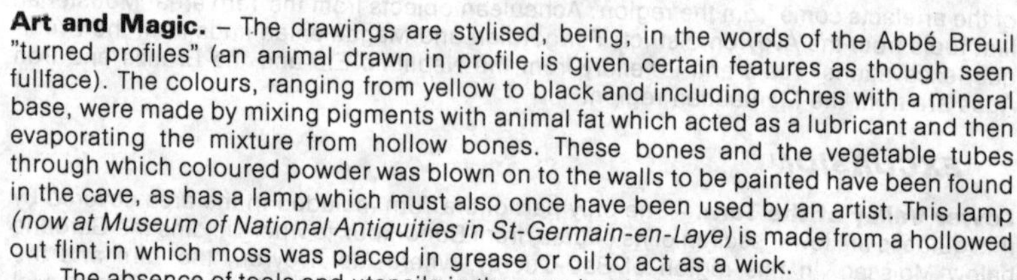

The Black Bull

An Exceptional Group of Paintings. – The four chambers of the cave contain many hundreds of paintings, some of which have been outlined with a pointed flint. A few belong to the Magdalenian Period, the majority to the Aurignacian *(pp 21-24)*.

The way the drawings are superimposed one upon another confirms the hypothesis that peoples of different civilisations decorated the walls with their own frescoes.

The unevenness of the walls was skilfully used by the artists to add relief to their drawings. The animals living in the Quaternary Era that were hunted by men can all be seen: oxen, cows, horses, deer, bison, ibex. Some of them are of impressive size.

Art and Magic. – The drawings are stylised, being, in the words of the Abbé Breuil "turned profiles" (an animal drawn in profile is given certain features as though seen fullface). The colours, ranging from yellow to black and including ochres with a mineral base, were made by mixing pigments with animal fat which acted as a lubricant and then evaporating the mixture from hollow bones. These bones and the vegetable tubes through which coloured powder was blown on to the walls to be painted have been found in the cave, as has a lamp which must also once have been used by an artist. This lamp *(now at Museum of National Antiquities in St-Germain-en-Laye)* is made from a hollowed out flint in which moss was placed in grease or oil to act as a wick.

The absence of tools and utensils in the cave has led anthropologists to believe that Lascaux was not used as a dwelling but probably as a kind of temple.

While the majority of the animals that appear on the walls are female and pregnant – symbolising fertility – some appear transfixed by arrows. These drawings are thought to be sympathetic magic: the illustration of animals struck by arrows or caught in a trap signifies, it is believed, that our ancestors hoped thus to make easier the capture or killing of their prey.

■ ADDITIONAL SIGHT

Eugene Le Roy Museum. – *Open 15 June to 15 September, 10 to 11.15am and 3 to 5.15pm; 7F.*

Eugene Le Roy (Perigord writer, 1836-1907) lived in Montignac and the museum housed in the buildings of the tourist centre *(Syndicat d'Initiative)* bears his name. The room of the author of *Jacquou le Croquant*, the story of a peasant revolt, has been reconstructed. Other rooms are devoted to ancient crafts no longer practised and to reconstructions of scenes from local history. There is also a small prehistoric collection.

EXCURSIONS

Régourdou. – *3 km - 2 miles - local map p 143. Guided tours in season, 9 to 11.30am and 2 to 6pm; out of season 10 to 11.30am and 2 to 4pm; 6F.* Leave Montignac by a road which branches off the D 704 just beyond a 14C church and climbs the Lavraux Hill. Admire the view from the site marked "Bellevue", then take a road through the wood to the prehistoric site of Régourdou which was discovered in 1954.

Examples of Mousterian industry, the finds – a jawbone in particular – are exhibited near the site. Also discovered on the site is an animal burial ground said to be the work of vegetarians and which perhaps indicates a cult of the bear.

Le Thot. – *7 km - 4 miles to the southwest – local map p 143. Leave Montignac by the D 706 and after 5 km - 3 miles take the narrow road which climbs away to the right.*

Open May to October, 9 to 11.45am and 2 to 5.45pm; July and August 9am to 5.45pm; 8F.

A modern building houses the centre of prehistoric art. The art of cave painting is described by means of giant slides showing the most typical paintings, films, a tableau situating this period in its overall historical context and plaster casts.

You can round off the visit with a walk in the park where you will see in real life a selection of animals, most commonly depicted in the cave paintings: deer, stags, tarpan horses, wild boar and bison. From the terrace there is a fine view over the Vézère valley and Lascaux hill.

St-Amand-de-Coly. – *Round tour of 32 km - 20 miles – about 1 1/4 hours – local map p 143.* Leave Montignac by the D 704 running east between arable fields and walnut groves.

After 4 km – 2 miles take a small road on the right which runs under a railway bridge.

La Grande Filolie. – The picturesque castle of La Grande Filolie nestling in a small valley comes into view. It is a Renaissance structure with a 15C battlemented keep and outbuildings, covered with a stone-slate roof.

Return to the D 704 and turn right. After 2 km - 1 mile make a left turn. The winding road climbs gently across a wooded countryside to reach St-Amand-de-Coly.

St-Amand-de-Coly. – *Description p 162.*

The road then follows the floor of a valley where pastures alternate with fields of maize. The D 62 follows the course of the river Coly, a small tributary of the Vézère, wooded hills line the left river bank while rock formations rise from the right. Shortly after Condat, when you have crossed the bridge over the Vézère, turn left into the D 704 which follows the right bank of the river and brings you back to Montignac.

The Ans Country. – *Round tour of 69 km - 43 miles – 2 hours – local map adjoining.*

The name, Pays d'Ans, recalls an overlordship which, in the 14C, extended as far as the Auvézère across eighteen parishes. The lord of Hautefort, overlord of the whole region, married one of his daughters to one of the lords of Ans from Flanders. She brought him as dowry lands many of whose villages still have as part of their name the word "d'Ans": Badefols, Ste-Eulalie, Granges, St-Pantaly...

The D 704, follows the right bank of the Vézère upstream as far as Lardin-St-Lazare. At Lardin take the D 62 overlooking pretty valleys planted with vines and poplars. To the right stands **Peyraux Castle** on the side of a wooded mountain. A small road to the right leads to it.

From there the road to Badefols-d'Ans follows the crestline with many **views** of the Corrèze mountains to the east and glimpses of Hautefort Château to the north.

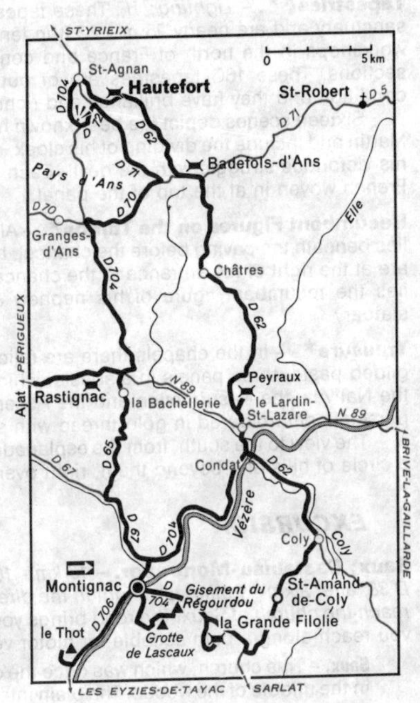

Badefols-d'Ans. – Pop 511. The 15C fortress restored after a fire belonged to the Born family.

The outline of Hautefort Château appears soon after you leave Badefols-d'Ans. The special features of the Périgord and Limousin countryside are seen cheek by jowl in this area – gentle fertile slopes where crops grow, fields cut by quickset hedges, walnut plantations, poplars and, close by, farmlands divided by trees, dense woods and red sandstone houses.

Hautefort Château★★. – *Description p 111.*

A short detour via St-Agnan by the D 704 and D 72, the road passes a point from which there is a fine **view** of Hautefort Château.

The D 71 and the D 70 cross a green and rolling landscape. Turn left into the D 704, then right into the N 89 which you follow for half a mile to visit Rastignac Château which is reached by a small road on the left.

Rastignac Château. – This elegant white building was built at the end of the 18C and comprises a rectangular structure surmounted by a terrace adorned with a pillared balustrade. A semicircular peristyle with Ionic columns forms part of the façade on the terrace side. The architectural design of the château is very similar to the White House in Washington. It was burnt down by the Germans in 1944 but has been restored.

Ajat. – Pop 297. *11 km - 6 miles from Rastignac by the N 89 and the D 68.* In this village, the Romanesque church which has an ovenvaulted apse roofed with stone slates, and the castle walls topped by battlements, make an interesting architectural group.

Return to Montignac by the D 65, the D 67 which runs along a small valley opening into the valley of the Vézère and finally by the D 704.

MONTPEZAT-DE-QUERCY★

Michelin map 79 fold 18 – Pop 1 412 – *Facilities p 38*

This small town in Bas-Quercy, which still has its covered arcades and old timbered or stone houses, owes its fame and its artistic treasures to the munificence of the Des Prés.

The Des Près Family. – Five members of this family, which came from Montpezat, became eminent prelates. Pierre Des Près, Cardinal of Préneste (now Palestrina), founded the collegiate Church of St-Martin consecrated in 1344; his nephew, Jean Des Près, who died in 1351, was Bishop of Coimbra in Portugal and then of Castres in France. Three other members of the family were consecrated bishops of Montauban: Jean Des Près (1517-1539), who gave his famous Flemish tapestries to the Collegiate Church at Montpezat, Jean de Lettes (1539-1556) and Jacques Des Près (1556-1589). This last was a warrior-bishop, an inveterate pursuer of the Huguenots.

■ COLLEGIATE CHURCH OF ST. MARTIN (Collégiale St-Martin)

time: 1/2 hour

This church, which is dedicated to St. Martin of Tours, was built in 1337 by an architect from the papal court at Avignon. Comparatively small in size, it has many of the characteristics of a Languedoc building: a single nave with no side aisles and the thrust of vaulting in the chapels supported by interior buttresses.

Nave. – The main part of the building has ogive vaulting, the bosses being painted with the founder's arms. There is simplicity and harmony in the proportions. In the first chapel on the south side stands a 15C Virgin of Pity in multicoloured sandstone. In the chapel opposite is a Virgin and Doves, a 14C statue in alabaster.

Tapestries★★. – *Lighting: 1F.* These tapestries, which were especially made to fit the sanctuary and are nearly 25 m - 82 ft in length and 2 m - 6 ft 6 in high, were woven in workshops in the north of France and consist of five panels, each divided into three sections. These 16C tapestries are of outstanding interest for they are in excellent condition and they have brilliance and richness of colouring.

Sixteen scenes depict the best-known historic and legendary events in the life of St. Martin and include the dividing of his cloak, many of the cures performed by the saint and his victorious struggle with the devil. Each scene is accompanied by a quatrain in Old French woven in at the top of the panel.

Recumbent Figures on the Tombs★. – Although the body of Cardinal Pierre Des Près lies beneath the paving before the chancel, his statue and tomb carved in Carrara marble are at the right of the entrance to the chancel where they were placed in 1778. Opposite lies the recumbent figure of his nephew Jean Des Près, a masterpiece of funerary statuary.

Treasure★. – In the chapels there are reliquaries and wooden caskets covered with a gilded paste, three panels in alabaster which originally came from England and depict the Nativity, the Resurrection and the Ascension, and several alms-purses. One of the purses is embroidered in gold thread with scenes for each month of the year.

The view to the south, from the esplanade near the collegiate church, stretches out to a circle of hills and beyond them, right over Bas-Quercy.

EXCURSION

Saux; Castelnau-Montratier. – *16 km - 10 miles. Leave Montpezat to the west by the D 38, after 2 km - 1 mile, turn right in the direction of Montpezat Station and finally left to reach the church of Saux.* The road brings you within 400 m - 440 yds of the church, which you reach along a path suitable for motor vehicles beside the wood.

Saux. – This church, which was once the centre of a large parish, now stands isolated in the middle of the woods. The plain interior consists of three domed bays decorated with fine 14 and 15C frescoes. The best preserved are in the chancel and show Christ in Majesty with the symbols of the four Evangelists, the Crucifixion and scenes from the Childhood of Jesus. In the south chapel may be seen the legend of St. Catherine; and in that on the north side, the legend of St. George.

Return to the D 38 and turn right onto the D 4 which leads to Castelnau-Montratier.

Castelnau-Montratier. – Pop 1 914. This hilltop town was founded in the 13C by Ratier, Lord of Castelnau, who gave it his name. It replaced a small village, built at the foot of the hill which was destroyed by Simon de Montfort in 1214 at the time of the Albigensian Crusade *(p 25)*. From a nearby hill on which stand three windmills, may be seen the layout of Castelnau, where old houses still line several of the narrow streets.

This region produces an excellent dessert grape known as the *Moissac (p 133)* and delicious peaches.

MOUTIER-D'AHUN★

Michelin map 72 fold 10 – Pop 234

The village of Moutier-d'Ahun lies between Guéret and Aubusson, near the upper valley of the Creuse which is spanned by an old bridge bristling with cutwaters. The village clusters round the church which contains remarkable 17C woodwork.

An Abbey's Fortunes and Misfortunes. – Shortly before the year 1000 Boson, Count of Marche, gave a church consecrated to Our Lady, which he owned on the banks of the Creuse, to Uzerche Abbey as a first step towards founding a Benedictine monastery. The monastery became independent of its mother house and took the name Moutier d'Ahun; in the 12C the monks replaced Boson's church by a larger building.

But the Hundred Years War put an end to this long period of prosperity; the abbey church was first destroyed by the English; it had scarcely been resurrected from the ruins, when, during the Wars of Religion, the nave was pillaged and set on fire.

It was in 1610 that the woodwork to ornament the chancel was made. When the monks fled at the time of the Revolution, the woodwork was whitewashed; patient restoration by the Abbé Malapert, priest of Moutier-d'Ahun, has restored its glory.

Church. – *Guided tours 9am to noon and 2 to 7pm; time: 1/2 hour; 3F.*

The church is now partly Romanesque – transept crossing, belfry and chancel – and partly Gothic – the 15C west door. The belfry is rectangular, pierced by three double bays on each side; traces of the 14C fortifications can still be seen in the chevet. The west doorway, built in granite, is adorned with six covings embellished with little figures – prophets and angels jostle jugglers, musicians and dancers.

The Woodwork★★. – The woodwork and the stalls entirely occupy the walls of the apse and chancel. All the carving was commissioned by the monks of Moutier-d'Ahun and was done between 1673 and 1681 by the master-craftsman of Auvergne, Simon Baüer.

On either side of the high altar, whose base was covered with 17C Cordova leather, are the two parts of a huge retable. These consist of ornately carved twisted columns bearing a broken pediment. The part of the chancel next to the retable is panelled with decorated woodwork which forms a monumental door which in turn gives access to a 15C chapel. The 26 stalls are magnificently sculptured portraying animals, flowers and fantastic scenes. The screen enclosing the chancel is surmounted by a double figure of Christ carved from the trunk of an oak tree. The lectern is made up of two lions back to back with the pulpit resting on their paws.

Items from the old monastery may be seen in the sacristy. They include 12C statues in multicoloured granite of St. Benedict and St. Antony the hermit, 15 and 17C reliquaries and, above all, a wonderful Christ skilfully carved in boxwood (17C).

NEUVY-ST-SÉPULCHRE

Michelin map 68 folds 18 and 19 – *Local map p 85* – Pop 1 842

The village of Neuvy-St-Sépulchre which lies near the *Vallée Noire (p 84)* gets the last part of its name from the basilica modelled on that of the Holy Sepulchre in Jerusalem.

Basilica. – *Time: 1/4 hour.* The building comprises two parts: a rectangular structure joined more or less happily to a circular one.

The building on the right was completed in 1049 and is dedicated to St. James Major.

A group of pilgrims led by Eude de Déols, undertook to built a church modelled on that of the Holy Sepulchre in Jerusalem to replace the original rectangular church. For this purpose, the belfry-porch was demolished and the rest of the building was left standing while the new church was being erected. In the meantime other pilgrims brought back the news that a rectangular structure had been added on to the rotunda in Jerusalem. It was thus decided to retain the existing building and join the two structures together.

The vast **rotunda★** is 22 m – 72 ft across; seven apsidal chapels are hollowed out of the thickness of the walls. The eleven round columns surrounding the sanctuary are crowned by interesting capitals: floral motifs, human and animal figures. The upper part of the rotunda was restored last century by Viollet-le-Duc, the architect and restorer of mediaeval buildings.

EXCURSION

Cluis. – Pop 1 375. *8 km - 5 miles to the southwest by the D 38.* A set of Aubusson tapestries may be seen in the 16C town hall. There are extensive ruins of a mediaeval fortress (12C) at Cluis-Dessous.

NOHANT

Michelin map 68 fold 19 – 6 km - 4 miles north of La Châtre – *Local map p 85* – Pop 480

Near the Indre valley, this quaint Berry village with its little square where century old elms group themselves closely round the church and its rustic porch, is the site of George Sand's château.

Life of George Sand. – The young Aurore Dupin de Francueil spent most of her childhood and adolescence in Nohant. She returned throughout her turbulent life to find peace and a sense of proportion.

After she had separated from her first husband, Baron Dudevant, she decided to live in Paris and joined Jules Sandeau; her life was free, her ways amazed – she cut her hair short and wore a frock-coat and a top-hat – and, wanting to be like her lover, who was a writer, in 1832 she published a novel entitled *Indiana* under the name of George Sand. She was then twenty-eight.

So great was the book's success that from then on George Sand never stopped writing. She wrote several novels which were socialistically inclined and which she set in the villages and castles of the *Vallée Noire* and peopled with Berry peasants – *Le Meunier d'Angibault, la Mare au Diable, le Péché de Monsieur Antoine, La Petite Fadette, François le Champi* and *Les Maîtres Sonneurs.* George Sand had an inexhaustible imagination, considerable aptitude, a style capable of conveying many shades of meaning and, at the same time, great fluency. Her love of nature may be seen in her memoirs (*Histoire de ma Vie*, 1854), stories and novels (*Les Beaux Messieurs de Bois-Doré*, 1858). She died at Nohant in 1876, an almost legendary figure having justified by gifts, the name given her by fellow-villagers of "the good woman of Nohant".

■ THE CHÂTEAU *time: 3/4 hour*

Leave the car at the car park beside the road.

Guided tours 1 April to 15 October, 9 to 11.15am and 2 to 5.30pm; the rest of the year, 10 to 11.15am and 2 to 3.30pm; closed Tuesdays, 1 January, 1 May, 1 and 11 November and 25 December; 10F; Sundays and holidays: 5F.

The fine 18C mansion, known locally as The Château stands deep in greenery. It has been turned into a museum and houses countless souvenirs of George Sand and her guests, Chopin and Liszt, Balzac and Flaubert, Delacroix...: pictures, drawings and a theatre for marionettes made by her son, Maurice Sand, portraits of the chief members of her family, the boudoir where she first began to write and wrote *Indiana*, as well as her bedroom and study.

NOIRLAC, Former Abbey ★ (Ancienne Abbaye de NOIRLAC)

Michelin map 69 south of fold 1 – *Local map p 162*

This abbey was founded around 1136 by Robert of Clairvaux, St. Bernard's cousin, on the right bank of the Cher, on the site known as Maison-Dieu on the edge of the wood, the Grand Bois de Meillant.

Guided tours 10.15, 11, 11.45am, 2.15, 3, 3.45 and 4.30pm (also 5.15 and 5.45pm, 1 April to 30 September); closed Tuesdays in October; 1/2 hour; 8F.

The monastery buildings built in the local pale stone and now fully restored, are on the regular Cistercian plan and are the most complete and best preserved examples of this kind in France. The splendid paving is an exact copy of the original. The monochrome stained glass by Jean Pierre Reynaud accords with the Cistercian style. Gregorian masses, concerts and other cultural events are held in this remarkable setting.

Church. – Work started in 1150 and lasted for a hundred years. The simplicity of line and the lovely pale stone add to the beauty of the architecture and to the sense of peace.

The nave with its ribbed vaulting is linked to the side aisles which have ogive vaulting by great pointed arches and rests on square pillars; the rectangular transverse ribs are supported by engaged columns with a simple tapered pedestal just above floor level.

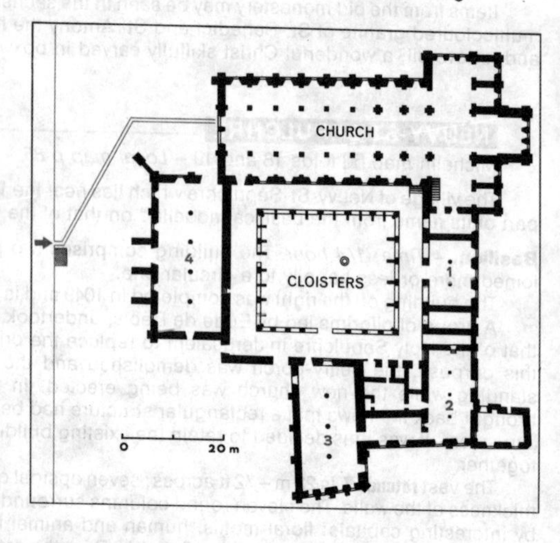

The chancel which is the oldest part, is roofed with broken barrel vaulting and ends in a flat chevet lit by a row of triplet windows topped by a six-lobed oculus.

Cloisters and Adjacent Buildings. – The cloisters now standing date from the 13 and 14C and replaced an earlier series built at the same time as the church. The east and south galleries have the most ornate carvings and all have fine ogive vaulting and rich ornamentation which contrasts with the simplicity of the church: corbels decorate the springing of the arches and capitals with different plant motifs crown the small pillars.

The chapterhouse (**1**) has a rounded doorway flanked by twin windows; the six square bays are divided by polygonal columns. There is a great chimneypiece in a corner of the heated common room (**2**) which is roofed with flattened pointed vaulting. The refectory (**3**), a tall room crowned with eight ogive domes and palm leaf mouldings adorning the capitals of the three columns, is lit by four large windows surmounted by two multilobed rose windows. In the vast cellar (**4**) there is an 18C wine press.

On the first floor is the **monks' dormitory** which was completely remodelled in the 18C as the quarters of the commendatory abbot and guest rooms with period furniture and hangings which are of interest.

NONTRON

Michelin map 72 fold 15 – Pop 3 954 – *Facilities p 38*

The town occupies the top of a promontory, crowned by ramparts and a castle which was restored in the 18C. From the war memorial at the end of the shaded terrace, there is an attractive view of the Bandiat valley spanned by a viaduct.

EXCURSIONS

Saut du Chalard★. – *Round tour of 36 km - 22 miles – about 1 3/4 hours – local map opposite.* Leave Nontron by the D 707 which crosses a rolling countryside to reach St-Pardoux. Then take the D 83 from which a road leads off to the right passing close to the church of Champs-Romain before coming out at a cemetery where you take a footpath signposted Saut du Chalard *(3/4 hour Rtn on foot)*. A precipitous path leads to a platform overlooking the Dronne which rushes, foaming over great rocks between steep and wooded slopes. *Return to Nontron by the D 83, D 79, D 85, D 79 and D 87.*

Étang de St-Estèphe; Roc Branlant. – *Round tour of 22 km - 14 miles – about 1 1/4 hours – local map above. Go out of Nontron to the north by the D 675 and continue for 4.5 km - 3 miles; then turn left before bearing right to Roc Poperdu.*

Roc Poperdu. – Great blocks of granite lie in a hollow of the valley.

Return to the D 675, which you follow to the left and as you approach the entrance to Augignac bear left again.

St-Estèphe Lake. – This lake, with shaded banks and a stretch of water 30 ha - 75 acres in extent, is a favourite outing for the people of Nontron.

Beyond the lake, a marked track which is suitable for cars, goes off to the left, opposite a bridge, to a pile of rocks.

Roc Branlant. – Follow the left bank of the stream which runs between the rocks. Beyond a large square block balanced on a rock table, the stream rushes down a series of falls in a woodland setting. Go along the left bank until you come to a large group of rocks known as the "devil's chaplet" and beneath which the waters thunder in a torrent.

The D 88, D 3 and D 675 lead back to Nontron.

La Chapelle-St-Robert. – *16 km - 10 miles to the northwest by the D 75 and the D 92 to the left.* The church is built of grey stone in a pure Romanesque style. The doorway is decorated with primitive capitals and the belfry over the transept crossing has three tiers of blind arcades.

ORADOUR-SUR-GLANE

Michelin map 72 south of folds 6 and 7 – *Local map p 122* – Pop 1 941

Ruined fire-scarred walls and a cemetery where the remains of 650 victims have been laid to rest will remind anyone visiting this spot of one of the cruellest events of the last war.

10 June 1944. – The people of Oradour, a large Limousin village, were going about their daily work; there was no warning of the drama to follow. At 2pm, as a cordon of German soldiers closed all the exits, a column of lorries and armoured cars entered the village. The operation was carried out by some 200 men of the special SS division "das Reich".

In Oradour anxiety replaced curiosity. On Nazi orders everyone gathered on the fairground: men, women and 247 schoolchildren brought there by their teachers. The women and children were locked in the church, the men in the barns and garages. Grenade explosions and machine-gun bursts killed a great many; fire and dynamite completed the massacre. A woman who managed to get out of the church through a window in the chevet, a young boy and a few men were the only ones to escape death.

Tour of the Ruins. – Go through the outer walls and along the streets of the ruined village. For a guide apply to the church where 500 women and children died. A visit to the *Maison du Souvenir* which contains objects which did not perish in the flames, and to the cemetery where lie the remains of the victims, is an unforgettable experience.

The New Oradour. – Nearby a new Oradour has been built. The modern church with its luminous stained glass windows and square belfry may surprise at first, but it has been designed to blend harmoniously with the neighbouring buildings and surrounding countryside.

PADIRAC Chasm *** (Gouffre de PADIRAC)

Michelin map 75 fold 19 – *Local maps pp 94, 108 and 166*

The Padirac Chasm provides access to wonderful galleries hollowed out of the limestone mass of the Gramat Causse *(p 108)* by a subterranean river. A descent of the vertiginous well and a tour of the mysterious river and the vast caves adorned with limestone concretions give the tourist a striking impression of this fascinating underground world.

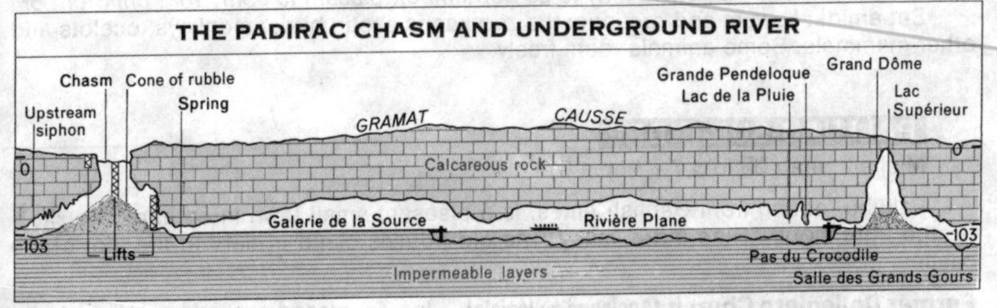

(From documents of the Société du Gouffre de Padirac)

From Legend to Scientific Exploration. – The Padirac Chasm was a fearful site to the local inhabitants right up to the 19C. The origin of this great hole was believed to be due to the devil. St. Martin, so the tale went, was returning from an expedition on the plateau where he had been looking unsuccessfully for souls to save. Suddenly his mule refused to advance: Satan, bearing a great sack full of souls which he was taking to hell, stood before the saint. Satan mocked the poor saint and made him a proposition: he would give him the souls he had in his sack on condition that St. Martin would make his mule cross an obstacle that he, the devil, would create on the spot. He hit the ground hard with his foot and the chasm yawned. The saint coaxed his mule forward and the beast jumped clear so that the devil, beaten, retreated to hell by way of the hole he had created.

The chasm served as a refuge for the people living on the plateau during the Hundred Years War and the Wars of Religion, but it would appear that it was towards the end of the 19C, following a violent flooding of the river, that a practicable line of communication opened between the bottom of the well and the underground galleries. The speleologist,

E.A. Martel, was the first to discover the passage in 1889. Between 1889 and 1900 he undertook nine expeditions and in 1890 reached the Chamber of the Grand Dôme. Padirac was opened for the first time to tourists in 1898.

Since 1900 there have been six exploratory expeditions under the leadership of G. de Lavaur. The 1947 expedition proved by fluorescein colouring of the water that the Padirac river reappears above ground 11 km - 7 miles away where the Lombard rises and at the St. George spring in the **Montvalent Amphitheatre** of rocks near the Dordogne. Further exploration of the course of the river and its tributaries has been carried out by later expeditions.

TOUR *time: 1 1/2 hours*

Open from the spring holidays to 30 June and 1 September to the 2nd Sunday in October, 9am to noon and 2 to 6pm; July, 8am to noon and 2 to 6.30pm; August, 8am to 7pm; 16.50F including lifts and boat trip.

Lifts and staircases take you into the chasm which is 99 m - 325 ft across and to the pyramid of rubble, debris of the original falling-in of the pot hole's roof, which lies in the centre of the chamber. From the bottom of the lift (75 m - 246 ft) there is a striking view of walls covered by the overflow from stalagmites, vegetation and a little corner of the sky at the mouth of the hole. Stairs lead down to the waters of the underground river, 103 m - 328 ft below ground level. Once at the bottom you start the 2 000 m - 1 1/4 mile underground journey of which 700 m - 1/2 mile is by boat.

Galerie de la Source (Gallery of the Spring). – This chamber is at the end of an underground canyon whose roof rises gradually; it is 300 m - 330 yds long and follows the upper course of the river that hollowed it out. At the far end is the landing-stage.

Rivière Plane. – A flotilla of flat-bottomed boats take you on an enchanted journey over the smooth and astonishingly translucent waters of the river. The depth of the river varies from 50 cm to 4 m (20 in to 13 ft), but the water temperature remains constant at 10.5 °C (51 °F) and that of the cave at 13 °C (55,4 °F). The height of the roof rises progressively to reach a maximum of 78 m - 250 ft; from the boat the different levels of erosion corresponding to the successive courses of the river may be seen. At the end of the boat trip, facing the **Lac de la Pluie** (Rainfall Lake), hangs the **Grande Pendeloque** (Great Pendant). This giant stalactite, whose point nearly touches the water, is the ultimate pendant in a chaplet of concretions 78 m - 250 ft in height.

Pas du Crocodile (The Crocodile Path). – A narrow passage between high walls links the underground lake and the chambers next to be visited. Look on the left at the **Grand Pilier** (the Tall Column), 40 m - 130 ft high.

Salle des Grands Gours (The Hall of the Big Humps). – A series of pools separated by humps – *gours* or natural limestone dams – divides up the river and the lake into superb basins beyond which can be seen a 6 m - 20 ft waterfall. This is the end of the area open to tourists.

Lac Supérieur (The Upper Lake). – This lake is fed only by water infiltrating the soil and falling from the roofs; the level is 20 m - 66 ft above that of the Rivière Plane. *Gours* or limestone humps ring the emerald waters of the lake.

Salle du Grand Dôme (Hall of the Great Dome). – The great height of the roof 91 m - 295 ft up, in this, the largest and most beautiful of the Padirac caverns, is most impressive. The belvedere, built half-way up enables the rock formations and the flows of calcite decorating certain parts of the walls to be seen. As you return to the landing-stage, you get interesting views of the Grand Pilier and the Grande Pendeloque. From the end of the Galerie de la Source, four lifts bring you back to the entrance.

■ ADDITIONAL SIGHT

Tropicorama Zoo. – *Open 15 May to 25 September, 8.30am to 8pm; 16F; children: 8F.*

Set amidst flowers and greenery the zoo keeps exotic birds, monkeys, ocelots and other mammals. Some animals roam freely.

PALLUAU-SUR-INDRE

Michelin map 68 fold 7 – Pop 1 017

Palluau, dating from Gaulish times, is a pleasant small town in an attractive **site★** on the right slope of the Indre valley. The old houses climb in tiers to the foot of the castle.

Former Collegiate Church (Ancienne collégiale). – Inside, placed around the chancel with its 15C stalls, are polychrome statues dating from the 15 and 16C. Among the most interesting are, on the right, St. James as a pilgrim, to the left St. Rock accompanied by his dog and his angel. The seignorial chapel in the north aisle built in 1514, contains remains of 16C tiling.

From the esplanade, behind the church there is a fine view over the valley. A staircase leads to the castle.

Castle. – *Guided tours 3 and 6pm, June to September; time: 1 hour; 5F.*

Perched on a rocky spur 120 m - 400 ft above the Indre valley the castle which is still inhabited has a fine park. The following parts of the castle are open to the public: the two perimeter walls; the 11C keep with its fine wooden ceiling is supposed to have been built by Foulques Rechin, Count of Anjou; the Flamboyant style chapel, decorated with frescoes, which were painted by an Italian artist during the Renaissance; the main building, in a pure Gothic style, contains rich Renaissance furnishings and is adorned by a series of tapestries presented to the Count of Palluau by Louis XIII; and finally the Philippe Auguste Tower, from which there is a wide view of the valley and the surrounding area.

EXCURSION

Indre Valley. – *Round tour of 23 km - 14 miles to the west.* Leave Palluau by the D 28 which affords plunging views over the river as it descends towards it. At Villebernin the road clings to the slope as it descends to the valley floor to a green countryside criss-crossed by hedges or lines of poplars, ash and willow trees.

Turn left at Tranger, taking the D 18 to cross the Indre and a canal which flows past the base of the château de l'Ile-Savary.

Château de l'Ile-Savary. – This fine 15C building located on an island *(no access to the public)* in the Indre river and built by Guillaume de Varie, a financier in the service of Jacques Cœur, has since been restored.

At Clion turn left onto the N 143 and after 9 km - 6 miles branch left again taking the D 63 B which leads to St-Genou.

St-Genou. – *Description p 168.*

Leave St-Genou by the D 63A lined with plane trees. After crossing the Indre there are fine glimpses of Palluau and its castle.

PECH-MERLE Cave ★★ (Grotte du PECH-MERLE)

Michelin map 79 fold 9 – *Local map p 125*

This cave was known to prehistoric man who performed his religious rites in it, but was then lost to history and was only rediscovered 200 centuries later in 1922. The natural decoration of the cave is interesting in itself; there are also wall paintings and carvings which are of great documentary value to prehistorians.

The Underground "Explorers". – Two boys of fourteen were the heroes of the rediscovery of the Pech-Merle Cave. Inspired by the expeditions and discoveries made everywhere in the region by the Abbé **Lemozi,** the Cabrerets priest who was a prehistorian and speleologist, the boys explored a small fault known only as having served as a refuge during the Revolution. The two friends pushed ahead, creeping along a narrow, slimy trench cut by wells and blocked by limestone concretions. After several hours their efforts were rewarded by the sight of wonderful paintings.

The Abbé Lemozi, who soon afterwards explored the cave scientifically, recognised the importance of the subterranean temple, and it was decided to open it to tourists. In 1949 the discovery of a new chamber led to the finding of the original opening through which men had entered the cave 20 000 years ago.

TOUR *time: about 1 3/4 hour*

Open from Palm Sunday to 1 November, 9.30am to noon and 1.30 to 6pm; 20F; museum: 11F.

In addition to the interest that there is for lovers of speleology in seeing caverns of vast size communicating with each other through wide openings and decorated with beautiful concretions, the Pech-Merle Cave offers prehistorians the sight of highly advanced paintings and engravings and material traces of prehistoric man's sojourn there.

Visitors may, at present, walk through 1 600 m - 1 mile of chambers and galleries.

The hall of the "broken column" is decorated with drawings of bison and mammoths outlined in black and forming a frieze 7 m - 23 ft long by 3 m - 10 ft deep. The drawings appear to date from the Aurignacian Age *(pp 21 to 24).*

The next cave, supported in the centre by three fine stalagmite columns, is known as the Galerie des Peintures (Picture Gallery): one wall is decorated with the silhouettes of two horses, covered and surrounded by dots, mysterious signs and outlined hand prints, known as "negative hands" *(illustration p 24).* These prints were made by stencilling in different colours round hands placed flat against the rock. On the roof of the Salle des Hiéroglyphes (Hieroglyphic Chamber) can be seen several strangely drawn feminine figures outlined on the clay with a finger.

The Salle des Disques (Hall of Discs) is ornamented with many strange concretions that look like discs; the origin of their formation remains unsolved. Farther on are huge, impressive columns, eccentrics with fine protuberances that defy the laws of gravity and cave pearls whose colours attract attention, ranging as they do from the shining white of pure calcite to red-ochre caused by the presence in the limestone of clay and iron oxide. The footprints made by a prehistoric man may be seen, petrified for ever, in the wet clay of a natural dam or *gour.*

In the last cave to be visited are the bones of cave-bears and the roots of an oak tree that bored down into the cave in search of moisture.

Amedée-Lemozi Museum. – *Same opening times as for the cave.*

This is a research and information centre on the prehistory of the Quercy. On the lower floor which is open to the public, there is an attractive and informative display of bones, tools, arms, utensils and works of art from 160 different prehistoric sites and ranging from the Lower Paleolithic to the Iron Age. In an adjoining room are exhibited colour photographs of the decorated caves in the region (in particular Pech-Merle and Cougnac). There is also a film show on paleolithic art in the Quercy.

The times indicated in this guide

when given with the distance allow one to enjoy the scenery
when given for sightseeing are intended to give an idea of
the possible length or brevity of a visit.

PELLEVOISIN

Michelin map 68 fold 7 – Pop 1 027

This is the site of an important pilgrimage to Our Lady of Pity *(first Sunday in September)* which goes back to the several apparitions of the Virgin to Estelle Faguette.

The town is situated in the heart of a rolling countryside. The church has a Romanesque chancel. Georges Bernanos (1888-1948) the French writer *(The Diary of a Country Priest)*, is buried here.

EXCURSIONS

Le Mée Castle. – *4 km - 2 1/2 miles by the D 11 in the direction of Ecueillé, soon afterwards bear left into the D 15 going towards Villegouin.* This feudal castle with its machicolated towers stands in an attractive site. It is protected by an outer wall with occasional small turrets.

Argy Château. – *5 km - 3 miles by the D 11 in the direction of Buzançais. Guided tours 9am to noon and 2 to 6pm; time: 1/2 hour; 5F.*

The château and the buildings near the 17C farm are under restoration.

This imposing château was fortified in the 12C and further altered in the 16C by Charles de Brillac, a companion in arms of Louis XII. The park and surrounding area have also been recreated.

The square 15C keep with trefoiled machicolations, is flanked by turrets and is a good example of military architecture. A curtain wall links the keep to the remarkable Brillac tower; on the upper floors are several beautifully decorated chimneys. During the Revolution the moat was done away with, the buildings to the southeast were rebuilt and windows were opened in the two towers.

The interior of the courtyard contrasts sharply with the sober exterior. The Louis XII style gallery (restored) is ornamented with accolades adorned with fleurons and pinnacles which prolong the small columns. Although the detail of the sculptured decoration is entirely French the superimposition of the galleries shows an Italian influence.

PENNE

Michelin map 79 fold 19 – *Local map p 163* – Pop 507

The old village, overlooked by its castle ruins, is perched in a remarkable **setting★** clinging to a rock spike which rises sheer above the left bank of the Aveyron in the prettiest part of its course *(p 164)*. There is a good view from the D 33 to the north of the village and from the D 133 to the south.

The complicated outline of the powerful mediaeval fortress with its jagged walls, in some cases poised on the very edge of the rock and seeming to defy all the laws of gravity, rises above the village houses with their almost flat roofs.

Leave the car on the D 9 at the entrance to the village or in the car park above the town hall and follow the street that leads to the ruins.

The street is narrow and is lined with old houses some of which have timber walls. Here and there is a carved doorway or a coat of arms. You go round the church which has a Classical doorway and a belfry in the tower, to a path which leads to the foot of the ruined towers.

Castle. – *Not open to the public.* The castle's singular position made it a key factor in the history of Quercy. At the time of the Albigensian Crusade *(p 24)* it became the stake in the bloody wars fought by the lord of Penne, supporting the revolt, and the followers of Simon de Montfort. Later, in the Hundred Years War, the English and the local troops seized it from each other time after time. It only fell into ruin last century.

From the tip of the promontory there is a good view of the towers and dilapidated walls of the castle, of Penne and the Aveyron valley.

PENNE D'AGENAIS

Michelin map 79 south of fold 6 – *Local map p 124* – Pop 2 167

This ancient stronghold, sometime fief of the Kings of England, was in ruins until the 1950s. Now extensively restored, it is a great attraction.

Place Gambetta. – Start from this shady terrace to tour the town. The Porte de Ville (Town Gateway) opens below two fine 16C houses. Go through the gate, take the Rue du 4 Juillet, then Rue Notre-Dame to the left.

Notre Dame de Peyragude. – This modern basilica built in the Romanesque-Byzantine style, stands on top of a hill from which there is an extensive view of the valley. From May to June, crowds throng to this church on pilgrimages to the Virgin.

View★. – From the viewing-table there is a bird's-eye view of the Lot Valley from Villeneuve to Fumel and to the Haut Quercy in the distance.

Upper town. – Take the Rue de Peyragude which affords fine vistas to the right as far as Porte de Ferracap. On the right the Rue de Ferracap and the adjacent alleys are lined with lovely, flower-decked houses which have been renovated. Some are corbelled and half-timbered. In Place Paul-Froment, the tourist centre *(syndicat d'initiative)* occupies a remarkable house in brick preceded by a porch with pointed arches. Pass between the town hall and the church to reach the "Ricard" gateway and fountain which are mementoes of Richard Lionheart who built the fortifications.

PÉRIGUEUX ★

Michelin map 75 fold 5 – Pop 35 392

See plan of built-up area in the current Michelin Red Guide France.

The white domes of the Cathedral of St-Front make the first view of Périgueux unique. The capital of Périgord is a very old city, built in the fertile valley of the river Isle and still retaining remarkable monuments to its long and tumultuous past. There is a good overall view of the town from the bridge beyond Cours Fénelon to the southeast.

Many tourists come to Périgueux, drawn by the ease of access it affords to beautiful settings, interesting buildings and outstanding prehistoric discoveries. The town's gastronomic specialities – among which truffles and *foie gras* (liver *pâté*) are outstanding – have given it an international reputation. Products are exported especially to England and the United States.

The Splendid Vésone. – The town of Périgueux derives from the sacred spring known as the Vésone. It was near the stream, on the left bank of the Isle, that the Gaulish Petrocorii (Petrocorci, which meant the «four signs» in Celtic gave its name both to Périgueux and Périgord) built their chief defensive town. After siding with Vercingetorix against Caesar, the Petrocorii had finally to accept Roman domination but benefited greatly from the *pax romana* which enabled the city to become one of the finest of all Aquitaine. Vesunna, as the town was then called, spread beyond the bend in the river Isle; temples, a forum, basilicas, an arena were built and an aqueduct over 7 km – 4 miles long was constructed to carry water to the baths. But in the 3C AD the city's prosperity was destroyed by the Alemans who sacked this and seventy other towns and villages throughout Gaul.

The Unfortunate City. – To avoid further disaster the Vesunnians enclosed themselves within a narrow boundary; stones from the temples were used to build powerful ramparts, the arena was transformed into a keep. In spite of all precautions the town suffered the depredations alternately of pillage and fire by such barbaric invaders as the Visigoths, the Franks and the Normans. Such misfortune reduced Vesunna to the status of a humble village and finally even its name died; it was known as "the town of the Petrocorii" or more simply still as "the town". St. Front later established the town as an episcopal seat and in the 10C it became the unassuming capital of the County of Périgord.

The Ambition of Puy St-Front. – A little sanctuary containing the tomb of St. Front, apostle of Périgord, was built not far from the city. Beginning as a point of pilgrimage, the sanctuary later became a monastic centre: a busy market town, Puy St-Front, grew up round the monastery soon eclipsing the other town in size.

The townspeople of Puy St-Front joined the feudal alliances against the English kings, established an emancipated consular regime and then sided with Philip Augustus against King John of England.

Little by little, the all-invading St-Front annexed the city's prerogatives; fights between the rivals increased. The city, unable to win against a neighbour under the protection of the king of France, had to accept union. In 1251 the two towns were united into a single consular community under the name of Périgueux.

Loyal Périgueux. – "My strength lies in the trust of my fellow-citizens" such is the proud device of Périgueux. The town, separated from France under the Treaty of Brétigny in 1360, was the first to answer the call of Charles V to take up arms against the English. It was in Périgueux that Du Guesclin planned the famous campaigns which enabled him to chase the English from the land.

Soon afterwards, Count Archambaud V, bribed by the English, openly betrayed the king and ill-treated the consuls. Protracted warfare began between the loyal townsfolk and their wicked overlord; when the royal troops arrived, Archambaud V fled and parliament claimed Périgord on behalf of the crown.

During the period of the Fronde (1649-1653) the loyalty of Périgueux was questioned unexpectedly by Condé. The Fronde supporters laid siege to the town; the Churches of St-Front and St-Étienne were badly damaged. Their patience exhausted the leaders forced the people to revolt; the garrison was rendered useless and soon afterwards the king's men entered the town in triumph.

■ OLD TOWN (BYZ) *time: 2 hours*

The cathedral, the Périgord Museum and picturesque 15-16C houses are crowded in an area barely 300 m – 330 yds wide.

Cathedral of St-Front★ (**BZ**). – This church, dedicated to St. Front, first Bishop of Périgueux, is one of the biggest in southwest France and one of the most curious.

A chapel first stood on the site of the saint's tomb in the 6C; later a larger church was built on the same site and consecrated in 1047. This second building was almost completely destroyed by fire in the year 1120 whereupon it was decided to construct an even bigger church by extending the damaged building.

This third basilica, completed about 1173, Byzantine in style, domed and with a ground plan in the form of a Greek cross which is uncommon in France, recalls St. Mark's in Venice and the Church of the Apostles in Constantinople. This was the first domed church to be built on the Roman road which was still used in the Middle Ages by many travellers going from Rodez to Cahors and on to Saintes.

In 1575, during the Wars of Religion, St-Front was pillaged by the Protestants, the treasure was scattered and the saint's tomb destroyed. Successive restorations, conducted without regard for the original plan, took away its early character. A thorough reconstruction was undertaken between 1852 and 1901 under the supervision of the architects Abadie and Boeswillwald. This systematic renovation was not appreciated by everyone: Abadie was criticised for increasing the number of architectural elements with the addition of seventeen turrets and thus virtually producing a new building.

St-Front has considerable appeal with its five domes, colonnaded turrets and four-storey **belfry** rising nearly 60 m - 200 ft in the air, crowned by a lantern tower surmounted by a conical spire.

From the Place de la Clautre, west of the cathedral, you can see the 11C church façade which had been built to complete a 6C sanctuary of which there are still some traces.

Domed Church. – *Enter by the north door.* The attraction of St-Front lies in its size and the bold imagination with which the domes have been built on pendentives. The east bay, which serves as a choir, ends in an oven-vaulted apse; behind the high altar is a splendid Baroque **retable** in walnut.

Old Church. – Steps emphasise the two axes and the different levels of the two churches; as you pass beneath the dome of the great belfry you enter what was the 11C "old church" and see traces of this earlier building.

The Cloisters. – *During the season apply to the western inner court or to the sacristan when services are not in progress.*

The cloisters date from the 12, 13 and 16C and are half-Romanesque, half-Gothic in architectural style. The galleries contain Merovingian tombs; the upper part of the original belfry now stands in the centre of the cloisters.

(After a photo by Arthaud, Grenoble)

Périgueux – The Cathedral of St-Front.

Tour of the roof. – *During the season apply in the inner court which is near the stairs or apply to the sacristan.*

After crossing the cloisters go up to the roof and walk round the cathedral going between the domes and turrets. From the apsidal roof look out over the old quarter.

Leave from Place Daumesnil, follow the Rue de la Clarté then turn right into Rue Limogeanne.

Rue Limogeanne (**BY 38**). – Renaissance houses are to be found at Nos 1, 3 and 5: note a corbelled three-sided turret, a façade adorned with moulded bands out of which open mullioned casements and in the inner courtyard of No 3, a fine door surmounted by scrolls, the salamander of François I in the pediment and an emblazoned coat of arms.

Turn right into the Rue de la Miséricorde.

At No 2, the former **Hôtel de St-Astier** (**B**) or Maison Ribette has a magnificent Renaissance staircase: the coffered ceilings of the entrance hall and the first floor are ornamented with roses. The ribs of the vaulting above the stairwell end in brackets.

Return to Rue Limogeanne.

An elegant door in the courtyard of No 12 opens beneath a double coving rising to an accolade and adorned with fleurons, pinnacles and floral carvings.

Take to the left, Rue Eguillerie.

At No 17 **Maison Tenant** (**D**) is a fine 15-16C mansion made up of two adjoining houses; much of the decoration of the façade shows the influence of the Italian Renaissance.

At the corner of Place St-Louis stands a modern fountain adorned with a fine bronze, The Spring by Ramon.

Turn back and walk along the Rue Limogeanne which is lined with old houses. Make for the Cours Tourny where you bear right.

Périgord Museum★ (**Musée du Périgord**) (**BY M**). – *Open 10am to noon and 2 to 5pm; closed Tuesdays and holidays; 2F.*

The museum, which stands on the site of the former Augustinian monastery, contains **collections of prehistory.** Most of the exhibits came from excavations undertaken in the area and are principally stones and tools dating from the Palaeolithic Age. Note in particular the skeleton of the Chancelade man, the red sandstone polishing tool, mammoths' tusks and engraved bones.

A gallery on the ground floor is devoted to **Gallo-Roman archaeology** and in particular to objects found during the excavation of Vesunna. Note the remarkable mosaics inset in the floor around an altar which was formerly used for the sacrifice of bulls and is adorned by a sculptured bull's head. Funerary steles are set up round the gallery.

In the former chapel there is an exhibition of Périgord popular arts and traditions: amidst the Limousin enamels note the finely executed pyx dating from the 13C.

In the ceramics section, the faiences from Nevers and the porcelain from Sèvres and from China are noteworthy.

In the section reserved for paintings, note the 13C **diptych from Rabastens** on the river Tarn, a large illuminated parchment, a portrait of Maréchal de Belle-Isle by C. Vanloo and a Canaletto. There are also paintings by local artists and portraits of Périgord's famous men and women.

The arcaded gallery surrounding the courtyard contains a lapidary museum.

Follow the Cours Tourny before turning right into the Rue du Plantier, with its old houses.

Turn right again into the Rue de la Constitution.

Rue de la Constitution (**BY 24**). – Note at No 3 a house with a Gothic doorway and mullioned windows. At No 7, the **Hôtel Gamanson** (**E**) or Logis St-Front is a fine 16C mansion. In the inner courtyard note the spiral staircase and the 17C well.

Take **Rue de la Nation** also lined with interesting houses to return to Place Daumesnil.

PÉRIGUEUX

Bugeaud (Pl.) .... BZ 16
Fénelon (Cours) .... BZ
Limogeanne (R.) .... BY 38
Montaigne (Crs. Pl.) ... BY 47
Prés.-Wilson (R.) ...... AYZ
République (R. de la) ... BZ 59
Taillefer (R.) .... BZ 70

Aquitaine (Av. d') ...... AY 2
Barbecane (R.) .... BY 6
Barris (Pont des) .... BZ 8
Chassaing (R. Clos) ..... AY 17
Clarté (R. de la) .... BZ 22
Constitution (R. de la) .... BY 24
Daumesnil (Pl. et R. A.) .... BZ 26
Éguillerie (R.) .... BY 27
Farges (R. des) .... BZ 32
Francheville (Pl.) .... BZ 33
Juin (Av. du Mar.) .... AY 37
Maurois (Pl. A.) .... BY 41
Miséricorde (R. de la) .... BY 45
Mobiles-de-Coulmiers .... AY 46
Nation (R. de la) .... BYZ 50
Papin (R. Denis) .... AY 51
Plantier (R. du) .... BY 55
Plumancy (Pl.) .... AY 57
St-Étienne de la Cité (⊟) .... AZ K
St-Front (R.) .... BY 62
St-Front (⊟) .... BZ
St-Georges (Cours) ...... BZ 63
St-Martin (Pl., ⊟) .... AY 66
Tourny (Cours) .... BY 72
50e Régiment-d'Infanterie (Av.) .... AZ 75

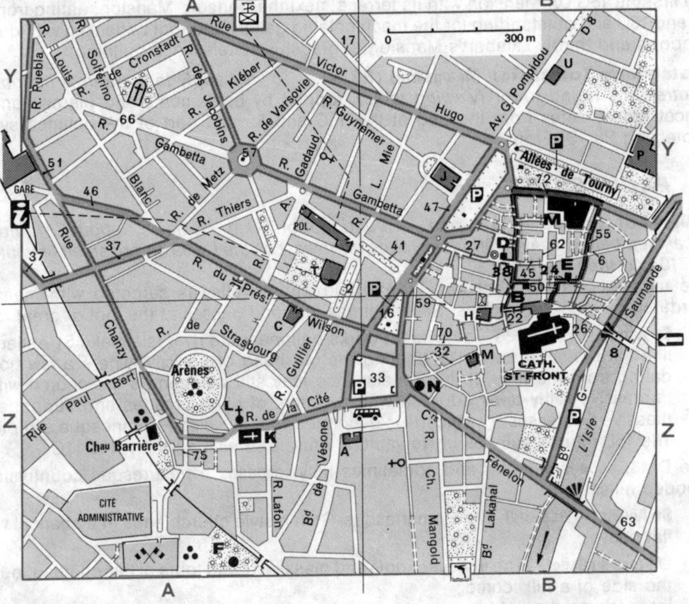

■ ADDITIONAL SIGHTS

Church of St-Étienne-de-la-Cité★ (**AZ K**). – *Restoration work in progress. Closed on Sunday afternoons.* St-Étienne-de-la-Cité was the cathedral church until 1669 when the title was transferred to St-Front. When it was built in the 12C the church was roofed with a line of four domes preceded by an impressive belfry-porch. When the town was occupied in 1577, the Protestants took down all but the two east bays. Restored in the 17C, mutilated again during the period of the Fronde, secularised during the Revolution, St-Étienne was reconsecrated at the time of the First Empire (1804-1814).

The church as it now stands is a good example of the pure Périgord-Romanesque style *(p 28)*. Outside can still be seen the beginning of a ruined bay and the torn foundations of a dome that was demolished. The eastern end of the chevet, which is plain, is pierced by three windows surmounted by arcades with double covings.

The two remaining bays are roofed with domes on pendentives; the east bay, with richer adornment, forms the chancel: graceful colonnaded blind arcades support the gallery.

A 17C **retable**★ of oak and walnut wood stands against the south wall of the west bay. In a sculptured arcade, once part of the tomb of Jean d'Asside, Bishop of Périgueux from 1160 to 1169, now stands a font of the same period.

Vesunna's Tower (Tour de Vésone) (**AZ F**). – *To visit the excavations apply to the tourist information centre.* This tower is all that remains of the temple dedicated to the titular goddess of the city. The temple which was built at the heart of the forum in the old city when the Antonines were in power in the 2C AD, originally had a peristyle with columns, was surrounded by porticoes and was framed by two basilicas.

The Tower of Vesunna, which is still impressive in spite of mutilation, is nearly 24 m - 79 ft high. It has an inner diameter of 17 m - 56 ft. Excavations near the tower have uncovered Gallo-Roman remains.

Arena (Arènes) (**AZ**). – Today a square surrounds the ruins of the vast elliptical amphitheatre that once held as many as 20 000 spectators. Great blocks of stone still mark the stairwells, the passages and the vaulting, but all the lower part of the building remains buried below ground. Demolition of the arena began in the 3C when the amphitheatre was turned into a bastion and became part of the city ramparts. In the 11C a count of Perigord built a fortress in the arena; this was only dismantled after Archambaud V's betrayal in 1391. The arena was next turned into a quarry, its stone being used to build houses in the town.

Barrière Castle (Château Barrière) (**AZ**). – This strange stronghold, built in the 12C and burned by the Protestants in the 16C stands near the arena. The keep, on Roman foundations, is the oldest part of the building.

A many-sided staircase tower, with a Flamboyant doorway, stands against the north wall.

Chapel of St-Jean (**AZ L**). – *To visit apply at the Ste-Marthe School.*

This chapel is all that remains of the episcopal palace destroyed by the Protestants in 1577.

The chapel which was built in 1521 has star ogive vaulting. The five keystones are ornamented with medallions on which are depicted God the Father and the four Evangelists. The triumphal arch and the two supporting columns are very ornate. The lateral niches rest on twisted columns and are surmounted by pinnacles decorated with angels and shells.

The Houses besides the River. – There is a **view★** from the Barris Bridge (**BZ**), of the many old houses built beside the Isle quay and, beyond, of the domes of St-Front. Left of the bridge stands an old timber-work house while on the right, each touching the other, are first the 16C Lur Mansion with its terrace, next the Consuls' Mansion, dating from the 15 and 16C and outstanding for the machicolated gallery and roof bedecked with dormer windows and thirdly Lambert's Mansion, a graceful Renaissance building.

Mataguerre Tower (Tour Mataguerre) (**BZ N**). – *To visit apply to the tourist information centre.* This round tower *(viewing table)*, topped by battlements and pierced only by lancet holes, dates from the end of the 15C and formed part of the defence system protecting Puy St-Front.

EXCURSIONS

Valleys of the Isle and Dronne. – *Round tour of 79 km - 49 miles – about 2 1/2 hours – local map below. Leave Périgueux to the northwest by the D 939 and bear left first into the D 710 and then the D 3.*

The road follows the right bank of the Isle whose valley is carpeted with meadows bordered by quickset hedges. Several times the road passes at the foot of great rocks.

St-Astier. – Pop 4 736. The cement works built near the river Isle make St-Astier look like an industrial town. Dominating the old heart of the city, where a few houses dating from the time of the Renaissance may still be seen, is the church with its impressive **belfry-tower** adorned with two tiers of blind arcades and supported by massive buttresses. The façade is decorated with recycled Romanesque sculptures. The 15C church still has ogive vaulting and its semicircular crypt is 11C.

The D 43, always winding and sometimes hilly, crosses a picturesque countryside of wooded hills.

St-Aquilin. – Pop 388. The Romanesque-Gothic style church ends in a chancel with a flat chevet.

Château du Bellet. – The fine tiled roofs and massive round tours of this château, built on the side of a hill, come into view on the right.

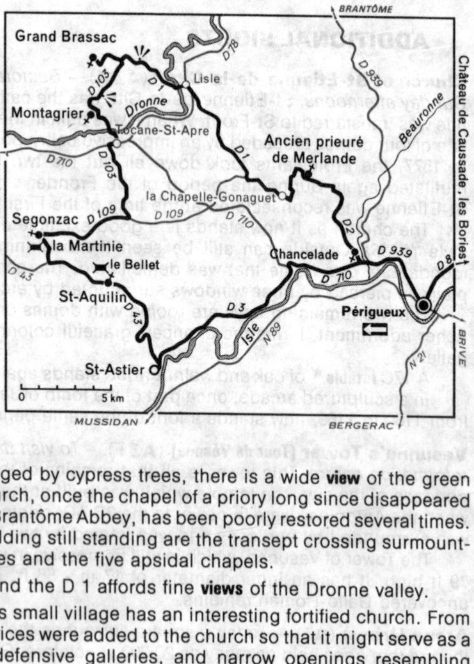

Château de la Martinie. – To the left stands this elegant Renaissance château which has now been converted into a farmstead.

Segonzac. – This hamlet has a small Romanesque-Gothic church which has been extensively restored.

You enter the Dronne valley at Tocane St-Apre. From the left bank you look across to the clumps of trees and crops on the hillsides opposite.

Montagrier. – Pop 385. From the end of a terrace near which stands the church of Montagrier ringed by cypress trees, there is a wide **view** of the green valley of the Dronne. The church, once the chapel of a priory long since disappeared which was a dependency of Brantôme Abbey, has been poorly restored several times. The only parts of the 12C building still standing are the transept crossing surmounted by a dome on pendentives and the five apsidal chapels.

The D 103 between Montagrier and the D 1 affords fine **views** of the Dronne valley.

Grand-Brassac. – Pop 528. This small village has an interesting fortified church. From the 13C onwards fortified devices were added to the church so that it might serve as a refuge. The crenellations, defensive galleries, and narrow openings resembling loopholes give the building a severe appearance.

The north doorway has a decoration which brings together sculpture of different periods: an arch adorned with fine covings and containing statuettes which formed part of a group depicting the Adoration of the Magi, has above it five 16C statues. These are sheltered by a porch. Among the figures are Christ between St. John and the Virgin and lower down St. Peter and another saint. Inside the church the narrowness of the nave increases the feeling of immense height.

Turn back. The D 1 crosses the Dronne river. Shortly after Chapelle-Gonaguet bear left onto a local road.

Former Merlande Priory. – In a deserted clearing in Feytaud Forest, near a spring favourable to the founding of a monastery stand a small fortified chapel and prior's house, both restored, solitary reminders of the Merlande Priory founded here in the 12C by the monks of Chancelade. The chapel appears to be a fortress-like structure due to its 4-sided plan. It is a Romanesque building with two bays: the first has a transverse rib and broken-barrel vaulting replacing the original dome, the second is roofed with an attractive dome on pendentives. The chancel, slightly above the level of the nave and preceded by a rounded triumphal arch, has barrel vaulting and a flat chevet. It is bordered by a series of blind arcades adorned with archaic **capitals**★ which are finely carved: monsters tangled one with another and lions devouring palm-leaf scrolls make up a bizarre but striking fauna.

A road through the woods leads to the D 2.

Former Abbey of Chancelade. – *Description p 81.*

Caussade; les Bories. – *32 km - 20 miles. Leave Périgueux to the northeast by the D 8. After 8.5 km - 5 miles turn right to reach Caussade Castle.*

Caussade Castle. – *Not open to the public.* Standing in a clearing of the Lanmary Forest this noble 14C fortress is protected by a perimeter wall with square towers.

Return to the road which you take to the left in the direction of Chariéras then turn left again. The white mass of Les Bories Castle comes into view on the right as you leave Antonne-et-Trigonnant.

Les Bories. – *Description p 57.*

The N 21 leads back to Périgueux.

PEYRAT-LE-CHÂTEAU

Michelin map 72 fold 19 – Pop 1 295 – *Facilities p 38*

Peyrat-le-Château presses close to a pool near which stands the square keep of a former fortress in a countryside of low mountains and hills where stretches of broom and heather alternate with pine and beech woods.

EXCURSION

Vassivière Lake★★ (Lac de Vassivière). – *8 km – 5 miles east on the D 13.* The twisting road affords wide views over wooded countryside and moorland covered with heather and broom. A road to the right leads to the Touring Club de France's (T.C.F.) sailing centre, from where you get a full view of the Vassivière Lake. This stretch of water (1 000 ha - 2 470 acres) made from a dam built on the Maulde River lies in a pleasant setting of wooded hills where, in springtime the gold of the broom mingles with the greens of the trees. Water sports are held in the summer *(see tourist calendar of events p 37).*

Beyond the Touring Club's centre a tourist road enables you to follow the lake shore which has many bays and promontories and provides occasional general **views.**

Vassivière Island. – *Take the scenic road to the south in the direction of Beaumont-du-lac.* This route overlooks the sailing centre and affords fairly wide **views** of the lake. *After 4 km – 2 miles turn left towards Pierrefitte. Leave the car in the car park.*

You can make an excursion on foot to Vassivière Island; from the bridge you can enjoy lovely **views**★ of the lake shores and of the surrounding mountains.

PLAIMPIED Former Abbey

Michelin map 69 fold 1 – 12 km - 7 miles south of Bourges

Of the great abbey founded by Richard II, Archbishop of Bourges, only the abbey church of the Augustinian Canons Regular can be seen today standing near the Auron river and the former Berry Canal.

St. Martin's Abbey Church. – Building began at the end of the 11C and continued for a hundred years. During the Wars of Religion (16C) the church was damaged and restoration work was not completed until the 18C.

In contrast to the simplicity of the façade and the side elevation, the chevet is surprisingly ornate: a line of blind arcades runs round the chevet and extends along the east walls of the two arms of the transept; the chevet windows are framed by small columns surmounted by delicately carved capitals.

The interior decoration owes its originality to the overall effect of the **capitals.** The oldest are in the chancel and are carved with monsters and demons. The influence of oriental art is plainly visible. One of the most remarkable capitals is on the pillar between the nave and the south transept and depicts the Temptation of Christ.

At the end of the south aisle there is a 16C Virgin carved in multicoloured wood.

POMPADOUR

Michelin map 75 north of fold 8 – *Facilities p 38*

Pompadour owes its place in history to Louis XV, who gave the castle together with the title of marchioness to his favourite, Madame de Pompadour, in 1745.

In 1761 the king established the famous stud at Pompadour; last century this became the nursery of the Anglo-Arab strain, making the area an important horse-breeding centre. A horse-show and race-meetings are held during the summer season.

Château. – *To visit the terraces apply to the caretaker. Guided tours in season 10am (9am Sundays and holidays) to 11.15am and 2 to 5.15pm; the rest of the year, 10 to 11.15am and 2 to 4.15pm; closed afternoons of race-meetings.*

This impressive 15C building, its majestic façade standing out against a background of greenery, is today inhabited by officials working at the stud. Round towers and square wings are linked by curtain walls topped by steep roofs resting on a line of machicolations. The terrace in front, is encircled by a moat and flanked by low towers.

National Stud (Haras National). – *Open 2 July to 28 February, weekdays 2.30 to 5pm, Sundays and holidays 10 to 11.30am and 2.30 to 5pm; when race meetings are held, 10am to noon and 6 to 7pm.*

The Puy-Marmont stallions stabled opposite the château number about 100 and are of many different breeds, including; thoroughbreds, Arabs, Ardennes, Bretons, Percherons; and especially Anglo-Arabs sought after in France and overseas for breeding and riding.

EXCURSION

Arnac Church; Ségur-le-Château. – *13 km - 8 miles to the northwest by the D 126.*

Arnac Church. – This 12C church is strikingly severe and impressively large. The doorway in the Limousin style is decorated with archaic capitals and blind arcades with corbels and medallions. In niches above the door are three statues; the Virgin has the two Limousin saints, St. Martial and St. Pardoux standing on her left and right respectively.

Inside the nave has ogive vaulting with emblazoned bosses and is adorned with interesting historiated capitals.

Continue along the D 126 then turn left onto the D 107 before taking to the right the D 6 which affords some fine views.

Ségur-le-Château. – Pop 304. Beneath the towering ruins of the fortress, the old houses of the ancient market village of Ségur-le-Château stand reflected in the waters of the Auvézère. Among the houses is one with timbered walls and mullioned windows known as the "House of Henry IV", for Ségur-le-Château was the native town of the first counts of Limoges and the ancestors of Henry IV.

The castle *(open 9am to noon and 2 to 6pm; apply to the guide at the foot of the castle walls)* stands in a picturesque setting at the top of a hillock encircled by a loop of the Auvézère. The visitor may see the castle courtyard and the ruins of the 14C chapel. From the watch-path there are good views of the old houses with their attractive roofs of brown tiles and the valley of the Auvézère.

PREUILLY-SUR-CLAISE

Michelin map 68 fold 6 – Pop 1 553

Preuilly built in tiers on the right bank of the Claise, has preserved certain old mansions. Recognized as the first Barony of Touraine, it was held by such famous families as the Amboise, Rochefoucauld, César de Vendôme, Galliffet and Breteuil. Preuilly has five churches and a collegiate church. Dominated in former times by a fortress which is now in ruins and beside which there is now a modern château, there are also the remains of the 12C collegiate church of St-Mélaine which was attached to the 12-15C castle.

Church of St-Pierre. – St. Peter's, a former Benedictine abbey church, is a Romanesque building which shows a mixture of Poitou and Touraine styles. Flying buttresses were added in the 15C. Restored with taste in 1846 by the architect, Phidias Vestier, the church however suffered from alterations in 1873 when the tower was added. The five bay nave is covered with cradle vaulting and has historiated capitals. The presbytery in a late 15C building, adjoining the south arm of the transept, formerly contained the chapter-house and monks' dormitory.

Near the church are 17C mansions one of which, the former Hôtel de la Rallière, is now an old people's home.

EXCURSION

Boussay. – Pop 271. *4.5 km - 3 miles to the southwest.* This château *(you can visit the exterior)* has 15C machicolated towers side by side with a 17C wing with Mansard roofs and an 18C façade. The surrounding park is in the French style.

PUYGUILHEM Château

Michelin map 75 north of fold 5 – 10 km - 8 miles west of St-Jean-de-Côle

Puyguilhem Château was built at the beginning of the 16C by Mondot de la Marthonie, first President of the Parliament of Bordeaux and Paris, and resembles many of the châteaux of the Loire Valley which were built in the reign of François I. It was taken over by the Fine Arts Department in 1939 and has been restored and refurbished after the 1940-45 War.

Open 9 to 11.30am and 2 to 6pm (9am to 6pm in July and August); closed Tuesdays and 15 December to 1 February; 8F.

The main building is flanked on one side by a massive round tower joined to an octagonal turret, on the other by an asymmetrical tower with cant walls, built to contain the main staircase. The decoration has considerable harmony of style. The pierced balustrade at the base of the roof of the main building, the dormer windows and the finely carved chimneys, the mullioned windows, the decorated battlements on the great round tower, all contribute to the elegance of this early Renaissance building.

Inside note the carved **chimneys**★: the one in the guardroom with its mantelpiece ornamented with foliage and medallions and especially the one in the great hall on the first floor. Its uprights are adorned with shell-shaped niches and on the entablature are depicted six of Hercules' labours.

Also of interest are the chestnut ceiling in the great hall on the second floor and the carved main staircase.

PUY-L'ÉVÊQUE

Michelin map 79 south of fold 7 – *Local map p 124* – Pop 2 333 – *Facilities p 38*

This little town which took its present name when it came under the overlordship of the bishops of Cahors, occupies one of the most picturesque sites in the valley outside Cahors. The best view of the town is from the left bank end of the suspension bridge: the old houses in golden stone rise in tiers on the right bank of the Lot, overshadowed by the church and the castle keep.

The church was built on the northeast side of the town at the tip of the defence system of which it was part. Before the church stands a massive belfry-porch flanked by a turret and buttresses. The doorway, surmounted by an accoladed pediment, is adorned with statues including figures of the Virgin and St. John at the feet of Christ on the Cross. The nave was built in the 14 and 15C and ends in a polygonal apse.

In the cemetery there are many old tombs and on the left of the church a Calvary ornamented with sculpture in the archaic style.

The keep, all that remains of the episcopal castle, dates back to the 13C. You can enjoy an extensive view of the Lot valley from the Truffière esplanade adjoining the keep and the town hall.

PUYMARTIN Castle

Michelin map 75 fold 17 – *Local maps pp 93 and 186*

The 15-16C castle (restored 19C) built in golden stone and roofed with stone slates comprises several wings linked by round towers and girt by curtain walls. During the Wars of Religion it was a Catholic stronghold.

Guided tours 1 July to 15 September, 10am to noon and 2 to 6.30pm; 4F.

Inside, the **decoration★** and **furnishings★** are remarkable. The state room is hung with 18C Aubusson tapestries in fresh green tones. The next room is adorned with interesting monochrome mural paintings on mythological themes. The main hall has a chimney decorated in *trompe l'œil* and a ceiling with beams painted in the 17C; note in particular a set of six Flemish tapestries illustrating the Trojan War, a table and chairs in Louis XIII style, a Regency chest of drawers and a Louis XV writing desk.

The oldest room in the castle is the hexagonal chapel which is crowned with star vaulting. The former guardroom which contains outstanding paintings, tapestries and furniture is also open to visitors. The splendid oak and chestnut framework which supports the roof is also of interest.

ROCAMADOUR★★★

Michelin map 75 folds 18 and 19 – *Local maps pp 94 and 108* – Pop 795 – *Facilities p 38*

Rocamadour, towered over by its slender castle keep, groups a mass of old dwellings, oratories, towers and precipitous rocks on the rugged face of a cliff rising 150 m - 490 ft above the Alzou Canyon.

Its setting is one of the most extraordinary in France.

Rocamadour from the south.

The Site★★★. – One should arrive in Rocamadour by the l'Hospitalet road. L'Hospitalet, which should be called Hôpital St-Jean, is a hamlet that still has a fortified gateway and contains the ruins of a hospital erected to succour pilgrims.

From a terrace-belvedere there is a remarkable **view** of Rocamadour: the Alzou winds its way between fields at the bottom of a gorge, while some 500 m - 1 640 ft up, pinioned to the cliff face, can be seen the extraordinary outline of this village whose unbelievably bold construction appears to defy the force of gravity. The religious buildings rise above the village centre and crowning all are the castle ramparts. The morning, when the sun shines fully on the rock, is the best time of all for looking at the view.

There is another striking view of Rocamadour to be had from the Couzou road, the D 32, as, dropping from the plateau, you pass a road going off to the left.

"Son et Lumière" (Sound and Light) (p 37).

HISTORICAL NOTES

The Enigmatic St. Amadour. – The identity of St. Amadour, who gave his name to the sanctuary village, has never been firmly established. A 12C chronicler reported that in 1166 "a local inhabitant having expressed the wish to be buried beneath the threshold of the Chapel of the Virgin, men began to dig a grave only to find in the soil, the body of a man. The corpse was placed near the altar so that it might be venerated by the faithful and from that time onwards miracles occured".

Who was this mysterious personage whose tomb appeared to be so old? The most contradictory theories have been advanced: some contend that he was an Egyptian hermit, others that it was St. Silvanus. The most accepted theory since the 15C is that the body was that of the publican Zaccheus, a disciple of Jesus and husband of St. Veroniça, who, meeting Christ on His way to Calvary, wiped His face, which was covered in blood and sweat, with her kerchief. Inspired by grace, Zaccheus and Veronica began to preach the Gospel in Palestine, but were forced to flee in the face of persecution and so came to Limousin to complete their mission. On the death of Veronica, Zaccheus retired to a rock on the plateau to end his days as a hermit. He was buried beneath this rock.

The rock served as a shelter; and the *langue d'Oc* expression – *roc amator* – he who likes the rock – named this sanctuary Roc Amadour which later became *Rocamadour.*

The Fame of Rocamadour. – From the time the miracles began until the Reformation the pilgrimage to Rocamadour was one of the most famous in Christendom. Great crowds came on days of major pardon and plenary indulgence. Henry Plantagenet, King of England, was miraculously cured and was among the first to kneel before the Virgin; his example was followed during the Middle Ages by the most illustrious personages including St. Dominic, St. Bernard, St. Louis and Blanche of Castile, Philip IV the Fair, Philip VI and Louis XI. Veneration of Our Lady of Rocamadour was established at Lisbon, Oporto, Seville and even in Sicily.

Penitents and the Pilgrimage. – Ecclesiastical, and in some cases, lay tribunals used to often impose the pilgrimage on sinners. It was a considerable penance, employed especially towards Albigensian heretics who were said to hate the Mother of God. On the day of his departure, the penitent attended mass and then set forth dressed in clothes covered with large crosses, a big hat upon his head, a staff in his hand and a knapsack on his back. On reaching the end of his journey, the pilgrim stripped himself of his clothes, climbing the famous steps on his knees in his shirt and chains were bound round his arms and neck. On being brought before the altar to the Black Virgin in this humiliating condition he pronounced his *amende honorable.* A priest recited prayers of purification and removed the chains from the penitent, who, now forgiven, received from the priest a certificate and a kind of lead medal bearing the image of the miraculous Virgin.

But the pilgrimages were not always conducted for pious ends: lords and town consuls sought the protection of Our Lady when making a treaty or signing a charter. Others came to Rocamadour to see the crowds and indeed to do business.

Decline and Renaissance. – Rocamadour reached its zenith in the 13C. Favours not even given to Jerusalem were granted to it; money poured in, but riches brought the covetous. For a hundred years the Abbeys of Marcilhac and Tulle disputed who should own the church at Rocamadour; Tulle was finally awarded the church by arbitration. During the Middle Ages the town was sacked several times: Henry Short Coat (Henri Court Mantel), in revolt against his father Henry Plantagenet, pillaged the oratory in 1183; during the Hundred Years War, bands of the English and the local soldiery plundered the treasure by turns; during the Wars of Religion the Protestant Captain Bessonies seized Rocamadour to desecrate and lay it waste; only the Virgin and the belfry miraculously escaped. Rocamadour did not rise from its ruins; the abbey remained idle until it was finally extinguished by the Revolution. In the 19C the bishops of Cahors tried to revive the pilgrimage and the churches were rebuilt. Though much of its splendour has vanished, Rocamadour is once again venerated by pilgrims.

■ SIGHTS *time: 3 hours*

Start from the Porte du Figuier. Some visitors may find the proposed tour too demanding and are advised to start the visit from the opposite direction by first driving via L'Hospitalet to the castle (car parks), and to go up by lift (6F).

The Village. – Once a fortified town, Rocamadour still retains much that bears witness to its past. Go through the Porte du Figuier which was already a gateway to the town in the 13C, and enter the main street which is now cluttered with souvenir shops. The narrow street, clinging to the living rock, is vertically overlooked by a peculiar tiered arrangement of houses, churches and the castle. The town hall can be seen to the right beyond the Porte Salmon, which is crowned by a two storey tower.

The Town Hall. – This is installed in a 15C house known as the Couronnerie or the Maison des Frères which has been restored. In the council chamber there are fine **tapestries★** by Jean Lurçat *(see p 48)* which portray the flora and fauna of the causse. *Open 1 May to 30 September, 9am to noon and 3 to 7pm; 3F.*

If you go farther along the Rue de la Couronnerie you will pass through the 13C Porte Hugon. The street continues, until it reaches the Porte Basse, to go through a picturesque quarter where little houses cluster down the slope to the very banks of the Alzou. Nearby stands the old fortified mill, known as the Mill of Roquefrège.

Return to the Place de la Carreta from whose entrance begins the Grand Escalier (Great Stairway) to the churches.

The Ecclesiastical City. – To reach it you have to climb the 216 steps of the Great Stairway *(Via Sancta).* Pilgrims often make this ascent, kneeling at every step.

The first 141 stairs lead, in five flights, to terraces on which once stood buildings for the canons to live in. These have now been converted into shops and hotels.

The Fort (**B**). – This vast and much restored building was formerly the palace of the bishops of Tulle; it has a military appearance and stands at the base of the huge cliff face. It was here that important pilgrims lodged.

The terrace on which the palace was constructed is known as the Place des Senhals from the pilgrims' insignia or *senhals* that were made there; coming out on to the square is the little Rue de la Mercerie.

Rue de la Mercerie. – The oldest street in Rocamadour, in which can be seen a curious 14C house (Maison de la Pomette), ends at the 13C Porte de Cabiliert, once flanked by a defensive tower.

Return to the Porte du Fort which goes through the palace perimeter wall and gives access to the Sacred Precincts.

A stairway with 75 steps leads up to the Parvis (square) which is encircled by several churches.

Le Parvis des Églises. – The square, which is also known as the Place St-Amadour, is fairly small and has seven churches rising at different levels from its sides: St. Saviour's Basilica opposite the stairway, St. Amadour's Crypt below the basilica, the Miraculous Chapel on the left, the three Chapels of St. John the Baptist, St. Blaise and St. Anne on the right and the Chapel of St. Michael standing on a terrace on the left.

Guided tours 1 June to 30 September, 9am to 5pm except Sundays; to visit apply to the sacristy or the shop, Magasin du Pèlerinage *on the parvis.*

St. Saviour's Basilica (Basilique St-Sauveur) (**D**). – The basilica is built in the Romanesque-Gothic style (11-13C) and has two equal naves, each of three bays, divided by pillars.

Standing in the centre of the church above the altar is a fine 16C figure of Christ carved in wood; the piercing by the lance is shown, unusually, on the right side.

Miraculous Chapel (Chapelle Miraculeuse) (**E**). – Seventeen steps rise in a stairway from the Parvis to the Miraculous Chapel of Our Lady considered as the "Holy of Holies" of Rocamadour. It is here that the hermit is believed to have hollowed out an oratory in the rock. In 1476 the chapel was crushed by a rock-fall; during the Wars of Religion and again in 1793 it was sacked; last century it was rebuilt.

On the Miraculous Chapel terrace may be seen an alms coffer with 13C bolts, and on the walls of the sanctuaries traces of 13 and 14C frescoes depicting St. Christopher and a *danse macabre* known as the "dance of death of the three living and the three dead men".

In the rock wall, above the door to the Miraculous Chapel is fixed a great iron sword which legend holds to be the "Durandal", the famous sword of Roland.

The interior is adorned with many votive items: banners, crutches, swords, offerings and the chains worn by penitents during certain ceremonies of repentance.

Suspended from the roof within the chapel, hangs the miraculous bell, dating back perhaps to the 9C, which rings out of its own accord to foretell miracles.

Above the altar is the statue of the Miraculous Virgin, also called the Black Madonna, seated with the Infant Jesus on her knees. Judging by the way this reliquary statue in wood was carved and the position of the Child, it may date from the 9C; the walnut base is covered by fine silver plating, of which traces remain.

St. Michael's Chapel (Chapelle St-Michel) (**F**). – This Romanesque chapel is sheltered by a rock overhang. The apse which houses a small oratory juts out towards the square.

On the wall outside are two **frescoes**★ representing the Annunciation and the Visitation of the Virgin: the skill in composition, the richness of colour – ochre, yellow, reddish-brown, and the royal blue background, protected from condensation and therefore well preserved – and the grace of movement all seem to point to the works having been painted in the 12C. They may well have been inspired both by Limousin reliquaries (note the figures in relief in the background) and Byzantine mosaics (note the swarthy complexions).

Inside, the chancel is adorned with paintings: Christ in Majesty is surrounded by the Evangelists; further down a seraph and the Archangel Michael weigh souls.

Go back down to the Parvis.

Museum-Treasure (**M¹**). – *Open 1 July to 31 August, 9am to 7pm; 1 April to 30 June and 1 September to 31 October, 9am to noon and 2 to 6pm; 5F.*

The museum contains certain valuable religious items; particularly outstanding are a 15C silver gilt chalice presented by Pope Pius II, a 14C *pietà* and another dating from the 17C, a 14C stained glass window, enamelled copper reliquary shrines, reliquary and processional crosses, insignia, vestments, sculpture and paintings.

Then take the side-walk known as the "tunnel" which passes beneath St. Saviour's to come out on a terrace from which there is a view of the Alzou Canyon.

Calvary. – A shaded Stations of the Cross winds up towards the castle. After passing the caves (grottes) of the Nativity and the Holy Sepulchre, you see the great Cross of Jerusalem (Croix de Jérusalem) brought from the Holy Land by the Penitential Pilgrims.

Château. – *Open 1 July to 31 August, 9am to 7pm; out of season 9am to noon and 2.30 to 6pm; closed 1 November to 1 April; 3F.*

The castle is built on the cliff spur. The present buildings adjoining a 14C fort, date from last century. From the ramparts *(car park)*, which rise above a sheer drop, there is an unforgettable **panorama**★★★ of the limestone plateau and of Rocamadour.

Eagles' Rock (Rocher des Aigles). – *Open 1 March to 15 November, 9am to noon and 2 to 7pm; flying displays several times a day during the season; 12F, children 7.50F.*

There is a breeding centre for birds of prey near the castle. Some of the birds are trained and give an amazing flying display.

Return to an esplanade which is at the same height as the religious centre of the town and take the lift to the main street near the Porte Salmon.

Tourists who wish to stay longer in Rocamadour might be interested in visiting the waxwork museum, **Roland-le-Preux** (**M²**). *Guided tours 9am to noon and 2 to 7pm – 10pm 1 July to 15 September; closed 1 October to Easter; 10F.*

ROCHECHOUART

Michelin map 72 north of fold 16 – Pop 4 053 – *Facilities p 38*

Rochechouart Castle rises above a rock promontory; the best view of it is from the D 3 BIS where it passes the foot of the cliff.

On the last day of the *ostension (p 37)*, held once every seven years, takes place a procession unique in the costumes that are worn and the shrines that are carried.

Immanent Justice. – In 1205 Viscount **Aymeric de Rochechouart** married the heartbreakingly beautiful Alix de Mortemart. Legend has it that the castle steward, mad with love for the Viscountess, tried to seduce her, but she repulsed his advances. In revenge the steward told his master that the viscountess had solicited him. The jealous viscount, on impulse, had his wife thrown to a lion in the east tower. Two days later, when he went to contemplate his act of justice, he found the lion crouched at his wife's feet. The guiltless woman was brought back into favour, the truth became apparent and the steward was dispatched to the lion, which, this time, proved to be hungry.

■ SIGHTS *time: 3/4 hour*

Castle. – The castle stands in a remarkable **setting**★ above the confluence of the Graine and the Vayres and is mostly late 15C. The 13C keep which flanks the northeast entrance fort, was razed level with the rooftops in the 16C. The second tower at the left end of the façade bears a lion carved in granite in a niche. Take a small bridge to the entrance fort.

Court of Honour. – The buildings which line the court on three sides were restored in the 18C and now house the public services including the sub-prefecture. They are adorned with a gallery supported on elegant twisted columns. The fourth side is closed by a curtain wall.

Municipal Museum (Musée municipal). – *Guided tours 1 July to 15 September, 10 to 11.30am and 3 to 6pm; the rest of the year, Saturdays, Sundays and holidays, 3 to 5pm; 5F.*

The museum was founded in 1894 by Albert Masfrand who was the chemist in Rochechouart. On the second floor of the castle there is a prehistoric collection of flint artifacts, and axes, flake tools and the contents of cave deposits. There is a model of a hypocaust – underground heating chamber – which existed at Chassenon *(see below)* and exhibits of pottery discovered in the Auvergne and the Charente Departments.

The gallery of the chase is on the ground floor and is decorated with early 16C **frescoes** depicting a deer hunt. The dress worn by the people and the setting – Rochechouart with its castle and the little town enclosed within the ramparts are recognisable – make the fresco an interesting document on the Louis XII period. There is another 16C keep of a later period than in the north wing.

Promenade des Allées. – On leaving the castle turn left to reach les Allées, a shaded path forming a terrace. From the site of the calvary at the end of the walk you get a good view ot the valleys of the Graine and the Vayres and the front of the castle. This façade flanked by round towers, opens on to the terraced garden.

EXCURSIONS

Biennac. – *2 km - 1 mile to the east by the D 10.* The church dating from the 12 and 13C is topped by a hexagonal belfry and supported at each corner by buttresses. To reach the church pass a covered well and then go up the semicircular flight of steps.

Chassenon (Gallo-Roman Remains). – *5 km - 3 miles to the northwest. Leave Rochechouart by the D 54 which then becomes the D 29. Guided tours 1 July to 15 September, 10 to 11.30am and 2 to 6.30pm (5pm out of season); closed 12 November to Palm Sunday; 10F.*

The remains are sited to the left of the road 500 m - 545 yds before the village of Chassenon. This was the settlement of Cassinomagus in antique times and acted as a halt and place of worship on the Agrippa Roman road between Lyon and Saintes.

Excavations since 1958 have uncovered baths and twenty or so underground chambers which probably served as reservoirs for water and which were fed by aqueducts. The baths were part of a rural sanctuary and included 3 temples and a theatre.

La ROQUE-GAGEAC★★

Michelin map 75 fold 17 – *Local map p 97* – Pop 404

The village of La Roque-Gageac, huddled against the cliff which drops vertically to the valley of the Dordogne, occupies a wonderful **site**★★ – one of the finest in this part of the valley which within a few miles contains Domme, Castelnaud and Beynac-et-Cazenac.

View★★. – The best view of La Roque-Gageac is from the west: the late afternoon sun highlights the tall grey cliff-face covered with holm-oaks, while the houses, with their stone or tile roofs, stand reflected in the calm waters of the river below.

In the foreground can be seen the outline of Malartrie Castle built in the 19C in the 15C style; at the other end of the village, standing at the foot of the sheer rock-face, is the charming Tarde Manor, whose main building is flanked by a round turret. The manor is associated with the Tarde family: the 16C humanist, Canon Tarde and Gabriel Tarde the 19C sociologist.

The Village. – *Time: 1/2 hour.* It has been extensively restored. Picturesque alleys, where the houses of peasants and craftsmen stand next to noble mansions, lead to the church on the rock. The church affords a view of the Dordogne as it winds through meadows and fields.

ROUFFIGNAC

Michelin map 75 southeast of fold 6 – *Local map p 186* – Pop 1 429

The church alone escaped when the Germans set about burning the town in March 1944 as a reprisal for the harassing of their troops by the Resistance. The town has been rebuilt.

Church. – You enter through a belfry-porch containing a doorway built in the style of the first Renaissance. It was constructed about 1530 and is ornamented with Corinthian capitals and surmounted by a finely carved lintel: the decoration is profane and somewhat surprising since it consists of sirens and women. The church has three aisles of equal height built in the Flamboyant style; the ogive vaulting is supported by round pillars cantoned by twisted columns.

Rouffignac Cave★ **(Grotte de Rouffignac).** – *5 km - 3 miles to the south. Leave Rouffignac by the D 32. After 3 km - 2 miles bear left into a pine avenue.* You come on a farmstead standing alone; beyond this a road leads to the cave.

Open Palm Sunday to 31 October, 10 to 11.30am and 2 to 5pm (6pm 1 July to 15 September); 1 November to Palm Sunday on Sundays only, 11am and 3pm; apply to the farm; time: 1 hour; 14F. Wear warm clothing.

This dry cave, which is also called the Cro de Granville, was known as early as the 15C. The galleries and chambers extend for more than 8 km - 5 miles. The tour (4 km – 2 miles Rtn), which is made by electric railway, takes in all the principal galleries. In 1956 Professor L.R. Nougier discovered in the caves a group of **paintings and engravings**★ in outline which were produced between the end of the Aurignacian and the end of the Magdalenian Periods *(pp 21 to 24)*. These engravings are of horses, ibex, rhinoceros, bison and a great number of mammoths among which may be seen the «Patriarch» and an amazing frieze of two stags locked in combat. There is an outstanding assembly of drawings on the ceiling of the last chamber (disfigured with graffiti).

EXCURSIONS

L'Herm Castle. – *6 km - 4 miles to the northwest. Guided tours 1 July to 31 August, 10am to noon and 2.30 to 6.30pm; closed Wednesdays; time: 3/4 hour; 6F.*

The castle was built in the heart of the Barade Forest in 1512 by John III of Calvimont, president of the Parliament of Bordeaux and Louis XII's ambassador to Rome. A series of crimes cast a pall of blood over the castle's history. John IV, son of John III, died a violent death there; his grand-daughter Margaret was assassinated in the castle on the orders of her husband François d'Aubusson. Recollection of these tragic events gave **Eugène Le Roy** the idea of making the castle the setting for his novel *Jacquou le Croquant*.

Powerful crenellated towers emerge from the overgrown ruins; in one of these, which is octagonal in shape, is a carved doorway with crossed mouldings in the Flamboyant style and a spiral staircase. Monumental chimneypieces can also still be seen at the different storeys.

La Douze. – Pop 700. *14 km - 9 miles to the west by the D 6 and D 45.* La Douze church *(to visit apply at the Epicerie Claude)* was built in the Gothic style in the 14 and 15C. A massive belfry-porch leads to a nave with ogive vaulting.

The **altar** is one great stone carved with many figures among which may be seen Pierre d'Abzac, Baron of Ladouze, and his wife Jeanne de Bourdeille, kneeling; behind stand their patron saints.

The pulpit was probably carved by the same artist as the altar and is ornamented with three carved panels: in the centre is St. Peter, patron saint of the church; the two side panels, in the shape of a shield, bear the arms of Pierre d'Abzac and Jeanne de Bourdeille.

On the left of the entrance a baptismal font has been placed on the shaft of a Gallo-Roman column decorated with rosettes and figures in archaic style.

ST-AMAND-DE-COLY

Michelin map 75 fold 7 – *Local map p 143* – Pop 301

Tucked away in the fold of a small valley off the main valley of the Vézère, is St-Amand-de-Coly, its old houses clustering round the impressive abbey church.

Church★. – *Time: 1/2 hour.* This church, of fine yellow limestone, is one of Périgord's most amazing fortified churches. A considerable defence system, now almost entirely uncovered, protected the buildings of the abbey established in this spot in the 12C.

Exterior. – The huge pointed arch of the doorway supports the porch-keep. Once the keep was pierced by loopholes; in the upper part corbels supported watch-towers; within the porch are a tall round-topped window with, below, a doorway surrounded by motifs carved in archaic style. Bear left to look at the chevet. Here the apsidal chapels, protected by a defensive structure, contrast in their graceful design with the severe lines of the upper parts of the walls of the nave and transept which have stone roofs.

Interior. – Pure lines and decorative simplicity combine to increase the beauty of the lofty interior. Above the transept crossing is an archaic cupola on pendentives. The raised chancel ends in a flat chevet and is roofed with crossed ogive vaulting. There was once a passage running right round the eaves of the building which formed part of its defence system: there remain a cornice, supported by consoles, which extends round the chancel and part of the transept, traces of the square pillars that once stood in the transept, and the door leading to the upper chamber in the keep.

ST-AMAND-MONTROND

Michelin map 69 folds 1 and 11 – Pop 12 801 – *Facilities p 38*
See town plan in the current Michelin Red Guide France.

St-Amand-Montrond, now the capital of the Saint-Amandois area of rich pastures where the white Charollais cattle are raised, grew up round a monastery which was founded in the 7C by St. Amand, a follower of St. Columban. It was later protected by a castle perched on Mont-Rond hill.

Church of St-Amand. – The church stands in the southeast part of the town, south of the D 951 which goes to Decize and Nevers. This interesting 12C Romanesque building opens with a beautiful round arched doorway framed by two multilobed bays. In the south aisle note the fine late 16C carving of Christ Reviled and opposite, the early 16C stone figure of St. Rock. The organ-case in the south arm of the transept was gifted in 1668 by the Grand Condé.

St-Vic Museum. – *Open 10am to noon and 2 to 5pm; closed Sunday mornings and Mondays; 4.80F.*

The 16C St-Vic Mansion was the town residence of the commendatory abbots of Noirlac *(p 146)*. There are eight rooms housing an exhibition which traces the history of St-Amand and its surrounding area. A prehistory gallery includes collections from the Lower Paleolithic to the Bronze Age. The Gallo-Roman influence which was very strong in the Berry district is represented by architectural artefacts, coins, fibula and ceramics.

The late Middle Ages is illustrated by rustic furniture and 15C tableware. In the gallery reserved for the 18C is displayed a **ceramic collection** dating from the 17 and 18C. There are also rooms devoted to the ethnography of Berry and 19C exhibits; note an amazing sculpture "The Clog Tree" by the local craftsman Louis Touzet.

EXCURSIONS

Meillant★★; Noirlac★. – *Round tour of 23 km - 14 miles – about 1 hour – local map opposite. Leave St-Amand by ①, the D 10.* The road goes through the forest, Grand Bois de Meillant.

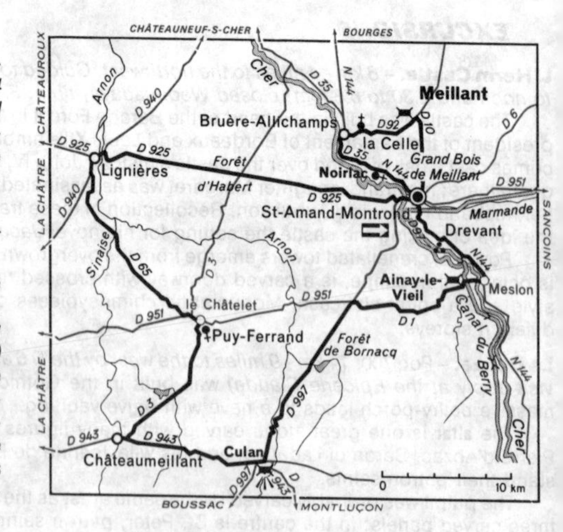

Meillant Château★★. – *Description p 131.*

La Celle. – Pop 264. The church of St-Blaise, originally a dependency of Déols Abbey *(p 83)* has an impressive square belfry and a chevet adorned with modillions and Romanesque capitals. The nave is supported by stout flying buttresses. Inside, the apsidal chapels are separated from the chancel by massive columns with interesting capitals. The church contains the tomb of St. Silvanus, the legendary apostle of Berry, whose relics were moved from Levroux to La Celle in the 15C.

Bruère-Allichamps. – Pop 638. A Gallo-Roman milestone was found in the town in 1757. It was erected in its present site at the junction of the N 144 and the D 92 in 1799. This point is now popularly held to mark the geographical centre of France.

The D 35 now follows the course of the picturesque Cher valley rich in meadowland.

Former Abbey of Noirlac★. – *Description p 146.*

The N 144 follows the right bank of the Cher back to St-Amand-Montrond.

Ainay-le-Vieil★; Châteaumeillant; Lignières. – *Round tour of 105 km - 65 miles – about 4 hours – local map p 162.* Michelin maps 69 fold 11 and 68 fold 20. *Leave St-Amand by ④, the D 97 which goes up the Cher valley.*

Drevant. – Pop 486. Ruins of a theatre and traces of a forum, baths and temples which were part of a Gallo-Roman rural sanctuary.

Take the N 144 through a rolling countryside affording views of the Cher valley.

Ainay-le-Vieil Castle★. – *Description p 43.*

The road winds through fields and meadows chequered by quickset hedges and after skirting Bornacq Forest enters the Arnon Valley bordered by heather clad rocks.

Culan★. – *Description p 89.*

The D 943 crosses hilly cattle rearing country.

Châteaumeillant. – *Description p 82.*

Puy-Ferrand. – The former abbey church of Puy-Ferrand, south of Le Châtelet, is a fine Romanesque building. The façade is ornamented with bays, finely carved capitals and geometrical designs.

At Le Châtelet take the D 951 to the left then the D 65 to the right.

Lignières. – *Description p 116.*

Return to St-Amand-Montrond by the D 925 which crosses the Habert Forest.

ST-ANTONIN-NOBLE-VAL

Michelin map 79 fold 19 – Pop 1 869

St-Antonin, an old city on the borders of Quercy and Rouergue, faces a vertical cliff of rocks known as the Rochers d'Anglars on the far side of the Aveyron valley. The houses with nearly flat roofs covered in round tiles rise above the right bank of the river.

So delightful was the setting of this Gallo-Roman resort, forerunner of the present town, that it was given the name of Noble-Val. An oratory founded by St. Antonin, who came to convert this part of Rouergue, was replaced in the 8C by an abbey.

The town developed rapidly during the Middle Ages as can be seen by the 13, 14 and 15C houses which were once the property of rich merchants.

■ SIGHTS *time: 1/2 hour*

Former Town Hall★. – This mansion was built in 1125 for a landowner, Archambauld, and is one of the oldest examples of civil architecture in France. In the 14C it was the consul's residence; restored last century by Viollet-le-Duc, it is now a museum.

The façade consists of two storeys. The gallery of small columns on the first floor is adorned with two pillars bearing statues of King Solomon and Adam and Eve; the second storey is divided into three sets of twin bays. The tall square tower that rises above the building is crowned with battlements.

Museum. – *Open 1 July to 15 September, 2.30 to 6pm except Mondays; 1 May to 30 June and 16 September to 31 October Saturdays and Sundays only same opening times; 5.70F.* The museum contains a collection on prehistory which is particularly rich in artifacts from the Magdalenian period. One room covers local traditions and folklore.

Old Quarter. – In front of the covered market is a strange 14C Calvary. Mediaeval houses stand in the alleys around the former town hall and in those winding down to the quays alongside the Aveyron.

EXCURSIONS

Grotte du Bosc; Upper Aveyron Valley. – *Round tour of 54 km - 34 miles – about 2 hours – local map opposite. Leave St-Antonin to the northeast by the D 75.*

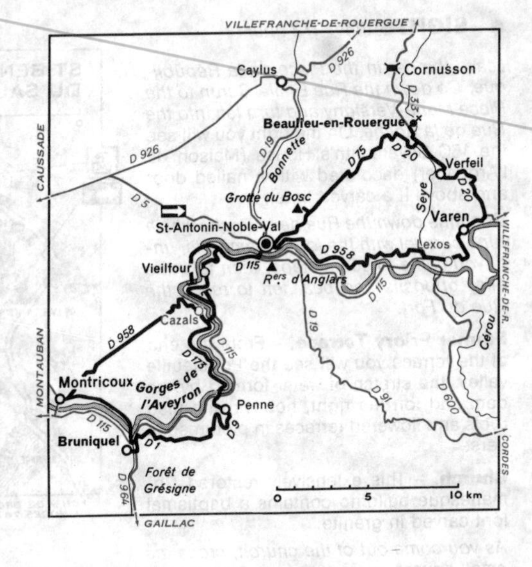

The Bosc Cave. – *Open 10am to noon and 2 to 6pm, 1 July to 31 August; afternoons only in June and September; closed 16 September to 31 May; time: 3/4 hour; 12F (including prehistoric museum).* The galleries once the bed of an underground river now dry, go back some 200 m - 220 yds beneath the plateau between the Aveyron and Bonnette valleys. Stalactites and eccentrics decorate the cave.

Continue along the D 75 then take the D 20 to the right and the D 33 to the left.

Former Abbey of Beaulieu-en-Rouergue★. – *Description p 79.*

Turn around and follow the D 33, then take the D 20 to the left.

Verfeil. – Pop 425. This small but charming bastion lies in the Seye valley. Its old houses with their flower decked façades, surround a covered market rebuilt of stone *(p 32)*. In the church, both the high altar and the 17C figure of Christ came from the former Abbey of Beaulieu.

Take the D 20 and then the D 958 to the right. The road follows the Aveyron which flows at this point along the wide valley floor, covered with meadows and crops.

Varen. – *Description p 184.*

The road passes a large cement works at the entrance to Lexos. *1 km – 1/4 mile beyond Lexos take the D 33 to the right, then bear left into a road marked "St-Antonin par le Coteau" (D 958).* The road climbs rapidly along the hillside, affording more and more glimpses of the Aveyron valley to which it returns after a winding descent. The river, outlined with a string of poplars, flows at the foot of tall cliffs barely covered with sparse vegetation. A little before St-Antonin the road and river run closely together along the narrow valley bounded by steep rocky sides.

Aveyron Gorges★. – *34 km - 21 miles – about 3 hours – local map p 163.* Leave St-Antonin by the south, cross the Aveyron and take the road on the right built along a disused railway track at the foot of tall limestone cliffs. *After 2.5 km - 2 miles turn left in the D 115 B*. This is a fine **corniche road★★** which rises rapidly. Pass through the hamlet of Vieilfour with its round tiled roofs. Shortly after passing through a tunnel there is a belvedere above a sheer drop from which there is a good view of the Aveyron enclosed by tall rock walls. Then as you descend towards the river the hamlet of Brousses comes into view.

At Cazals you cross again to the right bank of the river.

The roads begins to climb immediately and passes between vineyards, affording views of the meanders in the river Aveyron and the valley floor covered with peach and apple orchards and meadows intersected by lines of poplars.

Cross the Aveyron again to reach the old village of Penne in its pretty setting.

Penne. – *Description p 150.*

Leave Penne to the south by the D 9 which affords lovely **views★** of the village. The road drops down over the edge of the plateau before crossing this region of sparse vegetation with stunted bushes and the occasional vine. The road then descends again into the valley where the high, wooded hillsides are often strewn with rocks.

Bruniquel★. – *Description p 71.*

Follow the road built along the right bank of the Aveyron from Bruniquel to Montricoux.

Montricoux. – *Description p 71.*

Return to St-Antonin by the D 958 which runs through the Garrigue Forest, then take the D 115, a corniche road overlooking the Aveyron.

ST-BENOÎT-DU-SAULT

Michelin map 68 fold 17 – Pop 841

St-Benoît-du-Sault was built on a rocky spur above the smiling Portefeuille valley in a setting of green hills divided by small valleys and running brooks.

The village, erected on the site of the ancient Salis, fief of the lords of Brosse, also owes its renown to the Benedictine priory, founded there by the end of the 10C. Wandering through the narrow streets of the old town the visitor will find many ancient dwellings; these are all that remain of the once large walled town of the Middle Ages.

■ SIGHTS *time: 1/2 hour*

Leave the car in the Place de la République. Go down the Rue Émile-Surun to the Place Marie-Versigny and turn left into the Rue de la Roche. On the right you will see the 15C Silversmith's House (Maison de l'Argentier) decorated with a nailed door and above it a carved lintel.

Continue down the Rue de la Roche which runs parallel with the former ramparts, until you come to some steps, then take the alley opposite and bear left to reach the Rue du Fort.

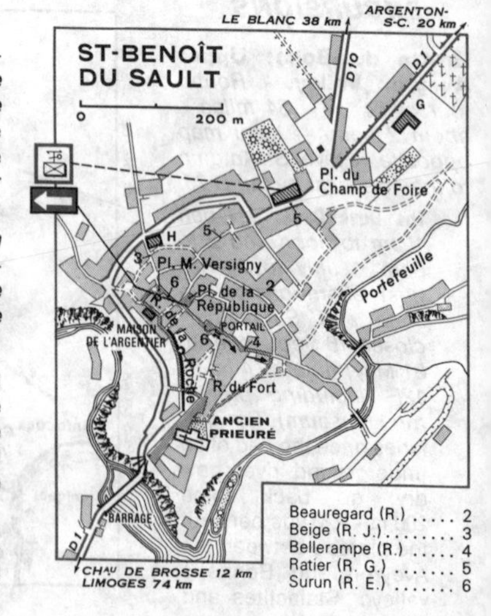

Former Priory Terrace. – From the end of the terrace you will see the Portefeuille valley, the stretch of water formed by the dam and, on the right, houses with tiled roofs and flowered terraces in picturesque tiers.

Church. – This extensively restored Romanesque building contains a baptismal font carved in granite.

As you come out of the church, cross the small square on your right to take the watch-path that goes round the old ramparts.

At the end a steep road leads off, left, to the Gateway (Portail). Go through the Gateway and you will see, on your right, a group of old houses.

Return by the Rue Émile-Surun to the Place de la République.

EXCURSION

Brosse; Château-Guillaume. – *27 km - 17 miles – about 1 1/2 hours. Leave St-Benoît-du-Sault by the D 1, going south. From the start this road gives a good view ahead.* Take the D 36 to Chaillac and then turn left into the road leading to "La Barytine" factory.

Brosse Castle. – As you walk down to the castle walls and circle them from the right, you get a view of the fortified perimeter walls perched on jagged rocks overhanging a small tributary of the Anglin. The fortress was owned successively by the lords of Brosse and Chauvigny and the Bourbon-Montpensier family. It was burnt down during the Hundred Years War by the English.

Return to Chaillac, turn left and shortly afterwards right onto the D 53.

Château-Guillaume. – This picturesque old village, whose houses are roofed with flat tiles, lies in the small valley of the Allemette. The village is dominated by the tall outline of a fortress which was an important strategic point in the Middle Ages. The fortress was altered and restored in the 19C in the manner of Coucy Castle (a masterpiece of military mediaeval architecture in the north of France).

ST-CÉRÉ ★

Michelin map 75 folds 19 and 20 – *Local map 94* – Pop 4 207 – *Facilities p 38*

The old houses of St-Céré cluster in the smiling Bave valley below the tall towers of St-Laurent. St-Céré stands at the junction of the roads from Limousin, Auvergne and Quercy, and has become a place to stay in its own right because of its pleasant **site**★ and because it is an excellent starting-point for walks and excursions in Haut-Quercy.

A Prosperous Town. – The Viscounts of Turenne, overlords of St-Céré, granted a charter giving the franchise and many advantages to the town in the 13C. It was enriched by the right to hold fairs and establish trading houses. Consuls and officials administered the town, whose defence was assured by the Castle of St-Laurent and a formidable line of ramparts. Even the Hundred Years War left the town practically unscathed. With the 16C dawned a new period of prosperity.

An Early Academician. – St-Céré had the honour to be the birthplace of Marshal **Canrobert** who won glory as a soldier in Algeria, was commander-in-chief in the Crimea and distinguished himself at St-Privat in the Franco-Prussian War of 1870.

The town can also count the poet **François Maynard** among her most famous citizens. The poet, son of a Member of Parliament, though born in Toulouse in 1582, spent many years of his life in St-Céré. While still young, he managed to obtain the post of secretary to Marguerite of Valois, at one time the wife of Henry of Navarre.

He soon became known as one of the most skilful court poets of the period. Malherbe noticed him as did also Cardinal Richelieu who honoured him by nominating him a member of the Academy which he had just founded. The story goes that Maynard, who enjoyed receiving honours but was not above receiving money, asked the cardinal for a tangible expression of the latter's confidence.

Blatantly he asked:

"But if I'm asked what you have asked me to do and what in return I've received from you 'What would you have me say?' 'Nothing' the Cardinal would dryly have replied.

The poet left Paris and came to live in St-Céré. He frequented literary circles and society and went to the fabulous receptions given at Castelnau. When he died in 1646 he was buried beneath the chancel of the Church of Ste-Spérie in St-Céré.

■ OLD TOWN

15, 16 and 17C houses give St-Céré a picturesque character all its own. Some houses still have their wooden corbelled façades and fine roofs of small brown tiles.

From Place de la République take Rue de l'Église.

Place de l'Église. – The Church of Ste-Spérie, a very old place of worship, was rebuilt in the 17-18C in the Gothic style. In the square near the chevet, **Puymule Mansion** (15C) is a turretted edifice pierced with doors and windows decorated with accolated arches.

Cross Rue de la République, a busy commercial street, to Rue du Mazel into which you bear left.

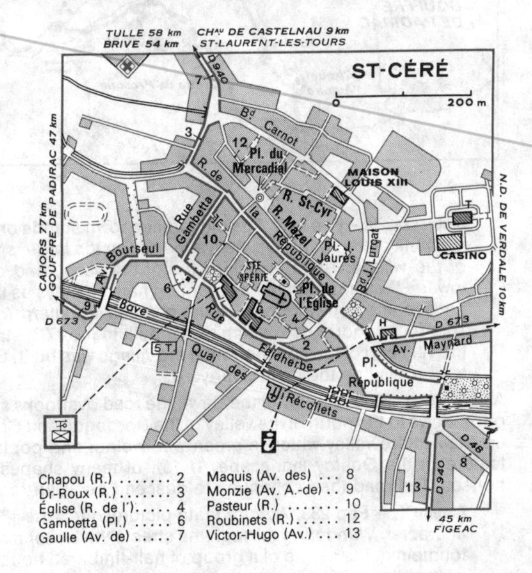

Rue du Mazel. – This street and the surrounding area form one of the most picturesque districts in the old town with old houses and fine doorways. At the corner of Rue St-Cyr, note the 15C **Ambert Mansion** with its two corbelled turrets and Renaissance doorway.

Further on the right, the narrow **Impasse Langarouste** (cul-de-sac) with a stream in the middle and paved with shingles, is overshadowed by tall corbelled houses.

Place du Mercadial. – This was the market square where fishermen brought their catch which was displayed on the *"taoulié"*, a stone slab along the 15C **house** of Jean de Séguier at the corner of Rue Pasteur. From this spot there is a lovely view of the square lined with half-timbered houses and the St-Laurent towers nearby.

The **Consuls' House** (Maison des Consuls) has an interesting Renaissance façade giving on to the Rue de l'Hôtel-de-Ville.

Rue St-Cyr. – At the beginning of the street stands a lovely mediaeval house with three corbelled façades. Further on, to the right, is the 15C **Miramon Mansion** flanked with a corner turret. The road which extends in a semi-circle and is lined with old houses, ends in Rue du Mazel.

On leaving Rue du Mazel take Boulevard Jean Lurçat to the left.

Louis XIII Mansion. – This splendid mansion has an elegant façade adorned with a balcony and is now occupied by a bank.

■ ADDITIONAL SIGHTS

Casino Gallery. – *Open 9.30am to noon and 2 to 7pm (6pm out of season); Sunday mornings, 11am to noon only; closed Tuesdays.*

In addition to temporary exhibitions, there is a large collection of **Jean Lurçat's tapestries**★ *(p 48)* on permanent display. The tapestries combine matter, form and colour and depict fabulous animals and cosmic visions.

St-Laurent Towers. – *2 km - 1 mile to the north by the D 940 and the D 48.* Perched on a steep hill which overlooks the town, the two tall mediaeval towers and perimeter wall – the residential section *(not open)* is the most recent – are a familiar local landmark.

Although the road to the right is a private road, the restriction is not strictly enforced. A track *(1 hour on foot Rtn)* skirts the ramparts and offers pleasant **views**★ of the town, the Bave and Dordogne valleys and the surrounding plateaux.

EXCURSIONS

Bave Valley★. – *Round tour of 35 km - 22 miles – about 4 hours – local map below. Leave St-Céré to the west by the D 673.* The towers of Montal Castle soon come into view on the left, rising above fields and meadows lined with poplars.

Montal Castle★★. – *Description p 138.*

The picturesque D 30 follows the course of the pleasant valley of the Bave towards the alluvial valley of the Dordogne. The D 14 rises steeply. From this road and the D 118 which you take at the hamlet of La Poujade, you get extensive **views** of the valley of the Dordogne dominated by the impressive outline of Castelnau castle.

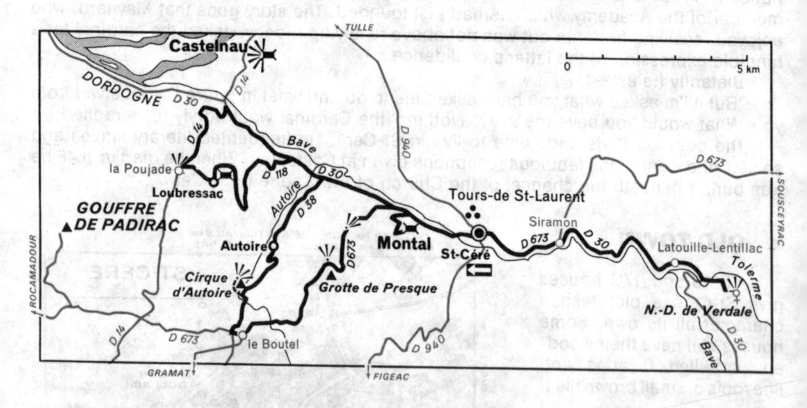

Loubressac★. – Pop 405. This old fortified town stands on a rocky spur overlooking the left bank of the river Bave. *Leave the car on the large, shaded square in the lower part of the village.* There is a fine **view** of the valley and of St-Céré with its distinctive towers. Walk through the enchanting narrow alleys as they wind between brown tiled houses and you will come to the château's postern *(not open)*.

This 15C manorhouse, which was rebuilt in the 17C, stands on a remarkable **site**★ at the very end of the spur on which the village was built. Several buildings with pointed tiled roofs line the main courtyard.

As it winds down the valley of the Bave, the road overlooks small green valleys and affords good views to the north of the valley of the Dordogne and Castelnau Castle. The D 38 goes up the Autoire valley which is green with walnut and poplar trees. Dovecotes, a typical feature of the Quercy landscape *(p 15)*, of many shapes and sizes stand beside the houses. The road then continues to descend between rocky slopes.

Autoire★. – Pop 233. Autoire in its picturesque **setting**★ is completely Quercynois in character. Wandering through the streets the visitor may see enchanting vignettes: a fountain at the centre of a group of half-timbered houses, old corbelled houses with brown tiled roofs, elegant turreted manors and mansions. From the terrace near the church there is a good view of the Limargue Mill and the amphitheatre of rocks that lies to the southwest.

The road rises above the valley between tall cliffs and comes to the floor of the amphitheatre.

The Autoire Amphitheatre★ (Cirque d'Autoire). – Leave the car in a parking area and take, on the right of the road, the path that overlooks the river Autoire which here forms a series of waterfalls (belvedere).
Cross the little bridge and go up the steep stony path cut in the rocks. Very soon you get a wonderful **view**★★ of the amphitheatre, the valley and the village of Autoire.

The picturesque D 673 crosses the Autoire after Le Boutel and descends the valley of the Bave affording wide views to the north of the valley of the Dordogne.

Presque Cave★ (Grotte de Presque). – *Guided tours 1 July to 31 August, 9am to noon and 2 to 7pm (6pm out of season); closed first Sunday in October to Palm Sunday; time: 1/2 hour; 10F.*
The cave consists of a series of chambers and galleries that go back 350 m - 380 yds into the rocks. Concretions, especially stalagmite piles in curious shapes and deposits along the walls with a thousand facets, have evolved in the Drapery Chamber, the High Chamber, the Chamber of the Great Basin and the Red Marble Hall. Slender columns of astonishing whiteness stand at the entrance to the Hall of Wonder.

Suddenly you catch sight of the St-Laurent towers overlooking St-Céré.

Chapel of Notre-Dame de Verdale. – *10 km - 6 miles plus 1 hour Rtn on foot – local map p 166. Leave the St-Céré to the east by the D 673.* The road passes wooded hills and meadows as it goes up the valley of the Bave. *Beyond Latouille a narrow road branches off to the left from the D 30; follow this to a hamlet where you will leave the car.* Walk up a path which runs beside the Tolerme, where it falls in cascades over the rocks. You will cross the stream twice on rough wooden bridges before the path starts to climb steeply between wooded slopes and brings you finally to the pilgrimage Chapel of Our Lady of Verdale which stands perched on a rocky crag.

From the crag there is a wide **view**★ of the Tolerme Gorges and the chesnut covered hills.

ST-CIRQ-LAPOPIE ★★

Michelin map 79 fold 9 – *Local maps pp 108 and 125* – Pop 179

St-Cirq-Lapopie (pronounced St-Sear) faces a semicircle of cliffs and itself stands perched on a rocky escarpment that drops vertically to the left bank of the Lot. This remarkable **setting**★★ is in the most picturesque part of the valley.

HISTORICAL NOTES

A Contested Stronghold. – It seems probable that men have been tempted to occupy this rock commanding the valley since Gallo-Roman times. The present name of the site commemorates the martyrdom of the young St. Cyr, killed with his mother in Asia Minor in the reign of Diocletian; his relics were brought back, it is said, by St. Amadour *(p 158)*. The La Popies, local lords in the Middle Ages, gave their name to the castle built on the cliff and, by extension, to the village that grew up at its foot.

The history of the fortress is a long series of sieges. In the struggle against Pepin the Short in the 8C, Waïfre, Duke of Aquitaine, placed his last hopes in this bastion. In 1198 Richard Lionheart tried in vain to seize the stronghold.

During the Hundred Years War, the English fought bitterly to take St-Cirq from the garrison commanded by the Lord of Cardaillac who remained loyal to the King of France. In 1471, Louis XI ordered the castle to be demolished but the ruins were still of sufficient strategic importance for the Huguenots to fight for them during the Wars of Religion. In 1580, Henry of Navarre, the future Henry IV ordered such walls of the valiant fortress as were still standing, to be knocked down.

The Craft that Died. – St-Cirq-Lapopie had a strong guild of wood-turners dating back to the Middle Ages. Even last century there were a considerable number of craftsmen still to be seen working their primitive lathes; their industry added a picturesque note to the old-fashioned village alleyways. Two craftsmen perpetuate the craft, producing wooden pegs (spigots or faucets) to stop the vent-holes of barrels, casks or taps for the wine industry.

■ SIGHTS *time: 1 hour*

It is a perennial pleasure to wander along narrow, steeply sloping streets lined with houses with lovely brown tiled roofs. The corbelled façades and exposed beams of some of the houses are further ornamented with Gothic windows, or bays with mullioned windows, in the Renaissance manner. Most of the houses have been diligently restored by artists, particularly painters and craftsmen who have been attracted by the beauty of St-Cirq-Lapopie and the valley of the Lot.

Church. – This 15C building stands on a rock terrace overlooking the Lot. A squat belfry-tower, flanked by a round turret, stands at the front end.

Inside the main body of the church has ogive vaulting and contains several Baroque statues.

There is a good view from the terrace to the right of the church.

La Gardette Museum (Musée La Gardette). – *Open 1 April to 15 October, 10.30am to noon and 2.30 to 6pm (7pm Sundays and holidays); closed Tuesdays out of season; 3F. Apply to Mme Lagarrigue or Mme Bizet in St-Cirq.*

Installed in the Maison Rignault, the museum contains 14 and 15C furniture and statues, lacquer work from China, frescoes dating from the Ming period and small African statues and masks.

La Popie. – You can reach the castle ruins and the highest part of the cliffs by taking a path that starts on the right of the town hall. From the cliff top *(telescope)* on which once stood the keep of La Popie Fortress, you get a remarkable **view**★★ right over the village of St-Cirq with the church clinging to the cliff-face, a bend of the river Lot encircling a chequerboard of arable fields and meadows outlined with poplars, and to the north, of the wooded foothills that border the Gramat Causse.

Le Bancourel. – *Follow the D 40 towards Bouziès for 300 m - 330 yds to reach this rock promontory overlooking the Lot.* A lay-by esplanade *(car park)* has been built where the D 8 branches off to the left from the tourist road that has been cut *corniche*-fashion in the cliff *(p 125)*. There is a **view**★ from Le Bancourel of the valley of the Lot and St-Cirq, with the rock of La Popie rising up out of the village.

ST-CYPRIEN

Michelin map 75 fold 16 – *Local map p 97* – Pop 1 730 – *Facilities p 38*

St-Cyprien clings to the side of a hill near the right bank of the Dordogne, in a setting of hills and woodlands characteristic of the Périgord Noir. It is dominated by the massive outline of its church around which cluster old houses.

Church. – The church, part of an abbey for Augustinian canons, built in the 12C, was restored in the Gothic period. Its size is impressive; it still has a Romanesque belfry-keep. Inside, the main body of the church, which is enormous, has ogive vaulting.

EXCURSIONS

Berbiguières. – Pop 185. *5 km - 3 miles to the south by the D 48 and then the D 50 to the left.* The village is dominated by a 17C château with ramparts flanked by watchtowers.

ST-GAULTIER

Michelin map 68 fold 17 – Pop 2 072

St-Gaultier is pleasantly situated on a hill overlooking the right bank of the Creuse. The town stands out from the background of wooded slopes where the scattered limestone outcrops have brought about the building of many lime-kilns. From the left bank west of Thenay, you get a good view of St-Gaultier, its roofs rising in tiers above the river, which is spanned by a fine stone bridge.

Church. – This was formerly the church of the neighbouring priory, and is now a college. It was built in the 12C and has a plain doorway adorned only with wide covings and small surrounding columns. Above the transept crossing rises a square tower with two tiers of blind arcades. Inside, the chancel which ends in an oven-vaulted apse, is ornamented with Romanesque capitals carved in archaic style.

A steep path goes down beside the old priory to the river bank where there is a pleasant view of the valley of the Creuse and the town's surroundings.

EXCURSION

Romefort Castle. – *15 km - 9 miles to the west by the N 151 and the D 44 to the left – local map p 68.* The castle *(not open to the public)* can be viewed from a bridge over the Creuse, in its picturesque setting on a rock shelf overlooking the left bank of the river.

The main 14C building is flanked by two towers and a 12C square keep. Both the castle and the keep have been restored. The triple perimeter wall is spiked by ruined round towers.

ST-GENOU

Michelin map 68 fold 7 – Pop 1 108

St-Genou has an abbey church; and three factories producing porcelain.

Church of St-Genou. – *Open during the week only.* This formerly belonged to a Benedictine abbey which was suppressed in 1772. Since the nave was destroyed in 1676 only the transept and the chancel remain and they are in the Romanesque Berry style. A series of blind arcades runs round the apse and the apsidal chapel is reinforced by column-buttresses, surmounted by capitals decorated with acanthus leaves.

Inside, beyond the triumphal arch, the vast chancel ends in an oven vaulted apse. The monumental columns have interesting historiated capitals showing Biblical scenes such as Daniel in the Den of Lions or episodes from the life of St. Genou, who was the apostle of the region in the 3C. St. Genou's tomb is placed under the high altar.

Lantern to the Dead (Lanterne des morts). – On a hillside above the hamlet of Estrées, standing isolated in a roadside field, is a 12C lantern to the dead. In the shape of a column, the lighted lantern on top symbolises everlasting life for the departed.

From this point which was at the intersection of two Roman roads there is a fine **view** of the Indre valley and Palluau-sur-Indre *(p 148)*.

You will find a selection of touring programmes on pp 34-36.

Plan your route with the help of the map of principal sights on pp 4-7.

ST-JEAN-DE-CÔLE ★

Michelin map 75 north of fold 6 – Pop 343

A strange church and a castle stand in a village, whose old houses and Gothic bridge give it an antique charm. All combine to produce a delightful setting where the golden stones tone in with the brown of the small roof tiles.

An old, narrow humpbacked bridge with cutwaters, spans the Côle, a tributary of the Dronne.

■ SIGHTS *time: 3/4 hour*

Church. – This former priory chapel was begun in the 11C; it is outstanding for the curious shape of the belfry pierced by windows, the nave which is high in proportion to its length, the capitals which divide the south chapel and the chancel and the sculpture found at roof level. The old covered markets are built onto the chevet.

Inside note the 17C woodwork in the chancel. The nave is covered by a wooden ceiling replacing the collapsed dome, the pendentives of which may still be seen; on the south side a chapel with oven vaulting, contains in a niche the tomb of a recumbent figure representing an abbot.

Marthonie Castle (Château de la Marthonie). – *Guided tours 1 July to 31 August, 10 to 11.30am and 2 to 6.30pm.*

A gallery houses a small collection of old publicity posters. In the guard room there is a demonstration of the production of hand-made paper. In three other rooms books and engravings, made in the same way, are on display.

All that remains of the 12C castle is the tower and its foundations (on the square); several mullioned windows are preserved from the 15 and 16C when the castle was rebuilt. The arcaded gallery and the staircase with straight ramps and eccentric or basket-handled arches, inside, date from the 17C.

Museum. – *Closed for restoration.*

In the Rue Fond-du-Bourg with its old half-timbered houses and overhanging porch roofs, one of the houses has been restored and is now a museum. Several rooms contain local arts and crafts: old tools and instruments belonging to the farmer, blacksmith, vine grower... as well as country-style furniture and a fortune teller's apparatus.

EXCURSIONS

Puyguilhem★; Grottes de Villars★. – *14 km - 9 miles. Leave St-Jean-de-Côle to the west by the D 98. In Villars take the road leading to Puyguilhem Château.*

Puyguilhem Château★. – *Description p 156.*

Return to Villars then turn left onto the D 82. After 3 km - 2 miles take the road to the right leading to the Villars Caves.

Villars Caves★. – *Guided tours 15 June to 15 September, 10 to 11.30am and 2 to 6.30pm; time: 1/2 hour; 11F.*

A winding corridor leads to chambers ornamented with beautiful concretions among which you will see yellow ochre draperies and particularly fine white stalactites hanging from the ceiling. The concretions in the last galleries to be passed through are formed from almost pure and very brilliant calcite and are amazingly white. Some of the chamber walls are decorated with prehistoric paintings done with manganese oxide and go back to Aurignacian times *(pp 21-24)*. The calcite coating covering some of the paintings proves their authenticity.

Thiviers. – Pop 4 215. *7.5 km - 4 miles to the east by the D 707.* This small busy town is famous throughout the region for its markets and fairs (*foies gras*, poultry and truffles). Vaucocour Château, which is Renaissance-Gothic in style and has been frequently restored, looks down from its towers and turrets on the valley of the Isle.

ST-JUNIEN

Michelin map 72 fold 6 – *Local map p 122* – Pop 11 194 – *Facilities p 38*
See town plan in Michelin Red Guide France.

St-Junien is a busy town, known for its paper-mills, taweries (leather dressing works) and particularly its glove factories. The collegiate church is Romanesque-Limousin in style.

The «Ostensions» of St. Junien. – A soldier named Junien went into retreat in a forest beside the Vienne early in the 6C. Renown of his piety spread throughout Limousin and a bishop of Limoges ordered a sanctuary to be built over his tomb. The monastery, later founded in the same place, formed the nucleus of the town that still bears his name.

Ostensions (p 37) commemorate, every seven years, the memory of St. Junien. When the ceremony is held the relics are shown and a picturesque spectacle unfolds: rich costumes are brought out, the main street is decorated with foliage and caged birds as a reminder of the forest in which the saint lived. Tableaux and groups of statues depict the principal events in the saint's life.

The Development of Glove-making. – St-Junien lies in the centre of a livestock rearing region and therefore had on hand the necessary raw materials – kid and lambskin. In addition the waters of the Vienne possess exceptional properties for tanning.

Glove-making began here in the Middle Ages and by the 15C had made the town famous. It is even said that Louis XI, on his return from Bayonne, was received in great style at St-Junien and permitted the master-glovers to present him with pairs of gloves.

Expansion of the industry has brought about many changes, but mechanisation is excluded as handwork alone can ensure a good finish. Today, 500 workers in eighteen workshops produce over 500 000 pairs of gloves each year.

■ SIGHTS *time: 1/2 hour*

Collegiate Church of St. Junien★ (Collégiale St-Junien). – The nave and transept of this remarkable Romanesque-Limousin building are late 11C; the main part of the building was completed when the façade was added at the end of the 12C; the plain, square chevet is 13C. The central bell-tower was rebuilt after it had fallen down in 1922.

The west doorway is divided into two bays and is framed by small columns. It is surmounted by a massive belfry-porch two storeys high, flanked by two stone bellturrets.

St. Junien's tomb★, a masterpiece of 12C Limousin sculpture, stands behind the high altar. Two-thirds of the tomb is of limestone adorned with sculpture; the remainder is only a plaster covering added last century when the high altar was moved and no longer formed part of the sarcophagus. On the east side, Christ is shown in glory surrounded by the symbols of the Evangelists; medallions depict the theological and moral virtues. On the north face the Virgin, within a glory, holds the Infant Jesus; seated on one side are the figures of twelve Old Men of the Apocalypse. On the opposite side the other twelve Old Men *(see illustration p 29)* are portrayed together with a medallion of the Holy Lamb. Against the pillars stands an interesting collection of 14, 15 and 16C multicoloured statues.

Chapel of Notre-Dame du Pont. – Standing on the right bank of the river Vienne beside a 13C bridge equipped with cutwaters is the elegant Chapel of Our Lady of the Bridge. There is a legend that the statue of the Virgin which now stands in the apse was originally found by the bridge on the river bank; the statue was immediately taken in solemn procession to the collegiate church, but the next day was found, once more, on the river bank. The people of St-Junien erected a chapel to the Virgin on the spot where the statue was found. The present church was built in the 15C on the site of the earlier sanctuary; it was enlarged and completed thanks to Louis XI, who came there twice on pilgrimage.

The overall architectural effect is of graceful flamboyance; a sculptured balustrade lines the base of the roof. The nave and two aisles of equal height are supported by elegant octagonal pillars; the vaulting is ornamented with finely carved keystones.

EXCURSION

Site Corot; Rochebrune. – *13 km - 8 miles. Take the V 8 out of the town to the northwest, following the left bank of the Glane. Leave the car opposite a factory.*

Corot's View (Site Corot). – *1/4 hour Rtn on foot.* Walk for a few minutes beside the river to reach the setting of the stream, flowing past rocks and trees, which inspired Corot and numerous other painters.

Return to the N 141 and turn right. At Rouillac take the D 948 to the right.

Rochebrune Château. – *Guided tours from Palm Sunday to 11 November 2 to 6pm; also 10am to noon, 1 July to 15 September; time: 1/2 hour; 10F.*

In the 16C the château became the property of Marshal Blaise de Montluc, who, during the Wars of Religion, distinguished himself by his implacable pursuit of the Protestants.

After admiring the outbuildings with their round tiled roofs, you cross the moat and enter the court of honour. Three main buildings link the four massive towers built in the 11 and 13C. Above the doors may be seen the arms of Marshal Blaise de Montluc. The apartments are furnished in the Empire and Renaissance style and contain many souvenirs of the Napoleonic period.

ST-LÉONARD-DE-NOBLAT★

Michelin map 72 north of fold 18 – *Local map p 122* – Pop 5 318 – *Facilities p 38*

St-Léonard-de-Noblat stands perched on a hill overlooking a vast depression crossed by the valleys of the Vienne, the Maulde and the Taurion. The church, which was once a collegiate church, is interesting as its belfry is an outstanding example of Romanesque architecture in the Limousin style. The town was the birthplace of the chemist and physicist, Gay-Lussac.

A Hermit. – The town was named after the hermit **Leonard,** godson of Clovis, who early in the 6C chose Pauvain Forest, which has since disappeared, as his place of retreat. He built a rustic sanctuary. His piety and the many miracles he performed made him one of the most popular saints in Limousin. A village was built alongside the retreat and took the name noblat (derived from *nobiliacum*) meaning noble site. His help was invoked in protecting horses and even more in the deliverance of prisoners. To remind us that St. Leonard was the patron saint of prisoners it is the tradition in St-Léonard, in the month of November *(p 37)* to celebrate the *Quintaine.* A small wooden fortress (representing a prison) or *Quintaine* is trampled down by riders on horseback armed with clubs.

The present town has spread far beyond its original site. Agriculture and the rearing of Limousin cattle *(p 18)* contribute largely to the town's prosperity. Industry also thrives with potteries, tanneries, shoe and plastics factories, paper-mills and timber yards.

A Great Scholar. – Joseph-Louis **Gay-Lussac** was born in St-Léonard in 1778 (died 1850). He distinguished himself in physics and chemistry: he discovered the law of expansion of gases and made ascents in a balloon to examine whether the earth's magnetic attraction decreased as the altitude increased. Later he devised the law of gaseous combination. In 1809 he demonstrated that chlorine was an element and discovered boron and fluoboric acid.

■ SIGHTS *time: 1/2 hour*

Church★. – This 12C church (restored) remains a fine specimen of Romanesque architecture. The side walls and the chapel of the Holy Sepulchre go back to the 11C. It is said that Richard Lionheart contributed to the construction of the church on his release from prison in Austria.

Exterior. – The **belfry**★★ *(illustration p 28)*, built above a porch which is open on two sides and embellished with remarkable capitals, adjoins the third bay of the nave. The bell-tower consists of four storeys built square, surmounted by two recessed storeys which are octagonal in shape. The transition from the square plan to the octagonal is managed by devising a sharply pointed gable for each of the four walls of the top quadrilateral. Each tier is adorned by beautiful blind arcades. The final touch of elegance is given by the stone spire which was constructed in the 12C.

The baptistry, between the belfry and the transept, now restored to its original appearance, was probably modelled on that of the Holy Sepulchre in Jerusalem.

The church's west façade, built in the 13C, has a wide door flanked by small columns decorated with finely carved crotcheted capitals supporting the covings. The east end rises harmoniously in tiers and the chapels are roofed with rounded tiles.

Interior. – There were different building stages *(model and resumé at the entrance)*. The powerful nave has cradle vaulting, the transept crossing is roofed with a high dome placed atop a drum pierced by 8 windows and resting on pendentives and smaller and less ornate domes rise above the end of each transept arm. The south transept contains the tomb of St. Leonard; his relics are kept in a small, lead, 11C reliquary casket in a nearby glass case. The chancel is wider than the nave and is cunningly constructed: each arch has been divided down its centre by a pillar or column supporting a suspension arch which is incorporated in the construction. The 15C oak stalls are decorated with satirical motifs. The ambulatory has asymmetrical groined vaulting resting on elegant small columns which stand between the apsidal chapels.

Old Houses. – There are several buildings of the 13, 15 and 16C still to be seen in the area round the church. A 13C house in the Place de la Collégiale, possesses a huge tiers-point window and above that two floors with twinned windows. In the Rue Gay-Lussac, No 18, built in the 16C, is complete with its triangular tympanum above the door and corbelled corner turret. There is a good **view** of this house and of the church tower from the Place de la République nearby.

EXCURSION

The Maulde Valley. – *Tour of 55 km - 34 miles – about 1 1/2 hours. Leave St-Léonard by the road to Limoges, then take on the left the D 39*^{A} *following the river Vienne.* Turn left *(road signposted "Circuits monts et barrages")*, at the confluence of the Vienne and the Maulde, which is dominated by the château de Muraud, perched on a promontory.

The road follows the Maulde valley traversing in this section a rocky wooded gorge. The small rushing river has been transformed by the E.D.F. (Electricité de France) into a great fluvial staircase formed by a series of eight dams *(barrages)*, controlled from one centre.

Artige Dam. – This the last dam of the series, serves to regulate the flow of water coming from the other barrages upstream. The road overlooks the dam and affords a fine view of the valley and the ruins of the former Priory of Artige.

Former Priory of Artige (Ancien Prieuré de l'Artige). – *Not open to the public.* A narrow road opposite the dam to the left leads to the entrance of the Priory. Founded in the 12C and secularised shortly before the Revolution, part of it was subsequently left to fall into ruin. From the road you can see the vast buildings with their round tiled roofs, the arcades between the chapterhouse and the cloisters, and the remains of emblazoned doors which create a romantic scene.

The road winds through wooded country before crossing the wooded farmland plateau.

Turn right on joining the D 14.

After crossing the reservoir, behind the Villejoubert Dam the road rises to Bujaleuf affording fine views on the left of the stretch of water retained by the Langleret Dam.

Bugaleuf. – Pop 1 079. Bear left to reach the bridge spanning the reservoir from which you can enjoy a good **view**★ of the two shores of the lake forming the recreation centre.

On leaving Bugaleuf, the D 16 descends into the valley affording lovely views of the stretches of water and the mountains on the horizon.

Fleix Dam. – Set in a fine wooded site this slim harmonious construction (50 m - 164 ft long and 16 m - 53 ft high) is supported by vertical buttresses.

The D 16 leads to the Martineix bridge – just before this take the narrow road to the right.

Martineix Dam. – A similar construction to the previous one, this dam stands in a wild but picturesque site.

Return to the D16 and turn left at the crossroads before going left again in the direction of Lafaux and then towards Artigeas.

After Artigeas the *corniche*-style road affords fine glimpses over the valley and the surrounding hills.

The Mont-Larron Power Station and Dam. – This stark looking building is the control centre for the series of dams. To the right of it a path, tarred to begin with, leads to the foot of the massive dam which is of the vaulted type. A path to the right climbs to the crest of the dam which is 183 m - 600 ft long.

Turn about and go right to join the D 5^{A1} *(in the direction of St-Moreil)* which skirts the wooded slopes of Mont Larron (altitude 624 m - 2 047 ft).

Take the D 5 to the left and then the D 13 which leads back to St-Léonard.

ST-MARCEL

Michelin map 68 folds 17 and 18 – *Local map p 88* – Pop 1 683

The old town of St-Marcel stands on a hill overlooking the right bank of the Creuse, on the site of the Gallo-Roman town of Argentomagus – forerunner of the present Argenton.

An archaeological dig *(not open to the public)* is being carried out on the site and in the surrounding area and a large number of items have been excavated. Some of these are now part of the collections of the local museum.

■ SIGHTS *time: 1/2 hour*

Church★. – The church of the former Priory of St-Marcel, which depended on the Abbey of St-Gildas in Châteauroux, was begun in the 12C by the Benedictines and only completed in the 15C.

The massive 14C bell tower, transposed to the north side of the nave, is covered with shingles and is crowned by a spire. The 12C chevet is attractive.

Inside the church is roofed with ogive vaulting whereas the Romanesque apse and apsidal chapels have oven vaultings; there is a double transept. The chancel is ornamented with 16C stalls, since restored. At the end of the nave, to the left above the door, a 15C Fresco of Our Lady shows St. Louis presenting a *protégé* to the Virgin who holds the Infant Jesus in her arms.

Treasure and Crypt. – *To visit apply to the priest in the presbytery, near the town hall.*

The treasure contains a 15C shrine of wood carved to depict the martyrdom of St. Marcellinus and St. Anastasius, another shrine made in the 13C of gilded copper and decorated with Limoges enamel and two other reliquaries: one of the arm of St. Marcellinus and the other (14C) of his bust.

The crypt extends beneath the apse and the south transept; it contains a few sculptured fragments from the tomb of St. Marcellinus.

Museum. – *Open 15 June to 15 September, 10am to noon and 2.30 to 6 pm, the rest of the year on Sundays and holidays only, same opening times.*

In the former priory, not far from the church, one gallery displays prehistoric artefacts from excavations in the region: bones, tools, arrowheads and engraved reindeer horns.

The other room is devoted to the Gallo-Roman period: a large ceramic collection classified in chronological order, coins, coffers and funeral urns, jewellery and sculpture. Among the **statuettes** note the Mother-Goddess (group) and a bronze votive offering depicting the god Mercury.

ST-MAURIN

Michelin map 79 fold 16 – Pop 433

The terraced houses roofed with round tiles cluster at the foot of the towers in the old village of St-Maurin, set in a pleasant, hilly region near the rich alluvial valley of the Garonne. A large square tower with battlements flanked by a turret now serves as the town hall; another square tower with two tiers of blind arcades is the sole reminder that the village once contained a Romanesque church which was part of a Cluniac abbey.

Church. – The present Gothic style church, has a porch tower flanked by buttresses and a bell-turret. It was restored in the early 17C and contains historiated capitals and a painted altarpiece in Cordova leather (Adoration of the Kings).

Old houses and an old covered market complete the picture of this original village.

EXCURSIONS

Castelsagrat. – Pop 483. *7 km - 4 miles to the southeast by the D 16 and then to the left by the D 127 and D 28.*

This former *bastide (p 32)* was founded in 1270 and still retains parts of its original plan. An interesting architectural group is formed by the arcades and houses on all four sides of the square, in the centre of which stands an old well. The oldest houses, some of which are corbelled, have attractive round tiled roofs.

The 14C **church** is built of fine grey stone with a plain façade and a Gothic nave. The chancel which ends in a flat chevet, is adorned with a huge 17C retable of carved and gilded wood.

Puymirol. – Pop 794. *10 km - 6 miles to the southwest by the D 16.*

From this *bastide (p 32)*, founded on a hill overlooking the Séoune valley in the 11C and still preserving a few old timbered houses, you get a view of the fertile plains of Agenais.

The church, which stands at one corner of the large arcaded square, has a deep 13C porch with multiple covings.

Beauville-Lacour. – *Round tour of 32 km - 20 miles. Leave by the picturesque D 16 to the north, after 8 km - 5 miles take the D 43 to the left.*

Beauville. – Pop 545. The village crowns a spur planted with vines and orchards. The arcaded street is lined with stone and wooden houses alternately. On the tip of the spur stands a small Renaissance chateau with a machicolated tower.

Go down by the D 402 which in the early stages offers views of the Petite Séoune valley and the Quercy hills. The D 7 to the right leads to Lacour.

Lacour. – Pop 180. This picturesque Quercy village, perched on the top of a hill has an interesting Romanesque church. A massive square belfry above the transept crossing accentuates the disproportion between the short nave and the chancel which ends in a flat chevet whose outer walls are supported by solid buttresses.

Go back to the D 7 and return to St-Maurin via Bourg-de-Visa.

ST-ROBERT

Michelin map 75 fold 7 – 5 km - 3 miles northwest of Ayen – *Local map p 143* – Pop 371

St-Robert is pleasantly situated amid hills facing a landscape typical of Dordogne, set with poplars and walnut trees. From the terrace of the town hall *(mairie)* there is a good view of the church chevet and of the surrounding countryside.

Church. – Of the 12C building only the transept, supporting an octagonal tower at the crossing, and the well-proportioned chancel remain. The turret and square tower which flank the chevet are evidence of the defences added to the building in the 14C.

The chancel is lit by a clerestory and is divided from the ambulatory by six columns topped by interesting capitals: some are historiated, others, attached to the ambulatory wall, were carved in a more archaic manner. On the left, as you enter the chancel, stands an unusual figure of Christ in wood (13C) from the Spanish school.

ST-YRIEIX-LA-PERCHE

Michelin map 72 fold 17 – Pop 8 037
See town plan in the current Michelin Red Guide France.

St-Yrieix (pronounced St-Irieh) stands at the centre of a rich stock rearing region and owes a large part of its prosperity to its regional cattle market; but the trades of shoe-making, chinaware and printing have also maintained a stout reputation in the town.

Darnet and Kaolin. – Limoges owes its position as china capital of France to St-Yrieix where kaolin deposits were discovered in the 18C. Kaolin already known in China in the 17C, was named after a hill called Kao-ling. It was first used in Europe since 1710, in great secrecy, by the Meissen factory near Dresden. Experiments on this pure white clay had been conducted by manufacturers of the translucent soft-paste porcelain *(p 118)*. Searches were being made all over southwest France, when, quite by chance, a surgeon by the name of Darnet who lived in St-Yrieix, came in touch with a chemist who was taking samples of clay and analysing them for the manufacturers. Darnet showed the chemist an earth used by his wife when doing her washing. Analysis showed this to be pure kaolin. In 1771 Darnet was charged by the king to supervise the mining of the kaolin. Thanks to Turgot, the General Intendant of Limousin, development was encouraged and St-Yrieix became the source of kaolin for Limoges and the whole region.

■ SIGHTS *time: 1 1/4 hours*

The Monastery Collegiate Church★ (Collégiale du Moûtier). – Built on the site of an abbey founded in the 6C by a hermit called Aredius or Yrieix, this collegiate church dating from the 12 and 13C was used by a chapter of canons who were dependants of the Abbey of St-Martin in Tours.

The church has the air of a fortress with its massive belfry-porch and stout buttresses capped with crenellations. The south door, however, is ornamented with fine covings and is surmonted by a Christ in Majesty dating from the 12C set in delicate blind arcades.

The nave has ogive vaulting and is very wide but the length is limited to two bays. A huge transept is followed by a long chancel. The walls are decorated with elegant blind arcades. A gallery which circles the nave, transepts and chancel is supported by modillions ornamented with carved heads, some of which are very beautiful. In the chancel the gallery is bordered by a fine wooden rail.

Treasure. – *Provisionally removed for restoration.* It includes the reliquary head of St-Yrieix made of wood plated with chased silver, the beard and eyebrows are picked out in gold. The bust dates from the 15C while the necklace is probably 18C. There are also a small 13C reliquary of enamelled gilt copper, adorned with 20 medallions showing angels with outstretched wings, a Eucharistic dove in gilded copper, with wings which open to reveal the Host, and several Limousin shrines in gilded wood dating from the 17 and 18C.

Plô Tower (Tour du Plô). – Near the collegiate church stands this 13C keep, decorated with twinned windows, which once formed part of the monastery's fortified precincts.

Porcelain Museum. – *Open 8am to noon and 2 to 6pm; closed Sundays, Mondays and holidays. Access by ①, the road to Limoges; after 2 km – 1 mile turn left towards the pond.*

There is a rich collection dating from the 18C to the present day. Next to the soft paste porcelain from Vincennes, Arras and Strasbourg, are fine specimens in soft and hard paste from the Count of Artois' factory. Presented in a glass case are items from Germany and England and two other cases display French ceramics of the 19C, mainly from Limoges. The absence of local production may seem surprising but although St-Yrieix did and still does manufacture porcelain, it is decorated at other factories.

EXCURSION

Le Chalard; Jumilhac-le-Grand. – *Round tour of 37 km - 23 miles – about 1 hour. Leave St-Yrieix to the northeast and follow the D 901.*

Le Chalard. – Pop 235. From the hillock on which the village church stands, there is a view characteristic of the smiling Limousin countryside.

The harsh outline of this Romanesque building supported by its many buttresses, is dominated by a massive square belfry. It was never completed and consists only of the chancel and one transept which were consecrated in 1100. During the Hundred Years War the English fortified the church. There is a good overall view of the chevet from the churchyard which contains many old tombs. The chancel is surrounded by beautiful Romanesque blind arcades and has roughly hewn granite capitals in the form of grimacing faces.

In the south arm of the transept a 15C historiated travelling chest exhibits the bust and reliquary containing the skull of St. Geoffrey, founder of the priory.

Continue along the local road through the hilly landscape.

Ladignac-le-Long. – Pop 1 245. The village has a Romanesque church with an octagonal belfry. The doorway is adorned with multilobed covings. The chevet is flanked at each corner by columns ornamented with historiated capitals supporting trilobar arches.

Take the D 11 to Jumilhac-le-Grand. As you approach this town, the picturesque road wends through the woods and enters the narrow valley of the Isle.

Jumilhac-le-Grand. – *Description p 113.*

The D 78 and the D 18 lead back to St-Yrieix-la-Perche.

SALIGNAC-EYVIGNES

Michelin map 75 folds 17 and 18 – *Local map p 186* – Pop 1 035

Not far from the valley of the Dordogne stands the impressive Castle of Salignac, built on a rock which stands out from the hillside on which the village is also perched.

Castle. – *Guided tours in season, 10am to noon and 2 to 7pm; Sundays, 10am to noon only; closed Tuesdays; time: 1/2 hour; 7F.*

There is a good overall view from the D 60, east of the village, of this mediaeval fortress which still belongs to the family from which came the Archbishop of Cambrai, François de Salignac de la Mothe-Fénelon *(p 76).*

The castle which was built between the 12 and 17C, is still encircled by ramparts. Mullioned windows lighten the façades of the main building, which is flanked by round and square towers. The whole building is enhanced by the warm colour of the stone and the lovely stone roofs.

Go up a Renaissance spiral staircase to visit several rooms with interesting furnishings mainly in the Renaissance and Louis XIII styles.

EXCURSION

St-Crépin-et-Carlucet. – Pop 310. *5 km - 3 miles to the southwest. Leave Salignac-Eyvignes by the D 60 and at Poujol take the D 56 to the left. Soon afterwards turn left again to St-Crépin.* This Périgord Noir village has a fine setting. Near the church stands the Cipières manorhouse, with its hexagonal tower and fine stone roofs.

SARLAT ★★

Michelin map 75 fold 17 – *Local maps pp 96, 97 and 186* – Pop 10 627 – *Facilities p 38*

Sarlat, capital of Périgord Noir (Black Périgord), with its many ancient buildings, gives the atmosphere and appearance of another age. The charm of this attractive city has been enhanced since 1964 when a plan was accepted for the safeguard and restoration of old Sarlat. Sarlat evokes the past, when it was the home of merchants, clerks, scholars and law students.

In 1837 a new road, the Rue de la République, was cut straight through the middle of the old quarter and it has since been known locally as the "Traverse". Much of the charm of the town is due to the building materials used: yellow ochre building stone, white limestone roof tiles or thick grey slates from the Corrèze.

The Completely Faithful Friend. – **Étienne de La Boétie,** who was born in Sarlat in 1530 in a house that can still be seen, became famous on many counts. He proved himself to be a brillant magistrate in the Bordeaux Parliament and an impassioned writer – he was only eighteen, when he wrote the compelling appeal for liberty, *Discourse on Voluntary Subjection* or *Contr'un – Against One,* which inspired Jean-Jacques Rousseau when he came to write the *Social Contract.* He also translated Greek authors and was a sensitive poet in his own right. He formed a friendship with **Michel de Montaigne** that was to last until he died and which has been immortalised by posterity. Montaigne was at La Boétie's bedside when the young man died all too early in 1563; thinking of his friend, Montaigne wrote his famous *Essay on Friendship* in which he propounded the maxim: "If I am pressed to explain why I was fond of him, I feel I can only reply: because he was himself and I am myself..."

■ OLD SARLAT★★ *time: 1 1/2 hours*

Start from the Place du Peyrou. It is bordered by La Boétie's House, the Cathedral and the former Episcopal Palace (extensively restored) which has retained its Renaissance loggia beneath the roof.

La Boétie's House★ (Maison de La Boétie). – This house, built about 1525 by Antoine de La Boétie, a criminal magistrate in the seneschal's court at Sarlat, was the birthplace of Étienne de La Boétie. The façade with its pointed gable and mullioned windows framed by pilasters decorated with medallions, is clearly Renaissance in style.

Cathedral. – Sarlat was an episcopal seat between 1317 and 1790. The Salignac Fénelon family ruled the diocese from 1567-1639 and 1659-1688. Although the present church was built during the 16 and 17C, the belfry adjoining the west façade is undoubtedly Romanesque. Of its three storeys, the lowest is formed of blind arcades, the second has open bays while the third was a 17C addition.

Inside the most striking features are the elevation and harmonious proportions of the vessel which is late Gothic in style, and the furnishings. *Leave by the south doorway.*

The first courtyard is bordered on the southeast corner by the **Chapel of the Blue Penitents** (Chapelle des Pénitents Bleus), a 12C building which originally belonged to the

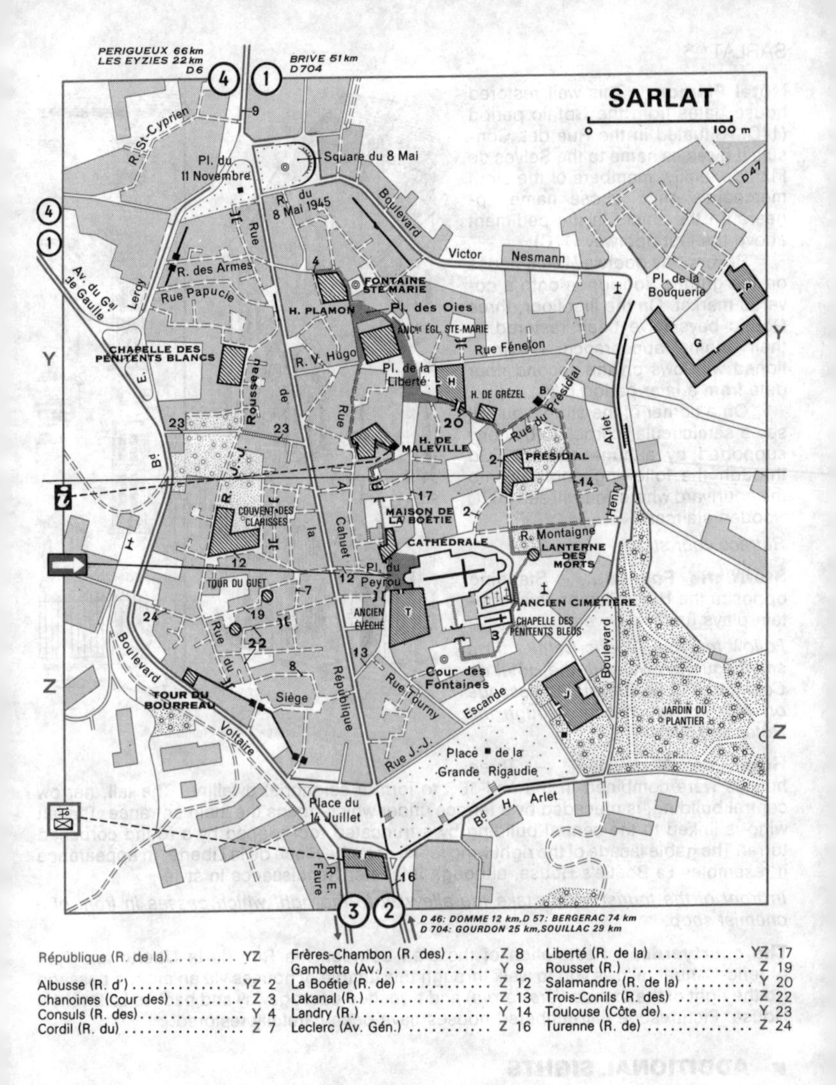

abbey around which the town of Sarlat grew. From here notice the south side of the cathedral supported by flying buttresses, the side chapels and the bulbous shaped lantern crowning the belfry.

Continue into the **Cour des Fontaines** and then turn left into the second courtyard, the **Cour des Chanoines** (**3**) which is enclosed on its north side by the Chapel of the Blue Penitents. Go round the chapel to reach the chevet of the cathedral which is adjoined by older buildings with stone tiled roofs.

Former cemetery. – Note the funeral niches in the wall behind the chevet and the former cemetery now arranged as a terraced garden which incorporates some of the 12-15C tombstones.

Go up the staircase.

Lantern to the Dead (Lanterne des Morts). – This rather strange 12C tower with its high conical stone roof was probably used as a funeral chapel. Good view of the chevet.

Make for the Rue Montaigne. The end of the alley, opposite, leads to the old rest-stop for post-horses (blacksmith).

Turn left into the Rue Landry which runs alongside the Présidial's garden.

Présidial. – This building was the seat of the civil and criminal courts from the 16C until the Revolution. The façade is original. Two superimposed bays are surmounted by a strange octagonal lantern tower crowned by a bell shaped roof.

Take the fork to the right which opens onto the Rue du Présidial. This gives a good view of a fine mansion (**Y B**) which has been rebuilt with its original rustic gallery.

Turn left into Rue du Présidial, then right into Rue de la Salamandre which slopes downwards.

Rue de la Salamandre (**Y 20**). – Pass on your right the elegant staircase tower of the Hôtel de Grézel with its 15C sculptured ogee arched doorway. There is a view over the crooked but enduring stone covered rooftops.

Rue de la Salamandre opens into Place de la Liberté, formerly Place Royale. *It is here that the open air performances are given during the Sarlat festival (p 37).*

Go right round the former Church of Ste-Marie, now secularized and deteriorating.

Place des Oies★. – Geese *(oies)* square gets its name from the Saturday morning markets held here.

Note the houses with their turrets, bell towers and corner staircases.

Hôtel Plamon. – This well restored house dates from the Gothic period (14C). Situated in the Rue des Consuls it owes its name to the Selves de Plamon family, members of the cloth merchant's guild whose name appears on the shield in the pediment above the first doorway (17C).

Beyond the doorway five arcades on the ground floor open onto a covered market. On the first floor, three Gothic bays have been restored to their original appearance. The mullioned windows on the second floor date from a later period (15C).

On a corner of the street you will see a semicircular corbelled balcony supported by a huge squinch. Go through the following doorway into the courtyard where you will see a 17C wooden staircase.

Retrace your steps.

Sarlat – Hôtel Plamon.

Ste-Marie Fountain. – Standing opposite the Hôtel Plamon this fountain plays under a cover.

Follow the Rue Albéric-Cahuet. In a small square, level with the Hôtel du Commerce, take the vaulted passage on your left which cuts through the Hôtel de Maleville.

Hôtel de Maleville*. – Three houses were combined in the mid-16C to form a seignorial dwelling. The tall, narrow central building, is preceded by a terrace under which opens the main entrance. The left wing is linked to the central building by a truncated roof topped by a round corbelled turret. The gable façade of the right wing looks onto the Place de la Liberté. In appearance it resembles La Boétie's House, although it is later Renaissance in style.

In front of the tourist centre take the alleyway to the right which passes in front of a chemist shop.

The courtyards. – Restoration of the area between the Rue de la Liberté and Rue Albéric-Cahuet, allows you to walk through this jumble of houses via an arch, a passage (to the right of the *Immobilière Jardin*) and a vaulted passageway and back to La Boétie's House. Picturesque half-timbered houses have been carefully restored.

■ ADDITIONAL SIGHTS

Western District. – The area west of the «Traverse» is a maze of narrow twisting and sloping alleys. During the renovation of the quarter in certain cases demolition was the only solution.

Rue des Trois-Conils (**Z 22**). – This street turns sharply left at the foot of a house flanked by a tower, which once belonged to consuls related to the La Boétie familly.

Tour du Bourreau (Executioner's Tower). – It was built in 1580.

Retrace your steps to the Rue du Siège.

Rue Jean-Jacques Rousseau. – You are now in a quarter which has several convents and walled gardens. The watch tower at the corner of Rue de la Boétie marks the site of a convent belonging to the order of St. Clare.

Chapel of the White Penitents (Chapelle des Pénitents blancs). – This 17C building, a former chapel, has a Classical doorway surrounded by columns; inside is a **museum of sacred art.** *(Open Easter to 10 October, 10am to noon and 3 to 6pm; closed Sunday mornings and holidays; 5F.)*

Most of the exhibits date from the 16 to 18C. There are several *Pietà* (a 17C one in the glass case), a 16C tabernacle in muticoloured wood, sections of magnificent wooden Baroque retables and in particular a lovely statue of an Angel in Adoration (on the left of the entrance).

EXCURSION

Puymartin Castle. – *9 km - 5 miles to the northwest. Leave Sarlat by ④, the D 47, then take a small road on the right which is signposted. Description p 157.*

SERMUR

Michelin map 73 southwest of fold 2 – Pop 155

The ruins of a tower rise from the top of a hill, at an altitude of 712 m - 2 365 ft in the green and valleyed country of Combraille. The tower is all that remains of a feudal fortress which was destroyed at the beginning of the Hundred Years War.

There is a path which leads to the foot of the tower. The view extends over the Marche and Combraille countryside.

SOLIGNAC *

Michelin map 72 fold 17 – 13 km - 8 miles south of Limoges – *Local map p 122* – Pop 1 244

Solignac has an interesting Romanesque church, once part of the famous abbey founded in 632 by St. Eligius. The town lies near the green valley of the Briance.

The Great Saint Eligius. – The legendary figure of St. Eligius dominated the Merovingian Age. This wise and saintly man was not only Dagobert's chief minister, but is also remembered as a goldsmith and loved as a man of inexhaustible charity.

He was born at Chaptelat in 588 and learnt his skill as a goldsmith in the workshops at Limoges. He went to work in Paris; but it was due to the confidence in him of good King Dagobert – so maligned in song – that St. Eligius was able to use his talents as a minister. St. Eligius, though titular Bishop of Noyon, felt the call of his native countryside and asked the king for land at Solignac on which to found a monastery where he could die in peace. "My king and master", the holy man said, "may you grant me this out of your bounty so that I may build a ladder, for by this ladder we shall climb to heaven, you and I." The king replied favourably to Eligius' request.

The abbey was built on a grand scale from the start, but in spite of its fortifications it did not escape the depredations of the Normans, the Saracens, the English and the Huguenots, each of whom plundered it in turn during its long history.

■ ABBEY CHURCH * (Église Abbatiale) *time: 1/2 hour*

The present church dates from the first half of the 12C and is the Limousin church which is most influenced by the Périgord style of architecture.

Exterior. – The big bell-tower built at the same time as the abbey was replaced in the 19C by a stark bell-gable. As you walk round the church you get a view of the fine grouping formed by the arms of the transept and the apse.

A frieze of blind arcades circles the upper part of the building adding further elegance; there is a fine bas-relief above the door which opens into the north transept.

Interior. – Go in through the door in the porch. From the top of the steps looking down into the nave you will be struck by the harmony of proportion, the purity of line, the strength of the architectural design and the warm colour of the granite of this church whose plan, with neither side aisles nor ambulatory, is that of a plain Latin cross.

The main body of the church is covered over with vast semicircular domes. An elevated passageway runs down both sides of the nave and is supported by blind arcading which in turn is carried by engaged columns and pilasters. Note also the carved archaic capitals and modillions which become more intricate towards the chancel.

The transept is assymmetrical. The south arm is roofed with cradle vaulting; note the 18C Virgin in multicoloured wood. In the north transept which is covered with an ovoid cupola pierced by a round window, a glass case *(lighting: 1F)* contains works of art including the 12C reliquary-bust of St. Théau in gilded copper and silver.

Apsidal chapels radiate from the chancel, which contains 15C stalls with expressive carved misericords and arm-rests. Note the restored distemper painting of St. Christopher on the pillar on the right of the chancel, which probably dates from the 15C.

Monastery Buildings. – The buildings which were reconstructed in the 18C and ravaged during the Revolution, have been occupied since 1945 by student missionaries of the Oblate of Mary Immaculate.

SORGES

Michelin map 75 fold 6 – Pop 911 – *Facilities p 38*

Sorges, a pleasant town famous as a truffle market, is situated on the road from Périgueux to Limoges, near the valley of the Isle, as the plateaux rise gently from the Périgord Blanc (White Périgord) to Nontronnais.

Church. – This Romanesque domed building has a massive square belfry with paired windows and a fine Renaissance doorway.

Truffle Centre (Maison de la Truffe). – *Open 2 to 6pm (5pm, 15 September to 31 May); closed Tuesdays; 9F.*

Truffles are an important Périgord speciality *(p 17)*. A museum housed in the tourist centre *(Syndicat d'Initiative)* features this product. With the help of tables, maps, photos, films and books, it traces the history of the truffle, the various species, the best soil and the selected trees, and the search methods. It also gives an idea of the economic and gastronomic importance of this mushroom.

A walk (time: 1 hour) to the truffle beds marked "A la découverte des Truffières" has been mapped out 2 km – 1 mile from Sorges. Enquire at the Maison de la Truffe.

SOUILLAC *

Michelin map 75 fold 18 – *Local maps pp 95, 96 and 108* – Pop 4 062 – *Facilities p 38*

Souillac, at the confluence of the Borrèze and the Dordogne, in the centre of a fertile region whose abundance contrasts keenly with the poverty of the causses or limestone plateaux of Martel and Gramat is a small town bustling with trade and tourists. It developed in the 13C, growing up round the abbey which was a dependency of the Benedictine Monastery at Aurillac; today, the town is traversed by the N 20.

When the Benedictines settled in the plain of Souillès – so called after a local word *souilh*, meaning bog or marshland where wild boar wallow – they replaced the community established there previously by St. Eligius *(see above)*. The monks drained the land continuously, transforming the marsh into a rich estate. Souillac Abbey was plundered and sacked several times by the English during the Hundred Years War, but rose from the ruins each time through the tenacity of its abbots. Greater disasters, however, befell it during the Wars of Religion: in 1562 Protestant bands pillaged the monastery; ten years later the monastery buildings were set on fire and only the abbey church, protected by its domes, escaped the flames.

The abbey was rebuilt in the 17C and attached to the Maurist Congregation, but it ceased to exist during the Revolution.

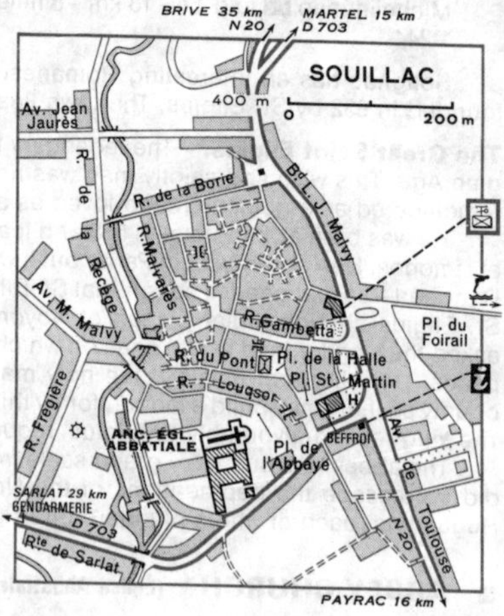

■ FORMER ABBEY CHURCH

(Ancienne Église Abbatiale) *time: 1/2 hour*

Leave the car in the Place de l'Abbaye, from where one can see the beautiful Romanesque chevet decorated with blind arcades and round arched bays.

Originally the abbey was dedicated to St. Mary; now it takes the place of the former parish church destroyed during the Wars of Religion. Of the old parish church all that remains is a large damaged tower known as the Beffroi – the Belfry. The church was built at the end of the 12C and bears a resemblance to the Romanesque-Byzantine cathedrals of Périgueux, Angoulême and Cahors, however, the size is less impressive.

The building has a wide main body surmounted by three deep domes resting on pendentives. To the left of the first bay stands a 16C polyptych painted on wood: The Mysteries of the Rosary, and in the second bay hangs a large canvas by Chassériau: Christ on the Mount.

The back of the doorway★. – There is mastery in the composition of this doorway, which was mutilated by the Protestants and was later placed inside the nave of the new church when it was erected in the 17C.

Above the door, framed by the statues of St. Peter on the right and St. Benedict on the left, is a bas-relief relating episodes in the life of the Monk Theophilus, Deacon of Adana in Cilicia: a new abbot, misled by false reports, removes Theophilus from his office of treasurer of the monastery of Adana; Theophilus, out of resentment, signs a pact with the devil to regain his office *(left)*. Repenting his sins, Theophilus implores forgiveness and prays to the Virgin Mary *(right)* who appears before him in his sleep, accompanied by St. Michael and two angels who guard her; they bring him the pact he made with the devil and she shows how she has had his signature annulled and has obtained his pardon. The right engaged pillar, which was originally the central pillar of the doorway, is richly decorated: monstrous animals grip and devour one another on the main facet; the sides show the sacrifice of Abraham and the origin of sin, which is illustrated by pride and lust.

By the door are fine bas-reliefs, in boldly decorative stances of the prophets **Isaiah★★** (right) and Joseph (left).

Beneath the narthex is a crypt containing sarcophagi.

The Prophet Isaiah.

La SOUTERRAINE

Michelin map 72 north of fold 8 – Pop 5 850 – *Facilities p 38*
See town plan in the current Michelin Red Guide France.

In the centre of a fertile depression in the Marche region stands La Souterraine, built on the site of the Gallo-Roman Villa Sosteranea. Many traces of its mediaeval fortifications remain, including the **Porte St-Jean** (St. John's Gateway), also known as the Porte de Breith (Breith Door) or the Porte Notre-Dame (Gateway of Our Lady), near the church. The gate (13-15C) is decorated with two encorbelled turrets and battlements.

Church★. – *Time: 1/2 hour.* Before the present building was erected, the monks from the Abbey of St-Martial in Limoges built a crypt which served as a tomb for the founder, Géraud de Crozant. This was in about 1020. Traces of a Gallo-Roman church (columns and inscriptions) erected round a well can still be seen.

Exterior. – Built of granite in the 12 and 13C, the church looks severe. The façade shows Arabic influence in the multi-lobed doorway with a slightly pointed arch flanked by two lantern towers. This influence was no doubt due to the pilgrims who passed through La Souterraine, which lay on one of the main routes to Santiago de Compostela. The tympanum over the south door is adorned with a Romanesque carving of the Virgin, Our Lady of La Souterraine. The style is typically Limousin as is that of the buttresses which support the transept. The 13C bell-tower had a belfry added last century.

Interior. – Inside, it is possible to follow the evolution of architectural styles from Romanesque to Gothic – from cradle vaulting in the second bay, through groined vaulting in the aisles, to the Gothic of the transept and chancel.

The nave is harmonious and is decorated with interesting capitals. The most original part of the building's design is the double transept: the crossing of the first bay is in the form of a trapezium with an oval dome rising above it on pendentives.

Note the 12C stone altar table which now stands on the altar in the Gothic chancel.

TOURTOIRAC

Michelin map 75 fold 7 – Pop 756 – *Facilities p 38*

This small market town, nestling in the greenery on the banks of the Auvézère, was the seat of a royal abbey in the 12C.

Orélie-Antoine I, King of Araucania. – Antoine Orélie de Tounens was born in Périgord in 1825. By 1858 he was practising as a lawyer in Périgueux, but was largely unknown. Suddenly he was seized by the ambition to live on a scale larger than life. He had become convinced that a bold man could subdue the backward tribes of South America and establish a powerful kingdom on the borders of Chile and Argentina. He borrowed a large sum of money and set sail for Chile, where he was greeted by the Indians as a liberator and in 1860 proclaimed himself King of Araucania under the title of Orélie-Antoine I. Chile became distrustful of what was going on and caught and imprisoned the "Libertador". The king repatriated to France, did not lose heart. In 1869 he landed secretly in Patagonia. After fantastic adventures, he was once more repatriated. Two further attempts were equally unsuccessful and in 1878, at Tourtoirac, where he had retired, this comic opera character who nearly gave France a kingdom, died.

Former Abbey. – *Open in season, 10am to 6pm; when closed apply at the presbytery or at the town hall near the church chevet.*

The remains of this former Benedictine abbey, founded in the 11C, stand in the gardens of the presbytery. To the right a small priorial chapel with cradle vaulting, stands side by side with the monk's bread oven and the watch-path. Of the former trefoil-shaped abbey church, only the transept surmounted by a powerful square belfry remains. The apse was destroyed during the Revolution. Note the fine capitals sculpted at the beginning of the 12C and the tall dome on pendentives. The much altered nave is now used for worship. The chapterhouse under the presbytery has been restored revealing remarkable Romanesque twin capitals. It gives access to the ruins of the cloisters.

TREIGNAC

Michelin map 72 fold 19 – Pop 1 800

Treignac is a picturesque town lying at the foot of the Monédières Massif *(p 135)*. Its houses rise in tiers above the Vézère which flows swiftly between boulders, having been dammed upstream from Treignac.

View of the Town. – You get a view of Treignac in its setting from the D 16, north of the town. For a different angle, go down a street that slopes steeply to the old Gothic bridge which spans the fast flowing Vézère. From the bridge you get a view of the ruins of the castle rising above the river, of the old houses with slate roofs and of the church.

Church. – This unusual square building flanked by a hexagonal belfry and covered by a vast slate roof, has ogive vaulting resting on huge pillars. The church, which has been restored, is lit by modern stained glass windows and has a granite altar.

Upper town. – Between Place de la République and Place de l'Hôtel-de-Ville, you will find groups of old houses adorned with turrets and carved doorways (note the scallop designs), and a 15C covered market built of granite.

The Mad Women's Rocks (Rocher des Folles). – *3/4 hour Rtn on foot. Road signposted southwest of the town.* Pretty views of Treignac. After climbing to the top of the hillock, take a narrow path which winds down through the heather to come out at the Mad Women's Rocks, a mass of great blocks of granite. From this point there is a pleasant view of the rocky Gorges of the Vézère and the surrounding wooded hills and heaths.

TULLE

Michelin map 75 fold 9 – Pop 20 642

Tulle extends over a couple of miles, its main street following the course of the narrow and winding valley of the Corrèze and its old houses rising in terraces on the hillsides overlooking the river. From the centre of the city rises the elegant stone steeple of the Cathedral of Notre-Dame.

A Litigious Abbey. – Tulle Abbey, founded on what is believed to be the site of a temple dedicated to the Roman Goddess Tutela, became powerful very early in its history. The monks frequently showed an aggressive zeal for affairs, as in the Rocamadour quarrel, in which for more than a century, the abbeys of Tulle and Marcilhac disputed possession of this wealthy sanctuary *(details p 127)*.

One of the abbots of Tulle, Élie de Ventadour, found an unusual method of replenishing his treasury which was all too often empty: he borrowed large sums at exorbitant rates of interest from the Jewish bankers of Brive; once the money was safely stowed in the abbey, the abbot, who controlled the court, charged the lenders with usury, condemned them and confiscated their property. Another abbot, Arnaud de St-Astier, obtained for himself in 1317 the title of Bishop of Tulle. This encroachment deprived Limoges of one of the most flourishing dependencies of its diocese: lawsuits dragged on endlessly bringing a bitterness that lasted for a long time between the two Limousin cities.

A Heavy Toll. – During the Hundred Years War the town fell twice, in 1346 and 1369, to the English. Each time the invaders were driven away by the local militia.

During the Wars of Religion, Tulle sided with the "papists"; the Protestant army under the Viscount of Turenne failed to take the city in 1577, but in 1585 Turenne came back and with bloody vengeance sacked the city after first assaulting it.

On 8 June 1944 Tulle was liberated by the men of the *maquis*, but the next day the Germans retook the town. Several hundred townspeople were arrested: 99 were hanged in the streets, the others were deported; 101 never came back.

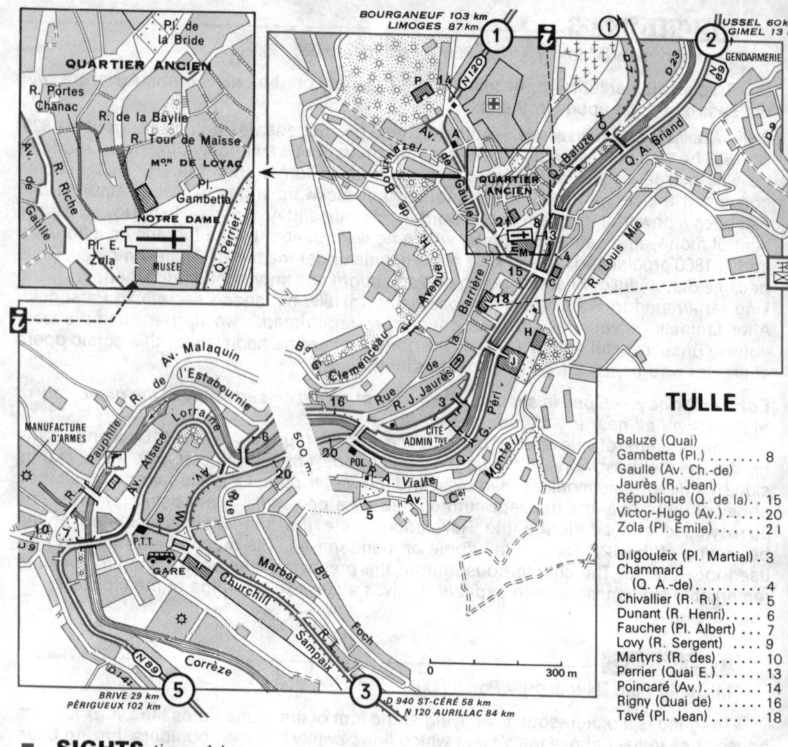

■ SIGHTS *time: 1 hour*

Cathedral of Notre-Dame. – In 1103, Abbot Guillaume wished his abbey, which was then very prosperous, to have a worthy setting, so he undertook the reconstruction of the church and the cloistral buildings. The 12C saw the building of the nave, the porch and the first storey of the belfry. The original plan was like that of many Benedictine churches, namely a nave and side-aisles, transept with dependent chapels, an apse and an ambulatory with apsidal chapels. The delays in construction explain why the columns and side walls are Romanesque while the vaulting is pure Gothic in style. In 1796 the dome above the transept and a part of the chancel collapsed. This caused the east part of the building to be taken down and the nave closed by a plain wall.

The **belfry**★ consists of three storeys surmounted by an elegant octagonal spire surrounded by bell turrets. This spire, which dated from the 14C, was struck by lightning in 1645, but has been restored in its original form. The ogive-vaulted porch contains a tiers-point doorway, adorned with moulding and small columns in the Limousin style. A much venerated 16C wooden statue of St. John the Baptist stands in the north aisle.

Cloisters. – *Open 1 April to 30 September, 9.30am to noon and 2 to 6pm; the rest of the year, 10am to noon and 2.30 to 5pm; closed Tuesdays out of season and holidays; 4F.*

Two restored galleries have fine ogive vaulting and afford a pleasant view of the cathedral and its belfry-porch. An interesting collection of decorative firebacks (16-18C) is on view. The 13C chapterhouse opens off the east gallery.

There is a **museum** *(reorganisation in progress)* adjoining the west gallery: religious and other sculpture in wood, firearms, pottery and porcelain exhibits.

The Old Quarter (Quartier Ancien). – This area, known as the "Enclos" (the Enclosure) retains a mediaeval atmosphere with alleys, stairways and old houses.

Maison de Loyac★. – This is the most outstanding secular building in Tulle. Built in the 15C it has an attractive façade: the windows and door are framed by small columns and are topped by accolades adorned with sculptured foliage, roses and animals.

A short walk *(1/4 hour Rtn on foot)* enables you to see characteristic parts of the old quarter. Turn left by the Maison de Loyac into the Rue de la Tour-de-Maïsse, a very narrow stepped street lined with corbelled houses whose porch roofs almost meet above the alley. Bear left again into the Rue de la Baylie and yet again into the sloping Rue des Portes-Chanac, where, among a group of old houses, you will notice on the left, at No 9, a fine sculptured doorway belonging to a late Renaissance mansion.

The Rue Riche – carved façade at No.13 – leads back to the cathedral.

EXCURSIONS

Étang de Ruffaud★**; Gimel-les-Cascades**★. – *Round tour of 31 km - 19 miles – about 2 1/2 hours – local map p 181. Leave Tulle by* ②. The N 89 as it climbs, affords pretty views of a rolling countryside cut by deep wooded valleys. At Corrèze-Gare take the D 26 to the right to reach the Étang de Brach (Brach Pool) in an attractive setting. *Continue along the D 26 and then take the D 53 to the right.*

Ruffaud Pool★. – This lovely stretch of water lies in a romantic setting.

As you come out of the small village of Touzac turn left in the direction of Gimel.

Gimel-les-Cascades★. – *Description p 106.*

Take the D 53 E which follows the smiling Montane valley.

On approaching Tulle by the D 9, there are fine glimpses of the town.

Corrèze Valley (upstream from Tulle); Naves. – *Round tour of 23 km - 14 miles - about 1 hour – local map below. Leave Tulle by the D 23, going northeast towards the town of Corrèze.* This pleasant road goes up the right bank of the Corrèze which here flows through a narrow and often enclosed valley. The road leaves the Corrèze to follow the Vimbelle valley until it reaches the village of the same name. The hills and meadows beside the river make a delightful picture. At Vimbelle bear left into the D 23^E and left again into the D 53 which climbs to meet the N 120, affording good views of the Vimbelle valley. *Follow the N 120 for 1 km 1/2 mile towards Tulle, then branch off right along a road which will bring you to Naves.*

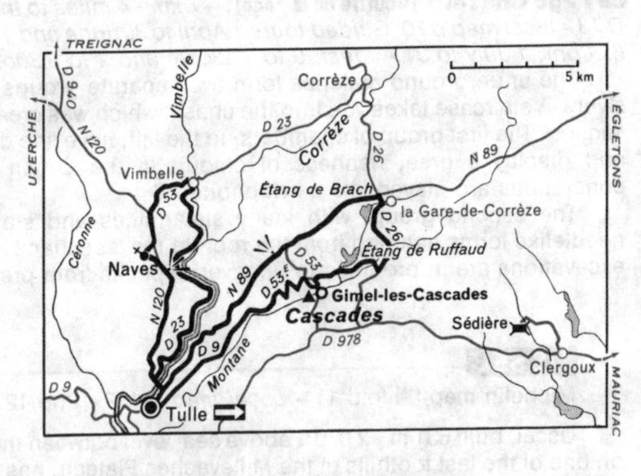

Naves. – Pop 2 176. The 15C church *(restoration in progress)*, flanked by a fortified turret, contains a gigantic retable carved in wood. Begun in 1652 and finished in 1704 it was the work of Pierre and Jean Duhamel. It swarms with naively carved characters and one recognises scenes from the Old and New Testaments – particularly those concerning St. Peter in chains, the patron saint of the church.

To return to Tulle take the D 58 which joins the N 120. This affords, on the left, a good view of the Corrèze valley, while on the horizon may be seen the crests of the Monédières. *The Corrèze valley between Tulle and Brive is described on p 87.*

TURENNE ★

Michelin map 75 southeast of fold 8 – *Local maps pp 70 and 94* – Pop 718

An old dictum ran that of Pompadour, Ventadour and Turenne, it was Turenne that reigned – such was the pride of this capital of the old *vicomté*, whose houses form a picturesque crescent round the castle ruins.

HISTORICAL NOTES

The Small Town with a Great Past. – From the earliest times in feudal history, Turenne held sway over 1 200 villages and a number of abbeys. The viscountcy, in its heyday, enjoyed enviable privileges: like the King of France, the viscounts ruled absolutely, ennobling subjects, creating offices and consulates, minting money and levying taxes.

The Great Turenne. – The name Turenne became famous through the family of La Tour d'Auvergne. In the 16C Henri de la Tour d'Auvergne was leader of the Limousin Huguenots and the most valiant supporter of the Reformation. As a reward for his zeal, Henry IV had him marry the heiress to the Duchy of Bouillon; The Turennes then went to live in Sedan and administered their own lands, which remained sovereign, from afar.

Another Henri de la Tour d'Auvergne, son of Henry IV's companion, inherited the ancestral lands in his turn: he was the great Turenne (1611-1675). He joined the Fronde when young, but later retreated to his own territory to escape the royal surveillance. He was joined by several nobles, and a joyous and crazy court was established which conspired against Mazarin; Condé himself even joined the man who was to become his rival. However, finally Turenne answered the king's command and left Limousin, though retaining the office of governor, to win glory on the battlefields. Louis XIV ordained that Turenne be buried beside Du Guesclin, at St-Denis. Napoléon considered him the greatest soldier of modern times. His tomb is now in the church of the Invalides in Paris.

Happy were the People of the Vicomté. – The inhabitants living in the reflected glory of their lord's prowess in battle, passed their days quietly within their small state and were envied since they suffered none of the tithes which fell so heavily on other French peasants. This golden age had to end: in the 18C a viscount sold his rights to Louis XV, and Turenne became united to the French kingdom.

■ CASTLE★ *time: 1 hour*

Leave the car on a large square at the foot of the mound.

Open 1 April to 30 September, 9am to noon and 2 to 7pm; the rest of the year on Sundays only, 2 to 5pm; 4F. Apply to M. Mallepeyre in the village or at the town hall (mairie).

On the way to the castle are old 15 and 16C houses, some flanked by towers and turrets, and the church built in 1592 by Charlotte de La Marck, wife of Henry I, Viscount of Turenne.

The ruins of Turenne Castle stand on the highest part of the mound, in a remarkable **setting**★. You get to Caesar's Tower, at the top of the promontory, by way of the flower-decked terrace, laid out just below the mound's summit. There is a stairway *(the steps are steep and some are worn)* to the actual summit. From the top there is a **panorama**★★: in the foreground you look down on to the slate roofs of the village houses while in the distance, in a green and valleyed countryside, you see the mountain, Plomb du Cantal, in the east.

At the other end of the promontory stands the Clock-Tower.

EXCURSION

La Fage Chasm★ (Gouffre de la Fage). – *7 km - 4 miles to the northwest by the D 8 and the D 13 – local map p 70. Guided tours 1 April to 30 June and 1 September to 31 October, 2 to 6.30pm; 1 July to 31 August, 9 to 11.30am and 2 to 6.30pm; time: 1 hour; 9F.*

The underground galleries form two separate groups which can be visited successively. A staircase takes you into the chasm which was created by the collapse of the roof section. The first group of chambers, to the left, have fine draperies in the form of jellyfish and display a great richness of colour. In the Organ Hall (Salle des orgues) the concretions are played like a xylophone.

The second group, with many stalagmites and stalactites, also has a forest of needlelike forms hanging from the roof. In the last chamber which is open to the public, excavations are in progress to uncover deposits from prehistoric times.

USSEL

Michelin map 73 fold 11 – *Local map p 132* – Pop 12 252

Ussel, built 631 m - 2 070 ft above sea-level between the Diège and Sarsonne valleys, on one of the last foothills of the Millevaches Plateau, has preserved several of the many secular buildings and monuments erected between the 15 and 17C.

■ SIGHTS *time 1 1/2 hours*

Old town. – Take Rue de la Liberté to reach Place Joffre with its fountain behind the church, and explore the side streets. There are goups of old houses decorated with turrets and with the coats of arms of their owners above the doorways. Most of them have been restored.

Behind the covered market, the **Ventadour Mansion** (Hôtel de Ventadour) is an elegant Renaissance house built by the Dukes of Ventadour at the end of the 16C to replace their feudal castle *(p 185)*.

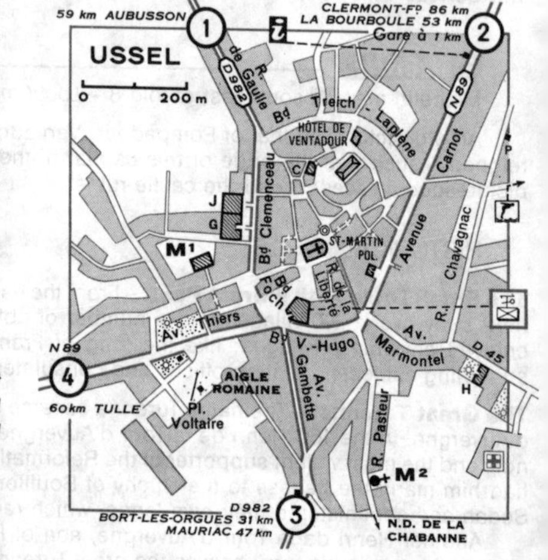

The Church of St-Martin has a belfry with a flat chevet dating from 1150. The nave and side aisles were rebuilt in the Gothic style in the 15-16C; the façade and sides are modern. The chancel contains fine woodwork and 18C stalls.

Ussel Museum (Musée du Pays d'Ussel). – *Open 1 July to 31 August, 10am to noon and 2 to 5pm; the rest of the year, apply to the town hall (mairie): ☎ (55) 72.27.27; combined ticket: 5F.*

The collections are shown in two buildings in different parts of town.

Choriol Mansion (Hôtel du Juge Choriol) (**M¹**). – This plain 18C mansion, which has been fully renovated, displays on three floors craftwork illustrating skills now no longer or little practised in the Ussel district. There is a remarkable 18C loom from a neighbouring village on view.

Penitents' Chapel (Chapelle des Pénitents) (**M²**). – There are outstanding examples of local art evoking the religious life of the region: a gilded wooden retable dating from 1711, a painting of Pentecost (1664) by the Cibille brothers, polychrome wooden statues (Angel at Prayer, 17C). Also of interest is an unusual 18C horse drawn hearse.

Roman Eagle (Aigle Romaine). – This statue was discovered beside the Sarsonne at Le Peuch Mill, the site of the Roman encampment of Le Peyrot which was the forerunner of Ussel.

Chapel of Notre-Dame-de-la-Chabanne. – *South of the town, access by Rue Pasteur.* From the esplanade near the pilgrimage Chapel of Our Lady of La Chabanne, there is a wide **view** of the Millevaches Plateau in the northwest, past the Monts Dore in the east, to the Cantal heights in the southeast.

EXCURSION

St-Angel. – Pop 562. *9 km - 6 miles. Leave Ussel by ④, the N 89.*

St-Angel is a small town grouped on a promontory overlooking the right bank of the Triouzone. Adjoining the **fortified church** are the buildings of the former Priory of St-Michel-des-Anges. The church façade supported by massive buttresses, has the severity of a fortress.

The **interior★** is surprisingly high: the nave and the aisles are of equal height and have ogive vaulting. Elegance and purity of style mark the chancel which has star vaulting; the apsidal chapels built in the walls are adorned with carved consoles.

The 15C sacristy, in the former chapterhouse, has beautiful ogive vaulting.

The maps and plans are orientated with north at the top.

UZERCHE★

Michelin map 75 northeast of fold 8 – Pop 3 185 – *Facilities p 38*

"He who has a house in Uzerche, has a castle in Limousin"; the number of attractive mansions and old houses to be seen in the city confirms this popular old saying.

Uzerche, a charming small Limousin town, stands on a promontory encircled by a bend in the River Vézère. On this picturesque site are crowded a surprising number of buildings with bell-turrets, watch-towers and pepper-pot roofs.

(After a photo by Arthaud, Grenoble)

Uzerche.

The Trick which Always Succeeded. – In 732 the Saracens, after being beaten back by **Charles Martel** at Poitiers, attacked Uzerche. The town was protected by solid walls and eighteen fortified towers and held out for seven years, but the population became decimated by famine and surrender seemed near until the besieged hit on a trick: they presented the emir of the Saracens with their last fatted calf, and with their last ration of corn. Amazed at such prodigality, the infidels raised the siege

The Uzerche arms – two bulls – recall this trick. The old town was never taken by force during any of the many sieges of the Middle Ages. Charles V, when he authorised the town to add three gold lilies to its arms, also gave it the appellation "Uzerche the maid", and its crest *non pulluta* (never sullied) confirms the glorious epithet.

View★. – At the Turgot Bridge, take the D 3, the Eymoutiers road, which climbs steeply and goes through the Ste-Eulalie suburb. Half a mile from the bridge, before a turning on the left you get a good **view★** of the site with the town perched on top of the rock and the Vézère running at its foot *(above)*: the church of St. Peter overlooks the many pinnacles adorning the slate-covered turrets, and, below the church, standing out amid the old terraced houses running down to the river, you see the outline of the towers of Pontier Château.

■ SIGHTS *time: 1 hour*

Leave from the Place Marie-Colein.

Rue Gaby-Furnestin. – On the left, you will see the 16C timbered house in which Alexis Boyer, surgeon to Napoleon I, was born. In this street which extends into Rue Jean-Gentet, note groups of renovated old houses with fine carved doorways.

Porte Bécharie. – This fortified gateway is the only one of the old city gates still intact: a modern statue of the Virgin stands in a niche above the arched passageway. Adjoining the gateway is a building known as the Château Bécharie, which is flanked by a square tower and a pendant turret; in the left wall is a great stone emblazoned with the Uzerche arms.

Turn right immediately beyond the Bécharie Gateway, into the Rue Escalier-Notre-Dame.

Place des Vignerons. – This little square, the Wine-Grower's Square, was formerly the fruit market. It is surrounded by old houses and the Chapel of Notre-Dame, the oldest church in Uzerche. The covered La Perception passageway leads to a small terrace which affords a bird's-eye view of the Vézère and of part of the town.

Leave the Tour du Prince Noir (Black Prince's Tower) on your left and walk along the Rue-St-Nicolas which will bring you out on the Place de la Libération. This square is dominated by the impressive mass of the Church of St-Pierre.

Church of St-Pierre. – This is an interesting Romanesque building dating from the 12 and 13C. The nave has broken barrel vaulting and is flanked by narrow aisles.

The capitals in the chancel are ornamented with tracery, foliage and animals; three others have been converted into holy-water stoups. On one may be seen monsters carved with lion's bodies and men's heads.

The 12C belfry is Limousin in style. Three square tiers with paired windows and gables are surmounted by a fourth octagonal in shape; this, in turn, is topped by a short roof covered in shingles which replaced the original stone pyramid roof.

To the southwest stands a massive round tower, erected as the defence point for the main door, built of rough-hewn stone with loopholes. Since restoration work on the church was undertaken last century, this tower is all that remains of the ancient defence system. The perimeter wall included 18 towers and five fortified gateways.

Crypt. – *Access through the chevet.* Beneath the chancel is an 11C crypt in the shape of a rotunda with three apsidal chapels supported by massive pillars. It contains a 14C tomb of unknown origin.

La Lunade Esplanade. – From this esplanade, built on the site of the former monastic buildings, there is a **view** immediately below of the La Pomme quarter which rises in terraces along the N 20, of the Vézère meander, and beyond, of the hills encircling the town.

Rue Pierre-Chalaud. – It is lined with old houses where you may see a Gothic or Renaissance door and timbered houses. At the end of the street the Château Tayac (12-14C) is a fine house with turrets and a door surmounted by a shield.

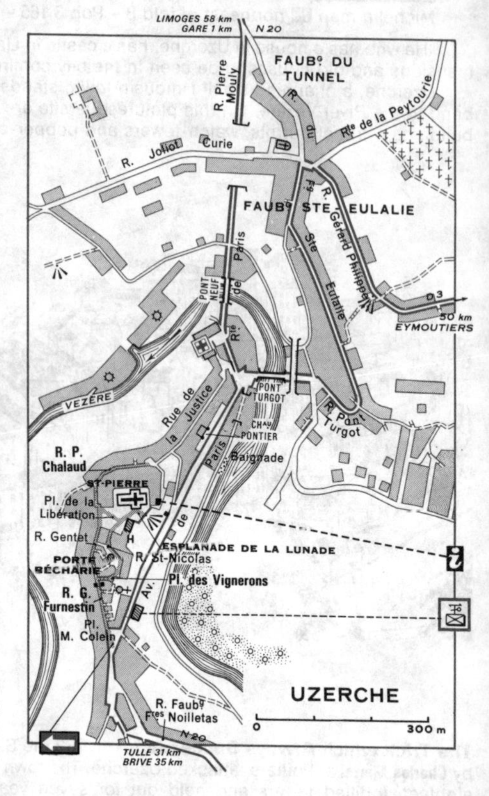

Return to Place de la Libération.
Walk along the Rue Jean-Gentet, where you will notice carved doorways, to the Bécharie Gateway and the Place Marie-Colein.

EXCURSIONS

Vigeois; Pompadour. – *25 km - 15 miles to the southwest. Leave Uzerche by the N 120. After 4 km - 2 miles turn right onto the D 3.*

Vigeois. – Pop 1 340. The Romanesque church *(restoration work in progress)* flanked by a Limousin belfry-porch is interesting. The north doorway with its multilobed arch shows a Languedoc influence. It is adorned with cusps and pairs of sculptured animals. The harmonious chevet with alternating bays and blind arcades, is ornamented with carved modillions and remarkable capitals crowning the engaged columns. Both the nave and the transept which is flanked by two apsidal chapels, are covered with broken barrel vaulting and date from the 12C.

There is a mediaeval bridge over the Vézère.

The bridge leads to the D 7 which you take to Pompadour.

Pompadour. – *Description* *p 155.*

VAREN

Michelin map 79 fold 19 – 16 km - 10 miles east of St-Antonin-Noble-Val – *Local map* *p 163* – Pop 909

The old market town of Varen stands on the right bank of the Aveyron, its houses clustered round the Romanesque church which is protected by large-scale defences.

■ SIGHTS *time: 1/2 hour*

Enter the old part of the town from south.

The old fortified gateway, the Porte El Faoure, leads to narrow streets lined by timberwork houses with corbelled upper storeys and flat roofs covered with round tiles.

Castle. – This is a massive keep topped by a battlemented watch-path and flanked by a corbelled turret. In this castle the Lord-Prior of Varen shut himself up when he challenged the decisions of the Bishop of Rodez and wished to prove his complete independence. In 1553 the Council of Trent replaced the monks in the priory.

Church of St-Pierre★. – The church was built at the end of the 11C. Its west face was included in the perimeter wall – the present doorway was opened in 1802 when the moats were done away with. Two archaic capitals of the original east end doorway still remain. A plain square belfry rises above the chancel which has a flat chevet and two semi-circular apsidal chapels.

The Romanesque style nave with nine bays is separated from the aisles by square pillars. The chancel and apsidal chapels are adorned with 17C stalls and interesting capitals with plant motifs, tracery, animals and cherubs surrounding the Tree of Life.

VENTADOUR Castle Ruins ★★

Michelin map 75 fold 10 – 7 km - 4 miles southeast of Égletons – *Local map p 93*

The ruins of Ventadour Castle rise in their wild setting on a rocky promontory commanding the Luzège Gorges.

Bernard de Ventadour. – Bernard, the son of a castle servant, was born in this Limousin fortress. He revealed unusual poetic talent and was to become one of the most famous troubadours, or singers of courtly love. He spent some of his time at the court of Eleanor of Aquitaine before she became the wife of Henry II and Queen of England. Upon her sailing to England he joined the court of the Count of Toulouse; and then retired to a monastery to die.

The Ventadour Fortress. – Ventadour appeared impregnable from its position and its defenses. It was taken, however, by treason and for thirteen years during the Hundred Years War the castle was in the hands of the English. At the time of the Renaissance the Viscounts, deserted it for an elegant mansion *(p 182)* which they had built in Ussel.

TOUR

The ruins. – From Moustier-Ventadour, a narrow road offers striking views of the ruins standing upright on the rocky spur. *Access by a path, 1/2 hour Rtn on foot.* Two towers, high defense walls, old inner couryards, traces of the main building and the outwork help us recall what once was an austere mediaeval fortress. Through the breaches in the walls there are plunging **views** onto the Luzège valley.

Tour of the "moat". – *7 km - 4 miles Rtn. Depart from the foot of the castle, bear right always.* Follow the access road, which leads into a narrow but tarred path and slopes *(gradient 1 in 6 1/2, very tight bend)* into the gorges of the Luzège – the famous "moat" of Ventadour – then halfway up the rocky slope to the foot of the ruins ending in the N 691. The road affords an awe-inspiring **views**★ of the ruins and the deeply incised meanders of the Luzège.

VÉZÈRE Valley ★★

Michelin map 72 folds 19 and 20 and 75 folds 7, 8, 16 and 17

This valley is a tourist route remarkable both for the beauty of the countryside it passes through and for the interest of prehistoric sites, particularly around Montignac and Les Eyzies-de-Tayac, which were once inhabited by generations of cave men *(see notes on prehistory pp 21-24).*

A Daughter of the Limousin. – The Vézère rises on the Millevaches Plateau, northwest of Meymac, and runs through the dull granite moorlands of Limousin, twisting along a stony course between heather-covered hills. Early on the river is tamed, spreading out in two great reservoirs controlled by the dams built at Monçeaux-la-Virole and Treignac where the valley narrows and the river once leapt in falling cascades.

Above Le Saillant, the only way of going up the gorges cut by the Vézère between Uzerche and the Brive basin is by rail.

However, you will get good **views** of the upper valley from certain roads that cut across it and from the larger towns built close to the river.

Treignac. – *Description p 179.*

Uzerche★. – *Description p 183.*

Vigeois. – *Description p 184.*

Le Saillant. – *Description p 43.*

■ THE PÉRIGORD'S VÉZÈRE

From Brive to Limeuil

108 km - 67 miles – about 1 day – local map p 186.

After Le Saillant, the Vézère enters the fertile countryside of the Brive bassin. Increased by the waters of the Corrèze, the river suddenly changes course and flows westwards to run through a typically Périgord countryside where willows, poplars and strangely hewn cliffs form a harmonious landscape.

Come out of Brive (p 68) by ⑥. The N 89 crosses the Brive Basin and joins the Vézère soon after its confluence with the Corrèze, near St-Pantaléon.

Between **Larche** (Pop 1 170 – *Facilities p 38)* and Terrasson the road leaves the valley to climb up to the plateau. *You follow first the D 60 then the D 63.*

As you drop down to Terrasson you will begin to notice vineyards on the hill slopes.

Terrasson-la-Villedieu. – Pop 6 309. Terrasson on the left bank of the Vézère is a busy little town with a prosperous trade in truffles and walnuts.

The **church** was built in the upper part of the town in the 15C and has undergone repeated restoration. The single aisle, transept and chancel have ogive vaulting.

From the terrace on the north side of the church you see the setting in which Terrasson stands: on the left, the slate roofs of the houses go all the way down the hillside to the Vézère, spanned by two bridges; in the distance beyond the part of the town built on the right bank, you see the Périgord countryside with its characteristic lines of poplars, walnut plantations and rich arable land.

The old bridge, Pont Vieux, was built in the 12C and is complete with cutwaters.

Between Terrasson-la-Villedieu and Condat, the road follows the floor of the valley before crossing to the right bank of the river. The river cuts through wooded slopes strewn with boulders.

Montignac. – *Description p 141.*

Régourdou; Lascaux Cave. – *3 km - 2 miles from Montignac. Description p 142.*

From Montignac to Les Eyzies the road follows closely the course of the river which is lined by magnificent poplars. This is the most attractive part of the valley. From the D 65, shortly after Montignac, you will see between the trees, the elegant outline of Losse Château towering above the Vézère.

(After a photo by M. Foucault, Éd. Tel)

Losse Château.

Losse Château. – *Guided tours, 1 July to 15 September, 10am to 12.30pm and 2 to 6.30pm; time: 3/4 hour; 10F.* This elegant 16C building stands perched high on a rock above the right bank of the river Vézère *(see illustration opposite)*. A terrace adorned with a balustrade supported by a fine basket-handled arch, stands before the main building which is flanked by a round tower at one corner. Inside there are splendid furnishings (16C Italian cupboard and coffers, Louis XIII furniture) and especially tapestries. Note the fresh colours of the Flemish tapestry in the tower chamber and the Florentine tapestry depicting the Return of the Courtesan in the main chamber; both are 17C.

Sergeac. – Pop 138. This village is pleasantly situated beside the Vézère at a spot where tall cliffs line the valley. Many prehistoric deposits (e.g. **Castel-Merle** *Description p 103)* have been discovered in the caves at the foot of the cliffs.
The village of Sergeac, which has an interesting and delicately carved 15C cross standing at its entrance, also possesses old stone slated houses and a turreted building, the last remains of a commandery which once belonged to the Order of St. John of Jerusalem.

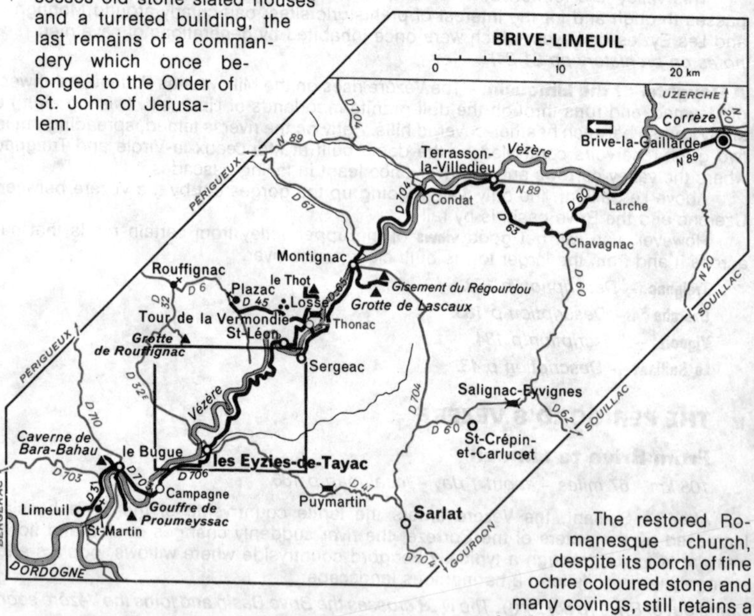

The restored Romanesque church, despite its porch of fine ochre coloured stone and many covings, still retains a fortified appearance with its loopholes, machicolations and bell-gable. The chancel with a flat ended chevet is adorned with sculptured capitals in the archaic manner.

Turn back and take the Thonac Bridge across the Vézère.

Le Thot. – *4 km - 3 miles from Thonac. Description p 142.*

La Vermondie Tower. – *3 km - 2 miles from Thonac.* This curious leaning tower, which, it is said, was demolished once by the Saracens in 732, stands near a 15C manorhouse on a hillside overlooking the Vézère. A delightful legend tells how, long ago, a young prince was held prisoner in the tower; every day his fiancée passed below; moved by the young people's misfortune, the tower leaned so low one day that the couple were able to exchange kisses.

Plazac. – Pop 502. *8 km - 5 miles from Thonac.* The Romanesque church in the centre of a picturesque churchyard planted with cypress trees, stands on a hillock overlooking the village. The 12C belfry-keep is roofed with lauze-stone slates *(p 48)* and embellished with blind arcades resting on Lombard bands.

From this point on, the road affords repeated and most pleasant views of typical Périgord landscapes: a background of meadows, a line of poplars or willows reflected in smooth waters and tall white and grey cliffs, spattered with scrub and evergreen oaks, in some cases hollowed out where they served as shelters for prehistoric man. Such scenery is often to be found south of St-Léon-sur-Vézère, as for instance at La Roque-St-Christophe, at Tursac and near Les Eyzies-de-Tayac, with castles and manorhouses adding a touch of elegance.

St-Léon-sur-Vézère. – Pop 391. St-Léon was built in an attractive setting of rocks half-hidden in greenery within a loop of the river Vézère. The small La Salle castle built of dry-stone and flanked by a massive square keep stands in the square. The small Romanesque church of golden stone partly roofed with stone is crowned with an interesting square belfry with two tiers of blind arcades. Clérans Château, in the village is an elegant building dating from the 15 and 16C with corner towers and battlemented turrets. Next to the churchyard stands a small chapel, also roofed with stone, which once served as a lantern tower to the dead.

La Roque-St-Christophe★. – *Description p 103.*

Le Moustier. – *Description p 102.*

Tursac. – *Description p 104.*

Les Eyzies-de-Tayac★★. – *Description p 100.*

Beyond Les Eyzies, the valley opens out, the hills disappear giving way to farmland. At Campagne you will see a little Romanesque church with a belfry-gable and a 15-16C castle.

Le Bugue. – Pop 2 784. *Facilities p 38.* This town is pleasantly situated on the inside of a meander of the Vézère river near where it joins the Dordogne.

Proumeyssac Chasm★ (Gouffre de Proumeyssac). – *Guided tours Palm Sunday to 30 September 8.30 to 11.30am and 2 to 6pm; in October, Sundays only, same opening times; time: 3/4 hour; 15F.*

A tunnel drilled into a hill overlooking the Vézère brings you to a platform built half-way up the chasm. From this platform you see the whole of this underground dome which is decorated, particularly at the base of the walls, with fine yellow and white concretions. Water seeps through abundantty, adding to the stalactites which, in some places, are very numerous and form draperies, pure coloured stalagmites and fantastic shapes such as the eccentrics and triangular crystallisations that are building up from the floor of the caves.

Bara-Bahau Cave (Caverne de Bara-Bahau). – *1 km - 1/2 mile from Le Bugue. Guided tours Palm Sunday to 30 September, 9 to 11.30am and 2 to 6pm; time: 1/2 hour; 10F.* The cave, which is about 300 ft long, ends in a chamber blocked by a rock fall. On the roof of the chamber, amid the protrusions in the rock, may be seen drawings of bears, bison, wild oxen and ibex. Most of the outlines were made with sharpened flints. The drawings were discovered in 1951 and appear to go back to the Aurignacian Age *(pp 21-24).*

The D 703 in the direction of Bergerac and the D 31 towards Trémolat will bring you to the **Chapel of St-Martin,** which is a delightful country church built at the end of the 12C.

Take the road to Limeuil (p 97).

VIC

Michelin map 68 fold 19 – 8 km - 5 miles northwest of La Châtre – *Local map p 84*

This village was built along the Roman road, thus its Latin name *Vicus* meaning village; it contains a small Romanesque church with interesting frescoes.

Church of St-Martin. – *Time: 1/2 hour; apply at the bakery by the church.* The church was presented by the Bishop of Bourges to the monks of Déols Abbey at the end of the 11C. It was decorated with frescoes the following century. The paintings were brought to light in 1849.

The **frescoes**★ adorn both sides of a wall that divides the chancel from the nave, as well as the walls of the chancel itself and the wall and vaulting of the apse. Redemption is shown as the main theme throughout the life of Christ from birth to death. Six colours are used in the paintings: carmine, red-ochre, yellow-ochre, ceruse white, black and grey-blue. Though the faces lack expression the composition is so skilled, the movement of the figures so alive and the detail so accurate, these paintings form a group whose technique was later copied in the pictorial and sculptural art of Limousin and the southwest. Note on the wall facing the main door, Christ in Majesty; on the right, a Descent from the Cross; on the vaulting of the apse, the four Evangelists and a Christ in Majesty; on the north wall of the chancel, the Washing of the Feet, Judas' Kiss, Simon Carrying the Cross and episodes in the life of St-Martin; on the south wall, Jesus entering Jerusalem; facing the altar, the Last Supper.

VIERZON

Michelin map 64 folds 19 and 20 – Pop 34 886

See town plan in the current Michelin Red Guide France.

Vierzon, a bridging town at the confluence of the rivers Yèvre and Cher, is at the intersection of several communication routes. The town is on the borders of the Berry-Champagne region with the Vierzon state forest to the north. The town's industrial products include agricultural machinery, ceramics, fertilizers, knitted goods, clothing and cement products. Vierzon is Berry's most important centre of porcelain production.

Old Town. – Winding streets lined with old timbered houses cover the mound which is dominated by a Gothic belfry. The **Church** of Notre-Dame *(closed for restoration)* has a belfry-porch with a basket handle arched doorway. Inside are paintings by Jean Boucher, a native of Bourges and master to Mignard. Note the one in the south arm of the transept showing St. John the Baptist.

A stairway to the left of the church leads to a garden from which you can enjoy an overall view of the church and look down on the roofs of the town and the valleys of the Cher and the Yèvre.

Town Hall. – This occupies the 17 to 18C buildings of the former benedictine Abbey of St-Pierre.

From the terraced gardens overlooking the Yèvre there is a view of the old town and of the church.

EXCURSION

Massay; Graçay. – *Round tour of 51 km - 32 miles – about 1 1/2 hours.* Michelin maps 64 folds 19 and 20 and 68 fold 9. *Leave Vierzon to the south by the N 20.*

Massay. – Pop 1 339. The church formerly belonging to a Benedictine Abbey founded in the 9C, was rebuilt between the 14 and 16C and has a square belfry-porch. Some of the abbatial buildings still remain, in particular the chapterhouse, parts of the 13C dormitory, the 12C storerooms and tithe-barns. The well preserved 12C abbot's chapel stands in the middle of the small cloisters. The abbot's residence dates from the 17C.

Follow the N 20.

Vatan. – Pop 2 052. The restored church of St-Laurian, has a 16C chancel with stained glass windows from the same period depicting the life of St-Laurian. Inside there are several interesting 18C paintings. The carved doorways date from 1498.

Take the D 922 out of Vatan in the direction of Graçay to the north.

Graçay. – Pop 1 844. This mediaeval city retains parts of its perimeter wall and several old houses. The 11C Church of St-Outrille has a striking twisted belfry.

The D 63 and the D 19 to the left lead to Genouilly.

Genouilly. – Pop 721. At the far end of the village rises the Church of St-Symphorien. Preceded by a fine porch and well restored this building has Romanesque capitals and Gothic style vaulting.

The D 108 and D 63 lead back to Vierzon.

VILLEGONGIS Château ★

Michelin map 68 fold 8 – 15 km - 9 miles to the northwest of Châteauroux

Visitors are allowed to walk round the outside of the castle any day of the week. Follow the route marked with arrows. Visit of the castle by appointment; ☏ *(54) 36.60.51.*

Harmonious and well balanced the architecture of this château is striking for its resemblance to the Château of Chambord in the Loire Valley. Started in 1530 and finished around 1575 for Jacques de Brizay and Avoye de Chabannes, the building of this château was probably the work of Pierre Trinqueau, one of the master builders who worked on Chambord from 1524 to 1538.

The plan of the château although simple in appearance is elegant, being composed of a main building flanked by two great round towers which are assymetrical. The whole is surrounded by water filled moats. Note the original form and balance of the roofs and chimneys, the mark of a master builder.

(After a photo by Roussel, Châteauroux)

Villegongis Château.

Built of white tufa stone the château is ornamented by decoration which equals the quality of its architecture. A frieze of scallop shells runs along the base of the cornice on the main building, and is accompanied by pilasters ornamented with diamond shapes and finely worked capitals.

It is however the superb chimneys which most clearly recall the château of François I. They are decorated with slates of varying shapes and are crowned by pediments and pinnacles. The monumental chimneys of the towers have ornate bases and niches containing the statues of St. James and St. Avoye. The staircase, lit by twin bays, with its coffered ceiling and straight flights, is typical of the Renaissance.

The furnishings date mostly from the 17 and 18C; there are several tapestries from Flanders, Beauvais and Aubusson. The frescoes are 16C.

VILLENEUVE

Michelin map 79 fold 10 – *Local map p 125* – Pop 1 649

Villeneuve, a former *bastide* surrounded by a circular boulevard, stands on the borders of Rouergue and Quercy, on a causse or limestone plateau bordered by the valleys of the Lot and the Aveyron.

The large cattle fairs held on the first of every month produce a lively bustle and vivid atmosphere.

Leave the car on the outskirts of the village near the Porte Haute. Follow the route marked with arrows to see the picturesque sights of Villeneuve.

The Arcaded Square. – Old houses surround the square; those on one side have mullioned windows adorning their façades. From the square you get a view of the massive outline of the Porte Haute, a great square tower which formerly served as a prison.

Church. – In the middle of the 11C Pierre Béranger, the Bishop of Rodez, founded the Monastery of the Holy Sepulchre (Saint-Sépulcre) at Villeneuve. The first church was built at the beginning of the 12C, in the shape of a clover-leaf round a central square marked by four pillars, the usual plan at that time for churches dedicated to the Holy Sepulchre. In the 14C the chancel was destroyed and a Gothic-style nave was added which ended in a five sided apse with ogive vaulting; painted on the vault of the northern apsidal chapel is a 13C Christ in Majesty. The Romanesque belfry above the transept crossing was raised during the Gothic period.

Tour Savignac. – This fortified gateway which stands near the church chevet was built in the 14C and formed part of the town's line of defence.

VILLENEUVE-SUR-LOT

Michelin map 79 south of fold 5 – *Local map p 124* – Pop 23 730
See town plan in the current Michelin Red Guide France.

Villeneuve-sur-Lot was one of the largest and strongest *bastides* of the southwest *(p 32)* when it was founded in 1253 by Alphonse de Poitiers on the borders of Périgord and Guyenne to back up the strongholds in Haut-Agenais.

The town which has kept traces of its mediaeval past, with its narrow alleyways and old houses, spreads far along the banks of the Lot. The richness of the alluvial valley, which produces large crops of fruit and early vegetables, has made Villeneuve into a lively business centre and, like Agen, a regional market for plums *(p 18)*.

■ SIGHTS *time: 1/2 hour*

Town Gateways. – The Porte de Pujols and the Porte de Paris stand erect, the only remaining traces of the former ramparts and marking what were once the southwest and the northeast limits of the old town. Both are built of brick and stone, topped by crenellations and battlements and brown-tiled roofs. The three-storeyed Porte de Pujols has mullioned windows.

Church of Ste-Catherine. – This church, built of brick in the Romanesque-Byzantine style was consecrated in 1937. Apart from the chancel, the church is adorned with a series of 14 and 15C stained glass windows (restored), which came from the earlier church and are attributed to the school of Arnaud de Moles, master enameller to Auch Cathedral. There are 17 and 18C gilded wooden statues.

Pont Vieux. – This bridge with uneven arches was built in the 13C by the English. There is a picturesque view from the bridge of the banks of the Lot and of the 16C Chapel of Notre-Dame du Bout-du-Pont with its chevet projecting over the water.

Gaston Rapin Museum. – *Open 3 to 6pm (2 to 6pm, 20 November to 30 June); closed Tuesdays, every other Sunday out of season, holidays and 20 October to 20 September; 4F.*

A villa situated at the corner of Boulevard Voltaire near the Porte de Pujols, houses the municipal museum. It was bequeathed by Gaston Rapin, a former town architect.

The basement is devoted to prehistory and to Egyptian and Gallo-Roman Antiquity. On the ground floor are a room reserved for Sacred Art (fine coloured boss of God in Benediction) and a gallery displaying etchings, drawings and contemporary sculpture. In a corner, the **Piranesi gallery** (Cabinet Piranèse) exhibits drawings and engravings on copper by this master famous for his feeling for the poetry of ruins.

The first floor is reserved for temporary exhibitions. On the second floor the Arts and Folklore of the region are featured. There is an interesting **Plum Museum** (Musée de la Prune) where instruments formerly used in the cultivation and marketing of plums are on show.

EXCURSIONS

Casseneuil. – Pop 2 822. *10 km - 6 miles northwest by the D 242.*

Casseneuil is built in a loop in the river where the Lède flows into the Lot. The warm brown tiled houses crowd round the church. Once the town lived of the river traffic; today the mainstay is the canning of foodstuffs.

As you stroll round the town, you get attractive glimpses along the banks of the Lède of **old houses** with balconies overlooking the river and of terraced gardens.

The church has a Gothic doorway surmounted by a rose window. The capitals in the nave have friezes of strange animals; on the vaulting in the chancel and in the aisles may be seen traces of old frescoes.

The Serres du Bas-Quercy. – *Round tour of 44 km - 27 miles – about 2 hours. Leave Villeneuve to the southwest by the D 118.*

Pujols. – Pop 3 411. This old village is perched upon a hill from which one can see the town of Villeneuve-sur-Lot and the wide fertile Lot valley.
A passageway built beneath a tower that serves as the belfry for the Church of St-Nicolas, leads to the old village which still lies close-packed within the 13C ramparts. The main street even today has many timbered houses with porch roofs. An old well, traces of the former fortifications, two churches – one St-Nicolas with fine ovige vaulting in the nave, the other Ste-Foy-la-Jeune with 15C frescoes (somewhat deteriorated) – and houses dating from the days of the Renaissance, all add to the pleasure of a visit.

Return to the D 118 and turn left. At the intersection with the D 220 turn left again in the direction of the Lestournelles Caves.

Lestournelles Caves (Grottes de Lestournelles). – *Guided tours 1 June to 30 September, 8 to 11.15am and 2 to 6.15pm; the rest of the year on Sundays only; closed 1 December to 1 March; time: 3/4 hour; 13F.* These caves have been hollowed out by underground streams. Small stalactites still in the process of formation can be seen hanging from the ceiling. Of the seven chambers the Hall of Pillars (Salle des Colonnes) is adorned with stout columns.

Continue along the D 220 till you come to the D 212 which you take to the left then turn left again in the direction of St-Antoine-de-Ficalba.

Fontirou Caves (Grottes de Fontirou). – *Guided tours Palm Sunday to 1 November, 9 to 11.45am and 2 to 6.45pm; the rest of the year Sundays and holidays only, same opening times, 13F.* These underground caves have been hollowed out of the grey Agenais limestone, and are bedecked with concretions coloured reddish-yellow by clay. Contrasting with the former are groups of pure white stalagmites. Bones of animals from the Tertiary period, which were discovered in the caves, are on display.

Continue to the N 21 then turn right before taking the D 110 to the left. The road crosses the Serres region, an area of limestone ridges separated by wide valleys.

Laroque-Timbaut. – Pop 1 201. This small town has a group of old houses to the south. Near the old covered market, go down a passageway that runs beneath a tower and, for about a hundred yards, follow an alley which is confined between the outer wall of the castle and old houses whose roofs are covered with round tiles.

The D 103 leads to Hautefage-la-Tour.

Hautefage-la-Tour. – Pop 520. Near the Church of Notre-Dame-de-Hautefage stands a fine hexagonal tower built at the time of the Renaissance. It serves as belfry to the church which is in the Gothic style with a Flamboyant doorway covered by a porch. A small round tower topped by a bell turret is built on to one side of the tower which has mullioned windows. The upper part is ornamented with a pierced balustrade, gargoyles and pinnacles. In the square shaded by plane trees there stands a pilgrimage fountain.

The D 103, D 223 to the left and N 21 to the right lead back to Villeneuve.

VILLESALEM, Former Priory (Ancien Prieuré de VILLESALEM)

Michelin map 68 fold 16 – 8 km - 5 miles northwest of La Trimouille

The Priory of Villesalem was founded at the end of the 11C by Audebert, Lord of La Trimouille, and was made a dependency of Fontevraud Abbey. The monastery buildings were sold as a State asset during the Revolution and were partly demolished. The church only just escaped being pulled down, but was converted by successive owners into a barn.

Church. – This early 12C church consists of a nave of five bays which are echoed by the flat buttresses of the south side aisles. The projecting transept opens onto the long apse flanked by two apsidal chapels.

Façade★. – The main façade is partly masked on the right side by a 17C building which was added by the Benedictines. The carved decoration of this façade is very rich. The doorways are adorned with capitals decorated with foliage, griffins, birds, lions and masks and with covings delicately carved with foliated scrolls and palm leaves.

Interior. – *Restoration work is in progress inside the church.* The walls which partitioned off certain parts of the church when it was in use as farm outbuildings, have been removed from the chancel transept and the three bays nearest the chancel. Some capitals are adorned with delicate carvings of foliage, tracery, birds and snakes.

YSSANDON Puy

Michelin map 75 west of fold 8

The Mound of Yssandon commands an extensive panorama since it stands in the centre of an undulating region where fertile fields and plantations of maize, tobacco, fruit and walnut trees alternate with pastures divided by quickset hedges and lines of poplars.

Access. – From the D 151 in the village of Prodelie a steep road, the D 151 E leads to the top of the hill (altitude 355 m - 1 165 ft) where many remains of the Gallo-Roman period have been found.

After 2 km - 1 mile there is a first viewing table. The remarkable **panorama★** includes, beyond the characteristic Dordogne landscape, the Limousin heights to the north, the Périgord hills to the west, the Brignac plain to the south with the Yssandon tower in the foreground and, to the east, the mountains of Auvergne. Pass the ruined tower that was once part of a massive 14C castle on your way to the top.

Leave the car in front of the church. A wide path leads round the churchyard to a second viewing table which gives details of the semicircular view over the Brive region.

INDEX

Lot (Lower Valley) . . . . . . Towns, sights and tourist regions.
Celle-Dunoise (La) . . . . . Other towns or places referred to in the text.
Sand (George) . . . . . Historical events, persons and local
Androne . . . . terms, explained in the text

The Department is given in brackets after the town, see abbreviations below:

Hte-Vienne: Haute-Vienne — L.-et-G.: Lot-et-Garonne
I.-et-L.: Indre-et-Loire — T.-et-G.: Tarn-et-Garonne

A

B

C

D

E

F

G - H

I - J - K

L

T - U

V - W

X - Y - Z

MANUFACTURE FRANÇAISE DES PNEUMATIQUES MICHELIN

Société en commandite par actions au capital de 700 000 000 de francs

Place des Carmes-Déchaux - 63 Clermont-Ferrand (France)

R.C.S. Clermont-Fd B 855 200 507

Dépôt légal : 9-84 - ISBN 2 06 013 611 - 3 - ISSN 0293-9436

Printed in France - 6-84-30

Photocomposition : KAPPA, Coulommiers - Impression : L'OFF-SET, Levallois nº 9212